ADAPTING FRANKENSTEIN

Manchester University Press

ADAPTING FRANKENSTEIN

The monster's eternal lives in popular culture

Edited by Dennis R. Cutchins
and Dennis R. Perry

Manchester University Press

Published by Manchester University Press
Altrincham Street, Manchester M1 7JA

www.manchesteruniversitypress.co.uk

British Library Cataloguing-in-Publication Data
A catalogue record for this book is available from the British Library

ISBN 978 1 5261 0890 6 hardback
ISBN 978 1 5261 0891 3 paperback

First published 2018

Typeset in Perpetua by
Servis Filmsetting Ltd, Stockport, Cheshire
Printed in Great Britain by
Bell & Bain Ltd, Glasgow

This book is gratefully dedicated to
Diane Long Hoeveler,
a friend whose untimely passing prevented her from
completing her contribution to this volume
and to
Laurence Raw,
a good friend and mentor

Contents

List of illustrations

Notes on contributors

Maria K. Bachman is Chair and Professor of English at Middle Tennessee State University and co-editor of the *Victorians Institute Journal*. Her books include *Fear, Loathing, and Victorian Xenophobia*, co-edited with Marlene Tromp and Heidi Kaufman (The Ohio State University Press, 2013) and *Reality's Dark Light: The Sensational Wilkie Collins*, co-edited with Don Richard Cox (University of Tennessee Press, 2003). She has published scholarly editions of Wilkie Collins's *The Woman in White* and *Blind Love* (Broadview Press, 2006, 2004), and Wilkie Collins's 'The Dead Hand' and Charles Dickens's 'The Bride's Chamber' (University of Tampa Press, 2009). She has also published numerous critical articles and book chapters on Samuel Richardson, Benjamin Disraeli, Edward Bulwer-Lytton, Charles Dickens, and Wilkie Collins.

Tully Barnett is a Research Fellow in the School of Humanities and Creative Arts at Flinders University in South Australia. She has published on new reading practices such as Kindle social highlighting and app-based reading platforms, posthumanism in new media art, and reading pedagogies in the tertiary literary studies classroom. She also researches in the field of cultural value as part of an Australian Research Council-funded project, 'Laboratory Adelaide: The Value of Culture'.

Kyle William Bishop directs the Honors Program at Southern Utah University, where he teaches courses in film and screen studies. He has published articles on a variety of popular culture subjects, including *Night of the Living Dead*, *Fight Club*, *Buffy the Vampire Slayer*, *The Birds*, and *The Walking Dead*. He has published two monographs on zombies: *American Zombie Gothic* (2010) and *How Zombies Conquered Popular Culture* (2015), both available from McFarland.

Véronique Bragard is Associate Professor in Comparative Literature at the Université catholique de Louvain (Belgium). She is the author of *Transoceanic Dialogues* (Peter Lang, 2008) and editor with Srilata Ravi of *Ecritures mauriciennes au féminin: penser l'altérité* (L'Harmattan, 2011) and with Christophe Dony and Warren Rosenberg of *Portraying 9/11: Essays on Representations in Comics, Literature, Film and Theatre*

(McFarland, 2011). Her recent publications include treatments of the representation of the Belgian colonial past in comics.

Dennis R. Cutchins is an Associate Professor of English at Brigham Young University, where he regularly teaches courses in adaptation and American literature. In 2000 he won the Carl Bode Award for the best article published in the *Journal of American Culture* for an essay on Leslie Silko's *Ceremony*, and in 2004 received the Charles Redd Center's Mollie and Karl Butler Young Scholar Award in Western Studies. He is currently working on a handbook to adaptation studies, and beginning work on ways to apply 'big data' theories to adaptation studies.

Joe Darowski received a PhD in American Studies from Michigan State University. He taught in the English Department a Brigham Young University-Idaho and is a member of the editorial review board of the *Journal of Popular Culture*. He is the author of *X-Men and the Mutant Metaphor: Race and Gender in the Comic Books* (2014), and editor of multiple books including *The Ages of Superman* (2012), *The Ages of Wonder Woman* (2014), *The Ages of the Avengers* (2014), *The Ages of Iron Man* (2015), and *The Ages of the Justice League: Essays on America's Greatest Superheroes in Changing Times* (2017).

Carol Margaret Davison is Professor and Head of the Department of English Language, Literature, and Creative Writing at the University of Windsor. She has published widely on the Gothic, cultural teratology, African-American literature, and Scottish literature. Her published books include *History of the Gothic: Gothic Literature 1764–1824* (2009), *Anti-Semitism and British Gothic Literature* (2004), and *The Gothic and Death* (2016). She also co-edited *Scottish Gothic: An Edinburgh Companion* (2018) with Monica Germanà.

Richard J. Hand is Professor of Media Practice at the University of East Anglia, UK. He is the founding co-editor of the international peer-reviewed *Journal of Adaptation in Film and Performance* and his interests include adaptation, translation and interdisciplinarity in performance media (with a particular interest in historical forms of popular culture, especially horror) using critical and practical research methodologies. He is the co-author of two books on Grand-Guignol horror theatre (Exeter University Press, 2002 and 2007), three books on radio drama (McFarland, 2006; Continuum, 2011; and Manchester University Press, 2014), two books on Joseph Conrad (Palgrave, 2005 and Rodopi, 2009), a book on Graham Greene (Palgrave, 2015), and has published translations of plays by Victor Hugo (Methuen, 2004) and Octave Mirbeau (Intellect, 2012). He has co-edited academic volumes on Conrad (2009), Horror Film (2007) and Radio (2012). As a practitioner he has written and directed radio and stage plays in the UK and US.

Jamie Horrocks is Associate Professor of English at Brigham Young University in Provo, UT, where she teaches courses on Victorian literature and culture and gender studies. Her research interests centre on Victorian aesthetics and the intersection of literature and art, especially in the later nineteenth century. She has published on Oscar Wilde, Vernon Lee, Virginia Woolf, the Aesthetic Movement, and Victorian periodical illustration.

Glenn Jellenik is an Assistant Professor of English at the University of Central Arkansas. His research explores adaptation, the productive intersections between mass culture and literature, and the cross-pollination between texts and the cultures that produce and consume them. He is co-editor of *Ten Years after Katrina: Critical Perspectives of the Storm's Effect on American Culture and Identity* (2015) and co-editor of the scholarly edition of Helen Maria Williams's *Peru and Peruvian Tales* (2015).

Kelly Jones is a senior lecturer in drama at the School of Fine and Performing Arts at the University of Lincoln. Her research focuses on theatrical realisations of the supernatural on the English stage from the Early Modern period to the present-day. In 2018 she co-edited, along with Benjamin Poore, *Contemporary Gothic Drama: Attraction, Consummation and Consumption on the Modern British Stage*.

Ben Kooyman completed a PhD in English at Flinders University, South Australia. His dissertation focused on film adaptations of Shakespeare. He currently works as an academic skills adviser at the Australian College of Physical Education. He is a scholar of Shakespeare, film, and horror cinema, His first book, *Directorial Self-Fashioning in American Horror Cinema*, was published in 2014. He writes regularly for the websites www.downunderflix.com and www.australiancomicsjournal.com.

Matt Lorenz is an Adjunct Assistant Professor at Farmingdale State College. His dissertation, 'Wordsworth's Philosophy of Wonder: Epistemology, Psychoanalysis, Phenomenology', won the award for best dissertation in the English Department at Stony Brook University. His article on Blake's *The Four Zoas* was published in the edited collection *Disabling Romanticism*, and his articles on Transatlantic connections between British Romanticism and American literature have appeared in *The Arthur Miller Journal*.

Kate Newell is the Chair of Liberal Arts at the Savannah College of Art and Design where she teaches courses in literature and adaptation. Her research interests include adaptation and other modes of intermediality. She has published essays on illustration and adaptation and is currently writing on novelisation, cartography, illustration, and other print-based modes of adaptation.

Morgan C. O'Brien is a PhD candidate at the University of Texas at Austin's Moody College of Communication. He has written about online gaming for the online journal *Flow*.

Dennis R. Perry is an Associate Professor of English at Brigham Young University, where he teaches courses in American literature and film adaptation. He is the author or editor of *Poe and Hitchcock* (Scarecrow, 2004), *Poe, 'The House of Usher' and the*

American Gothic with Carl Sederholm (Palgrave, 2009), and *Adapting Poe: Re-imaginings in Popular Culture*, edited with Carl Sederholm (Palgrave, 2012). In addition, his article on *Frankenstein* film adaptations appeared recently in *The Oxford Handbook of Adaptation Studies* (2017).

Paul C. Peterson is an expert on the U.S. Constitution and recently stepped down as Professor of Politics at the Coastal Carolina University. He taught there for more than thirty years. He has authored numerous articles and books on American government, political philosophy, and popular culture. His work has appeared in *Publius: The Journal of Federalism*, *The Political Science Reviewer*, *The John Marshall Law Review*, *The Journal of Media and Religion*, and *The American Political Science Review*.

Laurence Raw teaches at in the Department of English, Faculty of Education at Baskent University in Ankara, Turkey, and is one of the most prolific figures in contemporary adaptation studies. He has written several books, including *Character Actors in Horror and Science Fiction Films* (2013), and a chapter relating to *Frankenstein* parodies will appear in *Gothic Projections*, edited by Richard Hand and Jay McRoy (forthcoming). He is also the author of *The Ridley Scott Encyclopedia* (2009), *Adapting Henry James to the Screen* (2006), and *Adaptation Studies and Learning: New Frontiers* (2013), and edited or co-edited numerous books including *The Pedagogy of Adaptation* (2010), *Redefining Adaptation Studies* (2010), and *Nights at the Turkish Theatre* (2009). Raw also regularly updates his *Adaptation and Translation* blog, found at laurenceraw.blogspot.com.tr.

Farran L. Norris Sands is Professor of the Humanities at San Jacinto College in Houston, TX, where she currently teaches a course on monsters in literature, film, art, folklore, and religion. She holds a PhD in English Studies from Illinois State University, where she completed a dissertation on mad scientists in contemporary young adult novels and computer animated film. Her scholarly work can also be found in a co-authored chapter of *The Cambridge Companion to* Frankenstein, 2016. Her current interests include monsters, adaptation, children's literature, and young adult novels.

Jessica Straley is Assistant Professor of English at the University of Utah. Her book, *Evolution and Imagination in Victorian Children's Literature*, is forthcoming from Cambridge University Press. She has also published articles on evolutionary theory, vivisection, and Victorian literature in *Victorian Studies* and *Nineteenth-Century Literature*, and has contributed a chapter on the Victorian life and afterlife of images of dead children to *Comics Through the Looking-Glass*, edited by Anna Maria Jones and Rebecca N. Mitchell.

Lissette Lopez Szwydky is Assistant Professor of English at the University of Arkansas, specialising in nineteenth-century British literature and culture, the Gothic tradition, gender studies, and adaptation studies. Her publications include articles and book chapters on the popular histories of the Jamaican rebel bandit Three-Fingered

Jack, *The Hunchback of Notre Dame*, and *Dracula*. She is working on a book-length cultural history of adaptation focusing on the nineteenth-century entertainment industry.

Catherine Thewissen is a research and teaching assistant at Université catholique de Louvain (Belgium), where she specialises in the history and literature of World War I and the literature of Ireland. She recently published on the Belgian colonial past in *Breac: A Digital Journal of Irish Studies*.

Jeffrey Andrew Weinstock is Professor of English at Central Michigan University and an author or editor of twenty books. These include *The Age of Lovecraft* (University of Minnesota Press, edited with Carl Sederholm), *Return to Twin Peaks: New Approaches to Materiality, Theory, and Genre on Television* (Palgrave, edited with Catherine Spooner), *Goth Music: From Sound to Subculture* (Routledge, authored with Isabella van Elferen), and the *Cambridge Companion to the American Gothic*. Visit him at JeffreyAndrewWeinstock. com.

Introduction
The Frankenstein Complex: when the text is more than a text

Dennis R. Cutchins and Dennis R. Perry

*A*DAPTING *F*RANKENSTEIN APPROACHES THE seemingly endless adaptations, appropriations and re-appropriations, the prolific progeny of Mary Shelley's *Frankenstein or
the Modern Prometheus*, as inextricably intertextual pieces of popular culture. Arguably,
Frankenstein[1] has a greater presence in popular media than any other single narrative
over nearly two centuries,[2] only growing more extant and cogent as the popular
culture machine begins to ever more resemble the patchwork monster which Shelley's
precocious student created. In the context of this perpetual-motion phenomenon
Frankenstein invites a reading of itself in relation to what amounts to a potentially infinite
network of intertexts, or what we have termed the 'Frankenstein Network'. Unlike
other popular texts which generate adaptations periodically, *Frankenstein* has reached
a critical mass, to the point that adaptations flow forth continually at an unparalleled
rate.[3] Perhaps this is because Shelley touches the central nerve of our ambivalence
toward a modern world that interrupts the notion of the human. Or perhaps it is
simply her novel's recognition that any time a created thing becomes a sentient being,
capable of thinking for itself, complications will inevitably arise. Shelley could not have
imagined, however, the technology-saturated culture we now live in or the ways it has
forced us to adapt ourselves, and, in turn, continually to adapt *Frankenstein*.

Understanding the proliferation of Frankenstein adaptations, including many made
for young audiences, demands a creative and broad approach. Totalising mythic and
topical readings of *Frankenstein*, popular in the past, have addressed important issues
and cultural and historical themes such as sexual politics (Picart), race (Young), and
literary politics (Baldick). But mythic and topical approaches, as helpful as they have
been to Frankenstein studies, usually limit possible meanings by defining carefully circumscribed parameters of text (typically having a clear relationship to Shelley's novel),
genre (primarily literature to film), and criticism (often cultural criticism's focus on
race, gender, and class). But these approaches may not be comprehensive enough to
account for the Frankenstein Network. As Kamilla Elliott notes, scholars have rarely
'considered that the failure of adaptation studies to conform to theoretical paradigms
might arise from the inadequacies and limitations of the theories' (20). She goes on to
argue that adaptations are a special case in textual studies and that they may 'require

theories to adapt to *them*' (20–1 italics in original). We argue that this is particularly true in the case of *Frankenstein*. Straightforward literary theories, and even totalising mythic theories applied in the past, simply can't explain or describe the growing field of texts associated with *Frankenstein*. In an effort to comprehend this field, the adaptation studies approaches found in this collection focus on the complex relationships *between* the various texts, disparate traditions, and dynamic media in which *Frankenstein* has been adapted. From this perspective the meanings of any given adaptation, or of Shelley's novel itself, for that matter, are not perceived to be the result of a single text, a particular myth, or a set of cultural issues alone, but also the product of multiple relationships to other adaptations.

An adaptation studies approach to any work of art, including those associated with *Frankenstein*, requires that it be studied in the contexts created by other texts, since many of the perceived meanings are negotiated in webs of intertextual dialogue.[4] At its most basic level adaptation studies involves the comparison of one text to another, or to many others. We might argue that the distinguishing feature of an adaptation is that it is at least perceived by someone to be derived from the text to which it is compared. But it may be more accurate to say that adaptation is both a kind of text and a way of studying texts. Speaking specifically of *Frankenstein*, Thomas Leitch suggests that

> Adaptation theory tends to assume that adaptation focuses on the plot of the progenitor text, but arguments about fidelity to the earlier text's spirit should be equally open to adaptations based on a character like Sherlock Holmes or Frankenstein's monster with the ability to generate continuing adventures, especially if those adventures follow the same narrative formulas over and over again. (*Film Adaptation* 120)

There may, indeed, be no more fitting way to choose to understand *Frankenstein* than as a series of adaptations. Kyle Bishop suggests that some adaptations undergo what he calls a 'Frankensteinian process' by which they 'can no longer be seen as simply one side of a reductive dichotomy (original/copy), but neither can they be considered totally original products. Instead, seemingly new narratives are constructed from pre-existing pieces, pieces drawn from a complex system of related texts', and Shelley's novel is not the only source for these pieces (269). An equally weighty centre of the *Frankenstein* adaptation machine is, of course, James Whale's 1931 film, with its indelible and sympathetic portrayal of the monster by Boris Karloff in Jack Pierce's iconic make-up, German-Expressionist Gothicism, and dazzling electrical creation scene.

Mary Shelley's novel itself paves the way for the obsession with adaptation that has followed. Published in 1818, the title page, in fact, references texts that it adapts: the Prometheus myth noted in the title, three lines quoted from Milton's *Paradise Lost*, and the mention of *Caleb Williams* in the book's dedication to Mary's father, William Godwin. Among the most adapted texts in literature, *Frankenstein* was an immediate literary phenomenon upon publication, leading to fifteen different stage adaptations before 1851 – five in 1823 alone. Interestingly, Shelley revised her novel in 1831, making several significant changes that virtually amount to a minor adaptation. As

Figure 0.1 Boris Karloff as Frankenstein's Creature chained in a German expressionist dungeon.

Anne Mellor notes, 'the most striking thematic differences between the two published versions of the novel concern the role of fate, the degree of Frankenstein's responsibility for his actions, the representation of nature, the role of Clerval, and the representation of the family'. The most significant result of these revisions is the loss of some of the book's internal philosophical coherence (205).

While Whale was ostensibly adapting Shelley's novel, in truth his film was primarily adapted from Peggy Webling's then popular stage adaptation of the novel, which, in turn, followed many of the venerable stage traditions in practice since Richard Brinsley Peake's 1823 *Presumption; or, the Fate of Frankenstein*. *Frankenstein* (1931), for instance, made the monster mute and gave the doctor an 'Igor' assistant, both innovations introduced by Peake. In addition, Whale drew on German Expressionist *mise-en-scène* as well as on Gothic imagery to create an almost surreal atmosphere. These choices gave the story a look and feel that instantly transformed Shelley's philosophical and grotesque tragedy into a Gothic horror film – one that has not only been central to the development of horror cinema, but that has been more influential on most subsequent film adaptations than Shelley's novel.

Any understanding of *Frankenstein* in the twenty-first century will be delightfully riddled by such complex intertextual networks, and that makes these texts the ideal subject matter for an adaptation studies approach. In their introduction to *Adaptation Studies: New Challenges, New Directions*, Jorgen Bruhn, Anne Gjelsvik, and Eirik Frisvold Hanssen write that 'another detectable trend in adaptation studies is the movement away from a one-to-one relationship, that is, between *one* source (such as a novel) and *one* film. Instead, adaptation is viewed within a more comprehensive understanding of the cultural and textual networks into which any textual phenomena is understood' (8). They cite Christine Geraghty's analysis of Joe Wright's *Atonement* and her development of the idea that 'an adaptation necessarily relies on and cites a widespread web of influences' (8). Networked relationships like these have even changed the way the novel itself is read.[5] Traditionally, the many versions of *Frankenstein* have been viewed as mere exploitation, copies that are always inferior to the 'original'. But adaptation studies, as Harriet Margolis suggests, creates a space in which adaptations might be more than mimesis, more than an always-inferior copy. She argues that it is hard to imagine 'a literature class including [*Frankenstein*] without confronting the Hollywood versions of Mary Shelley's vision' (160). Imelda Whelehan and Deborah Cartmell argue, more specifically, that the cultural studies approach typically taken by adaptation scholars 'foregrounds the activities of reception and consumption, and shelves – forever perhaps – considerations of the aesthetic or cultural worthiness of the object of study' (as found in Elliott 'Rethinking' 580).

It is easy to imagine, for instance, a student reading Shelley's novel after[6] viewing Whale's *Frankenstein* interpreting Victor/Henry as a sympathetic and well-meaning, though ambitious, scientist with an unfortunate nervous incapacity to handle the results of his experiment. On the other hand, someone reading Shelly's Victor in the context of *I Was a Teenage Frankenstein* (Strock 1957) might see a very different man. The ruthlessness of Strock's Victor magnifies flaws underlying Shelley's romanticised characterisation, revealing a fundamentally cold, fierce, self-protecting man who refuses to do all he can to save Justine, Elizabeth, and the rest of his family. In *Mary Shelley's Frankenstein* (1994), Kenneth Branagh adapts the end of his story to allow a clearly desperate and even unreasonable Victor to use his horribly unaesthetic science to bring the dead and mutilated body of Elizabeth back to life.

Figure 0.2 Kenneth Branagh as Frankenstein feverishly working on his creation in *Mary Shelley's Frankenstein*.

This resurrection, and the ensuing scenes, highlight Frankenstein's character as a self-obsessed child, unable to respond to grief, form relationships, or generally function as an adult. This particular reading of *Frankenstein* aligns quite well with that of several contemporary scholars.[7] On the other hand, two other adaptations, both made for TV, *Frankenstein: The True Story* (1973), directed by Jack Smight, and *Frankenstein* (1973), directed by Glenn Jordan, emphasise the monster's childlike innocence. By so doing these adaptations heighten our sympathy for the monster, and stress Frankenstein's position as flawed creator/father.[8] Both of these adaptations actually anticipate the now popular reading of Frankenstein as a failed parent,[9] a thread picked up by Mel Brooks a year later in *Young Frankenstein* (1974).

As these examples suggest, from an adaptation studies point of view, any text is subject to multiple readings, or to put it another way, each text contains potentially innumerable meanings. Christa Albrecht-Crane and Dennis Cutchins reference this idea when they write in *Adaptation Studies* that there are any number of paths through a text, each potentially a source for an adaptation (18). Literary texts like Shelley's *Frankenstein*, by their very definition, retain a plenitude of both intentional and unintentional meanings, indicating the various paths that may be taken through the text. Adaptations may or may not adopt these meanings, but the very act of adaptation inevitably creates even more meanings, more possible paths with which future adaptors may engage. This makes future adaptations ever more suggestive and meaningful, certainly more daunting for scholars, and fitting subject matter for what we have

termed a 'Complex' approach. Because there have been important innovations from
plays, films, and from the language itself, one purpose of this volume is to demonstrate
that because *Frankenstein* has been refracted through so many media, and processed by
so many diverse audiences, it has become innately plural and unstable, the possession
of millions of individual reader/viewers. In *The Lives and Times of Ebenezer Scrooge*, Paul
Davis notes the same kind of trajectory for Dickens' *A Christmas Carol*. He suggests that
any contemporary audience can only understand *A Christmas Carol* in the light of all
the other Carols they have experienced. 'The Carol,' he writes, 'is the sum of all its
versions, of all its revisions, parodies, and piracies' (5).

Thomas Leitch complicates this matter even further when he, with some reserva-
tions, proposes that 'the question of whether a particular adaptation counts as an
adaptation rests not with any properties of the adaptation as such but with its audience'
('Adaptation and Intertextuality' 95). Recognising an adaptation, in other words, is
not the result of structural elements of the text so much as it is the result of perceptions of an audience. Matt Lorenz, in this collection (Chapter 7), discusses *I, Robot*
(2004) as a Frankenstein adaptation, though others may not notice the connection.
Thus, when someone experiences a new *Frankenstein* adaptation, acknowledged by the
creators or otherwise, the meanings they apprehend are automatically filtered through
the internal and personal palimpsest of other 'Frankensteins' they have experienced.
Hence, each person's aesthetic experiences become a personal collection of texts;
or, we might say, they become part of a personal, rather than global, mythology of
their own, a Frankenstein Complex, if you will. *Adapting Frankenstein* rests on this
critical premise. We contend that an adaptation studies approach, and the idea of a
Frankenstein Complex located in the minds of individuals, in fact, may offer the only
real way to comprehend the web of texts that Frankenstein has become. This is true
because none of us has experienced every Frankenstein adaptation. Our complexes,
then, are all idiosyncratic. They include those Frankensteins we have actually experienced, along with the more general cultural knowledge we have been able to absorb.
Thus a complex is created by what Judith Buchanan terms 'random accidents of critical
attention' (158).

If the 'Frankenstein Complex' is the personal experience of Frankenstein that each
of us carries within, then the entire potential collection of Frankenstein texts, the
repository, if you will, may be labelled the 'Frankenstein Network'. It includes easily
identified texts such as *Mary Shelley's Frankenstein*, but may also consist of texts like
Wally Pfister's *Transcendence* (2014), Doug Liman's *The Bourne Identity* (2002), or
Stephen Spielberg's *Jurassic Park* (1993), films that could be identified by audience
members as Frankenstein narratives.[10] Obviously, tracing the many potential ideological and thematic connections within the vast Frankenstein Network is all but impossible, given the number of genres, texts, and media involved, as well as the fact that each
adaptation reflects its own version of the Frankenstein Complex, and each audience
member potentially sees new connections. This isn't finding a needle in a haystack, this
is finding a particular needle in a barrel of needles.

Edison's 1910 *Frankenstein*, the novel's first film adaptation, was heavily influenced by the many early stage productions of *Frankenstein*. But the concept of Frankenstein and his monster which most of us carry around was archetypally established with Whale's two films *Frankenstein* (1931) and *The Bride of Frankenstein* (1935), followed distantly by the rest of the Universal series. These films deeply influenced radio, comics, and other media. In the 1950s Hammer's *Frankenstein* series added colour, sex, and more graphic violence, and centred on an essentially evil Baron Frankenstein who creates a different monster for each film. In turn, both the Universal and Hammer series continue to be reimagined by campy-ironic, nostalgic, and even pornographic Frankenstein films, adult and young adult books, stage plays, graphic novels, games, transmedia, comics, art, and so forth. And each of these media generates its own traditions in which the monster, not to mention its creator, takes on all imaginable roles – victim, superhero, clown, tragic figure, PhD, child, teenager, parent, avenger, and on and on. The aim of *Adapting Frankenstein* is to present a sampling of readings addressing aspects of this miasmic composite; in short, it represents a collective attempt to probe individual texts and media to make as many connections among them as possible.

The approaches taken by the chapters in this book engage popular as well as under-represented adapting genres to examine Frankenstein as an unrestricted network, an intertextuality writ large. The twin ideas of the Frankenstein Complex and the Frankenstein Network act as a liberating negative capability, demanding that scholars examine simultaneously numerous genres and meanings relevant to Frankenstein. These chapters tend to involve multiple texts in the analysis of any one text or set of texts, rather than one-to-one case study comparisons. In 2006 Linda Hutcheon introduced the term 'palimpsestuous' to adaptation studies, suggesting that adaptations allow audience members to experience multiple texts at once, as one text becomes a layer through which another text is experienced (6). We would add that artists, as well as audiences, also operate within these textual layers or palimpsests, at least some of which they have chosen. This idea is reiterated in a number of the chapters that follow. Since intertextual adaptation studies teach us that a text's meaning derives from its relationship to other texts, the more of these texts that become part of the conversation, the more meanings can accumulate. For example, in light of *Mary Shelley's Frankenstein*, Danny Boyle's National Theatre production of *Frankenstein* (2011), and *Frankenstein's Wedding: Live in Leeds* (Teague and Hampton 2011), one might be tempted to note a trend towards re-enshrining Shelley's novel as the preferred source for adaptations. The wider contemporary field, however, including Dean Koontz's Frankenstein series (2004), *I, Frankenstein* (2014), *Victor Frankenstein* (2015), and recent television appearances of Shelley's characters in *Penny Dreadful* (Showtime 2014–16) and *Once Upon a Time* (ABC 2011–), demonstrates an equal interest in adapting Whale's film, exploring Shelley's characters through new contexts such as graphic novels and fairy tales, and creating completely new backstories.

The awesome task of making sense of such a vast network of texts forces scholars to adopt innovations, not the least of which is a non-linear, hypertextual notion of reading. Thus the Complex/Network approach to Frankenstein is not a simple methodology but, rather, a recognition of the interrelatedness of Frankenstein texts that opens doors to multiple possibilities. How, for example, do we compare texts from differing genres, such as DC Comics' *Frankenstein: Agent of S.H.A.D.E.* (Lemire 2005–), Marvel Comic's *The Hulk* (1962–), and James Whale's *Frankenstein*? We might begin by comparing the dual natures of David Banner and the Hulk to the Creature as it was portrayed by Karloff. These characters are dangerous as well as sympathetic, and both the Hulk and the Creature have their origins as collateral damage of imperfect science. We might also observe the way both the Creature as an agent of S.H.A.D.E. and the Hulk as an Avenger are forced to negotiate the problems of working within groups. Not stopping there, questions might then be asked about the influence of these characters on the creation of other comics and on recent cinema. Ultimately, broader meanings might be explored about all of this in terms of the ways both Frankenstein and his Creature are brought into various imaginative universes. In short, recognising the complex nature of Frankenstein tends to illuminate unexpected and even revelatory pathways through many texts.

Clearly, Frankenstein is more than a text. It's more than a novel, more than a film, and even more than a series of films. And this continuous and ongoing popularity demands scholarly attention. As Susan Hitchcock put it, 'the monster's story says something important. Otherwise we would not keep telling it' (Hitchcock 11). Thomas Leitch suggests that the 'something important' is 'to explore the mystery of human identity', a pattern which he notes in all the great Hollywood monster franchises (*Film Adaptation* 106). Leitch is right, of course, because what it means to be human is one of the central questions that drives Shelley's narrative, as well as many of the adaptations. But it's more complicated than that. Writers, filmmakers, new media artists, playwrights, and storytellers of all kinds don't just keep retelling the *same* story. Instead they continue to reinvent Frankenstein and his Creature – reinscribing them with meanings, and remaking them in their own images over and over again. It's not just that these characters can't die; instead we have actually fulfilled the fictional scientist's worst nightmare and provided the monster with an endless progeny 'propagated upon the earth' (Shelley 119). Evidence for this may be found in the fact that early readers were less focused on the Creature that runs amok, and more concerned with the good doctor's 'presumption'. Later nineteenth-century readers and theatre goers saw an analogue of social unrest. Mid-twentieth-century readers and viewers often focused on the fear of out-of-control technology, while scholars in the late twentieth century discovered a tale of male usurpation of the birthing process. Each of these readings would suggest a different central question and a focus on different anxieties that a Complex approach can highlight. Hence, the 'Frankenstein Complex' is constantly evolving ideologically, culturally, technologically, and generically.

The causes and cultural significance of this seemingly endless reinvention are really the subject matter of this collection, but a clue to the reasons for *Frankenstein*'s fecundity may be found in the ideas of Mikhail Bakhtin. Ellen Cronan Rose has suggested that 'certain texts become "canonical"' because of 'their plasticity [and] capacity for adaptation to the complex, often bifurcated needs and sensibilities of successive generations of readers' (809). Bakhtin would likely agree with this notion, but he employs a metaphor to describe this 'plasticity' that is particularly fitting for the study of *Frankenstein* adaptations. In his analysis of Rabelais's writings Bakhtin defines what he calls the 'grotesque body'. He describes it as 'a body in the act of becoming. It is never finished, never completed; it is continually built, created, and builds and creates another body' (*Rabelais and His World* 317). As examples, Bakhtin suggests images of consumption, regurgitation, birth, or copulation. A body or bodies engaged in these kinds of acts becomes difficult to delineate or distinguish. 'Thus,' he continues, 'the artistic logic of the grotesque image ignores the closed, smooth, and impenetrable surface of the body and retains only its excrescences (sprouts, buds) and orifices, only that which leads beyond the body's limited space or into the body's depths' (318).

These grotesque bodies are literal for Bakhtin as well as metaphorical. He equates the grotesque body, typically associated with ribald humour, with grotesque texts that tend to open themselves to interpenetration by other texts, symbolic interpretations, and the constant generation of other texts. 'If we consider the grotesque image in its extreme aspect,' he writes, 'it never presents an individual body; the image consists of orifices and convexities that present another, newly conceived body. It is a point of transition in a life eternally renewed, the inexhaustible vessel of death and conception' (318). Thus, grotesque texts for Bakhtin are those which seem constantly to generate other texts. Perhaps it should not be surprising that Bakhtin's grotesque bodies resemble, at least in some respects, Frankenstein's Creature. The monster, in essence, becomes the dark side of Rabelais's grotesque creations. Upon first seeing what he has created from the parts collected at the slaughter and charnel houses, Shelley's Victor Frankenstein finds it difficult to 'delineate' or define his creation. Then, as it comes to life, he notices with horror the Creature's thin 'yellow skin' that 'scarcely covered the work of muscles and arteries beneath' (Shelley 60). The Creature may not have Bakhtinian 'orifices', but its insides, nevertheless, are nearly on display. Images of the monster from television, stage, and film seem, if anything, to emphasise the grotesque nature of the Creature's body, which is often covered with oozing wounds and bursting stitches – all threatening to split open at any moment. But let us be clear that Bakhtin sees this literal lack of a thick skin, at least in so far as it applies to texts, as a positive thing in that it engenders new texts. 'The events of the grotesque sphere,' he writes, 'are always developed on the boundary dividing one body from the other and, as it were, at their points of intersection. One body offers its death, the other its birth, but they are merged in a two-bodied image' (322). At least part of the attraction of *Frankenstein*, then, may be the monster's grotesque body – a body that never seems completely closed or finished.

Bakhtin contrasts this image of the grotesque body or grotesque text with that of the canonical or closed body or text. These he characterises as smooth, finished, and impenetrable. With the closed body the 'opaque surface and the body's "valleys" acquire an essential meaning as the border of a closed individuality that does not merge with other bodies and with the world' (320). Thus, these closed bodies or texts tend to lose their symbolic value, along with their ability to generate new texts (321). Shelley's *Frankenstein*, on the other hand, seems to retain the ability to generate new texts and simultaneously leave itself constantly open to new interpretations. Thus, as Hitchcock puts it, 'the very "plasticity" of the novel, as more than one critic has mentioned, goes far in explaining Frankenstein's longevity' (323).

Louis James explored some of this plasticity when he outlined the varied ways in which just one aspect of the Frankenstein phenomenon, the monster, has been inter-preted, including as 'a type of the unconscious', as a Jungian shadow, as Rousseau's natural man, as a Wordsworthian child of nature, as a Romantic rebel, as Mary Shelley's abandoned babe, as part of the Darwinian debate on evolution, and as a representation of the colonised other (James 78). Interpretations of this single element are definitely varied, and many of those interpretations have served as the foundations for strikingly different adaptations, some of which are treated in the pages of this col-lection. But the ubiquitous nature of Frankenstein may lead us to make the mistake of treating individual texts or iterations of Frankenstein as undistinguished and ahistorical parts of a greater whole. Chris Baldick warns against this when he suggests that a truism like Frankenstein plays on 'our deepest fears' 'refuses to recognise that fears are themselves subject to history' (6). Thus, to write about Frankenstein is to grapple with the problem of writing about specific texts in specific historical, biographical, political, or cultural contexts, without losing sight of the larger, sprawling context that is the Frankenstein Network.

Some scholars have chosen to solve that problem by grounding any discussion of Frankenstein in the relatively solid foundation of the novel. But even that is not always safe or simple. Until fairly recently the many adaptations of Shelley's work were typically viewed by the literati as pop-culture ephemera, unworthy of scholarly attention. In the words of Linda Hutcheon, 'even in our postmodern age of cultural recycling, something – perhaps the commercial success of adaptations – would appear to make us uneasy' (3). Early on, the popularity of the many commercial, seemingly simplistic, adaptations took a heavy toll on the novel's prestige, intellectual elites apparently assuming that anything this popular with the general public simply could not be the highest form of art. Upon its publication the novel, too, was criticised by some as 'uncouth' and 'disgusting' Gothic sensationalism, a trend that was reinforced by the early stage adaptations – several of which were parodies or farces (Hitchcock 74). As late as the early 1970s Levine and Knoepflmacher were afraid that their book on *Frankenstein* would 'be received as a self-parody of the solemnity of academic criti-cism' (xii). With the advent of feminism, cultural criticism, and other more flexible critical tools, however, the justification of Frankenstein criticism, dealing with either the novel or its progeny, has become unnecessary.

But choosing to focus exclusively on the novel does not solve the problem of under-standing individual 'Frankensteins' in specific historical contexts at the same time that we recognise them as parts of a larger whole. As poststructural theory teaches, the story exists only in the reading or the telling, but unlike, say, James Joyce's *Ulysses*, which is experienced almost exclusively by reading the novel that Joyce wrote, the balance of what we identify as 'Frankenstein' is not experienced in the novel. The solution that became popular in the late 1980s was to view Frankenstein as a 'myth'. This makes some practical sense, and several of the major critical statements concerning Frankenstein adaptations since that period agree that, having moved beyond the status of a mere novel to that of a myth, Frankenstein's adaptations are, in fact, engaged in a myth-making process that reinterprets and adds new dimensions to Shelley's story (Hand; Baldick; Picart). The Frankenstein 'myth', the 'essence' of Frankenstein, if you will, is defined by Baldick as a two-part structure that he believes may be found in most adaptations: (a) that Frankenstein makes a living creature out of bits of corpses; and (b) that the Creature turns against his creator and runs amok (3). In addition to Baldick's basic framework, many scholars also agree that adaptations have tended to grow out of the cultural anxieties of the time when they were produced (Botting; Baldick; Picart). Botting, for example, notes that since the monster is usually the locus of cultural anxieties, many adaptations become warnings (*Making Monstrous* 192). For Picart these cultural anxieties typically revolve around issues of power, gender, and technology (*Cinematic Rebirths* 20), while Baldick, following the novel-centred current we mentioned earlier, insists that although a cultural focus is inevitable in criticism and adaptation, it should be historically grounded in the anxieties originally part of Shelley's novel – the non-sexual creation of life and technology run wild (5–7).

We are not convinced, however, that 'myth' is the best way to conceptualise the Frankenstein phenomenon, at least when our intention is to study adaptations. Identifying a body of texts as representative of a myth has a tendency to hide or ignore the idiosyncrasies and differences of a particular adaptation while emphasising shared motifs and similarities. As Richard Hand and Jay McRoy put it, 'a myth lives, and the "truth" of it is not to be found in the earliest version but, as Lévi-Strauss claims, in all its versions' (2). Baldick, also citing Lévi-Strauss, carries this argument even further, suggesting that 'the mythic value of myth remains preserved, even through the worst translation' (2). But we find this statement highly problematic for the study of adaptation, since the 'translation' is exactly the thing we are hoping to study.[11]

When scholars identify Frankenstein adaptations as iterations of a myth they tend to ignore the specific *tellings* in favour of defining an archetypal or overarching and generalised version of the myth. This is exactly what Baldick's 'skeleton story' is, his attempt to define the 'essence' or central motifs shared in the adaptations, since, as he argues, a myth's true substance 'does not lie in its style, its original music or its syntax, but in the story which it tells' (2). A great deal of important information is lost, however, when we ignore a particular text's style, music, or syntax. Hence Baldick's two-line 'least common denominator' version of Frankenstein is not really the 'essence' of *Frankenstein*, but simply another adaptation. In addition, nor does such a narrow reduction of the 'myth' account for various types of indirect adaptations or appropriations, which may use some elements from a source text but not others. *I, Robot* or *Her* (2013), for instance, can certainly be read as Frankenstein stories even though the man-made beings in both of these films are not created from 'bits of corpses'.

Moreover, a mythic approach to Frankenstein does not account for much of our pleasure with adaptations. When we read a new novel with 'Frankenstein' in the title, or watch a new film adaptation, we do so not only to remind ourselves of what it has in common with other texts, but also because we hope to be surprised and to find something new *combined* with something familiar. Afterwards we may return with pleasure to Shelley's novel or to an older film, texts that we may have known for years, but that we have suddenly learned to see with new eyes. This is one of the marvellous gifts that any adaptation can offer us: the chance, the excuse, to return to a familiar text and read it or watch it over again. Perhaps this happens when we see *Young Frankenstein* and then return to the Whale films, or when we read Brian Aldiss's *Frankenstein Unbound* (1973) and then return to Shelley's novel. And the pleasure we experience is usually not found in either text alone but, rather, in between them, in the places where the texts meet in shocking dissonance or unexpected harmony.[12] Any new adaptation of *Frankenstein* will, no doubt, introduce new elements, but will also steal parts from the still living body of work that has come before.

The relationships among texts in the Frankenstein Network are complicated, to say the least. As Bakhtin put it in the early part of the twentieth century, all texts, including any new adaptations of Frankenstein, are intertexts. 'The living utterance,' he writes,

> having taken meaning and shape at a particular historical moment in a socially specific environment, cannot fail to brush up against thousands of living dialogic threads, woven by socio-ideological consciousness and around the given object of an utterance; it cannot fail to become an active participant in social dialogue. After all, the utterance arises out of this dialogue as a continuation of it and as a rejoinder to it – it does not approach the object from the sidelines. (*The Dialogic* 276–77)

In effect, Bakhtin defines the Frankenstein Complex here. So, although the plot of *I, Frankenstein* (2014) may have nothing to do with the plot of Shelley's novel, the filmmakers explicitly ask the audience to see their film in conversation or dialogue with other Frankenstein texts, including the graphic novel of the same name. And there are good artistic and practical reasons for that. The dialogues create in the minds of the viewers, at least potentially, a richness that a similar fantasy film without these sorts of explicit dialogues might lack. Shelley herself, in fact, began this dialogic process by incorporating into her novel Giovanni Aldini's radical experiments in galvanism, the Prometheus myth, Rousseauian philosophy, *Paradise Lost* (1667), the Faust legend, *Caleb Williams* (1794), and arguably François-Félix Nogaret's *Le Miroir des événemens actuels, ou La Belle au plus offrant* (1790)[13] and Senjūshō's 'Making a Humanoid at Mt Kōya' (ca. 13th century),[14] among others. The more of these texts that a reader of

Shelley's *Frankenstein* has in her or his mind – the more, in other words, they are part of the reader's Frankenstein Complex – the more likely those texts will be drawn into conversation with each other. This dialogue between texts is precisely the locus for intertextual adaptation studies.

And the 'influence' which these texts have on each other, based on an individual's Frankenstein Complex, likely has little to do with the historical order in which they appeared. Anyone who reads Shelley's novel for the first time today inevitably brings to it their own version of the Complex. The consequence of this saturation is that our various experiences with Frankenstein bring emotional and intellectual baggage with them that inescapably conditions our reactions to the new adaptations which we encounter. Such an intertextual definition of our relationship with proliferating Frankenstein adaptations becomes a natural model for our approach to Frankenstein in this study, since the Complex approach to Frankenstein suggests that the 'meaning' of any given text is to be found not in the text itself, but only in its relationship to other texts around it. Frankenstein, in fact, may offer the adaptation version of the 'wave-particle duality' found in physics, in that individual texts may be studied as 'particles', discrete from other texts, or as part of a 'wave' of texts, all interrelated. Just as physicists have had to come to terms with the fact that the definition of light depends on how it is studied, so those approaching the vast Frankenstein Network will inevitably need to come to terms with intertextual relationships to explore its 'wave' effect.

In the twenty-first century that network has become increasingly more complicated as Frankenstein has been reimagined in many novel environments. These include providing new back stories for characters such as Igor (*Victor Frankenstein* 2015), featuring the monster in comic-styled supernatural action adventures (*I, Frankenstein* 2014), updating the science used to create the Creature (*Frankenstein* 2015), building a family drama in which a dead cop is brought back to life to try to mend his ways (*Second Chance* 2016), making Frankenstein into a 200-year-old who uses his techniques to keep himself alive while creating an army of 'monsters' in a plot to rule the world (*Frankenstein* 2004), turning the tale into a dark, Victorian detective television series (*Penny Dreadful* 2014–16, *The Frankenstein Chronicles* 2015–), setting the key characters in a fairy tale to help the evil Maleficent (*Once Upon a Time* 2011–), historicising post-World War II as a grisly, camp, gore-fest (*Frankenstein's Army* 2013), targeting mass audiences with animated comedy adaptations (*Hotel Transylvania* 2012, *Igor* 2008), and, harkening back to James Whale's masterpieces, animating with stop-motion a boy's attempts to bring his dead dog back to life (*Frankenweenie* 2012). While adaptations in the 1960s and 1970s added sexuality to Frankenstein (*Flesh for Frankenstein* 1973), contemporary adaptations often push the boundaries of violence and gore, add human interest and dark mystery, and appeal to children. Perhaps most significant is how television has begun finally to invest in the Frankenstein franchise with expensive, well-produced series. In the past, aside from children's Saturday-morning animated shows like *Frankenstein Jr. and the Impossibles* (Hannah-Barbara 1966) and *Milton the Monster* (Seeger Productions 1965), television only periodically came out with films that were, for the most part, not innovative. Clearly the Frankenstein Network 'is alive' and well in a broad variety of inventive adaptations.

The present study includes chapters in five categories of adaptation media: dramatic presentations on stage and radio, cinema and television, literature, illustrations and comics, and new media. Part I, on stage and radio, begins with two chapters on nineteenth-century stage adaptations by Lissette Lopez Szwydky and Glenn Jellenik, who explore how these become models of adapting Shelley's novel to various media, particularly film, identifying ways in which addressing audience-specific needs have been a crucial component to the ongoing fascination with Frankenstein. While Szwydky (Chapter 1) focuses on the early key innovations to Shelley's story in Peake's *Presumption* and other early nineteenth-century stage adaptations that eventually became foundational in subsequent adaptations in various media, Jellenik (Chapter 2) approaches Peake's play in terms of its intertextual model of adaptation, claiming that the play created Shelley's *Frankenstein* as much as the novel structured the play. Laurence Raw (Chapter 3) then analyses a companion media, radio, in terms of its special conventions relevant to its more general listenership, particularly noting how radio adaptations reflect their historical and cultural contexts.

Film and television, arguably the most influential genres of Frankenstein adaptations, are covered in Part II through crucial moments as they have developed from the 1950s to our day, reflected through the lens of modern critical theory. Dennis R. Perry (Chapter 4) looks at how *Forbidden Planet* (1956), a science fiction film not before linked to Frankenstein, explores the Atomic Scientist Movement's attempt to wrest control of the bomb from the military as a reflection of the Frankenstein power motifs in the film. Kyle Bishop (Chapter 6), on the other hand, examines television, an under-explored medium of Frankenstein adaptations. TV adaptations of *Frankenstein*, he argues, tend to be more fragmented and tangential than full-length films, often appearing as special episodes in series like *Buffy the Vampire Slayer* and *X-Files*. Unsurprisingly, Victor and his monster seem quite at home within the fragmented structure of television. Morgan C. O'Brien (Chapter 5) traces the production paper trail to unfold how Hammer Studios made Shelley's tale meaningful to a post-World War II audience and simultaneously effected a paradigm shift in horror films generally. Also looking at Hammer's Frankenstein franchise, Maria K. Bachman and Paul Peterson (Chapter 8) view these films within an evolutionary context which is focused almost exclusively on the creator, rather than the Creature. They argue how and why Hammer makes the scientist the monster and his creation the victim. Further blurring the boundaries between the creator and the created, Matt Lorenz, too (Chapter 7), focuses on two indirect adaptations (*I, Robot* and *X-Men First Class*) to examine questions of the psychological creation of the Creature character, rather than merely its physical creation.

Literary adaptations of *Frankenstein* (Part III) discover a range between new identities (personal and literary), and the function of mad scientists. While Farran Norris Sands (Chapter 11) examines mad scientists in young-adult dystopian literature, wherein the Frankenstein figure, not his creation, becomes the locus of cultural anxieties and a harbinger of the apocalypse, Jessica Straley (Chapter 11) looks at how children's books have appropriated the Frankenstein monster's 'glorious grossness' as children's comedy, at the same time helping young readers examine infirmities, diets, and what counts as a normal body. Jamie Horrocks (Chapter 9) explores how new adult literary genres, like neo-Victorian novels,[15] use the Frankenstein trope as models for textual resurrection – an apt allegorisation of this emergent literary genre. The creation of Frankenstein's Creature becomes a symbol for the textual reincarnation that takes place in neo-Victorian literature on both narrative and meta-narrative levels. Carol Davison (Chapter 10) examines Scotland's featured role in Shelley's novel in terms of Scottish literary reimaginings of the bride motif in *Frankenstein* in order to engage issues surrounding transgressive female power in relation to Scottish history, politics, and national identity. Jeffrey Andrew Weinstock (Chapter 13), on the other hand, examines H.P. Lovecraft's Frankenstein-inspired tale, 'Herbert West – Reanimator', in terms of the new object-oriented materialism theory, noting how Frankenstein tales tend to demolish human exceptionalism.

Art and comic adaptations of Frankenstein (Part IV) often become metaphors for the monster's creation itself from used body parts. Kate Newell (Chapter 14) suggests the term 'repurposing' to describe how illustrations for various editions of Shelley's novel are sometimes recycled or recaptioned – like old body parts – and then applied to different moments in the book. She nicely defines how the choice and use of illustrations can reinforce an essential reading of the novel or suggest new ways of apprehending it. In a similar way, Joe Darowski (Chapter 15) discovers in issues of Marvel's *X-Men* both an alien Frankenstein monster and an articulate leader of a subterranean race. In classic comic book fashion, the monster is repurposed to fit the fanciful Marvel universe of changelings and mutants. Finally, Veronique Bragard and Catherine Thewissen (Chapter 16) note similar repurposing with the un-superhero-like Frankenstein monsters found in *bande dessinées* Franco-Belgian comics. Here forlorn monsters, often traumatised outsiders, struggle to find their place in lonely landscapes and in solitude.

In Part V Kelly Jones' chapter (Chapter 18) moves firmly into the twenty-first century, examining live-broadcast stage and television productions in terms of the uncanny effects of the theatrical Gothic as a product of its 'liveness'. More specifically, she emphasises the effect produced on the audience by the horrific playfulness of the corresponding liveness of monster and medium. Tully Barnett and Ben Kooyman (Chapter 17), on the other hand, consider how the themes of Shelley's novel interact with notions of hybrid textuality in Shelley Jackson's *Patchwork Girl* (1995) and Dave Morris's *Frankenstein* iPad app (2012). Both of these texts, Barnett and Kooyman argue, create new media identities that explore the boundaries of the human offered by an engagement with digital frameworks for storytelling. Richard Hand (Afterword) wraps up the book by turning our attention briefly to the unexplored range of the Frankenstein Network. He touches on pop-culture Frankenstein ephemera, including *Night Gallery* (1969–73) shorts, a *Black Mirror* (2011–) episode, political campaign appearances, and a surprising number of Frankenstein adaptations premiering at the 2016 Edinburgh Festival Fringe.

Shaping many of these studies of adaptation, and linking them to their various critical perspectives, is a crucial dimension of the Frankenstein Complex: the monster's patchwork creation. This, in fact, is a central feature of adaptation itself. In this sense, of course, we are following in Shelley's own footsteps, as she appropriated a number of sources in creating her masterpiece. This collection is intended to broaden the scope of future research on Frankenstein by focusing on the important relationships between texts, especially as they are processed in the minds of their diverse audiences and demonstrate the Frankenstein Complex at work.

Notes

1   The sheer number of adaptations in virtually every medium makes the Frankenstein phenomenon difficult to approach, to say the least. In fact, it is hard to know exactly what we mean even when we do something as simple as write the word 'Frankenstein'. Are we referring to Shelley's novel, a particular adaptation, the popular culture phenomenon, or something else entirely? To lessen confusion we have adopted the convention of writing 'Dr Frankenstein' or 'Victor Frankenstein' when referencing the character, '*Frankenstein*' or 'Shelley's *Frankenstein*' when discussing the novel, '*Frankenstein* (1931)' when dealing with specific film adaptations, the 'Frankenstein Complex' when referring to a given person's personal experience with Frankenstein, and the 'Frankenstein Network' or simply 'Frankenstein' when working with the body of related texts that are the subject of this collection.

2   Paul Davis has suggested that Dickens' *A Christmas Carol* should hold this title, and he may be right. Both *Carol* and *Frankenstein* are unquestionably culture-texts that continue to generate adaptations on a regular basis.

3   As of September 2016 the IMDB lists six films (*I, Frankenstein*, *Victor Frankenstein*, *Frankenstein*, *Baby Frankenstein*, *Frankenstein's Monster*, and *Frankenstein Created Bikers*) released in 2014–16, and no fewer than five new Frankenstein films in development. In addition, it lists two new television series adaptations, ITV's *Frankenstein Chronicles* (2015–) and Fox's *Second Chance* (2016), as well as dozens of individual television episodes with 'Frankenstein' in the title. It also notes *Frankenstein*, a full-length ballet production by Lian Scarlett (2016), as well as several live simulcasts.

4   We, along with Thomas Leitch and others, 'begin with the axiom that adaptation is a subset of intertextuality – all adaptations are obviously intertexts'. ('Adaptation and Intertextuality' 89)

5   For a discussion of the notion of a 'two-way' change see page 25 of Kamilla Elliott's 'Theorizing Adaptations/Adapting Theories'.

6   The order of reception may be more important here than the order of production.

7   See, for example, Mellor (48–59).

8   One actually has the impression when watching both of these adaptations that if Frankenstein had had access to quality day care the resulting problems never would have arisen.

9   As in the work of Randel (195).

10 We note that two of these films, *The Bourne Identity* and *Jurassic Park*, were adapted from novels by Robert Ludlum and Michael Crichton, making the question of adaptation that much more complicated for these films. Were Ludlum and Crichton influenced by Shelley? Did the film adaptations bend toward Frankenstein and away from the ostensible source texts? The potential points of influence, if not infinite, are certainly numerous.

11 While Frankenstein likely does *function* as a myth in contemporary culture, we need to recognise what myths are in order to understand what that means. Myths are not, as Lévi-Strauss would have us believe, timeless truths, unbound by culture or language, and able to survive 'even the worst translation'. Folklorist George Schoemaker defines myth, as many folklorists would, as a 'sacred narrative … about the beginnings of things', and often associated with 'ritual and ceremony' (237). In most of its iterations Frankenstein certainly is a story about the beginning of something, a creation story, if you will. And this is, perhaps, the most valuable reason to identify Frankenstein as a myth. If Frankenstein is about the creation of new life, or even the creation of a new kind of being, then it is a myth in this technical sense of the word. Professor of religion Robert A. Segal, in a broader definition of 'myth', begins by suggesting that myths are stories 'about something significant', in which the main figures are personalities rather than 'impersonal forces' (4–5). That part of Segal's definition would apply to many narratives, but he goes on to propose that myth 'accomplishes something significant for adherents', who deeply believe and hold to the myth 'tenaciously' (6). Hence, the Frankenstein phenomenon functions as something like a myth for millions of readers, listeners, and viewers in that it expresses, through narrative and characters, central, or even core beliefs that many people find deeply significant.

12 Linda Hutcheon goes a long way toward defining what is, perhaps, the central pleasure of adaptations, generally, and at least some of the pleasure we derive from adaptations of Frankenstein. She argues that imitation is second nature for human beings, something we do largely without thinking (20). In short, we love repetition because it is safe and predictable, but it is also boring. And we enjoy variation, though it can be chaotic and frightening.. It's ironic that Shelley's *Frankenstein*, which may be the most adapted literary text ever written, concerns itself precisely with the creation of a copy of a human being, but one who is deeply uncanny, since he is both familiar, and yet quite different from other humans. The monster, in short, is himself a living, breathing adaptation.

13 See Julia Douthwaite and Daniel Richter, 'The Frankenstein of the French Revolution: Nogaret's Automaton Tale of 1790.' *European Romantic Review*. 20.3 (2009): 381–411.

14 Thanks to Professor Jack Stoneman for introducing us to this tale.

15 Neo-Victorian novels and films have become, themselves, the subjects of adaptation studies, and Imelda Whelehan has pointed out that they have 'garnered an astonishing amount of interest and yet, in common with adaptation, the area inspires fascination and loathing in equal parts' (272).

Bibliography

Albrecht-Crane, Christa and Dennis Cutchins, eds. *Adaptation Studies: New Approaches*. Madison, NJ: Fairleigh Dickinson UP, 2010.

Aldiss, Brian W. *Frankenstein Unbound*. London: Jonathan Cape, 1973.

Baldick, Chris. *In Frankenstein's Shadow: Myth, Monstrosity, and Nineteenth-century Writing*. Oxford: Clarendon Press, 1987.

Bakhtin, M.M. *The Dialogic Imagination*. Trans. Caryl Emerson and Michael Holquist. Ed. Michael Holquist. Austin: University of Texas Press, 1981.

————. *Rabelais and His World*. Trans. Hélène Iswolsky. Bloomington: Indiana UP, 1984.

Bishop, Kyle. 'Assemblage Filmmaking: Approaching the Multi-Source Adaptation and Reexamining George Romero's Night of the Living Dead.' *Adaptation Studies: New Approaches*. Ed. Christa Albrecht-Crane and Dennis Cutchins. Fairleigh Dickinson UP, 2010. 263–277.

Botting, Fred. *Making Monstrous: Frankenstein, Criticism, Theory*. Manchester and New York: Manchester UP, 1991.

Bourne Identity, The. Dir. Doug Liman. Universal, 2002.

Bride of Frankenstein, The. Dir. James Whale. Universal, 1935.

Bruhn, Jorgen, Anne Gjelsvik, and Eirik Frisvold Hanssen. '"There and Back Again": New Challenges and New Directions in Adaptation Studies.' *Adaptation Studies: New Challenges, New Directions*. Eds Jorgen Bruhn, Anne Gjelsvik, and Eirik Frisvold Hanssen. London: Bloomsbury, 2013. 1–16.

Buchanan, Judith. 'Forbidden Planet and the Retrospective Attribution of Intentions.' *Retrovisions: Reinventing the Past in Film and Fiction*. Eds Deborah Cartmell, I.Q. Hunter, and Imelda Whelehan. London: Pluto Press, 2001. 148–162.

Davis, Paul. *The Lives and Times of Ebenezer Scrooge*. New Haven and London: Yale UP, 1990.

Douthwaite, Julia and Daniel Richter. 'The Frankenstein of the French Revolution: Nogaret's Automaton Tale of 1890.' *European Romantic Review* 20.3 (2009): 381–411, DOI: 10.1080/10509580902986369 (accessed 22 January 2015).

Elliott, Kamilla. 'Rethinking Formal–Cultural and Textual–Contextual Divides in Adaptation Studies.' *Literature Film Quarterly* 42.4 (2014): 576–593.

————. 'Theorizing Adaptations/Adapting Theories.' *Adaptation Studies: New Challenges, New Directions*. Eds Jorgen Bruhn, Anne Gjelsvik, and Eirik Frisvold Hanssen. London: Bloomsbury, 2013. 19–45.

Frankenstein. Dir. J. Searle Dawley. Edison Manufacturing, 1910.

Frankenstein. Dir. Danny Boyle. National Theatre, London. 2011.

Frankenstein. Dir. Glenn Jordan. Dan Curtis Productions, 1973.

Frankenstein. Dir. James Whale. Universal, 1931.

Frankenstein: The True Story. Dir. Jack Smight. Pinewood Studios, 1973.

Frankenstein's Wedding: Live at Leeds. Dir. Colin Teague. BBC 3. 19 March 2011.

Hand, Richard and Jay McRoy, eds. *Monstrous Adaptations: Generic and Thematic Mutations in Horror Film*. Manchester and New York: Manchester UP, 2007.

Hitchcock, Susan Tyler. *Frankenstein: A Cultural History*. New York and London: W.W. Norton & Company, 2007.

Hutcheon, Linda. *A Theory of Adaptation*. London and New York: Routledge, 2006.

Internet Movie Database, The. IMDb.com, Inc, 2009.

I, Robot. Dir. Alex Proyas. 20th Century Fox Film Corporation, 2004.

I Was a Teenage Frankenstein. Dir. Herbert L. Strock. Santa Rosa Productions, 1957.

James, Louis. 'Frankenstein's Monster in Two Traditions.' *Frankenstein, Creation and Monstrosity*. Ed. Stephen Bann. London: Reaktion Books, 1994.

Jurassic Park. Dir. Steven Spielberg. Universal, 1993.

Leitch, Thomas. 'Adaptation and Intertextuality, or What Isn't an Adaptation, and What Does it Matter.' *A Companion to Literature, Film and Adaptation*. Ed. Deborah Cartmell. West Sussex, UK: Blackwell's Publishing, 2012. 87–104.

————. *Film Adaptation and its Discontents: From* Gone with the Wind *to* The Passion of Christ. Baltimore: Johns Hopkins UP, 2007.

Lemire, Jeff. *Frankenstein, Agent of Shade*. National Comics Publications [D.C. Comics]. 2011–13.

Levine, George and U.C. Knoepflmacher, eds. *The Endurance of Frankenstein: Essays on Mary Shelley's Novel*. Berkeley: U of California P, 1979.

Margolis, Harriet E. 'Lost Baggage: Or, The Hollywood Sidetrack.' *Approaches to Teaching Shelley's* Frankenstein. Ed. Stephen C. Behrendt. New York: Modern Language Association of America, 160–165.

'Marionette.' *Fringe*. Fox. KSTU, Provo. 9 December 2010.

Mary Shelley's Frankenstein. Dir. Kenneth Branagh. Tri Star Films, 1994.

Mellor, Anne K. 'Making a Monster.' *Mary Shelley's Frankenstein*. Ed. Harold Bloom. New York: Chelsea House, 2007, 43–59.

Picart, Caroline Joan S. *The Cinematic Rebirths of Frankenstein: Universal, Hammer, and Beyond*. Westport, CT: Praeger, 2002.

Randel, Fred V. 'The Political Geography of Horror in Mary Shelley's *Frankenstein*.' *Mary Shelley's Frankenstein*. Ed. Harold Bloom. New York: Chelsea House, 2007. 185–211.

Rose, Ellen Cronan. 'Custody Battles: Reproducing Knowledge about Frankenstein.' *New Literary History* 26.4 (1995): 809–832.

Schoemaker, George. *The Emergence of Folklore in Everyday Life: A Fieldguide and Sourcebook*. Ed. George Shoemaker. Bloomington, IN: Trickster Press, 1990.

Segal, Robert A. *Myth: A Very Short Introduction*. New York: Oxford UP, 2004.

Shelley, Mary. *Frankenstein*, 2nd Edition. Ed. J. Paul Hunter. New York and London: W.W. Norton, 2012.

Smith, Johanna. 'A Critical History of *Frankenstein*.' *Frankenstein*, 2nd Edition. Ed. Johanna M. Smith. Boston and New York: Bedford/St Martin's, 2000.

Stoneman, Jack. 'Zombie Poetics of Medieval Japan.' Stanford University. Stanford, CA. 8 March 2014.

Transcendence. Dir. Wally Pfister. Alcon Entertainment, 2014.

Whelehan, Imelda. 'Neo-Victorian Adaptations.' *A Companion to Literature, Film and Adaptation*. Ed. Deborah Cartmell. West Sussex, UK: Blackwell's Publishing, 2012. 272– 291.

Young, Elizabeth. *Black Frankenstein: The Making of an American Metaphor*. New York and London: New York University Press, 2008.

Young Frankenstein. Dir. Mel Brooks. Gruskoff/Venture Films, 1974.

Part I

Dramatic adaptations of *Frankenstein* on stage and radio

1

Frankenstein's spectacular nineteenth-century stage history and legacy

Lissette Lopez Szwydky

M UCH OF THE SIGNIFICANCE of Mel Brooks's *Young Frankenstein* (1974) lies in its
engagement with *Frankenstein*'s adaptation history and early cinema conventions, which it accomplishes through a brilliant mix of parody and homage. The more
they are well versed in *Frankenstein*'s film history, the more viewers are able to appreciate the jokes in *Young Frankenstein* that cover a full range of characters, scenes, props,
and film techniques, alongside literary, film, and cultural critiques.

Audiences familiar with *Frankenstein*'s full adaptation history might find another
layer in *Young Frankenstein*. In one of the film's most memorable scenes, the Creature
dances a duet to Irving Berlin's 'Puttin' on the Ritz' and performs tricks for treats to a
sold-out theatre audience (Figure 1.1).

Figure 1.1 Gene Wilder as Frederick Frankenstein and Peter Boyle as the Creature in *Young
Frankenstein* (1974). Directed by Mel Brooks. © 20th Century Fox.

The scene may be original to *Frankenstein*'s film history, but it directly invokes the novel's nineteenth-century stage history, which also took many forms – melodramas, farces, and burlesques. Song-and-dance routines such as the one in *Young Frankenstein* were common in nineteenth-century stage productions, such as *Frankenstein; or, The Vampire's Victim*, a musical first staged at London's Gaiety Theatre in 1887. Like the 1974 parody, the 1887 burlesque took its most immediate inspiration from several earlier *Frankenstein* adaptations, Gothic thrillers, and other popular entertainments. One might say that *Frankenstein; or, The Vampire's Victim* was the *Young Frankenstein* of its day. Both adaptations recycle scenes and situations from previous dramatisations, suturing them into new fabrications of the Frankenstein legend. Where *Young Frankenstein* both lampoons and pays homage to the *Frankenstein* films of the 1930s and 1940s produced by Universal Studios, *Frankenstein; or, The Vampire's Victim* borrows from early melodramas and comedies that began the work of transforming Frankenstein's monster into a cultural icon, starting in 1823 (Figure 1.2).

Figure 1.2 Promotional image of Fred Leslie as the Creature in *Frankenstein; or, The Vampire's Victim* (1887). First performed at the Gaiety Theatre. Photo credit: Mander and Mitchenson / University of Bristol / ArenaPAL.

Although much of *Frankenstein*'s film history is well known to scholars and fans alike, the nineteenth-century dramatisations are less known outside of specialised circles. The most influential study to date is Steven Forry's ground-breaking book, *Hideous Progenies: Dramatizations of* Frankenstein *from Mary Shelley to the Present* (1990), which includes a comprehensive list of plays appearing between 1823 and 1986 and production details and commentary for many of those plays. Audrey A. Fisch's *Frankenstein: Icon of Modern Culture* (2009) builds on Forry's formative work, providing extensive summary and analysis of the nineteenth-century plays, as well as Victorian political cartoons (also discussed by Forry), and twentieth-century adaptations on stage and screen. Two twentieth-century plays are given extended discussion: Peggy Webling's *Frankenstein* (1927), the most direct predecessor to James Whale's iconic treatment of the monster; and *The Last Laugh* (1915, co-written by Paul Dickey and Charles Goddard), the first original Frankenstein drama of the twentieth century, which also happened to take cues from a comic 1849 predecessor, *Frankenstein; or The Model Man* (Fisch 156). Fisch brackets her study of Frankenstein's adaptation history with discussions of the novel's literary history, early reception, and later critical history. Ultimately, Fisch demonstrates how feminist scholars in the 1970s and 1980s paved the way for the literary canonisation of Shelley's novel, while adaptations transformed *Frankenstein; or The Modern Prometheus* from novel idea to cultural icon.[1]

Like all narratives that are repeatedly repurposed, *Frankenstein* adaptations must be considered within their respective historical, political, and cultural contexts, as Susan Tyler Hitchcock does in *Frankenstein: A Cultural History* (2007). While Forry and Fisch delve into the specific details of the early plays, including their reception and production details, Hitchcock's socio-historical approach narrates the evolution of the Frankenstein Complex across multiple media from the nineteenth century to the present, showing how these adaptations provide unique takes on the relevance of the Frankenstein Complex.[2]

Frankenstein is certainly one of the most adapted novels, but it is not alone. Adaptations were a common sight on London's nineteenth-century stages. Diane Long Hoeveler's 'Victorian Gothic Drama' shows the overwhelming proliferation of adaptations, including stage versions of John Polidori's *The Vampyre* (1819), Victor Hugo's *The Hunchback of Notre Dame* (1831), and Alexandre Dumas's *The Corsican Brothers* (1844), to name a few. Victorians saw at least eight adaptations of Charlotte Bronte's *Jane Eyre* in the fifty years following the novel's publication.[3] Charles Dickens's works were staples of the Victorian stage, often while the novels were still in serialisation.[4] Robert Louis Stevenson's *The Strange Case of Dr Jekyll and Mr Hyde* was transformed for the stage only months after its publication in 1886.[5] Gothic narratives in particular found themselves at the centre of the century's fascination with adaptation. Hoeveler's *Gothic Riffs: Secularizing the Uncanny in the European Imaginary, 1780–1820* (2010) tracks popular Gothic narratives and themes through the multiple media and genres available to nineteenth-century consumers, including opera, drama, melodrama, ballads, and chapbooks.[6] Of all of these, nineteenth-century popular theatre provides the most obvious legacy to contemporary afterlives of nineteenth-century novels like *Frankenstein*. As Hoeveler explains, 'There is no question that contemporary viewers of the horror film … owe a visual and cultural debt to the many advances and experiments made by the Victorian Gothic drama' (69). The proliferation of adaptation in the age of film and digital media is an extension of the nineteenth-century's fascination with emerging technologies and commercial popular culture.

   Much of the existing *Frankenstein*-focused scholarship has worked to recover, catalogue, and contextualise *Frankenstein*'s early stage history, bringing to light for modern audiences pieces that have long been forgotten, despite their importance in shaping the Frankenstein story over nearly two centuries. The trend in scholarship is, unsurprisingly, to focus on individual adaptations and highlight their respective distinctions. My work builds on the earlier scholarship by taking a different approach – foregrounding trends (as opposed to individual plays) established by the early dramatisations that have become central to the iconography of Frankenstein. In this chapter, I track several major scenes and trends that have come to dominate the Frankenstein Complex today – creation scenes, death scenes, and rehabilitation plots – and trace their developments to the nineteenth-century stage. By better understanding the origins of iconic moments and trends in *Frankenstein*'s adaptation history, we not only better understand the connections between past and present but also gain a stronger awareness of adaptation's role in *Frankenstein*'s narrative evolution from novel to what Paul Davis calls a 'culture text'. Unlike most existing scholarship, I treat melodramas and comedies based on *Frankenstein* with equal interest because the latter genre is typically ignored but has equal cultural force as the more 'serious' adaptations of the nineteenth-century stage and later films.

Presumption sets the stage

Returning to England from Italy in the summer of 1823, Mary Wollstonecraft Shelley wrote to Leigh Hunt (her late husband's long-time friend and publisher), 'Behold! I found myself famous!' (378). The reason? A melodrama based on *Frankenstein* was a hit at the English Opera House and a second printing of the novel now featured her name (the novel was originally published anonymously). The 1823 printing (arranged by her father, William Godwin) owed its appearance to the drama's popularity. Shelley attended the play on 29 August and was impressed, as she tells Hunt:

> The play bill amused me extremely, for in the list of dramatis personæ came, ——— by Mr. T. Cooke: this nameless mode of naming the un[n]ameable is rather good. … The story is not well managed – but Cooke played ———'s part extremely well – his seeking as it were for support – his trying to grasp at the sounds he heard – all indeed he does was well imagined & executed. I was much amused, & it appeared to excite a breath[less] eagerness in the audience. (378)

Shelley enjoyed the excitement Cooke's performance produced for the audience, but was less pleased with the plot changes. As in the novel, the Creature in Peake's drama is nameless. His creator's name is Frankenstein. They don't get along. These were some of the only similarities between Shelley's *Frankenstein* and the version staged nightly in London.

Richard Brinsley Peake's *Presumption; or, The Fate of Frankenstein* premiered on 28 July 1823 at the English Opera House and forever changed the fate of *Frankenstein* in popular culture. The play notably introduced several alterations that would set new standards for subsequent adaptations. For example, the hunchbacked assistant Fritz (often Ygor/Igor in later film adaptations) was introduced in a comic role written expressly for Robert Keeley, the theatre's resident comedian. The character was a hit with audiences and would be reconfigured in most nineteenth-century dramatisations as well as in twentieth-century adaptations such as James Whale's *Frankenstein* (1931).[7] Sometimes this 'assistant' is more of an intellectual equal who collaborates on experiments, such as the diabolical, and humorous, Dr Pretorius in *Bride of Frankenstein* (1935) or the ethically conscious, and more serious, Dr Krempe in *The Curse of Frankenstein* (1957), as well as several other assistants in the Hammer Films. In *Mary Shelley's Frankenstein* (1994), Victor is joined by both Henry Clerval and Professor Waldman in his initial experiments (although they remain unaware of the human project that builds on their earlier findings). All examples differ widely from Shelley's novel, where Victor Frankenstein's isolation not only enables his experiments but also shapes his mental and emotional instability.

Since the introduction of the lab assistant character in 1823, one is hard pressed to find an adaptation where Frankenstein works alone. On the nineteenth-century stage, Fritz served as an interlocutor between Frankenstein and theatre audiences by narrating the creation scene in the first two stage adaptations. He became a 'fall guy' of sorts in James Whale's 1931 film by bringing the well-meaning scientist an 'abnormal' brain and then serving as a convenient and justifiable first victim, due to his cruel treatment of the monster. In *Bride of Frankenstein* (1935), Fritz is temporarily replaced by the forgettable Karl (played by Dwight Frye, who also played Fritz in the previous film), before Bela Lugosi introduced 'Igor' to the Frankenstein lexicon in *Son of Frankenstein* (1939). Karl makes a comeback in *The Revenge of Frankenstein* (1958), becoming a willing (although tragic) participant in the scientist's monstrous experiments. 'Eye-Gor' is one of the most memorable characters of *Young Frankenstein* (1974), where he serves as Frederick's guide in navigating the Frankenstein castle, its secrets, and the family history, while also guiding audience interpretation through his exaggerated inferences and inflections. Some more recent reimaginings expand the role significantly. The animated film *Igor* (2008) makes the hunchback assistant's role central to the mad scientist trope. *Victor Frankenstein* (2015), the most recent big-budget release, starring James McAvoy and Daniel Radcliffe, tells the story that everyone 'already knows' from Igor's perspective. All of these lab assistants find their ancestor in Peake's 1823 play.

Peake's *Presumption* had other permanent influences on the Frankenstein Complex. For example, although many of the 1820s melodramas included avalanches or nautical imagery from the novel's frame narrative, Peake eliminated the frame narrative featuring Robert Walton's Arctic expedition. Later adaptations followed suit and Walton was omitted in most adaptations for the next two centuries.[8] Instead of the cross-continental travel that we get in the novel, the action in Peake's play is confined to a single geographical setting and all scenes take place very close to the Frankenstein home. Forry and others have chalked up this change to the necessity of nineteenth-century dramatic conventions that would have required the plot to unfold over a shorter time period with fewer scenic changes. However, films are typically more flexible with regard to scene changes and timelines, suggesting that the continuation of this trend in later adaptations is less easily explained. Why, for example, is Frankenstein's laboratory located in his own cellar in the first Hammer film, *The Curse of Frankenstein* (1957)? Budgetary limitations are often used to explain the change; however, much of this film's plot plays up the proximity of home and family, and although it seems a major departure from the portrayal of the Frankenstein family's demise in the novel, the relocated lab still enables the domestic destruction seen in this film.

The revision introduced in *Presumption* that has garnered the most scholarly scrutiny was stripping the Creature of speech. Thomas Potter Cooke performed the part in pantomime – becoming the first in a long line of mute monsters in Gothic melodramas and horror films where exaggerated gestures, emphatic groans, and shrieks replace the eloquent arguments and literary allusions found in Shelley's novel. Pantomime acting was a staple of the nineteenth-century stage, and the part was likely configured this way to reduce the total number of spoken lines so that the piece could be played in any theatrical venue. (Traditional spoken-word drama was allowed only at London's two major theatres, Covent Garden and Drury Lane; melodramas and pantomimes could be staged at any theatre.) Like Boris Karloff in the twentieth century, Cooke would become famous for playing Frankenstein's monster in the early half of the nineteenth century. In 1853, the *Illustrated London News* estimated that Cooke had played the Creature more than 300 times (Forry 11).[9] The number is likely much higher when one considers the different adaptations that featured Cooke as the Creature, later revivals of *Presumption*, and Cooke's performances outside of London. Contemporary reviews lauded Cooke's performance for years as the following review published for an 1826 revival shows: 'T.P. Cooke seems, from the frequency of repetition, to have acquired still greater perfection, and added additional interest to the part of the Monster, the performance of which is certainly one of the finest specimens of pantomime acting we remember ever to have witnessed' ('Theatre'). In 1826, Cooke also played Frankenstein's Creature in *Le Monstre et le Magicien*, a French adaptation by Jean-Toussaint Merle and Antony Béraud staged in Paris.

While the effect that *Presumption* had on later versions of the story may seem a major loss to some literary scholars, nineteenth-century theatregoers were quite happy with most of the changes that Peake introduced into *Frankenstein*'s popular history.[10] As one review from the *Morning Post* on 30 July 1823 makes clear:

> Whatever may be thought of Frankenstein as a novel, or of the principles of those who could indite [sic] such a novel, there can be but one opinion of it as a drama. The representation of this piece upon the stage is of astonishing, of enchaining, interest. In the novel the rigid moralist may feel himself constantly offended, by the modes of reasoning, principles of action, &c. – But in the Drama this is all carefully kept in the back ground. Nothing but what can please, astonish, and delight, is there suffered to appear … ('Review')

Both positive and negative reviewers agreed that the theatrical production far outweighed its literary presentation. Theatregoers could rest assured that they would be treated to a spectacle that would certainly 'please, astonish, and delight' them, instead of a didactic, philosophical narrative.

Presumption brought together the perfect mix of performers, spectacle, and story – crushing its immediate stage competitors. Forry documents four *Frankenstein* dramatisations premiering between 28 July and 1 September 1823 during *Presumption*'s first season. Henry Milner's *Frankenstein; or, The Demon of Switzerland* was staged eight times at the Coburg Theatre in late August, and two anonymously penned pieces premiered in September. *Humgumption; or, Dr. Frankenstein and the Hobgoblin of Hoxton* saw six performances at the New Surrey Theatre. *Presumption and the Blue Demon* (a piece borrowing both the title of Peake's play and the practice of Cooke's blue make-up) closed after two showings at Davis's Royal Amphitheatre.[11] Because there are no existing scripts for any of these pieces, it is difficult to say exactly why they failed while *Presumption* took the lead in providing visual cues for the Frankenstein Complex for generations to come. But reasons for the novel's theatrical success are easier to discern.

Despite its limited first run of 500 copies, Shelley's *Frankenstein* was a shocking publication, ripe for theatrical representation (and exploitation). As the play moved to different venues, theatres staging *Presumption* benefited financially from the controversy stirred by the novel's contents and its author's infamous family.[12] But why put on a dramatic production that only meagrely resembled the original story? For theatre managers and popular dramatists it made sense to capitalise on a tale that possessed significant controversy if not widespread visibility. Purging novels of their political sympathies was a standard stage practice, given contemporaneous censorship requirements dating back to the Licensing Act of 1737. Peake strategically picked out the most spectacular elements of the story and pieced together a drama that would satisfy both the Examiner of Plays and the management at the English Opera House.[13] *Presumption* would be revived at many of London's major theatrical venues for the next three decades, as well as in theatres across the country. Forry identifies at least fifteen different adaptations that were staged in England and France between 1823 and 1832.

Much of the iconography associated with the Frankenstein Complex originated with *Presumption* and the more successful adaptations that immediately followed. The Paris production of *Le Monstre et le Magicien* also became a major influence by inspiring two additional well-known early English melodramas (all appearing in 1826): Henry Milner's *Frankenstein; or, The Man and the Monster* and John Kerr's *The Monster and the*

Magician; or, The Fate of Frankenstein (a loose translation of the French play). Many elements that are often erroneously attributed to *Frankenstein*'s afterlife in film such as creation scenes, spectacular death scenes, the calming response that music has on the monster's rage, stunning uses of fire, and the possibilities (when imaginable) of educating or rehabilitating the Creature that we have come to expect from Frankenstein adaptations find their origins in these early plays.

Spectacular creation and death scenes

In James Whale's *Frankenstein* (1931), Henry Frankenstein fervently and repeatedly announces, 'It's alive!' at the moment of animation. These famous lines are a verbal riff on Peake's *Presumption*, where Frankenstein announces the Creature's birth by screaming 'It lives!' (Act 1, Scene 3). The iconic 1931 film thus blends Peake's language with visuals added in later pre-cinematic adaptations. *Presumption*'s creation scene takes place off stage, but the Creature makes his spectacular stage entrance marked by an action-packed sequence chock-full of special effects. According to printed stage directions, he breaks through doors, destroys props, and executes two impressive leaps while fire burns in the background. Unfortunately, his creator is not impressed by his amazing strength and acrobatics. Frankenstein recoils. The Creature makes friendly gestures at him. Frankenstein rejects him. The monster gets angry. He grabs Frankenstein's sword, snaps it in two, tosses his creator onto the stage floor, and escapes while the scientist lies senseless. The curtain closes on the first act amid loud thunder and lightning. On the nineteenth-century stage, the first meeting between Frankenstein and the Creature typically followed this format. Whale's 1931 film appears to be the first major departure from this narrative, as Henry Frankenstein is initially sympathetic toward the monster (though eventually turns against him).

The first melodrama to stage the creation scene was Henry M. Milner's *Frankenstein; or, The Man and the Monster* (1826), which premiered at the Royal Coburg Theatre on 3 July 1826. O. Smith played the unnamed monster.[14] The scene blends monologue, music, and spectacle, to build up the tension for the monster's reveal, rejection, and rebellion:

> *Fran.* Now that the final operation is accomplished, my panting heart dares scarcely gaze upon the object of its labours – dares scarcely contemplate the grand fulfillment of its wishes. Courage, Frankenstein! ... *(Music. – He eagerly lays his hand on the bosom of the figure, as if to discover whether it breathes.)* The breath of life now swells its bosom. ... *(Music. – He rolls back the black covering, which discovers a colossal human figure, of a cadaverous livid complexion; it slowly begins to rise, gradually attaining an erect posture, Frankenstein observing with intense anxiety. When it has attained a perpendicular position, and glares its eyes upon him, [Frankenstein] starts back with horror. ...* (Milner 1826, reprinted in Forry 194)

Titillating language adds an implied layer of sexual tension leading up to the Creature's 'birth' (creation scenes in the Hammer Films era and later would emphasise this sexual tension). The spectacle would prove important for later adaptations, becoming the most memorable moment of *Frankenstein* adaptations to date. Yet even Milner's most 'original' scene borrows heavily from predecessors, and although *Presumption* wasn't billed as a source text, its influence is obvious. '*The Man and the Monster* takes from *Presumption* and *Le Monstre et le Magicien* Frankenstein's initial reaction: his attempt to stab the Creature with a sword, which the Creature snaps in two' (Fisch 99). The monster's creation proved novel on the stage. Audiences had previously 'witnessed' the creation through the lab assistant's second-hand description as he peered through a laboratory window. Now, they were first-hand witnesses, creating new audience expectations for later plays as the creation scene took centre stage.

Adaptations staged during the Victorian period expanded the creation scene significantly. *Frankenstein; or, The Model Man*, a comic harlequinade penned by brothers Richard and Barnabus Brough, premiered on 26 December 1849 at the Adelphi Theatre. *The Model Man* draws loosely on *Le Monstre et le Magicien* (and Kerr's English version) by having Frankenstein's animation potion come from a mystical source. Because of the play's comic conventions, the creation scene lacks the tension of Milner's melodrama (Figure 1.3). Instead of rebelling violently against his creator, the Creature sees Frankenstein's fear as egregiously rude and un-gentlemanly. The Creature in *The Model Man* is not a sinister monster, but a misunderstood orphan who ruminates on his unfortunate social position, in verse. As with many *Frankenstein* comedies, class difference plays a major role in the narrative that unfolds in this adaptation.

The Model Man is also notable for its self-awareness, situating itself as one more in a long line of *Frankenstein* adaptations. The play's debt to previous versions is implied

Figure 1.3 Creation scene from *Frankenstein; or, The Model Man* (1849) from *The Illustrated London News* (12 January 1850). Image ©The British Library Board. All Rights Reserved. Image reproduced with kind permission of The British Newspaper Archive (www. britishnewspaperarchive.co.uk)

at times, such as its silent incorporation of alchemy for animation or Frankenstein's insistence on painting his mechanical man with 'a touch or two / Of red just here – and a tinge of blue' (a nod to the established technique of using blue make-up to make the monster more ghastly). *The Model Man* explicitly acknowledges itself as a play dominated by spectacle, such as when the Creature Zamiel (played by O. Smith, who was by now too old to carry out the highly physical role of Frankenstein's monster as he did in Milner's melodrama) explains how to use special effects:

> Zamiel: You'll see; to make what's coming more terrific
> I'll turn the lights down by a charmed specific,
> And when the business of the scene requires
> I'll heighten the effects with colored fires.
> (*Frankenstein; or, The Model Man*, Scene 5. Reprinted in Forry243)

The Model Man points out one of the most important elements of a successful *Frankenstein* dramatisation in its use of stunning visuals and relative disregard for textual 'fidelity' to a source text, a trend that has only recently become accepted in adaptation scholarship.[15] We continue to see this type of explicit, self-referential acknowledgement in *Frankenstein*-inspired film comedies and musicals such as *Abbott and Costello Meet Frankenstein* (1948), *Young Frankenstein* (1974), and *The Rocky Horror Picture Show* (1975).

Spectacle-driven entertainment is often seen as the purview of contemporary big-budget films, yet similar techniques were used in nineteenth-century popular theatre. Scenes were staged with elaborate props and special effects, enabling canny theatre managers to profit accordingly. Managers who refused to update their theatres with modern lighting, props, and new stage technologies quickly found themselves financial flops.[16] As most nineteenth-century reviews make clear, theatre patrons expected to be entertained, and poorly financed pieces rarely generated ticket sales. Proper investment was paramount to a play's commercial success. We see this especially in the climactic close of the earliest *Frankenstein* melodramas – the death scene.

Frankenstein is full of death. Shelley's novel chronicles the deaths of seven characters. The Creature, however, does not die in the novel. Instead, he floats away on an ice-raft 'borne away by the waves, and lost in darkness and distance' (Shelley 186), affording the monster complete agency in determining his own fate. This ending is usually erased in adaptations.[17] The most famous Frankenstein films typically show the Creature being destroyed, usually by fire. In the 1931 film, the Creature collapses under a burning windmill set ablaze by an angry, torch-bearing mob. In *Bride of Frankenstein* (1935), the Creature blows up the laboratory containing himself, his intended mate, and Dr Pretorius. The Creature is also burned in the first instalment of the Hammer series, *The Curse of Frankenstein* (1957). Branagh's 1994 film ends with the Creature setting himself ablaze over the corpse of his 'father' as they float on an ice raft. Such spectacular special effects enhance the endings. Killing the monster brings finality to a narrative that resists closure on the page.[18]

Fire also dominated the most spectacular nineteenth-century dramas. An early review of *Presumption* provides insight into audience expectations:

> One moment he is a monster delighting only in blood; the next a 'lubber fiend,' and then even beneficent spirit. He sets fires to houses, plays with blind men, stabs ladies, scares children, and burns his own fingers! At length, when this gentleman has done much mischief and more foolery, and every body begins to wonder how he is to be disposed of in the end, the author gets rid of him by a stratagem, to say the least of it, original. ('English Opera-House' 3)

Elizabeth Nitchie provides the following survey of how stage dramatisations distinguished themselves through the originality and sensationalism of their respective death scenes:

> The Monster seemingly had as many lives as a cat, and each necessitated a different end. In 1823 at the English Opera House he perished in an avalanche, at the Coburg in a burning church. In 1826 he was killed by a thunderbolt in Paris and at the West London Theatre, he leapt into the crater of Mount Aetna at the Coburg, he died in an Arctic Storm at the English Opera House. In the twentieth century, on the stage he committed suicide by a leap from a crag in 1927 and was shot to death in 1933. (225)

Diverse in method, the various death scenes on stage share spectacular qualities that are dramatic departures from the Creature's slow 'fade-to-black' exit in the novel. Often Frankenstein perishes alongside his Creature; sometimes the scientist is allowed to survive at the end of the production. Yet whether both main characters survived or only one, all of the earliest melodramas of the 1820s concluded with a spectacular *tableau* eradicating the monster.

Detailed stage directions for the three earliest melodramas underscore the importance of action and effects in the final scene, as detailed in stage directions for *Presumption*'s first season:

> (*Music. – Frankenstein discharges his pistol – The Monster and Frankenstein meet at the very extremity of the stage. – Frankenstein fires his second pistol – the avalanche falls and annihilates the Monster and Frankenstein. – A heavy fall of snow succeeds. – Loud thunder, heard, and all the characters form a picture as the curtain falls.*) (Peake, Act III, Scene v. Reprinted in Forry 160)

Presumption closes with a traditional *tableau*, a standard stage technique signifying the end of a play where actors would pose as if captured in a still picture – an image that would leave a memorable impression. The avalanche scene was so popular with audiences that Peake returned to it later that year in a parody of his own adaptation, *Another Piece of Presumption* (1823), with Frankenstitch and his monster buried under an avalanche of cabbages in the village square.

The prominence of death scenes in the 1820s melodramas suggests that adapters were closely following Peake's vision. Milner's *The Man and the Monster* ends with Victor murdered by the Creature, who is then chased down by soldiers and armed peasants (possibly the earliest inspiration for the finale of Whale's 1931 film).

Wounded and cornered, the Creature leaps into Mount Etna '*vomiting burning lava*', and the stage directions call for '*torrents of fire, sparks, smoke, &c.*' to simulate a volcanic eruption. Contemporary reviews focused on these special effects. The play's Duncombe printed edition even published a diagram of actors' stage positions at the curtain's close, further emphasising the impact of effective staging. (Milner, Act 2, Scene 8. Reprinted in Forry 204).

Le Monstre et le Magicien and Kerr's English translation both return to the nautical imagery of the novel for purely spectacular reasons. Escaping the flames of his burning castle, Frankenstein finds himself on a small boat in a tempestuous sea. As Frankenstein's cohorts attempt to rope and pull him aboard a larger, more stable vessel,

> … the Monster appears on the rock uttering a shout of demonic joy on beholding him, Frankenstein
> utters a shriek of despair. The Monster darts from the rock into the boat, seizes Frankenstein – a
> moment after a thunderbolt descends and severs the bark, the waves vomit forth a mass of fire and
> the Magician and his unhallowed abortion are with the boat engulphed in the waves. (Kerr, Act
> 3, Scene 4. Reprinted in Forry 226)

There are slight, situational variations between the French and English versions, but ultimately the scenes have similar outcomes – the spectacular demise of the monster and his creator by carefully crafted special effects, including lightning and fire. The premise proved popular with theatregoers, and later revivals of Peake's *Presumption* would replace the play's original avalanche with scenic sea deaths, as evidenced by playbills advertising a new finale (Figure 1.4).

The spectacular finales of all the early *Frankenstein* melodramas demonstrate not only theatregoers' tastes for elaborate stage sets and action-packed dramas, but also

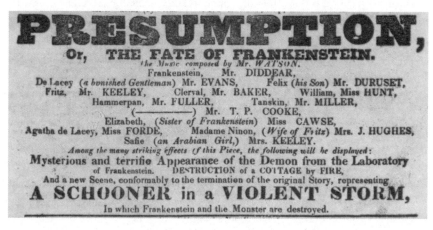

Figure 1.4 Detail from 'Playbill announcing a revival of Peake's *Presumption* for December 7, 1830 at the Theatre Royal Covent Garden.' Downloaded from 'A collection of playbills from Covent Garden Theatre, 1829–1830.' Nineteenth Century Collections Online (NCCO). Gale. ©The British Library.

the technological advances that dominated nineteenth-century popular theatre. All of these elements combined to create the iconography that continues to dominate the Frankenstein Complex to date. As Jeanne Tiehen explains:

> The very word Frankenstein conjures distinct images: the mad scientist, the strange laboratory, the unstoppable Monster…. Through these components, the story of Frankenstein reflects social anxieties and mirrors a hope for returning to normative conditions through the demise or punishment of the Creature and Dr. Frankenstein in almost every adaptation. (66–7)

The playbill for the 1830 Covent Garden revival of *Presumption* makes clear that the images and stage effects are the real draw. There is no worry of leaking 'spoilers', since the playbill outlines the details of the final scene. Audiences are told beforehand that Frankenstein and the monster will die at the end. Perhaps audiences even expect it. The novelty here is not if or why, but how those deaths will occur. That said, there were three typical ways to dispatch the monster on the nineteenth-century stage. When the Creature died, he typically succumbed to the natural elements – avalanche, fire, or lightning.

Domesticated creatures and creators

Near the end of *Young Frankenstein*, the Creature acquires his creator's intellectual abilities. Addressing the villagers with an eloquent, sympathetic speech, the Creature is accepted into the community and even marries Frankenstein's former fiancée. In the comedy's final scene the Creature reads the *Wall Street Journal* and groans sexually as Elizabeth comes to bed in full Bride-of-Frankenstein-style costume. The Creature is transformed into a full member of society. Bolts and stitches no longer define him. No one is afraid of this educated, domesticated Creature. This trend dominates *Frankenstein*-inspired comedies, including loose appropriations of the narrative such as the American sitcom *The Munsters* (1964–66), and children's films such as *Alvin and the Chipmunks Meet Frankenstein* (1999) and *Frankenweenie* (2012).

Given their natural light-heartedness, comedies tend to allow the Creature to survive the narrative. Throughout the nineteenth century, Frankenstein monsters in farces, parodies, and burlesques were often lucky enough to escape the unfortunate fate of their ill-fated stage brothers who appeared in melodramas (although there are some exceptions such as Peake's 1823 parody, *Another Piece of Presumption*). Victorian adaptations envisioned models for rehabilitation that predate *Young Frankenstein*'s comic vision of domestic bliss. Education and acculturation are central to this rehabilitation, and these issues play out differently in the two documented Victorian comedies.

The Creature is able to speak in most comedies, a further marker of his ability to be rehabilitated and integrated into society. For example, in *Frankenstein; or, The Model Man* (1849), education is set up as a central thematic concern, established by the monster's first words:

> *Monster.* .... But stop. Where am I, aye & likewise who?
> How did I get here? that's a poser too.
> How is it too that in my situation,
> With no advantages of education,
> My thoughts in words an utterance are seeking,
> Though unaccustomed quite to public speaking?
> (Brough and Brough, Scene 3. Reprinted in Forry 239)

The monster in this mid-century harlequinade emphasises the importance of first impressions. Lack of familial support and formal education are the reasons for the monster's rage. When the characters contemplate how to deal with the monster in Scene 7, Otto (the hero of this piece) scoffs at the idea of hurting him, explaining that the modern way to deal with criminals is to 'teach them to grow better', which mirrored contemporaneous ideas about the modern prison system.[19] Music, dance, and other markers of 'culture' are the permanent solution for both the Creature and greater social ills. As Fisch notes, 'With its allusion to education as the key to "calm subordination" for the unruly masses, the play can allow an unthreatening Creature ... into polite society' (Fisch 117). Invoking previous adaptations' use of the power of music to enthral the monster, Otto plays his magic flute and, '*The monster, neatly dressed a la happy Villager with his hair and moustaches curled, enters smiling & following the music. .... The monster dances pleased*' (Brough and Brough, Scene 7. Reprinted in Forry, 249). Frankenstein and the monster hug. The reconciliation is complete once Frankenstein agrees to find his ward 'a situation' to support himself financially and become a productive, model citizen.

Richard Henry's *Frankenstein; or, The Vampire's Victim* (1887), the most long-running adaptation of the Victorian period, also plays up the possibility of social integration.[20] The plot of this 'burlesque extravaganza' is complicated as it involves not one, but two Creatures: the Monster (made of clay) and a progenitor called the Model (made of terra-cotta), both of which may harken back to the Jewish legend of the Golem, which some scholars have linked to the visual inspiration for Boris Karloff's make-up in the Universal Films.[21] Both Creatures can talk, and they immediately question their social positions and possibilities for mobility:

> Monster *(to Model)*: I say can you speak?
> Model *(Grinning)*: I think so.
> Monster: What's your name?
> Model: I dunno ...
> Monster: *I* dunno?
> Model: What's yours?
> Monster *(With a happy thought.)* The same! Perhaps they'll christen us soon to give us
>   status.
> Model: And later on perhaps they'll vaccinate us. (Henry. Reprinted in Forry 57)

The Monster and the Model identify names, religion, and vaccination as markers of 'status' – putting this adaptation in conversation with cultural and scientific movements of its day. They also situate the *Frankenstein* narrative within debates about empire and race during the Victorian period (in addition to class conflict, as earlier comedies had done). *The Vampire's Victim* subtly couches in its comedy a more serious history of power abuses, inequality, and disenfranchisement, all while offering another version of the *Frankenstein* narrative's intersection with larger political policies and debates.[22] *The Vampire's Victim* thus incorporates the image of Frankenstein's monster as a model for political unrest that had become popular in several Victorian political cartoons, where he was used to debate working-class enfranchisement, the abolition of slavery, and the struggle for Irish independence.[23] While previous adaptations had played up Cooke's blue makeup as a marker of difference, *The Vampire's Victim* takes this implied connection from a specific visual cue to widespread cultural practices and builds on arguments circulating in other visual media of the Victorian period.

Although the methods for rehabilitation in these two Victorian comedies differ significantly, the ultimate goal is the same – reintegrating the rehabilitated monster into society. When compared to the earlier melodramas, the Victorian comedies are also notable for including the Creature's desire for a mate and domestic happiness – a central theme in Shelley's novel that is not fully realised until Brooks's *Young Frankenstein*.[24] Mary Jacobus notes that this domestic possibility is first introduced in Whale's 1935 sequel, 'In *Bride of Frankenstein*, Frankenstein and his maniacal collaborator Dr Pretorius undertake what neither Mary Shelley nor her hero could quite bring themselves to do – embody woman as fully monstrous' (133). The possibility is thwarted, however, when the female Creature in *Bride of Frankenstein* rejects the monster, just as Victor predicts in the novel. On the nineteenth-century stage, the only dramatisation to address the Creature's request for a companion is the 1887 burlesque *The Vampire's Victim*. According to Forry's description of the piece, the monster becomes an unwilling participant in a comic romantic triangle featuring two vampires named Mary Ann and Visconti. The monster wants nothing to do with either, instead preferring Frankenstein's fiancée, Tartina, whom he kidnaps in the second act, and whose rescue determines much of the remaining plot (Fisch 2009). Although the monster's love life is treated very differently in *Young Frankenstein* (where he actually marries his creator's former fiancée), we see here yet another connection between the parodies of 1887 and 1974 that imagine domestic futures for the lonely monster.

Just as the Creature is tamed or contained at the end of each dramatisation, Frankenstein is also 'domesticated' in most stage and screen adaptations, a trend begun by Peake in 1823. In *Presumption*, Frankenstein's family features more prominently throughout the play, and domestic relationships are emphasised explicitly (a notable change from the novel, which relies heavily on implicit arguments for the importance of domestic affection). Relationships are reconfigured, with Agatha De Lacey replacing Elizabeth Lavenza as Frankenstein's betrothed; Elizabeth is paired with Henry Clerval. Fritz and his wife provide comic relief and foil to a perfect picture of domestic bliss. When Frankenstein animates his Creature, he immediately thinks of the potential damage to his family:

> Frankenstein: It lives! ... miserable and impious being that I am! Elizabeth! brother!
> Agatha! – fairest Agatha! Never more dare I look upon your virtuous faces. Lost! lost!
> lost! (Peake, Act I, Scene III. Reprinted in Forry 144)

As Jeffrey Cox explains, 'Even the story of Frankenstein's animation of the creature
and then his struggle with it is firmly imbedded in a vision of domestic relations' (Cox
69). Cox is referring to *Presumption*, but his observations apply to most *Frankenstein*
adaptations. Whether Frankenstein dies (in the melodramas of the 1820s) or survives (in later comedies and many films), the domestic comforts that he side-lines in
Shelley's novel are central themes in most adaptations. Frankenstein is dead at the end
of *Presumption*, yet three happy, heterosexual couples remain 'to find domestic bliss'
(Cox 69). The French and English versions of *Le Monstre et le Magicien* both include
multi-layered domestic plots, and Milner's melodrama follows suit (as do many films
in the Frankenstein Network).

The nineteenth-century stage comedies continue the expanded role of the domestic sphere established by the melodramas. In Peake's *Another Piece of Presumption*,
Frankenstitch (a tailor who creates a 'made man' out of the bodies of his nine competitors) not only regrets creating the monster, but also immediately laments that he is no
longer worthy of his family's love and affection. Mrs Frankenstitch complains that she
gets lonely when her husband is away at work, but he reassures her that she is important
to his happiness. Domestic plots take different forms in later adaptations, but still remain
notable for their importance in creating happy endings. In *The Model Man* Frankenstein
is engaged to Agatha, who hates him and tells her father that forcing her to marry him
would be a crime because 'He's to his works so wedded by the wig-o-me / That if he
marries me as well, 'tis bigamy' (Brough and Brough, Scene 2. Reprinted in Forry 235).
In the 1849 play Agatha elopes with her lover Otto, leaving Frankenstein unpaired,
although not for long. The play restores domestic happiness as Undine (the water fairy
who gives Otto the magic flute) takes Frankenstein home to meet 'Rhine's fairy daughters' (Brough and Brough, Scene 7. Reprinted in Forry 250), assuming that he will find a
suitable wife. This trend continues in several film versions, notably *Frankenstein* (1931),
its sequels, and *Young Frankenstein* (1974). When Frankenstein survives the adaptation,
he is typically integrated back into family life. (A notable departure are the Hammer
films, which characterise Baron Frankenstein as a sociopath.)

By sparing most of the members of the Frankenstein family and/or providing
Frankenstein with a domestic future, adaptations bypass Shelley's nuanced critique
of ambitious individualism (coded masculine) that destroys home and family (coded
feminine).[25] Feminist scholars such as Mary Poovey have argued that the novel is a
feminist critique of individualism, emphasising the importance of community, the
domestic sphere, and by extension, women's influence. 'Frankenstein's fatal impulse
... has profound social consequences,' writes Poovey.

> Mary Shelley is more concerned with th[e] antisocial dimension ... primarily in terms
> of [Victor's] social relationships. After animating the monster, the product and symbol

of self-serving desire, the exhausted scientist is immediately confronted with a dream explication of his crime: having denied domestic relationships by indulging his selfish passions, he has, in effect, murdered domestic tranquility. (334–5)

In the novel, Victor destroys the domestic sphere by shunning his family and his parental responsibilities to his 'child', and then refusing to provide the Creature with a partnered, domestic future. In adaptations, by contrast, the home is always the site of unquestioned stability.

The promise of domestic happiness remains intact in many adaptations, such as when the 1931 film ends with the Baron Frankenstein toasting 'the future of the House of Frankenstein' and the upcoming marriage. Caroline Picart has argued that by eliminating Margaret Saville, Caroline Beaufort-Frankenstein, and Justine Moritz, and consequently allowing Elizabeth and Frankenstein to survive and marry, the changes in Whale's film are 'indicative of the degree to which the original novel seems to have been purged of its implicit criticism of a patriarchal politics of gender' (392). The argument is true, except that it is not original to Whale's film or the adaptations that followed. None of the female characters listed above is included in any major dramatisation of *Frankenstein* from 1823 through to the Universal films of the 1930s. Justine does return in a few later films. In Hammer's *The Curse of Frankenstein* (1957), Baron Frankenstein allows the monster to kill her when she threatens to expose Frankenstein's experiments as well as the fact that she is pregnant with his child. *Mary Shelley's Frankenstein* (1994) contains the most 'faithful' portrayal of Justine to date. Safie appears in Peake's *Presumption*, her first and only appearance in the Frankenstein Network. Elizabeth and Agatha, the two female characters who do make it into the nineteenth-century stage adaptations, are sometimes conflated and are always very much background figures. Despite being a minor role, Frankenstein's fiancée usually survives at the end of the nineteenth-century plays. The stage and film adaptations side-step Shelley's insistence that the Creature understands the importance of domestic ties and family more so than Frankenstein, who takes it for granted.

Conclusion: textual history, cultural history

Frankenstein's adaptation history is closely tied to the novel's textual history. As William St Clair explains in *The Reading Nation in the Romantic Period* (2004), Shelley's novel was published anonymously in 1818 with a limited run of only 500 copies. *Frankenstein*'s second printing came in August 1823 – only weeks after *Presumption*'s premiere. The second run, of 1,500 copies, quadrupled the number of available copies of the novel in print. Still, with a total of 2,000 copies of the novel in circulation, that number equalled the approximate attendance of one performance of *Presumption*. In short, on any given night, more people were able to see the stage progeny of Shelley's text than read the novel.[26] When we consider all of the *Frankenstein* adaptations circulating during the nineteenth century, including movement between theatres, regions, and later revivals, it is clear that more people were likely to encounter some version of *Frankenstein* on the stage rather than on the page.

To date, *Frankenstein* has been adapted (both directly and loosely) for stage, screen, textual, and digital media hundreds of times, making it difficult to locate an 'original' Frankenstein. Paul O'Flinn explains that 'There is no such thing as *Frankenstein*, there are only *Frankensteins*, as the text is ceaselessly rewritten, reproduced, refilmed, and redesigned' (194). O'Flinn is referring to a phenomenon driven by adaptation, which transforms narratives (be they plays, novels, or other singular works) into 'culture texts', a term coined by Paul Davis and developed by Brian A. Rose as a 'body of adaptations extended over time that ... has the potential of becoming a larger, reflexive body of narratological, performative, and cultural elements' (2). Each adaptation not only adds another layer to the 'network of texts' collectively known as 'Frankenstein', but also implicitly or explicitly engages with previous adaptations, blurring the lines between old and new, original and derivative. Together, all the pieces make up the Frankenstein Network.

Identifying and understanding adaptation trends from *Presumption* to the present highlights the nuances and interdependence of *Frankenstein*'s adaptation history. One of the most important takeaways from this approach is that a one-to-one model of adaptation does not accurately explain why or how Frankenstein's Creature has become one of the most recognisable 'monsters' of our time. Readings that focus too much on a single adaptation and its return to Shelley's text as the only 'original' miss how much new adapters of the story are influenced by the adaptations that have come before. *Frankenstein*'s cultural history is so indebted to adaptation that the monster himself can easily be seen as a symbol for adaptation studies, a concept eloquently summed up by Julie Grossman's term 'elastextity' and its relationship to both Shelley's novel, which she called her 'hideous progeny', and the monster created therein. Grossman writes, 'Adaptations conceived as 'hideous progeny' change not only the *way* we view but also our ideas about *what* we are viewing. They "destroy" other texts, even as they create new ones, revealing new perspectives on human identity and culture' (1). Given the ubiquitous presence of the Frankenstein narrative in popular culture across myriad media, it is nearly impossible for one's first encounter with this narrative to be Shelley's novel. Each adaptation functions as both destroyer and descendant, introducing new takes on the 'original', questioning its 'authority' as 'source text', and yet ensuring that Frankenstein's name has a culturally relevant lineage – from the first stage offspring in 1823 to the present and all the *Frankenstein* descendants yet to come.

Notes

1 For an overview of *Frankenstein*'s feminist criticism, see Diane Long Hoeveler, 'Frankenstein, Feminism, and Literary Theory.'
2 Additionally, Hitchcock discusses new editions of the novel, textual adaptations, comics and illustrated versions, sequels, parodies, musicals, and a wide range of cultural

appropriations. Financial and commercial issues are also addressed, as well as careful considerations of questions of authorship and ownership of a cultural myth situated outside of the bounds of contemporary notions of copyright and licensing.

3   See Stoneman. *Jane Eyre on Stage, 1848–1898*.

4   See Glavin. *After Dickens*; and more recently, Glavin, ed. *Dickens Adapted*.

5   See Rose, *Jekyll and Hyde Adapted*.

6   See Hoeveler, *Gothic Riffs*.

7   Whale's Fritz is a more diabolical character than Peake's comic lackey, and the film monster eventually kills him because the demented assistant continuously tortures him with fire.

8   Peake's play ends with an avalanche that recalls the Arctic setting of the novel's frame. The reintroduction of nautical imagery in Milner's *Frankenstein; or, The Man and the Monster* (1826) likely had more to do with the vast popularity of nautical melodramas during the first half of the nineteenth century than with a strong desire to return to a more 'authentic' representation of the novel's frame narrative. The most famous reinsertion of the Artic frame narrative in film adaptations is Kenneth Branagh's *Mary Shelley's Frankenstein* (1994), starring Aidan Quinn as Captain Robert Walton.

9   For more on Thomas Potter Cooke, see Nichols, 'The Acting of Thomas Potter Cooke.'

10 For a discussion of audience interpretations from visualising the monster from page to screen (or stage), see Heffernan, '"Looking at the Monster".' For a discussion of how nineteenth-century audiences would perceive the mute Creature, see Raub, 'Frankenstein and the Mute Figure of Melodrama.'

11 Forry notes that Peake's self-parody *Another Piece of Presumption*, which premiered on 20 October 1823 at the Adelphi Theatre, did better than any of these competitors, with nine performances. It's important to rehash this brief history of *Presumption*'s earliest competitors because some of the scholarship on the early dramas conflates the pieces or provides contradictory (or no) information about their dates or locations. I have streamlined Forry's history for ease of reference and comprehension, as this information appears in a less unified format in his book.

12 The negative criticism launched at the novel followed *Frankenstein* to the stage. The premiere of Peake's *Presumption* was met with protests from groups such as the Society for the Suppression of Vice and Immorality. *Presumption*'s playbills promoted the moral message of the drama. For the full exchange, see Forry 5–9.

13 For more information on *Presumption* and its licensing, see Cox, *Seven Gothic Dramas, 1789–1825*.

14 Although Thomas Potter Cooke was the most famous actor to portray the monster in early stage adaptations, O. Smith (full name Richard John Smith) quickly became the second-most famous actor associated with the role.

15 The most frequently cited book-length study arguing against a fidelity model of adaptation is Linda Hutcheon's *A Theory of Adaptation*. For a solid overview of major shifts in the conversation around adaptation studies see Simone Murray's introductory chapter to *The Adaptation Industry*.

16 Forry describes an unsuccessful staging of *Presumption* in Birmingham when theatre manager Alfred Bunn decided to short-change the production. The event is recorded in *Recollections of O. Smith*, ed. William W. Appleton, *Performing Arts Resources* in 5 (1979), and also

quoted in Forry, 7. An altered version of this anecdote taken from Peake's letter to Charles Matthews can be found in H. Barton Baker, 'Theatrical Make-Shifts and Blunders,' *Belgravia: A London Magazine* 37 (December 1878): 221–22.

17 Spivak, 'Three Women's Texts and a Critique of Imperialism.'

18 The resistance to closure is a characteristic treatment of monsters in literature as noted by Jeffrey Jerome Cohen in 'Monster Culture (Seven Theses).' *Monster Theory: Reading Culture.* Minneapolis: University of Minnesota Press, 1996.

19 For a historical and philosophical examination the evolution of prison systems and their influence and effects in the age of industrialisation, see Foucault, *Discipline and Punish.*

20 Forry identifies 'Richard Henry' as the pseudonym for Richard Butler and Henry Chance Newton. *Frankenstein; or, The Vampire's Victim* premiered on 24 December 1887 at the Gaiety Theatre and ran for 106 performances during the season. The play is notable for being the only documented dramatisation of the late Victorian period and also for being one of the most difficult to piece together due to lack of availability of an easily accessible script. Forry and Fisch both quote liberally from the only known typescript archived at the British Library, which is difficult to track down. The sections that they reproduce and commentary in their respective studies are currently the only way to piece together the contents of this play.

21 See Jane P. Davidson, 'Golem – Frankenstein – Golem of Your Own,' *Journal of the Fantastic in the Arts* 7.2/3 (1995): 228–43; also Norma Rowen, 'The Making of Frankenstein's Monster: Post-Golem, Pre-Robot.' *State of the Fantastic: Studies in the Theory and Practice of Fantastic Literature and Film.* Ed. Nicholas Ruddick. Westport, CT: Greenwood Press, 1992), 169–77.

22 For in-depth discussions of *Frankenstein*'s intersection with nineteenth-century racial politics see Malchow, *Gothic Images of Race in Nineteenth-Century England* and Mellor, '*Frankenstein*, Racial Science, and the Yellow Peril.' Elizabeth Young's *Black Frankenstein* traces transatlantic appropriations from the nineteenth century to the present showing how Frankenstein's monster has been reappropriated as the ultimate metaphor of 'blowback' for various political, social, and scientific wrongs. Young shows how the Frankenstein monster figures into discussions of slavery, racial and national identities, gender and sexual conventions (especially the construction of American masculine identity), and international relations.

23 For example, in 1832 the Frankenstein Monster was portrayed in at least three political cartoons that featured the Creature as the monstrous embodiment of enfranchisement achieved through the Reform Bill. Politicians alluded to the story in arguments against emancipation, enfranchisement, and colonial independence and there are several political cartoons depicting each. For a full overview see Forry and also Hitchcock.

24 Alain Jessua's French comedy *Frankenstein 90* (1984) also explored the humorous potential of human/Creature relationships.

25 Four decades of feminist scholarship have offered various readings of *Frankenstein* as a critique of nineteenth-century gender politics and the limits of the domestic sphere. For an excellent overview of feminist scholarship on Shelley's novel see Hoeveler, '*Frankenstein*, Feminism, and Literary Theory.' For a foundational feminist reading, see Jacobus, 'Is There a Woman in This Text?'

26 For these figures see both St Clair and Stephen Behrendt's 'Introduction' to *Presumption*.

Bibliography

Behrendt, Stephen C. 'Introduction.' Romantic Circles, August 2001.

Brough, Richard and Barnabus Brough. *Frankenstein; or, The Model Man*. (1849). Reprinted in Forry, 227–250.

Cox, Jeffrey N. *Seven Gothic Dramas, 1789–1825*. Athens: Ohio University Press, 1992.

Davis, Paul. *The Lives and Times of Ebenezer Scrooge*. New Haven: Yale University Press, 1990.

'English Opera-House,' *The Times* (London). 29 July 1823. Page 3.

Fisch, Audrey A. *Frankenstein: Icon of Modern Culture*. Hastings: Helm Information, 2009.

Forry, Steven Earl. *Hideous Progenies: Dramatizations of Frankenstein from Mary Shelley to the Present*. Philadelphia: University of Pennsylvania Press, 1990.

Foucault, Michel. *Discipline and Punish: The Birth of the Prison*. Vintage, 1977.

Glavin, John. *After Dickens: Reading, Adaptation and Performance*. Vol. 20. Cambridge University Press, 1999.

Glavin, John, ed. *Dickens Adapted*. Burlington: Ashgate, 2012.

Grossman, Julie. *Literature, Film, and Their Hideous Progeny: Adaptation and ElasTEXTity*. London and New York: Palgrave, 2015.

Heffernan, James. '"Looking at the Monster": Frankenstein and Film.' *Critical Inquiry* (1997): 133–158.

Hitchcock, Susan Tyler. *Frankenstein: A Cultural History*. New York: Norton, 2007.

Hoeveler, Diane Long. '*Frankenstein*, Feminism, and Literary Theory,' *The Cambridge Companion to Mary Shelley*. Cambridge University Press, 2003. 45–62.

———. 'Victorian Gothic Drama.' *The Victorian Gothic: An Edinburgh Companion*. Eds Andrew Smith and William Hughes. Edinburgh: Edinburgh University Press, 2012. 57–71.

Jacobus, Mary. 'Is There a Woman in This Text?' *New Literary History* 14.1 (1982): 117–141.

Kerr, John Atkinson. *The Monster and Magician: or, The Fate of Frankenstein: A Melo-dramatic Romance, in Three Acts*. London: J. & H. Kerr, 1826. Reprinted in Forry, 205–226.

Malchow, Howard L. *Gothic Images of Race in Nineteenth-Century Britain*. Stanford University Press, 1996.

Mellor, Anne K. '*Frankenstein*, Racial Science, and the Yellow Peril.' *Nineteenth Century Contexts* 23.1 (2001): 1–28.

Milner, Henry M. *Frankenstein; or, The Man and the Monster! A Peculiar Romantic, Melo- dramatic Pantomimic Spectacle, in Two Acts* (London: John Duncombe, 1826). Reprinted in Forry, 187–204.

Nichols, Harold J. 'The Acting of Thomas Potter Cooke.' *Nineteenth Century Theatre* 5.2 (1977): 73.

Nitchie, Elizabeth. *Mary Shelley: Author of Frankenstein*. New Brunswick: Rutgers University Press, 1953.

O'Flinn, Paul. 'Production and Reproduction: The Case of *Frankenstein*.' *Literature and History* 9.2 (1983): 194–213.

Peake, Richard Brinsley. *Presumption; or, The Fate of Frankenstein* (London: J. Duncombe), 1824. Reprinted in Forry, 135–160.

———. *Presumption; or, The Fate of Frankenstein*. Ed. Stephen C. Behrendt. *Romantic Circles*. August 2001. Available online www.rc.umd.edu/editions/peake/index.html.

Picart, Caroline Joan S. 'Re-Birthing the Monstrous: James Whale's (Mis)Reading of Mary Shelley's *Frankenstein*.' *Critical Studies in Mass Communication* 15 (1998): 382–404.

'Playbill announcing a revival of Peake's *Presumption* for December 7, 1830 at the Theatre Royal Covent Garden.' Downloaded from 'A collection of playbills from Covent Garden Theatre, 1829–1830.' British Library. Nineteenth Century Collections Online (NCCO).

Poovey, Mary. 'My Hideous Progeny: Mary Shelley and the Feminization of Romanticism.' *PMLA* 95.3 (1980): 332–347.

'Review,' *The Morning Post* (London). 30 July 1823.

Raub, Emma. 'Frankenstein and the Mute Figure of Melodrama.' *Modern Drama* 55.4 (2012): 437–458.

Rose, Brian A. *Jekyll and Hyde Adapted: Dramatizations of Cultural Anxiety*. Westport, CT: Greenwood Press, 1996.

'Theatre,' *The Morning Post* (London). 21 September 1826. Issue 17398. Nineteenth-Century British Library Newspapers: Part II.

Tiehen, Jeanne. '*Frankenstein* Performed: The Monster Who Will Not Die.' *The Popular Culture Studies Journal* 2.1–2 (2014): 65–86.

'Scene from the Extravaganza of "Frankenstein, Or, the Model Man," at the Adelphi Theatre.' *Illustrated London News* (London, England) 12 January 1850: 28.

Shelley, Mary Wollstonecraft. 'Letter to Leigh Hunt dated September 9, 1823.' *The Letters of Mary Wollstonecraft Shelley*. Ed. Betty T. Bennett. 3 vols. Baltimore: Johns Hopkins University Press, 1980–88. 1: 378.

Spivak, Gayatri Chakravorty. 'Three Women's Texts and a Critique of Imperialism.' *Critical Inquiry* 12.1 (1985): 243–261.

St Clair, William. *The Reading Nation and the Romantic Period*. Cambridge: Cambridge University Press, 2004.

Stoneman, Patsy, ed. *Jane Eyre on Stage, 1848–1898: An Illustrated Edition of Eight Plays with Contextual Notes*. Ashgate Publishing, Ltd., 2007.

Young, Elizabeth. *Black Frankenstein: The Making of an American Metaphor*. New York University Press, 2008.

2

A Frankensteinian model for adaptation studies, or 'It lives!': adaptive symbiosis and Peake's *Presumption, or the fate of Frankenstein*

Glenn Jellenik

*F*RANKENSTEIN (1818/1823/1831) HAS A life of its own. It is perhaps our culture's most adapted text, and also one of our most adaptable metaphors. The mere mention of the word conjures almost 200 years of versions, images, meanings, cautionary tales, and arguments. Specifically, Frankenstein's Creature has been used as a metaphor for a motherless child, out-of-control technology, a vast number of 'out-of-control' Others such as 'the mobs that were seen as threats to the established orders of society' (Gupta xxxii), as well as a myriad of 'all kinds of [perceived] political monstrosity' (Armitage 224). And we can add adaptation theory to the metaphoric cultural possibilities of the Frankenstein trope. This chapter argues for the productivity of what I call a Frankensteinian model for adaptation studies, which attempts to systematically trace and account for the work of intertextuality in the act of adaptation.

The Frankensteinian model, or 'Not things learned so much as things remembered'

In imagining *Frankenstein* as a model for adaptation, we must first assume that there is no single source to inaugurate a one-to-one compare/contrast case study. Julie Grossman's *Literature, Film, and Their Hideous Progeny: Adaptation and ElasTEXTity* (2015) illustrates this assumption. Grossman uses the Creature as a central metaphor in her re-visioning of adaptation through the lens of intertextuality. From that perspective, she positions and considers adaptation as a creative rather than a derivative act, 'a re-animation that is connected to the preceding work, but not chained to it' (6). Her book makes the claim that 'hideous progeny and the mutating narrative of the Frankenstein story can be considered a critical lens for understanding adaptation' (25); in the end, such an approach clears a critical space, one 'that moves viewers and readers beyond their comfort with inherited boundaries and pre-existing patterns' (1).

The idea that a further unpacking of the specific work of intertextuality is necessary within adaptation studies is far from new. Robert Stam's seminal 2000 essay, 'Beyond Fidelity: the Dialogics of Adaptation', identifies adaptation as an 'intertextual dialogism' that 'is less an attempted resuscitation of an originary word than a turn in an ongoing dialogical process' (64). Ilana Shiloh's 'Adaptation, Intertextuality, and the Endless Deferral of Meaning' picks up Stam's thread to argue that adaptation functions as 'an intertextual practice, contributing to a dynamic interpretive exchange … in which each text can be enriched, modified or subverted' (4). That concept jibes with a shift by many critics in the field toward productively developing and exploring the 'dynamic interpretive exchange', specifically, what is enabled by positioning adaptation as the product and catalyst of an ongoing intertextual dialogic that actually creates meaning, rather than as a discrete and contained 'translation' that simply conveys meaning.

The Frankensteinian model joins that exploration by stressing the productive multiplicity of sources in order to circumvent the fidelity model and the one-to-one case study, both of which tend to radically under-read and/or flatten the act and product of adaptation. Such approaches excise much of what is productive, complex, interesting, and troubling about adaptation by ignoring the work of intertextuality. As Linda Hutcheon posits, 'to interpret an adaptation *as an adaptation* is to treat it as what Barthes called, not a "work", but a "text", a plural "stereophony of echoes, citations, references" … it is only as inherently double- or multilaminated works that they can be theorized *as adaptations*' (6). Hutcheon offers the metaphor of a palimpsest: 'adaptation is a form of intertextuality: we experience adaptations (*as adaptations*) as palimpsests through our memory of other works that resonate through repetition with variation' (8). Adaptations, in short, are not created in a sterile source/copy laboratory but, rather, seem to spring from our own 'workshop of filthy creation' (Shelley 58).

Frankenstein's Creature is the perfect metaphor for a critical approach that centres the palimpsestic nature of adaptation. He exists as a new being cobbled together from previous 'texts', each with the capacity to express, create, and drive meaning. Kenneth Branagh's 1994 film adaptation of Shelley's novel engages this potential, offering the Creature's body, itself, as a palimpsest. The Creature (Robert DeNiro) references his intertextual capacity in order to explain his ability to play a pipe, despite never having learned. He posits his knowledge as 'not things learned so much as things remembered'. Some component part of him knows how to pipe, which suggests the palimpsestuous nature of not only his cobbled-together body, but also his mind. The Creature exists as both the sum of and more than the sum of his parts. Traditional adaptation studies have exhausted the critical approach that dissects an adaptation as the sum of its parts. The Frankensteinian model invites critics to consider adaptation and source as participating in a symbiotic cycle, one that creates rather than merely reiterates.

Pedro Javier Pardo Garcia's 'Beyond Adaptation: Frankenstein's Postmodern Progeny' productively challenges adaptation studies' desire to worship at the source/copy shrine. In place of that monolith, he installs intertextuality: 'The concept of intertextuality explains much better than adaptation the complex interplay of sources and different kinds of relationships involved. This is not just to substitute a new, trendier term for an older one, but to replace the classical conception of adaptation as a one-way relation running from text to film … [with] a dialogue involving many shades and nuances, and running in both directions' (239). For most scholars adaptation doesn't function as, nor is it read as, a binary, but it exists in a web or a constellation. Yet Garcia creates a false dichotomy between adaptation and intertextuality that the Frankensteinian model collapses. Intertextuality is an integrated and inextricable part of the act of adaptation. As such, the model explores the ways that an adaptation cycle such as *Frankenstein*'s not only reflects the concept of cultural intertextuality, but also accounts for the simultaneous existence of multiple versions, evidences the symbiotic nature of postmodern cultural production, and questions traditional notions of originality and derivation.

In centring the work of intertextuality, the Frankensteinian model tracks and accounts for what gets produced in an intertextual adaptive cycle. It does this by viewing adaptive changes as inherently productive. To construct a presiding poetics for the field of adaptation studies, we must acknowledge that adaptation is not only a method of constructing a text; it is also a reading strategy.[1] Reading an adaptation *as an adaptation* involves a distinct process. The traditional critical reading strategy for adaptations has been a rear-view-mirror process, one that guarantees the primary status of the source by using the adaptation to construct a one-to-one binary that logically reflects back on the source; as Leitch points out, 'Adaptations will always reveal their sources' superiority because whatever their faults, the source texts will always be better at being themselves' (161). The Frankensteinian model uses the adaptation, and specifically what gets changed in the process of adaptation, to project into the culture. It reads forward to track and process the work of the (inevitable) alterations, rather than backward to judge or evaluate them.

Within the Frankensteinian model, adaptations invoke, suggest, and are cross-pollinated by a series of precursor texts, by creative and interpretive changes worked *by* the adapters, and by cultural and industrial concerns that work *on* the adapters. This chapter will look at the first adaptation of Mary Shelley's novel, Richard Brinsley Peake's 1823 play *Presumption, or the Fate of Frankenstein*, in order to explore both the contemporary function of Peake's changes and their far-reaching engagements, implications, and afterlives, since so much of the Frankenstein cycle is based on *Presumption*.

'It lives!'; or On symbiotic transformations

Peake's play was the first adaptation of *Frankenstein*, and, as with many subsequent adaptations, it was a commercial but not a critical success. From the traditional critical perspective, it functions as what David Cowart derisively terms 'literary parasitism … the monstrous alteration' of a literary source by its adaptation (8). Yet a vibrant symbiotic relationship exists between the texts, to the point that the argument could be made that Peake's play created Shelley's novel as much as her novel structured his play. As will be shown, many aspects of what we now understand to be 'Frankenstein' originate in the play, rather than in the novel. *Presumption* set in motion the revitalisation process that has produced a cycle with a life of its own, one that has clearly become more than the sum of its parts. The play's box-office success meant that Romantic-period audiences would wait less than a month for the second adaptation, Henry M. Milner's *The Demon of Switzerland*. William St Clair points to Peake's *Presumption* as the direct catalyst for the second edition of the novel (360–1), and Shelley herself acknowledged the effect on the fate of her novel: 'On the strength of the drama, my father had published a new edition of *Frankenstein*' ('To Leigh Hunt' 96). A second edition for such a novel was relatively rare at the time. St Clair reports that, despite its quickly selling out its initial run of 500 copies, the publisher had no plans to reissue the novel: 'For [publisher James] Lackington, the selling out of the first edition was the end of the matter. In making that decision Lackington was following the usual practice' (360).[2]

The strength of the play's symbiotic boost had an afterlife beyond publishing; Peake's title, *Presumption, or the Fate of Frankenstein*, positions the novel in its subtitle. Dramatic adaptations of novels were quite common in late eighteenth- and early nineteenth-century theatre, with theatre managers looking to cash in on the emerging genre's rise in popularity (P. Cox 2; Nicoll 91). Similar to today's film adaptations, theatres would leverage a popular novel's title. *Presumption*'s advertising and publicity suggest that there was little to gain by referencing the novel. However, by 1826, following the initial adaptations and the reissue of the novel, Milner's second adaptation foregrounds Shelley's title (*Frankenstein, or the Man and His Monster*) and, in posters publicising its performance, pointedly credits the novelist: 'Founded principally on Mrs Shelley's singular work, entitled, *Frankenstein, or the Modern Prometheus*'. The use of Shelley's title, as well as her name and the full title of the novel, in promotions attests to a rise in *Frankenstein*'s popularity and cultural recognition after the initial production of Peake's play.

Obviously, there is no way to know how much Shelley's version owes its afterlife to its adaptations, but it is certain that some well-worn and iconic aspects of our cultural consciousness of *Frankenstein* originate not with Shelley's novel, but Peake's *Presumption*. These include industry concerns, such as the generic shift from a philo-sophical novel that subverts its Gothic-romance plot to a decidedly non-subversive musical melodrama that centres love and romance plots; textual concerns, which also depend on industry concerns, such as the playwright's productive addition of the lab assistant Fritz (who in some later adaptations would become Ygor, Igor, or EYE-gore); and the production's enhanced attention to the creation scene and to the physical body of the Creature. Each of these changes/additions has played forward in multiple permutations to become an established element of the Frankenstein Network. While free to employ a rear-view reading strategy that considers how such alterations filter back to the source text, we can also read such changes forward to consider what they signify about the culture/environment that adapted and consumed these mutated texts.

The first thing that should be said about Peake's *Presumption* is that it is not a very *good* play. But then, academia has already dictated that such is the case for any and every play of the period. To give a history of the London stage from the second half of the eighteenth century through the end of the Romantic period is to chart the decline of drama, a decline that began with a specific and identifiable moment: the passage of the Licensing Act of 1737. In response to withering political criticism from Tory playwrights such as John Gay and Henry Fielding, Robert Walpole's Whig government imposed the Licensing Act, which severely censored British playwrights, making the performance of plays subject to the approval of the Lord Chamberlain. The Licensing Act scrubbed the stage of any perceived political criticism and, indeed, virtually all overt reference to politics. In addition to purging the stage of political engagements, it rigorously censored the language and subject matter of dramatic works. Finally, it mandated that new dramas could be performed only at the city's 'legitimate' patent-holding theatres.[3] All plays performed at non-patent, 'illegitimate' theatres had to be comedies, pantomimes, or musicals. These strictures pushed the stage's most talented authors toward other genres – cue the rise of the English novel. The Act also gave rise to the melodrama, a fusing of drama, comedy, and the musical. The genre consistently transferred its focus away from any overt processing of public, political, and social issues and towards an anodyne centring of private domestic concerns. In the melodrama, all tensions are sublimated to romantic urges (love drives), which function as the narrative engine. Unlike a parallel move made in an eighteenth-century English novel such as Samuel Richardson's *Pamela* (1740), melodrama's political and social issues function as little more than a *mise-en-scène*, props that set the stage and the mood for the beating heart of the story: romance. All dramatic tensions revolve around and become processed and resolved through the love story.

There is a long critical history of marginalising and dismissing the genre of melodrama as a monstrosity: 'As the theater succumbed completely to the demand of pure entertainment … the place of tragedy was usurped by that bastardly imitation known as the romantic melodrama' (Quintana ix–x). However, co-existent with the late twentieth-century shift in adaptation studies, critical efforts to read the genre in a different light have begun. Jeffrey Cox's 'The Death of Tragedy; or, the Birth of Melodrama' reassesses the cultural work of melodrama and positions it as 'one key popular way to deal with the aesthetic, cultural, social and political tensions' of the Romantic period (163). Cox posits melodramas as focal points that provide an enhanced understanding of Romantic-period cultural processes. In that way, the rise of melodrama can be read less as an artistic abomination and more as a systematic artistic containment of radical ideas. On a nightly basis, these plays rehearsed specific iterations of an emerging British subject/character. Amid shifting sets of cultural dynamics, demographics, and social structures, British audiences processed the emergence of the systems of capitalism and imperialism through melodrama.

The content-based aspects of the genre are established not only through repetition of various permutations of the form of the domestic melodrama, but also through familiarity of characters and sources, which were serially recycled in the plays. Actors, stock characters, history, novels, poems, music, and other plays came to function as aspects of a productive intertextual relay that grafted the plays onto many other areas of the culture, and, in turn, grafted that culture to the ethos established by the plays.

That said, the melodrama's aesthetic qualities suffer in the economy developed by Romanticism's critical ethos. Julie Carlson associates popular melodramas 'with all the dirty words of romanticism: senses, body, collaboration, labor, money, failure' (15); Jane Moody echoes Carlson: '[Such plays] do indeed pose an uncomfortable challenge to an idealist history of Romanticism which has privileged imagination, solitude and critical self-consciousness over the claims of the body, the institution and the market' (3). Yet, as one of the goals of twenty-first-century adaptation studies has been to challenge Romanticism's definition of originality and creative genius (Hutcheon 3–4), melodrama is an ideal object of inspection.

The critical narratives surrounding melodrama and adaptation are similarly arced. And in *Presumption*, we have a melodrama and an adaptation, because the only way to stage a version of Shelley's novel in 1823 was as a musical melodrama. In his posthumously published review of the novel, Percy Shelley offers a socio-philosophical reading of the condition of the Being (his term for the Creature): 'Treat a person ill, and he will become wicked. Requite affection with scorn; – let one being be selected, for whatever cause, as the refuse of his kind – divide him, a social being, from society, and you impose upon him the irresistible obligations – malevolence and selfishness. It is thus that, too often in society, those who are best qualified to be its benefactors and its ornaments, are branded by some accident with scorn' (418). The 'accident' is birth into the lower class, as here Shelley's review interprets the novel as pushing on emerging issues of democracy in Britain. From its initial publication, *Frankenstein* was recognised as politically radical. And there was, literally, no place on the London stage for that.

Peake's *Presumption* replaces all socio-philosophical engagements with marriage engagements. Of course, Shelley's novel does have a love story – or at least the place-holder for a love story. However, romance plays little role in the novel, to the point that Shelley seems to actively subvert the trope. Beyond the figuratively incestuous nature of Victor and Elizabeth Lavenza's romantic involvement, Shelley represents no passion between the characters.[4] Their relationship is sketched out in two letters from Elizabeth to Victor. The first, after his post-creation breakdown, functions mainly as an expository summary of the family's activities in his absence (65–68). The second, after their engagement, acknowledges so little passion on Victor's end that Elizabeth wonders if he has another lover (161). For Shelley, the romance functions as a circum-stantial plot device, a convenient and stock Gothic crisis that the novel wastes no space to establish. Such de-emphasis highlights the text's socio-philosophical themes.

Presumption not only emphasises and centres romance, but multiplies it. The play washes away any figurative incest by coupling Elizabeth with Clerval rather than Victor. Victor's neglected and star-crossed partner then becomes Agatha De Lacey, whose brother Felix, as in the novel, loves the Arabian girl Safie. And, for good measure, the play adds a comic 'love' story between Victor's servant Fritz and his shrewish French wife, Madame Ninon (French for neither/nor). The play's melodramatic structure ensures that, with the exception of Victor and Agatha, both of whom die at the hands of the Creature, all these couples end up together.

This romantic centring should look familiar. Cowart claims a similar tendency in Hollywood adaptations, pointing out cinema's odd desire to transmogrify a source's tragedies into happy marriages. He labels such moves 'vulgar myth fulfillment' and 'monstrous alteration' (8). Rather than dismiss such adaptive changes as vulgar and monstrous, the Frankensteinian model acknowledges the potential cultural work activated by these mutations. These decisions certainly function as 'myth fulfillment', but all texts function, to an extent, as myth fulfilment. The question, in the end, becomes: what myth is being fulfilled? Shelley fulfils, among others, the Promethean myth: that science, technology, obsession, and the hubristic thirst for progress lead to personal destruction. Peake actually offers a similar conclusion, but filters it through romance and marriage: in the end, Victor's crime may be one of presumption (hubris), but his punishment suggests that his fundamental error was putting scientific pursuit before love. Indeed, all other characters in the play are saved/spared only when they prioritise love and foreground union.

From a philosophical standpoint, it is easy to sympathise with the urge to dismiss the melodrama's love-as-panacea argument. But such a dismissal fails to explore the cultural work performed by love/marriage in such texts. Indeed, Cox's 'Birth of Melodrama' reads the genre as particularly suited to a British public anxiously balanced between war and peace. For Cox, the liminal genre exploited a liminal national space to construct an essentially conservative moral structure amid the rapidly accelerating culture of the early nineteenth century. Yes, love-as-panacea is an insultingly simple argument, but it was one that was rehearsed on a nightly basis in the centre of the culture, one that worked to establish and solidify an emerging British identity and ethos. While the censors deemed it politically neutral, there is a clear political advantage – to the status quo – to serially centring love/marriage.

Presumption performs that work not only by adding multiple love stories, each of which pulls focus from the socio-political implications of the overall plot, but also through the neutralising effect of music. The play sprinkles eight love songs throughout its three acts. Each number appears at a point where the text seems ready to engage with the thorniest implications of its plot engine. Music famously soothes the savage Creature, but it also functions to dissolve philosophical and social tension. Further, the performance of music, the insertion of harmony into a text that serially threatens and then absolutely reaffirms harmony, reveals melodrama's (moderately) conservative core. The genre is obsessively occupied with establishing a harmonious social structure that strengthens and preserves existing hierarchies.

The adaptive centring of love and romance in the Frankenstein story did not, by any means, end with *Presumption*. In fact, it is a staple of film adaptations, from the first (the 1910 Edison *Frankenstein*), which ends with Frankenstein and Elizabeth embracing, to Whale's 1931 version, which ends with Frankenstein and Elizabeth embracing, to

Branagh's 1994 version, which, despite its titular nod to fidelity to Shelley's novel, is structured as a torrid love story, complete with extended passionate love scenes and a rewritten ending, adapted from Jack Smight's *Frankenstein: The True Story* (1973) and Roger Corman's *Frankenstein Unbound* (1990) and perhaps a bit from Whale's *Bride of Frankenstein* (1935), where Victor, unable to accept Elizabeth's death, reanimates her murdered corpse.

While the concept of lost love as tragedy/punishment shifts the cultural implications and arguments of the text, *Presumption* also uses love-as-comedy to do the same. Peake adds the characters of Fritz and Madame Ninon, the requisite servant-class old couple whose incessant bickering is a staple of the period's popular plays. She carps about his fecklessness, he about her nagging. Both complain about the other's age. But in the end, they love one another. The addition of such stock characters is perfectly within the ordinary. While the employment of such comic racking between tension and harmony pulls some focus from larger issues, it might pass unmentioned except for the fact that Peake's addition of Fritz sets off a rich intertextual cycle of lab assistants that runs through Dwight Frye's Fritz (*Frankenstein*, 1931), Bela Lugosi's Ygor (*The Son of Frankenstein*, 1939, *The Ghost of Frankenstein*, 1942), J. Carol Naish's Daniel (*The House of Frankenstein*, 1944), Charles Bronson's Igor (*House of Wax*, 1953), Marty Feldman's Eye-gore (*Young Frankenstein*, 1974), all the way forward to John Cusack's (voice) 2008 postmodern bit-player-becomes-main-character Igor, star of his own eponymous feature-length animated children's film (*Igor*). Significantly, the character of Igor (Daniel Radcliffe) becomes a co-lead, and the lens through which the audience receives the story, in Paul McGuigan's recent *Victor Frankenstein* (2015) (Figure 2.1).

Figure 2.1 James McAvoy as Frankenstein and Daniel Radcliffe as Igor in *Victor Frankenstein*.

A focus on Fritz/Igor offers an opportunity to explore the potential productivity of another oft-marginalised aspect of adaptation studies: economic concerns. Too often, critics shy away from viewing the adaptation as a capitalist endeavour. However, it is clear that a desire to reach a broad audience has great implications for the composition of the adaptation, its popular reception, and what it says about the culture that produced and received it. As a look at the industry pressures that participate in the construction of a dramatic or film adaptation would not be complete without a consideration of economics, we would do well to consider such concerns.

Peake wrote the character of Fritz into *Presumption* in order to create a role for Robert Keeley, a celebrated comedian and box-office draw whose participation in the project guaranteed a broader audience. Though primarily the move functions to satisfy an industry concern, it has a narrative function as well. In many ways, the Fritz/Igor character serves as an avatar or surrogate for the audience. Frankenstein is obsessed, basically functionally insane. To ask an audience to relate to and rely on such a character risks alienating it. As Harold Bloom has pointed out, the Creature, by virtue of his more comprehensible desires (love, kindness, comfort) becomes the character with whom the reader/audience can relate (*Shelley's* Frankenstein 4). In that way, the novel enacts an identity crisis, since the Creature's response to his treatment cannot be sanctioned. Yet Frankenstein's behaviour makes him equally unworthy, leaving the reader in a sympathy vacuum. By inserting Fritz, a character with the requisite fear of the situation, the play offers a remove from Frankenstein and keeps us from depending, narratively, on such a flawed character. Fritz also keeps us from going over entirely to the Creature's side. In his fear of both Frankenstein and the Creature, we gain perspective – we see clearly the danger of the madness of literature's first mad scientist, as well as the danger of the power of the Creature he creates.

Presumption opens on Keeley's Fritz, singing a comic number that suggests the Gothic horror of his master's off-stage laboratory: 'Oh, dear me! what's the matter?/ How I shake at each clatter' (I, i). Fritz's abject fear is played for laughs; he is cast as the rustic rube: 'Why couldn't you be happy in your native village … instead of coming here to the city?' (I, i). Interestingly, that clownish anxiety pushes on a broader cultural anxiety surrounding emerging issues of modernity, namely, industrialisation and the huge population migration away from the English countryside and into the city.

William Wordsworth's 'Preface to the Lyrical Ballads' (1800 edition), the poet's unofficial manifesto of Romanticism, touches directly on this anxiety. The Preface sketches out Wordsworth's parameters for a 'new' poetry, one inspired by and reacting to the rapid changes in British culture and society: '[A] multitude of causes, unknown to former times, are now acting with a combined force to blunt the discriminating powers of the mind, and, unfitting it for all voluntary exertion, to reduce it to a state of almost savage torpor. The most effective of these causes are the great national events which are daily taking place, and the increasing accumulation of men in cities' (xv–xvi). The poet attaches his call for a poetic revolution directly to the conditions produced in Britain by encroaching industrial capitalism, namely, 'the increasing accumulation of men in cities'. The rise of industrialism led to mass urbanisation, and the jobs it produced cut men off from the diversity of their natural intellectual state, a native intelligence and genius of the rural English that Wordsworth sought to channel in his poetry, both in style and in content. Jacqueline Labbe refers to this intelligence as one in which 'urban culture corrupts while the countryside purifies' (96). Wordsworth reflects and drives the emerging cultural concept that there exists a clarity in the thinking and values of the countryside that is obscured by the concerns of the city.

Presumption's Fritz demonstrates and fosters this ideology. While the servant's case of the yips is patronisingly dismissed by his 'betters' in the play, his general fears about the dangers and consequences of his master's work are proved to be altogether well founded. He functions for the audience as both object and subject, fluctuating between serving as an object of humorous scorn and standing in as our voice of reason. He occupies the other end of the physical spectrum from the Creature, utterly non-threatening and weak, producing humour rather than horror. At the same time, he acts as a foil for Frankenstein, simple and completely lacking in anything resembling presumption or ambition. Even considering the argument for money as the genesis of Peake's creation of Fritz, once given life, the character catalyses a cultural motion and effect. Indeed, in later adaptations in the cycle, Fritz/Igor's role expands, with his ineptitude becoming a specific explanation for the Creature's damaged brain (Whale and Brooks), or becoming the main character or co-lead as in *Igor* and *Victor Frankenstein*. In all of these retellings, the character offers an increased opportunity to rehearse issues of class, labour, education, and superstition. Of course, the adaptations engage such issues obliquely. The philosophy is mainly implied by the fact of the physical existence of the character.

This is in keeping with the fact that many of the adaptations' most complex arguments are contained in and expressed by the Creature's body. As such, audio-visual adaptations of *Frankenstein* pay outsized attention to that physical body, as well as its literal construction/creation. If I were to say 'It's alive!' everyone would immediately get the reference. Yet, as with Sherlock Holmes's 'Elementary, my dear Watson', the phrase comes not from the novel, but from the first stage adaptation: *Presumption* gives us the line 'It lives!' More than an interesting trivia tid-bit, the spoken line testifies to the audio-visual text's heightened attention on the creation and body of the Creature. Shelley, upon seeing *Presumption*, noted the productive attention to the Creature's body: '[The Creature] presents his unearthly and monstrous person on the stage … I was much amused, and it appeared to excite a breathless eagerness in the audience' (*The Life and Letters* 95). And, as with any change, the adaptation's increased focus on the body refocuses its textual/cultural engagements.

For its part, the novel offers a creation scene without a manic moment of triumph. '[M]y candle was nearly burnt out, when, by the glimmer of the half-extinguished light, I saw the dull yellow eye of the creature open … breathless horror and disgust filled my heart' (60–1). Shelley depicts the scene in terms of exhaustion. Frankenstein's triumphant, hubristic cry of 'It's alive!' originates in Peake's enervated 'It lives!' (I, iii), as does the decision to morph the Creature from a brilliant and philosophically astute autodidact (he teaches himself to read with *Plutarch's Lives*, Goethe's *Sorrows of Young Werther*, and Milton's *Paradise Lost*) into a dumb brute. These changes also appear in James Whale's iconic – and in many ways culturally definitive – 1931 film adaptation. And therein lies the utility of the Frankensteinian model – these changes are not random, nor the mere whims, butcherings, or mad science of their creators. They are produced from specific cultural and interpretive catalysts. Most importantly, they have an afterlife. And tracing out the cultural impacts and implications of those afterlives is one of the tasks of adaptation studies.

One potential reading of *Presumption* explains Peake's specific heightened attention to the Creature's body as reflecting an early nineteenth-century cultural anxiety about imperialism, and specifically, issues of slavery and emancipation. In the original production of *Presumption*, the Creature was played by T.P. Cooke in blue face paint, and the colouring of the actor in the role functioned to immediately code the character for the audience. In a review of the play's opening night, the critic for *The Examiner* identified Cooke's Creature as 'a revengeful North American savage, painted blue' ('Review' 504). The critic also suggests that the play functions 'as a satire on our Irish system' (505). And Elizabeth Nitchie points out that, in all subsequent stage adaptations, 'the Monster ... was always painted blue' (392). With that in mind, the decision to morph the Creature from a brilliant autodidact into a dumb brute becomes socially and politically significant. According to Chris Baldick, '[the] decision to give the monster an articulate voice is Mary Shelley's most important subversion of the category of monstrosity' (45). *Presumption* completely undermines that subversion.

Audio-visual representations of the story, across the board, give much greater attention to the creation scene than does Shelley's novel. Interestingly, Peake most extensively quotes from *Frankenstein* in the creation scene. At the same time, the play departs from the novel in vital ways, even within those quotations. For instance, Peake's stage directions and dialogue repeatedly describe the Creature as 'the demon'. Shelley never does so; rather, she uses the word 'daemon', which can be read as an alternative spelling of 'demon', but can also be read as far more complex. Within mythology – and remember, the subtitle of the novel is 'the Modern Prometheus' – a daemon is a guardian spirit/double.[5] The case could be made that Shelley's use of the term functions deconstructively rather than descriptively – that is, it does not, like 'demon', code the Creature as evil but, rather, leaves open the possibility that the Creature is Frankenstein's double, and is neither evil nor good. *Presumption*'s less ambiguous terminology for the Creature supports its alteration of him into a dumb brute, which enacts a conflict between body and mind. The play's monster is all body, and the crisis for the stage production becomes that of the body run amok. The Creature's mind is woefully undeveloped compared to the physical capacity of his body. As Peake's Frankenstein puts it, 'What have I cast on the world? a creature powerful in form, of supernatural and gigantic strength, but with the mind of an infant' (II, i). Whale makes the same move, allowing his film to focus on the out-of-control body. In that way, it can be read as a primarily Other/colonial interpretation. Shelley's Creature, on the other hand, has a keen mind, allowing him (and us) to figure his mistreatment as more injustice than cruelty. The novel explores the social causes and effects stemming from the consequences of Victor's creation: 'I ought to be thy Adam; but rather I am the fallen angel, whom thou drivest from joy for no misdeed. Everywhere I see bliss, from which I alone am irrevocably excluded. I was benevolent and good; misery made me a fiend' (93–4). Here we see both the echo of Shelley's *Paradise Lost* epigraph, which treats Victor's responsibility – 'Did I request thee, Maker, from my clay/ To mould Me man? Did I solicit thee/ From darkness to promote me' – and the catalyst for Percy Shelley's socio-philosophical reading. The move to a Creature with a supernatural strength that his intellect cannot govern or control shifts the text's central problem from social (see Percy Shelley's review) to physical. Who would blame the society that fears and/or casts out such a chaotic, destructive force? *Presumption* demonstrates the devastating effect of the Creature's lack of control in the moment when he is rejected by the De Laceys. After being driven from the cottage by Felix, the 'Demon' burns down the hut 'with malignant joy' (II, v). Whale replicates the burning of the cottage in *The Bride of Frankenstein* (1935). Shelley, however, gave her Creature volition and a mind powerful enough to control his supernatural strength. He is similarly devastated and outraged when he is driven from the cottage by Felix. 'I could with pleasure have destroyed the cottage and its inhabitants, and have glutted myself with their shrieks and misery' (121), yet he reins in his rage rather than acting on it. By morphing the Creature into a destructive brute whose strength outstrips his mental faculties, Peake and Whale contain the radical socio-political implications of the novel's argument, perhaps aligning it with conservative defences of imperialism and slavery.

Indeed, in an 1824 Parliamentary debate in the House of Lords, George Canning used *Presumption* to argue against the emancipation of British-held slaves in the West Indies.[6] Canning's argument specifically hinged on the concept of slaves' overdeveloped bodies and underdeveloped minds: 'In dealing with the negro, Sir, we must remember that we are dealing with a being possessing the form and strength of a man, but the intellect only of a child. To turn him loose in the manhood of his physical strength, in the maturity of his physical passions, but in the infancy of his uninstructed reason, would be to raise up a creature resembling the splendid fiction of a recent romance' (Canning col. 1103). Canning would not have been able to use Shelley's Creature to advocate his position, since she put him in possession of an intellect as fully developed as his body. Clearly, there were those in the culture who recognised the utility and potential of Peake's shift. For the adaptation critic seeking to move beyond the fidelity model, it is vital to track the cultural implications and arguments of these changes as they functioned in the text's moment of construction.

Conclusion: Frankenstein as the postmodern Prometheus.

In the end, the Frankensteinian model shifts away from what we might call the local model, the one-to-one case study that has dominated adaptation studies since its inception. That model imposes a marginalising compare/contrast structure, leading to rear-view reading strategies. The Frankensteinian model offers a more global approach that allows critics to play adaptations forward, to consider them as existing in a web of cultural connection rather than a hermetic textual binary. It assumes that, as Hutcheon argues, 'there must be something particularly appealing [and culturally productive] about adaptations *as adaptation*' (4), and allows critics to position and consider the constructive work of adaptations. John Ellis argues that the 'adaptation trades upon the memory of the novel, a memory that can derive from actual reading, or, as is more likely with a classic of literature, a generally circulated cultural memory. The adaptation consumes this memory, aiming to efface it with the presence of its own images' (3). The first half of Ellis's concept is wonderfully productive: literature, whether read or not, adapts into elements of collective cultural memory. But then Ellis veers into an odd and objectionable turn back to the bizarre idea that our 'cultural memory' has room for only one version of a given story. The adaptation doesn't consume; it is consumed; its images don't efface; they inscribe themselves into the living cultural palimpsest.

Perhaps we could respond to Ellis's Romanticism – and Bloomian *Anxiety of Influence*-inflected Oedipal dynamic of cultural memory – with a Borgesian postmodern formula. The short story 'Pierre Menard, Author of the *Quixote*', offers the obituary of a twentieth-century author who has rewritten, word for word, two chapters of Cervantes's *Don Quixote*. Despite the fact that the texts are identical, the story insists on their simultaneous and individual existence in the culture. Accordingly, it distinguishes separate cultural implications of the identical texts: 'To compose the *Quixote* at the beginning of the seventeenth century was a reasonable undertaking, necessary and perhaps even unavoidable; at the beginning of the twentieth, it is almost impossible. It is not in vain that three hundred years have gone by, filled with exceedingly complex events. Amongst them, to mention only one, is the *Quixote* itself' (7–8). Borges posits reception as a constructive factor in a text. An experience of Menard's *Quixote* does not efface or threaten the existence of Cervantes' text; rather, it occasions a thinking forward: 'Cervantes' text and Menard's are verbally identical, but the second is almost infinitely richer' (9). While the story seems to be about writing, it is more about reading; Borges presents postmodernism as a reading strategy. Menard's text is the richer thanks to the conceptual contextual work performed by the reader. Such a strategy questions notions of originality. And a similar dynamic is at work in the reading of any adaptation.

As adaptations enter the culture, they reanimate their sources. In doing so, they engage with, activate, and even create intertexts. The adaptation is not merely a copy – it lives! It is its own creation, no mere assemblage of reconstituted plot points, but a text with a life and intentions of its own, its own drives and urges. *Presumption* evidences the use and construction of productive intertexts. In accounting for them, our cultural reception of the Frankenstein story comes to have at least two sources: Shelley's novel and Peake's play. And as we scroll forward, other radically intertextual versions, such as Mel Brooks's *Young Frankenstein*, Whale's two films, which draw so heavily from Peake, clearly begin to function as third and fourth source texts, and so on and so on. This, the Frankensteinian model argues, is the organic make-up of adaptations and our reception of them. To paraphrase (or adapt) Branagh's Creature (or DeNiro's Creature), the components are not so much a novel adapted as cultural details remembered. This adaptive pastiche, this suturing of intertexts, parallels *Frankenstein*'s own creation, making it the perfect adaptive cycle and the perfect metaphor for adaptation as creative act.

As the Introduction to this collection suggests, to attempt to assert a single source for any version of *Frankenstein* is patently absurd. Each iteration of the Frankenstein story, whether direct or oblique, is inflected by other iterations, both consciously and unconsciously, and subject to intertextual influences beyond the Frankenstein story. In turn, that iteration both enters and pulls more into the web. A productive example of this can be found in Danny Boyle's radically intertextual 2013 stage version of *Frankenstein*. The play cast Benedict Cumberbatch and Jonny Lee Miller as Frankenstein and the Creature. The fact that Miller and Cumberbatch were both playing Sherlock Holmes in separate popular TV adaptations at the time of the production intertextually knit the Frankenstein story to the Sherlock Holmes story. And the fact that Cumberbatch and Miller alternated roles night to night intertextually knit the play to Sam Shepard's *True West*. The casting alternation also nods to the critical reading of Frankenstein and the Creature as doppelgangers. Bloom centres that reading in critical *Frankenstein* studies: 'A critical discussion of *Frankenstein* needs to begin from an insight first recorded by Richard Church and Muriel Spark: the monster and his creator are the antithetical halves of a single being' (*Shelley's Frankenstein* 2). Here we see yet another facet of adaptation: critical interpretations or readings as adaptations (Stam 62–3). Significantly, Bloom's 'first' recordings of the doppelganger reading appear decades apart, Church's in 1928 (*Mary Shelley*) and Spark's in 1951 (*Child of Light: Mary Shelley*). Further, even Church's earlier observation misses the 'first' recording of the critical insight of the doppelganger reading by eighteen years. The Edison *Frankenstein*, directed by J. Searle Dawley, offered the same reading in 1910, using an ingenious camera trick to resolve the text's fundamental conflict between Frankenstein and his Creature. At the denouement, Frankenstein confronts his creation. However, the confrontation takes place not face to face but in a mirror, suggesting that man and monster are both components of Frankenstein's personality. The film diffuses the threat of the monster by dissolving him into the mirror image of Victor, implying that he has banished his daemon. In that way, we see that adaptations can function as critical readings. With that intertextual relay in mind, Boyle's production feeds critically from and back into Bloom, Spark, Church, Dawley, and likely others.

Perhaps this capacity for intertextual multiplicity is Frankenstein's most productive characteristic. Even when it's bad – and it's often bad – it's wildly creative. Each version functions as a Barthesian 'tissue of quotations', consciously (and sometimes unconsciously) 'drawn from [and feeding into] innumerable centres of culture' (146). As Hutcheon points out, adaptation is not just an act, it is also the product of that act (7). Those products live in the culture, not as mutually exclusive units, but as a perpetually morphing set of simultaneously available, and interpretable, variations. The task of the adaptation critic, among other things, is to chart and account for the afterlife and implications of symbiotic variation. In the end, a field that doesn't attempt to theorise and account for the critical possibilities of multiplicity and adaptation's challenges to concepts of originality risks suffering the fate of Frankenstein, a character doomed by his failure to fully consider and understand the complexity and capacity of his creation.

Notes

1 For another iteration of this concept, see *The Pedagogy of Adaptation* (2010), where Cutchins, Raw, and Welsh seek 'to stimulate new theoretical interventions in the discipline … [by] treat[ing] adaptation as an approach to texts, a trope, if you will' (xv).

2 Further attesting to the symbiotic relationship between stage and page, Susan Tyler Hitchcock notes, that 'in 1825, there appeared a two-penny chapbook … called The Monster Made by Man, or The Punishment of Presumption. … [The book], published anonymously, leaned more on Peake's play than the original novel' (91).

3 These were the Theatre Royal (Drury Lane), Covent Garden, and, in 1767, the Haymarket.

4 Though Elizabeth is adopted and not related to Victor by blood, they were raised as brother and sister. And interestingly, the Creature's impassioned desire/demand for a mate is frustrated by the text (Ch. XVII).

5 Interestingly, Peake leaves the Creature's name blank in his credits, a strategy noted and appreciated by Shelley: 'This nameless mode of naming the unnameable is rather good', and a practice that will be picked up by Whale in 1931. The refusal to name the creature leaves open the various readings of him: 'Being' (P. Shelley), 'Creature', 'Monster' (movies), 'Demon' (Peake), 'Daemon' (novel and Bloom, *Shelley's Frankenstein* vii)).

6 While the Slave Trade Act of 1807 outlawed the slave *trade*, slavery itself was not abolished in the Empire until the Slavery Abolition Act of 1833, and even then not completely.

Bibliography

Armitage, David. 'Monstrosity and Myth in Mary Shelley's *Frankenstein.*' *Monstrous Bodies/ Political Monstrosities*. Eds Laura Lunger Knoppers and Joan B. Landes, Ithaca, NY: Cornell UP, 2004. 200–226.

Baldick, Chris. *In Frankenstein's Shadow: Myth, Monstrosity, and Nineteenth-Century Writing*. Oxford: Clarendon, 1987.

Barthes, Roland. *Image, Music, Text*. New York: Hill, 1978.

Bloom, Harold. *The Anxiety of Influence*. Oxford: Oxford UP, 1973.

————. *Mary Shelley's* Frankenstein: *Updated Edition*. New York: Chelsea, 2007.

Borges, Jorge Luis. 'Pierre Menard, Author of the Quixote.' *Everything and Nothing*. Trans. Donald Yates. New York: New Directions, 1999.

The Bride of Frankenstein. Dir. James Whale. Perf. Boris Karloff, Elsa Manchester, and Ernest Thesiger. Universal, 1935.

Canning, George. 'Amelioriation of the Condition of the Slave Population in the West Indies (House of Lords).' *Hansard's Parliamentary Debates*. n.s. 10 (16 March 1824): cols. 1046–1198.

Carlson, Julie. *In the Theatre of Romanticism*. Cambridge: Cambridge UP, 1994.

Cowart, David. *Literary Symbiosis*. Athens: U of Georgia P, 1993.

Cox, Jeffrey. 'The Death of Tragedy; or, The Birth of the Melodrama.' *The Performing Century: Nineteenth-Century Theater*. Eds Peter Holland and Tracy Davis. New York: Palgrave, 2007. 161–181.

Cox, Philip. *Reading Adaptations: Novels and Verse Narratives on the Stage, 1790–1840*. Manchester: Manchester UP, 2000.

Cutchins, Dennis. 'Introduction.' *The Pedagogy of Adaptation*. Eds Dennis Cutchins, Laurence Raw, and James Welsh. Lanham, MD: Scarecrow, 2010.

Ellis, John. 'The Literary Adaptation: an Introduction.' *Screen* 32.1 (1982): 3–5.

Frankenstein. Dir. J. Searle Dawley. Perf. Charles Ogle, Mary Fuller, and Augustus Phillips. Edison, 1910.

Frankenstein. Dir. James Whale. Perf. Boris Karloff, Clive Owen, and Dwight Frye. Universal, 1931.

Frankenstein. Writ. Nick Dear. Dir. Danny Boyle. Perf. Benedict Cumberbatch and Jonny Lee Miller. Royal National Theatre, London, 22 February 2011.

Frankenstein; or, The Demon of Switzerland. Writ. Henry M. Milner. Perf. O. Smith. Coburg Theatre, London, 18 August 1823.

Frankenstein; or, The Man and His Monster! Writ. Henry M. Milner. Perf. O. Smith. Coburg Theatre, London, 3 July 1826.

Frankenstein: The True Story. Dir. Jack Smight. Perf. Michael Sarrazin, Jane Seymour, and James Mason. Hammer, 1973.

Frankenstein Unbound. Dir. Roger Corman. Perf. John Hurt, Raul Julia, and Bridget Fonda. 20th Century Fox, 1990.

Garcia, Pedro Javier Pardo. 'Beyond Adaptation: Frankenstein's Postmodern Progeny.' *Books in Motion: Adaptation, Intertextuality, Authorship*. Ed. Mareia Aragay. New York: Rodopi, 2005. 223–242.

The Ghost of Frankenstein. Dir. Erle Kenton. Perf. Lon Chaney Jr. and Bela Lugosi. Universal, 1942.

Grossman, Julie. *Literature, Film, and Their Hideous Progeny: Adaptation and ElasTEXTity*. New York: Palgrave, 2015.

Gupta, Nilanjana. 'Introduction.' *Frankenstein*. By Mary Shelley. Delhi, India: Pearson, 2007.

Hitchcock, Susan Tyler. *Frankenstein: A Cultural History*. New York: WW Norton & Company, 2007.

The House of Frankenstein. Dir. Erle Kenton. Perf. Boris Karloff, Lon Chaney Jr., and J. Carol Naish. Universal, 1944.

House of Wax. Dir. Andre de Toth. Perf. Vincent Price and Charles Bronson. Warner, 1953.

Hutcheon, Linda. *A Theory of Adaptation*. 2nd Edition. New York: Routledge, 2012.

Igor. Dir. Tony Leondis. Perf. John Cusack, Molly Shannon, and Steve Buschemi. MGM, 2008.

Labbe, Jacqueline. *Writing Romanticism: Charlotte Smith and William Wordsworth 1784–1807*. New York: Palgrave, 2011.

Leitch, Thomas. '12 Fallacies in Contemporary Adaptation Theory.' *Criticism* 45.2 (2003): 149–171.

Moody, Jane. *Illegitimate Theatre in London, 1770–1840*. Cambridge: Cambridge UP, 2000.

Nicoll, Allardyce. *The History of English Drama, 1660–1900*. Cambridge: Cambridge UP, 1955.

Nitchie, Elizabeth. 'The Stage History of Frankenstein.' *The South Atlantic Quarterly* 41(1942): 384–398.

Presumption; or, The Fate of Frankenstein. Writ. Peake, Richard Brinsley. Perf. T.P. Cooke, and J.W. Wallack. English Opera House, 28 July 1823.

Quintana, Raymond. Introduction. *18th-Century Plays*. New York: Modern Library, 1952.

'Review of *Presumption*.' *The Examiner* 3 August 1823: 504–505.

Shelley, Mary. *Frankenstein; or, the Modern Prometheus*. New York: Bedford, 2000.

———. 'To Leigh Hunt,' 9 September 1823. In *The Life and Letters of Mary Wollstonecraft Shelley*. Vol II. Ed. Mrs Julien Marshall. New York: Haskell, 1970.

Shelley, Percy Bysshe. 'On "Frankenstein"'. *The Prose Works of Percy Bysshe Shelley from the Original Editions*. Vol I. London: Chatto, 1906.

Shiloh, Ilana. 'Adaptation, Intertextuality, and the Endless Deferral of Meaning: *Memento*.' *M/C Journal* 10.2 (2007). 30 April 2016 http://journal.media-culture.org.au/0705/08- shiloh.php.

The Son of Frankenstein. Dir. Rowland Lee. Perf. Boris Karloff, Bela Lugosi, and Basil Rathbone. Universal, 1939.

St Clair, William. *The Reading Nation in the Romantic Period*. Cambridge: Cambridge UP, 2004.

Stam, Robert. 'Beyond Fidelity.' *Film Adaptation*. Ed. James Naremore. New Brunswick: Rutgers UP, 2000.

Victor Frankenstein. Dir. Paul McGuigan. Perf. James McAvoy and Daniel Radliffe. 20th Century Fox, 2015.

Young Frankenstein. Dir. Mel Brooks. Perf. Gene Wilder, Marty Feldman, Peter Boyle, and Teri Garr. 20th Century Fox, 1974.

3

The Gothic imagination in American sound recordings of *Frankenstein*

Laurence Raw

I N NOVEMBER 2014 THE BBC broadcast a television documentary, 'Gothic Goes Global', part of a three-part series with the overall title *The Art of Gothic*, in which presenter Andrew Graham-Dixon argued that one of the main reasons for the endur- ing popularity of texts such as Shelley's *Frankenstein* and Stoker's *Dracula* lay in their attempts to deconstruct imperialist rhetoric. Human beings at the end of the eight- eenth century, he insisted, were no longer willing to accept without question the authority of (mostly self-appointed) rulers, and were searching for alternative means of self-expression. They found those means, at least in part, in the Gothic novel, with its emphasis on mysterious and troubling worlds dominated by a restless spirit of human inquiry, a desire to extend psychological knowledge and construct new worldviews. Although both Victor Frankenstein and his Creature are destroyed at the end of Shelley's novel, their revolutionary visions continue to stimulate the collective imagination.

In a 1999 work, *The Power of Now*, Eckhart Tolle corroborates the power of the Gothic by suggesting that most human beings operate exclusively based on either memory or anticipation and, by so doing, develop 'an endless preoccupation with past and future and an unwillingness to honor and acknowledge the present moment' (27). This time-based view, Tolle argues, lies at the heart of most problems of perception: '[If] all your problems or perceived causes of suffering or unhappiness were miracu- lously removed [...] you would soon find yourself with a similar set of problems [...] like a shadow that follows you wherever you go' (33). Tolle suggests that this form of perception is not confined to isolated individuals but represents a 'collective dysfunc- tion' creating 'a very unhappy and extremely violent civilization that has become a threat not only to itself but also to all life on the planet' (40). The best solution, he believes, would be for everyone to recognise their 'inner purpose' that is unrelated to the conscious mind and helps promote the imaginative 'consciousness of the moment' (62). Surprisingly, Graham-Dixon makes much the same claim. He suggests that the Gothic emphasises the 'consciousness of the moment', especially in the novel, and hence becomes a popular subject for adaptation into other media – especially radio, where directors have seemingly limitless options to create innovative and disturbing sonic landscapes. Richard J. Hand's books on horror radio in the United States and Great Britain outline a number of popular strategies for creating these sonic landscapes. These include: using a framing narrator who not only tells the story, but establishes a sense of atmosphere; creating unexpected sound-effects like the crash of a gong or the slamming of a door; commissioning atmospheric music, with piano, trumpet and organ among the most favoured instruments; and introducing subtle variations in pace. Hand remarks in *Listen in Terror* that 'the place of sound is inherently important in the works of the most influential of Gothic writers' (14), and the importance of sound in radio is unquestioned. 'Although we may well be inured to the concept of disembodied voices talking to us on our radios, computers, phones and iPods,' Hand writes, 'it is not difficult to remind ourselves how extraordinarily uncanny this is.' (20)

Such uncanniness, as applied to *Frankenstein*, might encourage listeners to rethink the Creature's role in the novella. Radio listeners are placed in a position not dissimilar to that of De Lacey, the Parisian-turned-blind-peasant in the source text. He comes across as sympathetic and kindly, and is the only person to treat the Creature sympathetically, telling him not to despair. Unlike De Lacey, most listeners already understand the Creature's capacity to scare off rather than attract humanity (drawing on their previous knowledge of films and/or other visual media). But, since listeners cannot see the Creature on radio, they are invited to reconsider their prejudices and view him in the same fashion as De Lacey, as an object of sympathy rather than prejudice.

To illuminate this point, this chapter will analyse three American sound versions of *Frankenstein* from different periods in history. Elliott Lewis's adaptation for the anthology series *Suspense!* was a half-hour drama broadcast on CBS Radio on 11 March 1952 with British character actor Herbert Marshall (Figure 3.1) as Victor Frankenstein.[1]

Eighteen years later an LP recording of the tale was issued in the Super 8 Monsters series with Jackson Beck as the Narrator and Peter Fernandez as Victor. Most recently, Quicksilver Radio Theater created a one-hour adaptation that premiered on American public radio in 2007 and was twice rebroadcast on Frederick Greenhalgh's valuable *Radio Drama Revival* podcast in 2009. There are several other English radio adaptations of *Frankenstein*, originally broadcast on both sides of the Atlantic, readily available, but I have limited my attention to these three adaptations in an attempt to demonstrate the variety of strategies adopted by audio adapters.[2]

Anthony Ellis's *Suspense!* script reshapes Shelley's *Frankenstein* into a family melodrama in which Victor Frankenstein encounters his vicar friend James (Paul Frees), who decides to tell the world about the doctor's experiments. Meanwhile, the doctor has to struggle to keep his wife, Elizabeth, from discovering his guilty secret. The 1970 LP version of the tale is dominated by the Narrator setting the scene as well as guiding our responses to the action taking place. Both of these adaptations illustrate Thomas Leitch's point that all adaptations have a multitude of source texts; they not only draw inspiration from the Shelley novel but are also stylistically influenced by James Whale's 1931 film, as they both represent the Creature as inarticulate and

Figure 3.1 Herbert Marshall, at right, in an NBC radio studio.

highly destructive (120–1). In these adaptations the Creature, as well as the doctor, need to be eliminated before social order can be restored. The Quicksilver version, on the other hand, follows Shelley's *Frankenstein* by creating a battle of wills between the doctor (Joseph Franchini) and the Creature (Craig Wichman). In this version our judgemental loyalties are divided: the doctor puts his case eloquently, but so does the Creature, who comes across as a sympathetic rather than repulsive personality. Both are highly articulate, and their discussions raise important questions of power, colonialism, and free will – the kind of topics that have been perennially popular with those concerned with the Gothic imagination. The adaptation envisages what might have happened in the source text, had De Lacey been able to humanise the Creature through sympathetic treatment.

The reasons why the three versions were shaped so differently certainly have something to do with the creators, but all three are also institutionally as well as culturally determined. Popular taste had been so effectively shaped by the Whale film adaptation that it would have been unwise for the *Suspense!* series to have offered a radically alternative view: their sponsors were mostly interested in high ratings, not artistic integrity. The 1970 LP adaptation was also fiscally motivated, intended, as it was, for the burgeoning market for commercially produced sound recordings. By contrast, the Quicksilver adaptation was premiered on public radio, with professional actors taking minimal fees in an enterprise primarily conceived for artistic purposes. As the publicity claimed, it tried to be 'intelligent and very faithful' to the source text while making it 'spring into robust life' ('Frankenstein' 2007). I propose that the different treatments of the source texts in the three adaptations rehearse a familiar conflict between enlightenment rationalism, which upholds certain preconceived conventions of rational behaviour, and the Gothic imagination that inspired Mary Shelley to write the ghost story at Diodati that purportedly inspired the novel (originally conceived in a dream). The response to her work from directors across the decades indicates the extent to which they are prepared to embrace or reject her radical vision.

Suspense! was originally conceived as a vehicle for Alfred Hitchcock, who is credited with directing the pilot for the series in 1940, a radio version of *The Lodger*, which the director had filmed in Great Britain fourteen years previously. When the series proper was launched in June 1942, CBS presented adaptations of whodunits by Dorothy L. Sayers and Agatha Christie, but by 1943 the focus had radically changed, with the emphasis shifting from logic to psychology, from surprise endings to sustained tension. Offering between $150 and $500 per script by the early 1950s, producers advised prospective dramatists to produce material that was 'believable from the start', preferably using first-person narration and containing at least one plum role for a Hollywood star (Heuser 183).

Herbert Marshall, cast as Frankenstein, regularly appeared on *Suspense!* as part of a radio career that flourished in the late 1940s and early 1950s. After playing the Narrator in *The Lodger* he had taken over as the host of *Hollywood Star Time*, beginning in 1946, while also playing globe-trotting secret agent Ken Thurston in *The Man Called X* for CBS, a thriller designed not only to entertain but to alert 'an anxious war-weary world to the inherent dangers of resting on its laurels during the brief peace after war' (Crosby). Marshall was ideally suited to play Victor Frankenstein in Elliott Lewis's production, which, like *The Man Called X*, was designed to alert listeners to the destructive power of science in the post-war world (Figure 3.2).

The casting of Marshall was an inspired decision, part of *Suspense!*'s deliberate policy of casting well-known performers against type ('Old Time Radio Downloads'). Marshall plays not only the main character, but also the narrator, telling much of the story in the past tense as a first-hand account of his experiments. His Victor Frankenstein, highly reminiscent of Colin Clive's performance in Whale's film, comes across as a tortured genius, unable to contemplate the sheer magnitude of his achievement. This was no coincidence — as members of Hollywood's British community, Whale and Marshall regularly fraternised with one another at a variety of social events, and hence Marshall would have been well aware of the director's earlier work (Baxter 99). While Marshall, in common with contemporaries such as Frank Sinatra and Lucille Ball, relished the chance to play against type on radio (where their faces could not be seen and they could rely solely on their vocal abilities), his presence in the *Frankenstein* adaptation serves a more important thematic purpose. If performers with a trustworthy voice like Marshall can no longer be trusted, then listeners have to be

Figure 3.2 The 'trustworthy' Herbert Marshall from a late 1930s cigarette advertisement.

extra vigilant about not taking the people they encounter at face value, especially those with whom they are ostensibly familiar. This notion works both ways: if listeners should approach Marshall's Frankenstein with caution, perhaps they should follow De Lacey's example in the source text and view the Creature more sympathetically.

Like many other horror adaptations, Lewis's production takes full advantage of radio's intimacy between performers and listeners. Marshall speaks in quiet, confidential tones as he sets the scene for us; in the background we hear the chiming of a bell and the sound of cows mooing. We are not in Central Europe, as in Shelley's novel or the Whale film, but, rather, in a quiet English village where Frankenstein's friend James (Joseph Kearns) serves as the local vicar. The change of location is deliberate, designed to lull listeners into a sense of false security. In such a tranquil environment peopled by reliable-sounding men like Marshall, nothing can go wrong ... or can it? Hand remarks that the use of familiar sound-effects and voices was a deliberate ploy designed to make listeners feel that 'there is very little that separates them from the hero/celebrity' (Hand 46).

Director Elliott Lewis highlights Victor Frankenstein's frailties by contrasting him with the more stable James. The broadcast begins with Victor's mundane conversation with James's wife and a brief exchange of pleasantries with James. At this point Marshall's Victor sounds a little worried, but perfectly normal. As the conversation continues, however, he describes the creation scene and struggles to describe what he has done, finally blurting out the line 'I've … made … a …thing!' with each word interrupted by a short pause. He takes a deep breath and delivers the triumphant phrase, 'I've created a man!' in a half-scream of delight. Clearly he has been driven almost insane by his experiments. This apparent insanity forces us, as listeners, to reconsider our relationship to him, thereby adapting ourselves to make sense of 'complications of surprise and suspense, and possibly even betrayal' (Hand 50). As Victor and James discuss the experiment they walk, and eventually arrive at Victor's house. They descend to his basement laboratory and Victor shows James the lifeless Creature. The more the doctor talks about his creation, the more insistent the vicar becomes in his opposition. 'It's wrong,' he cries, 'Victor, bury it, let it be at peace!' Victor Frankenstein's discourse, on the other hand, becomes more and more hyperbolic. He declares, 'What would it mean to me [to publicise the creation] to the world!' A moment later he insists, 'I'm not ashamed! I think I'm a little frightened at the incredible greatness of what I've done! It's bigger than anything since the world began.' Against James's wishes, Victor demonstrates the process he plans to use to bring the Creature to life, but insists that the amount of the drug he injects will allow the Creature to live for only a moment. The Creature comes fully to life, however, and the first half of the adaptation ends with the sound of his heavy breathing.

The adaptation bears only a passing relationship to Shelley's source text: Elliott seems far more concerned with reshaping his production according to the requirements of a half-hour time slot, as well as fulfilling the series' long-established remit of providing a drama calculated to keep listeners 'in suspense!' Leslie McMurtry argues that productions like this have been critically under-served by scholars and critics, especially those productions whose 'collage-like techniques' of dialogue supplemented by sound-effects 'are often dismissed as unoriginal and not worthy of study' (147). McMurtry's observations have been echoed by Heuser, who claims that most literary adaptations of this period were inadequate, sacrificing the nuances of the source texts in a misguided effort 'to condense plot and dramatize narration' (88).

This judgement seems particularly unfair for at least two reasons. In common with most adaptations produced for anthology series, Elliott and Lewis had less than a week to adapt and record *Frankenstein*, and together they concentrated on the story's basic analysis of the ethics involved in the doctor's experiments (Raw, 'Austen' 88). Thus their version takes the somewhat simplistic route of serving as a warning to anyone foolish enough to challenge the basic laws of nature, since God, as the vicar points out, is the sole creator. The point is reiterated in James's closing speech, which recounts how, after his friend's death, he returned to the laboratory and 'destroyed every single evidence of Victor Frankenstein's terrible experiment'. He continues, 'the result of that experiment has never been found, nor have I been able to convince authorities that such a thing ... ever existed!' As he speaks, a piano can be heard on the soundtrack thumping out a series of discordant notes; this changes into a funeral dirge as the production closes. Victor Frankenstein's efforts have apparently resulted in the creation of an unnatural force over which humanity has no control. The music, by Lucien Alfred E. Moraweck, emphasises this impending sense of doom.[3] Yet perhaps this is only half the story. We do not hear anything from the Creature's perspective, but remain aware that he is meting out punishments only to those who want to destroy him. If Victor had treated him as a human being rather than as an object for experimentation, then perhaps the Creature would not have been regarded as an unnatural force.

In terms of listener response, *Suspense!* had achieved much of its success by challenging prevailing moral and social certainties (Hand, 58). Radio plays such as *Sorry, Wrong Number* established the series' reputation as a place where writers regularly questioned what it was to be good or bad, civilised or uncivilised.[4] The series received a Special Citation of Honor in the Peabody Awards of 1946 for its efforts. *Frankenstein* offers a prime example of this approach through its characterisation of Victor and the Creature.

The adaptation acquires a further level of meaning when considered in terms of its first broadcast date. With the publication of the pamphlet *Red Channels* in 1950, listing 151 actors, writers, broadcast journalists, and others in the context of alleged communist manipulation of the media, employees at CBS were required to sign a loyalty oath declaring that they had not been associated with any organisation deemed subversive by the Attorney General of the United States. William Paley, the company's chair, cast this demand in the most positive light when he recalled in his memoirs that this measure relieved everyone of 'any threatened blackmail, accusations, or pressures by outside crusaders' (qtd. in Raw, *Hawthorne* 30). Yet this did not prevent the network from dismissing anyone who refused to sign the oath on the grounds of belief. Confronted with this radically conservative atmosphere, many scriptwriters shied away from potentially contentious subjects and toed the company line by reminding viewers and listeners of the importance of guarding against those who might threaten the democratic status quo. Anthony Ellis's script for *Frankenstein* casts the doctor in the role of potential subversive, threatening the laws of nature with his creation. The Creature becomes the victim of blind prejudice, with everyone quick to condemn him as a monster. It is not surprising that Ellis omitted the De Lacey episodes. James's speech at the end of the drama reminds us of the importance of eradicating such figures. In this way Mary Shelley's endorsement of the Gothic imagination was reshaped into an anti-communist tract that plays on listeners' fears of the unknown or intangible.[5]

By 1970 the tradition of radio drama had all but vanished in the United States; *Suspense!* had come to an end eight years earlier, and thereafter CBS broadcast very little if any drama until 1974, when *Radio Mystery Theater* was created under the aegis of Himan Brown, one of the leading producers of the inter-war era.[6] Spoken-word recordings were still produced commercially, however, notably under the Caedmon label, which had begun in 1952 by issuing an LP of Dylan Thomas reading his own poetry,[7] and subsequently expanded its catalogue to encompass many of the twentieth century's leading writers – W.H. Auden, T.S. Eliot, Robert Frost, Wallace Stevens – as well as selections read by star actors such as Richard Burton, John Gielgud, and Vanessa Redgrave. Caedmon harvested material from all over the world – their releases included works by Colette, Thomas Mann, Tolkein, and Shakespeare – and thereby laid the foundations for the contemporary audiobook industry. By the end of the 1960s their products enjoyed substantial sales, appealing both to 'college educated men' and 'busy housewives who had to get the ironing done' (Rubery).

Caedmon paved the way for these recorded literary adaptations, and in 1970 *Frankenstein* was recorded in the Super 8 Monsters series and issued as an LP. Very different in terms of tone and style to most of Caedmon's products, which tended to preserve as much of the source texts as they could, this project represented an attempt to extend the range of dramatic material on sale to prospective listeners. The time of release was significant. As Hand has suggested, even the British did not seem especially interested any more in horror adaptations, except as subjects for comedy: 'This is why Stephen Gallagher, the writer of several horror plays for [the BBC Radio 4 series] *Fear on Four* cannot remember any distinctive horror radio from [his] growing up years in the 1960s' (Hand 128).[8] It was not until 1973, when Vincent Price starred in the anthology series *The Price of Fear*, that the genre reoccupied a serious place in the BBC schedules.[9] Thus the Super 8 Monsters *Frankenstein* was both after and before its time.

This recording begins with the Narrator describing the young doctor's journey to Inglestadt; we learn later that his studies sowed 'the seed of dreadful inspiration within him'. Arriving at Inglestadt, the doctor encounters Dr Waldman (also played by Hernandez) who tells him that humankind will soon have discovered 'the elements that create life. Man will be created in his own image.' The sound of a bottle opening can be heard on the soundtrack, followed by the regular drip of liquid, as Waldman shows Victor Frankenstein the elixir that will expedite the process of discovery. The action shifts to the doctor's study as he reads from his diary, describing in particular his enthusiasm for 'life's mysteries' as a dirge-like melody, strongly reminiscent of that used in the *Suspense!* adaptation, plays softly. As Victor Frankenstein continues his life's work, the dark atmosphere intensifies: the Narrator describes the 'horrible destiny' awaiting us as a consequence of 'the corruption of the human body'. Victor continues his 'most morbid research' in Burke and Hare mode as he opens a grave to find a suitable corpse. The soundscape captures the sombre mood, with the creak of the coffin lid competing for our attention with the sound of howling dogs and deliberately discordant church bells. The production subsequently contrasts the Narrator's pronouncements as he describes the doctor's visits to 'graves ... and vaults ... and morgues!' and Victor Frankenstein's cry of elation as he uncovers 'the cause of generation and life!'

We are left in no doubt as to the moral scheme imposed on this adaptation: the doctor possesses no redeeming features whatsoever, despite his scientific accomplishments. The Narrator repeatedly reminds us about Victor's 'ghostly creation' that challenges our understanding of what it means to be human. Victor Frankenstein himself remains oblivious to such strictures as he exclaims, 'Is this my creation?! It moved!' The Narrator immediately deflates this mood with the observation that the Creature resembles nothing more than 'a mummy imbued with life'. The prejudices that will blight its future existence are firmly in place. We hear a muffled combination of grunts, groans, and intermittent footsteps, interspersed with the same sonorous melody that we heard previously, stressing the danger which the Creature poses as well as his bestial nature. The remainder of the action follows a predictable path as the Creature wreaks havoc on the neighbouring village before turning on his creator. The doctor insists that he is the Creature's ally, but to no avail; fuelled by prejudice and hate, and unable to detect the presence of good in the world, the Creature crushes him to death, leaving the Narrator to reflect sorrowfully that both the doctor and the Creature contributed to their own deaths. Social order, apparently, can return only once both have been eliminated.

With its strident sound-effects and music, coupled with the Narrator's seemingly endless moralising, this adaptation veers towards melodrama in its creation of a universe of moral absolutes. By such means we are asked to reflect on prejudice directed against most scientific research – in individual as well as societal terms. We are left in no doubt that Victor Frankenstein's mental corruption dates back to when he was a student, listening intently to Dr Waldman's pronouncements while remaining unaware of their consequences. Education can be advantageous, the production seems to suggest, but it should be tempered by a suspicious attitude towards progress, especially the kind of progress that puts the collective well-being at risk.[10]

Even by 1970 standards this adaptation seems old-fashioned, a throwback to the golden age of radio drama, when adapters deliberately crafted melodramas in order to sustain the medium's 'middlebrow appeal' (Heuser 38). Listeners have little or no opportunity to make up their own minds about the characters and are asked simply to accept 'the lessons expected in the overheard action; staying attuned through radio' (Heuser 145). Such strategies had helped to transform radio into an effective instrument of propaganda during World War II, as well as in the immediate post-war years. But by 1970, at a time when the Gothic spirit flourished in various areas of American culture, this consciously didactic approach to adaptation seemed incongruous. In 1967 the so-called 'Summer of Love' represented the apotheosis of the counter-culture movement in which people were invited to question everything about themselves and the environment they inhabited. An unprecedented gathering of young people in San Francisco (as many as 100,000 in number) advocated alternative lifestyles based on gender equality, communal living, and free love. They propounded revolutionary ideas as well as advocating psychedelic drug use to explore new modes of expression. This movement extended beyond San Francisco into other parts of the United States, as well as to Europe; and its effects reverberated throughout the remainder of the 1960s and into the 1970s. The Super 8 Monsters LP repudiates the lessons of that movement – and, by extension, of the Gothic – particularly in its reluctance to acknowledge the possibilities of psychological and emotional progress in the Creature, if he were treated with kindness and understanding rather than prejudice. Such conservatism might help to explain the sluggish sales at the time of the LP's initial release: just over 2,000 copies were sold. Believed lost for several years, this recording resurfaced in 2008 on YouTube, where, as of February 2016, it had achieved just under 3,500 views. These numbers might suggest a continuing reluctance on the part of potential listeners to embrace its views.

With the advent of the internet, the scope for creating and sharing new forms of audio drama increased significantly, providing creative artists with what Sarah Kember and Joanna Zylinska describe as 'a singular stabilisation'. No longer dependent on sponsors to guarantee a series' future life, they can work on new performative relationships involving human and machinistic elements (laptops, PCs, smartphones) (64). Moreover, the boundaries between radio and other forms of sound recording have dissolved: like the Super 8 recording, many recordings issued on LP or broadcast on commercial as well as public stations are now readily available to listeners at any time. Web-based dramas are more international, promoting greater access and mutual exchange between listeners and performers worldwide.

Quicksilver Radio Theater's revival of *Frankenstein* (2007) can be downloaded from a variety of sites, including *Radio Drama Revival*, SFF Audio, and iTunes, while listeners can share their views of the production through Facebook and Twitter ('Frankenstein: Modern Prometheus'). Taking advantage of this new facility for performer/listener exchange, adapter Craig Wichman returned to Mary Shelley's source text in 2007 and had Captain Walton (Craig Baldo) narrate the tale. Baldo begins this production by speaking softly, as if sitting by the fireside, taking listeners into his confidence. It is only after two or three minutes that his voice rises as a single piano in the background signals the start of the doctor's account of his experiments. With Walton making occasional interjections, listeners are offered the kind of emotional security markedly absent from the other two revivals. The doctor's experiments might be sinister, but we are secure in the knowledge that the tale is being told at second hand by Walton. Nothing appears to faze him, therefore we can share his feelings.

As the Creature springs into life, the tone abruptly alters: curtains open, footsteps click, a clock chimes, and a door opens. For a few moments we have no clue as to what is happening; the steady Walton is not around to explain things. Our confusion is resolved only after a few agonising moments, when the sound of birds cheeping in the trees can be heard as the doctor leaves his laboratory to return home. Director Jay Stern deliberately toys with our emotions by placing the sounds at different distances from the microphone, thereby distancing listeners from, and subsequently bringing them in closer proximity to, the narrative. The clicking footsteps, the chiming clock, and the open door are all heard in the distance – unlike the birdsong, which proves uncomfortably obtrusive to our ears. Listeners might have heard the tale several times before, but Stern and Wichman seem to suggest that it is still of paramount significance to an understanding of humanity. To return to the source text, we are placed in De

Lacey's position, unable to see anything, but understanding that something significant is about to happen. The importance of this narrative is reinforced when Stern introduces a third narrator – the Creature. As in Shelley's source text, he recounts his adventures in a form of discourse whose diction and vocabulary far surpasses that of his creator. The Quicksilver revival suggests that this narration is a notable feat by having the piano play a triumphant melody in the background as the Creature begins his tale of searching for berries in the forest. We are transported into a context wherein the distinction between human beings and the Creature no longer seems important – no longer a frightening presence, the Creature gradually acquires the kind of survival skills necessary for any living being.

Yet, once again this feeling of calm is abruptly dispelled as the Creature recounts his experiences with De Lacey and his family. The music becomes discordant once more, though we can hardly hear it above the din of fighting and screaming. This is followed by a few moments of agonising silence, leaving us wondering what will happen next. The silence is broken by the throaty cackle of a crow, followed by four gunshots that we soon discover have left the Creature wounded. Our favourable view of the Creature's social standing has been shattered; despite his accomplishments in speaking and fending for himself, he is still treated as a potential threat to human stability. Stern indicates that this view is caused by ignorance: human beings, it appears, are both unwilling and unable to accept alternative constructions of existence. There might be little intellectual difference between ourselves and the Creature, but the villagers who find the Creature insist otherwise.

Due to this violent treatment, it is hardly surprising that the Creature should thirst for revenge against his creator. He eventually exclaims ominously to the doctor, 'I will be with you on your wedding-night!' This is followed by the rustling of a leather bag and the chink of glass, followed by a splash as the doctor makes a hasty move to rid himself of anything that might identify him as the Creature's originator. The move proves futile, as suggested by the ominous sound of a Hammond organ in the background, as the Creature carries out his threat, kills the doctor's wife and disappears. The story subsequently comes full circle as we return to Walton finishing his narrative.

Yet, matters have certainly not been straightened out. In contrast to his complacent attitude earlier on, Walton starts as he hears an unexpected cry of anguish. The Creature makes an unexpected reappearance into the frame narrative – not as part of Walton's or the doctor's stories, but as a protagonist in his own right. In Stern's version he is not the dishevelled figure with 'long locks of ragged hair' as described by Shelley (237), but a living, healthy presence repenting for his past sins despite a basic self-loathing. The Creature announces his intention to commit suicide, and speaks his lines in a series of short phrases ('my spirit ... will sleep ... in peace') in a vocal style reminiscent of Herbert Marshall in the 1952 adaptation, but without any feeling of pain or suffering. The Creature knows his destiny and has prepared himself for it. Stern's slight alteration to the source-text narration reinforces our belief in the

Creature's indestructability. Although we apparently hear his death wail at the end of the show, he remains in our minds a living metaphor for the power of the Gothic imagination to withstand all possible attempts to destroy it. Stern's version ends on a tranquil note: after the Creature's cry nothing can be heard except for the faint crash of the waves, the wind howling and the creak of Walton's ship's timbers. It is tempting to suggest that, with the advantage of a longer time-slot (one hour instead of thirty minutes), Stern had both the time and the space to create a more 'faithful' version, one that celebrated the power of the Gothic imagination.

So far this chapter has shown how the Creature has been interpreted in two opposite ways, as a figure of pure evil, and as a victim of human indifference. Yet there is a sense in which both readings represent different sides of the same psychological coin, and this interpretive flexibility helps to explain why Shelley's text has proved enduringly popular as a subject for radio adaptation. The same is also true for adaptations in other media, but radio has always had the advantage, especially over the visual arts, of appealing to the imagination through creating sonic landscapes designed to stimulate listeners. We neither have to worry about issues of verisimilitude (is the actor playing the Creature giving a convincing performance?); nor do we have to make comparative judgements concerning whether the visual aspects either conform to or depart from our mental images of the novella. Because such formal issues are not as significant as they are in other forms of adaptation, the radio adaptations can directly comment on contemporary issues, providing suggestive perspectives on the 'Frankenstein Complex' that tell us a lot about their contexts of production. The radio *Frankenstein*s of 1952 and 1970 depict worlds dominated by collective dysfunction, with people unable to tolerate the presence of difference. Both adaptations run under thirty minutes, and both have clear and rather simplistic moral messages. They show how people's reactions have been shaped by past knowledge of human behaviour. This view might have been tolerated in 1952, when CBS's creative personnel had to deal with the fall-out emanating from the publication of *Red Channels*, but it nonetheless denotes a highly intolerant society. The Quicksilver version seems at first to posit an equally pessimistic interpretation, as it shows the Creature willingly accepting death, but Stern made a conscious effort to depict the Creature as something of a Noble Savage whose shifting states of mind indicate a being of limitless potential. When Shelley described the process of creating *Frankenstein* she likened the moment of creation to a similar moment of potential – the time when she 'first stepped from childhood into life' (qtd in Sunstein 117). In the Introduction to the 1831 edition she described this transformative process thus:

> My imagination, unbidden, possessed and guided me, gifting the successive images that arose in my mind with a vividness far beyond the usual bounds of reverie. I saw – with shut eyes, but acute mental vision, – I saw the pale student of unhallowed arts kneeling beside the thing he had put together. I saw the hideous phantasm of a man stretched out, and then, on the working of some powerful engine, show signs of life, and stir with an uneasy, half vital motion. (9)

The Quicksilver adaption of *Frankenstein* captures some of the mix of wonder and dread clear in Shelley's novel.

Although the Quicksilver version recreates the spirit of the novel for contemporary listeners, it would be erroneous to describe it as a 'faithful' adaptation. 'Fidelity' is an elusive concept, especially in a transmedial context where the novel has been completely reshaped for radio adaptation. Even if we were to introduce fidelity discourse into our analysis, we would be faced with the problem of determining which source text Stern actually used: the first anonymous edition published in London (1818); the second edition appearing in France four years later with Shelley's name on it; a modern version with editorial emendations; or the Whale adaptation, which has proved so influential since its premiere in 1931. If we set aside issues of 'fidelity' and consider Stern's version as a creative response to the novel, it is evident that we are being encouraged to 'adapt' ourselves – understood in this context as accommodating new experiences and new phenomena.[11] Stern's production advocates 'adaptation' on two levels, textual and psychological. By adapting the Shelley novel into sonic form, with the emphasis placed on the Creature's nobility, even at the point of death, he suggests that the best way to improve our lives is to follow a similar imaginative path, to cast aside the opinions of others and follow our instincts. This might seem a romantic, even idealistic, interpretation, quite out of step with modern psychological thinking, which emphasises the power of reason behind all the decisions we make. On the other hand, as psychologist Jerome Bruner has observed, we are also *bricoleurs*, blessed with the capacity to 'improvise in how we tell about ourselves to ourselves, improvise in the interest of keeping our investment in our balance from getting undone' (100). The improvisatory spirit helps to establish our unique identity so that we can meet, and perhaps redefine, the situations where we will go on living. Stern's Creature is also a *bricoleur*, whose improvisatory spirit enables him to adapt to and ultimately transcend the indignities of his situation, which is precisely what the Gothic encourages. The aural medium is ideal for depicting the positive aspects of this process of transformation, with the characters communicating to us via the microphone and thereby establishing the kind of emotional closeness that is generally impossible on television or film. Our experience of listening to *Frankenstein*, especially in its 2007 incarnation, can help us to understand why Mary Shelley's process of writing the novel should prove such a life-changing moment for her, and how we can experience a similar process of imaginative adaptation, if only we trust in our instincts. By doing so we come to understand the significance of how and why the Gothic went 'Global', as described by Andrew Graham-Dixon. He envisions the creation of a global community of purpose dedicated to reading and being inspired by Gothic material (and its adaptations), and using their experiences to redefine their place in the world and their relationship to it.

Notes

1 Marshall's grandfather Godfrey Wadsworth Turner was the grand-nephew of Edward Wollstonecraft, first cousin of Mary Shelley.

2 The archive.org site lists the following American adaptations: a ten-part serial (1931) produced by George Edwards; a half-hour version (broadcast 8 January 1944) in *The Weird Circle* anthology series from RCA; another half-version in Ronald Colman's *Favorite Story* series (broadcast 13 December 1947); an unaired transcription in the *NBC Short Story* series (1952); and another version for *Suspense!* (broadcast 7 June 1955). More recently the BBC has broadcast an adaptation in its *Classic Serial* strand (28 October/4 November 2012) with Shaun Dooley as the Creature and Jamie Parker as the doctor (dir. Marc Beeby). The British independent company Big Finish released a 6-hour version on podcast in September 2014, with Arthur Darvill as the Creature and Nicholas Briggs as the doctor (dir. Scott Handcock). A complete version of the 1931 adaptation is available online in its full ten-part version, as well as a two-and-a-half hour adaptation by W.D. Sherman Olson. I have chosen not to discuss this adaptation on the grounds that it is an Australian rather than an American version that lifts most of the lines out of the Shelley source text, and resembles a dramatised reading rather than an adaptation planned for radio drama performance.

3 Moraweck usually consulted with producer William Spier as well as Elliott about the kind of music required, immediately before each episode of *Suspense!* was broadcast. The smallest details were calculated for dramatic effect (Dunning 647).

4 Directed by William Spier and starring Agnes Moorehead, *Sorry, Wrong Number* appeared first on CBS on 25 May 1943.

5 Lawrence Buell describes Shelley's novel as a series of 'fable-like thought experiments that [...] belie the appearance of factual solidity and narrative closure by conjuring up an aura of the mysterious' (75).

6 *Radio Mystery Theater* ran on CBS Radio from 1974 to 1982.

7 The album sold over 500,000 copies before its release on other formats – cassette, CD and online.

8 *Fear on Four* ran on BBC Radio 4 from 1988 to 1999.

9 *The Price of Fear* ran on BBC World Service from 1973 to 1974 and 1983.

10 Not surprisingly, the *Suspense! Frankenstein* is highly reminiscent of another adaptation that was also originally broadcast in 1952, this time on ABC's television series *Tales of Tomorrow*. In this adaptation the Creature (Lon Chaney Jr) goes on a brief rampage that results in the death of the housekeeper. Frankenstein (John Newland) afterwards admits, 'I created a being with no thought of what would become of him, no thought of the danger involved, no thought of a tragedy like this.' He then proceeds to destroy his own notes and equipment to prevent anyone from repeating his mistake.

11 Tony Gurr and I have explored this process in more detail elsewhere by drawing on the work of psychologist Jerome Bruner (Raw and Gurr 75–83).

Bibliography

Baxter, John. *The Hollywood Exiles*. London: Macdonald and Jane's, 1976.

'Blood for Sale: Gothic Goes Global.' *Art of Gothic*. Perf. Andrew Graham-Dixon. Dir. Paul Tickell. BBC Four. 6 November 2014.

Bruner, Jerome. *Making Stories: Law, Literature, Life*. Cambridge: Harvard UP, 2002.

Buell, Lawrence. *The Dream of the Great American Novel*. Cambridge: Belknap – Harvard UP, 2014.

Crosby, John. 'Air Villains Chased Again by "Mr. X".' *Oakland Tribune* 9 July 1948. 31 December 2014. www.digitaldeliftp.com/DigitalDeliToo/dd2jb-Man-Called- X.html.

Dunning, John. *On the Air: The Encyclopaedia of Old-Time Radio*. Oxford: Oxford UP, 1998.

'Frankenstein.' *Tales of Tomorrow*. ABC. *Youtube*. 2 October 2014.

'*Frankenstein: Modern Prometheus*' (2007). http://frankensteinia.blogspot.co.uk/2007/10/listen-to-frankenstein.html (accessed 30 December 2014).

Greenhalgh, Fred. 'Bonus! Quicksilver's Frankenstein Stalks Again …' Weblog posting. *Radio Drama Revival*. 20 October 2009. www.radiodramarevival.com/bonus-quicksilvers-frankenstein-stalks- again/ (accessed 30 December 2014).

Hand, Richard J. *Listen in Terror: British Horror Radio from the Advent of Broadcasting to the Digital Age*. Manchester: Manchester UP, 2014.

Heuser, Harry. *Immaterial Culture: Literature, Drama and the American Radio Play 1929–1954*. Bern: Peter Lang AG, 2013.

Kember, Sarah and Joanna Zylinska. *Life after New Media: Mediation as a Virtual Process*. Cambridge: MIT, 2012.

Leitch, Thomas. *Film Adaptation and its Discontents: From* Gone with the Wind *to* The Passion of the Christ. Baltimore: Johns Hopkins UP, 2009.

McMurtry, Leslie Grace. 'Revolution in the Echo Chamber: Audio Drama's Past, Present, and Future.' Diss. U of Swansea, 2014.

Raw, Laurence. *Adapting Nathaniel Hawthorne to the Screen: Forging New Worlds*. Lanham, MD: Scarecrow, 2008.

——— . 'Jane Austen on Old-Time Radio: Creating Imaginative Worlds.' *Global Jane Austen: Pleasure, Passion and Possessiveness in the Jane Austen Community*. Eds. Laurence Raw and Robert G. Dryden. New York: Palgrave Macmillan, 2013. 37–51.

Raw, Laurence and Tony Gurr. *Adaptation Studies and Learning: New Frontiers*. Lanham, MD: Scarecrow, 2013.

Red Channels: The Report of Communist Influence in Radio and Television. New York: Counterattack, 1950.

Rubery, Matthew. 'Interview with Barbara Holdridge.' *LA Review of Books*, 19 August. 6 January 2015. lareviewofbooks.org/author/barbara-holdridge.

Shelley, Mary. *Frankenstein; or, The Modern Prometheus*. 1818. Oxford: Oxford UP, 1998.

——— . 'Introduction: Preface to the 1831 Edition of *Frankenstein*'. 2009. 22 February 2016. www.rc.umd.edu/editions/frankenstein/1831v1/intro.

Sunstein, Emily W. *Mary Shelley: Romance and Reality*. Baltimore: Johns Hopkins UP, 1991.

Tolle, Eckhart. *The Power of Now: A Guide to Spiritual Enlightenment*. Nevato, CA: Namaste, 1999.

Part II

Cinematic and television adaptations of *Frankenstein*

4

A paranoid parable of adaptation: *Forbidden Planet*, *Frankenstein*, and the atomic age

Dennis R. Perry

*F*ORBIDDEN *PLANET* (WILCOX 1956), MGM's big-budget entry into the 1950s 'golden age' of cinema science fiction, has long been considered the best science-fiction film from the decade, only surpassed by Kubrick's *2001: A Space Odyssey* some twelve years later. Beyond its spectacular special effects and memorable robot, Robby, *Forbidden Planet*'s story has had the added prestige of being considered a thoughtful adaptation of Shakespeare's *The Tempest*, with Morbius as Prospero, Robby as Ariel, Altaira as Miranda, Commander Adams as Ferdinand, and Morbius' monster as a psychologically spawned Caliban. It's a nice fit: science stands in for magic during a time of atomic paranoia and concerns about the dangers of technology. Rick Worland and David Slayden, however, go against this interpretive grain, suggesting that *The Tempest* is more an 'interpretive red herring' than a relevant source. They argue that the story of Adam and Eve cast out of Eden is thematically more to the point (142). Judith Buchanan, on the other hand, reminds us that early reviews linked the film first with either *King Kong* (1933) or Stevenson's *Strange Case of Dr Jekyll and Mr Hyde*, with Morbius and his id monster as the scientist with an evil double (149). Noting that such connections depend on 'random accidents of critical attention' (158), she herself identifies *Island of Lost Souls* (1932), an adaptation of H.G. Wells' *The Island of Dr Moreau*, as an equally likely source text for the film (155). Technology proves problematic in both films, and Moreau, like Morbius, is eventually destroyed by his own creations. Obviously, a story as richly suggestive as *Forbidden Planet* might be an intertextual match for any number of relevant parables of mad scientists who inadvertently create a monster, or avatar-double, that is beyond control.

   The film begins as a rescue ship arrives on the planet Altair IV and finds that the only survivor of a previous mission twenty years before is Professor Morbius, who explains that the rest of the crew were killed by some unknown planetary force. Tensions mount between the rescue party and the reclusive scientist, who is busy studying the scientific marvels of a dead race, the Krell. Eventually Morbius's fear of being taken back to earth releases a monster spawned from his own id and made real by Krell technology. After several of the rescue crew are killed by this monster, Morbius faces the fact that he is responsible for their deaths, and is himself killed by the monster. The list of related stories noted above concerning the unwelcome consequences of science is useful, but ignores the fact that Mary Shelley's *Frankenstein* actually undergirds many of these tales, including *Forbidden Planet*. Recognising the relationships between *Frankenstein* and *Forbidden Planet* provides a good example of the how the Frankenstein Complex can expose unexpected affinities between texts to reveal unrecognised adaptations.

While the source texts suggested by Buchanan and others are plausible lenses through which to read *Forbidden Planet*, none takes account of the film's Cold War context. It is this anxious post-war period, combining fear of a nuclear holocaust with unprecedented economic bounty (Worland and Slayden 140, 143), that sets the stage for seeing the film as a contemporary Frankensteinian meditation on both the dangers and the benefits of science and technology. Importantly, the film also examines the relative merits of scientists themselves, who, while they may have helped to win the war and save the world, are just as likely to be responsible for destroying it. And any discussion of scientific advances that cannot be controlled by the creators inevitably evokes Mary Shelley's prophetic fable of modernity, along with its nearly endless train of adaptations. Her cautionary tale has become part of our very language for describing questionable effects of science and technology, including everything from the atomic bomb to Dolly the cloned sheep.

This chapter makes a case for the importance of *Frankenstein* and its popular-culture progeny as important intertexts of *Forbidden Planet*, particularly in terms of the related ties between Frankenstein and his monster, atomic scientists and theirs, and Morbius and his id monster. All three pairs embody variants of a process associated with information networks called feedback loops, in these cases connecting creator and creation. Further, this feedback process becomes a metaphor for understanding the infinite palimpsest of adaptation itself, which enables recognition of new meanings as we see the source text(s) in new ways. These new meanings, in the case of a text like *Frankenstein*, often become the source for more adaptations, and so on.

In the wake of the bombing of Hiroshima and Nagasaki, during the ensuing Cold War, a debate opened up concerning the role of scientists in society. Seeing themselves now as potentially important players in world affairs, a group of Manhattan Project scientists began to campaign for civilian control of atomic research, and for international jurisdiction over its development. The scientists involved in this 'liberal' crusade, known as the Atomic Scientists movement, claimed authority over atomic weapons by virtue of their expertise, and, in some sense, their collective guilt. J. Robert Oppenheimer described this guilt when he said, 'In some sort of crude sense ... the physicists have known sin; and this is a knowledge which they cannot lose' (88). Albert Einstein, who had first suggested to US President Franklin D. Roosevelt that building the atomic bomb was possible, later condemned the use of the bomb against Japan, and was sympathetic toward the Atomic Scientists movement (Clark 752). Having helped determine the outcome of World War II, the scientists involved in the movement had become important players on the world stage and changed the course of international politics. At the same time, more practical military and government officials pushed back against the idea that civilian scientists should regulate nuclear research. They recognised that less reasonable forces were playing nuclear catch-up and would never be amenable to what the scientists were demanding. These tensions illustrate the paranoid perspective that Susan Sontag would aptly name the 'imagination of disaster' (*Against Interpretation*).

For post-World War II audiences living in the United States in such a charged atmosphere, *Forbidden Planet*'s back story of a technologically advanced and prosperous race, the Krell, whose scientific advances led directly to their apocalyptic demise, would have hit close to home. This theme is part of the reason that similar science-fiction films were popular in the 1950s. Many Americans in the late 1940s and early 1950s were beginning to fear the seemingly unlimited power of science. They also feared that scientists, not unlike the extinct Krell, were creating powerful engines of destruction without reckoning on the myriad potential dangers involved. In *The Cosmic Man* (1959), released three years after *Forbidden Planet*, the scientist hero says of public opinion, 'Everyone seems to be afraid of scientists these days, as if we know some deep dark secret about the mystery of life.' Wisely or not, and fed by pro-military arguments, such fears led to the growing public concern over Manhattan Project scientists weighing in on public policy. As Cyndy Hendershot notes, many of the post-war scientists viewed themselves as 'mystics who impart political and ethical wisdom to a frightened American public' (26). This attitude may have grown out of a sentiment typified by the messianic Manhattan Project recruiting slogan aimed at scientists: 'Help win the war to end all wars' (25). The debate over who would control nuclear weapons would remain unsettled until the Cuban Missile Crisis, when it was resolved in favour of military control. In the meantime, the dispute over whether to trust the military, as Cold War heroes, or to trust the scientists, who were often depicted as soft on communism, inevitably spilled over into the ideology of many 1950s films. The conservative *The Thing from Another World* (1951) suggests the danger of scientists who get so lost in the wonder of discovery that considerations like public safety are overlooked. In fact, the film compares some scientists explicitly to excited children with a new toy. On the other hand, representing a more liberal, science-friendly view, films like *The Day the Earth Stood Still* (1951) present scientists like Sam Jaffe's Professor Barnard as being wiser than the petty world leaders and trigger-happy military personnel whose paranoid squabbling endangers world peace and planetary survival.

Viewed in the context of these debates, which were centred on the uses and abuses of atomic weapons, Commander Adams's (Leslie Nielsen) comment about the horrific results of Dr Morbius's and the Krell's science – 'We are, after all, not God' – firmly situates the film in favour of military rather than scientific control of potentially dangerous technologies. Such twentieth-century scepticism about science should not be surprising, since Mary Shelley defined many of the same fears in 1818. In fact, part of the resonant power of Adams's declaration is its linking of Morbius to the titular character in James Whale's *Frankenstein* (1931), who, having created life, euphorically screams, 'Now I know what it feels like to be God'. This theme continues in *Bride of Frankenstein* (1935), when Frankenstein's colleague, Dr Pretorius, proposes a toast to Frankenstein and his ambitious plans for an ongoing project of human creation: 'To a new world of gods and monsters'. While Percy Shelley and Lord Byron were enthusiastic about experiments in electricity and galvanism, and the wonder of seemingly bringing momentary life back to frogs and humans, Mary clearly anticipated the moral and ethical pitfalls of such science. Her novel, thus, turns the possibilities of science fiction technology into the stuff of horror. By the 1956, the year *Forbidden Planet* was released, life was again imitating art, and nuclear science was indeed starting to feel like something out of a horror movie. Many centuries before Morbius arrived on Altair, the Krell had perfected the instrumentality by which whatever they wished to have would be instantly created for them, thus linking mind and machine. As becomes clear in the film, however, they had not anticipated that the desires of their unconscious minds would also draw on this power. Hence, their ids, representing lust, jealousy, envy, hate, and murderous anger, had full power to act, causing the Krell to unconsciously annihilate one another almost overnight. The Krell's godlike scientific aspirations not only created a technological monster, but reached forward 200,000 years to make a Frankenstein out of Morbius. *Forbidden Planet* creates a kind of perfect storm by harnessing nearly infinite creative power to fallible human (or Krell) wills. That also seems to be one of the basic problems explored in Shelley's novel, which illustrates the potential dangers of creation. *Forbidden Planet*, with its more advanced science, takes this trope to its logical extreme.

Surprisingly, *Forbidden Planet* has gone mostly unremarked as a Frankenstein tale, a peculiar oversight, considering that Shakespeare's *Tempest*, intertextually joined at the hip with *Forbidden Planet*, is often itself associated with *Frankenstein*. In fact, as early as 1818 the *Edinburgh Literary Magazine and Miscellany* review of Shelley's *Frankenstein* compares it to *The Tempest* (Review of *Frankenstein* 252). This perpetual oversight of *Forbidden Planet* as part of the Frankenstein Network is even more astonishing, considering the way that both the Krell and Morbius become naively obsessed with implementing a technology that proves destructive as well as uncontrollable. Thus, *Forbidden Planet* is actually two Frankensteinian cautionary tales in one. In fact, there are a number of other significant connections between Victor Frankenstein and Dr Morbius. Like Frankenstein, Morbius is an obsessive scientist with a God complex who dreams of unlimited power. And like Frankenstein, Morbius creates a monster. Like Frankenstein, Morbius is also deeply secretive.

Frankenstein, in Whale's 1931 film, at first insists that his fiancée Elizabeth, his friend Victor Moritz, and his mentor Dr Waldman are interrupting his work and must leave his castle. In a similar fashion, as Adams's ship is circling Altair IV, Morbius tells Adams and the visitors from Earth to leave immediately, warning them that he cannot be held responsible for the consequences of their landing. Once they do arrive and visit Morbius's home, he further demonstrates his impatience with and hostility toward the crew, even demonstrating Robbie the Robot's inhibition about harming human life

Figure 4.1 Advertising poster from *Forbidden Planet*.

by pointing a gun at Adams and then commanding the robot to fire it. Morbius tries quickly to get rid of the would-be rescuers by showing them that he is in no danger, does not need or want rescuing, and that he cannot leave his work for several years to make reports on Earth.

The tour Morbius is later forced to give of the extensive Krell labs shows the stereotypical scientist's dream of endless, 'top priority' funding. To Morbius the

well-meaning rescue party is like a government oversight committee, there to inter-
fere with his research Eden. But Morbius is also associated with Frankenstein, and,
like Frankenstein, Morbius is obsessed with doing and understanding the seemingly
impossible. In fact, the Krell, like the alchemist-inspired Victor Frankenstein, imitate
God by seeking to create life where there is none. Morbius shows Commander Adams
and Dr Ostrow (Warren Stevens) how the Krell measured and boosted their intellects,
and how they harnessed near-infinite power with 9,200 thermonuclear reactors, all in
an attempt to create matter using pure intellectual power.

Following Morbius's tour, an argument develops over what to do with the Krell
technology. While Commander Adams, from the military perspective, sees it as 'too
big' for any one man to control, Morbius insists that with his 'brain-boosted intellect'
only he is capable of studying, applying, and distributing Krell technology responsibly.
At least on some level, Morbius understands the potential dangers involved with the
Krell technology. Clearly the post-war battle of words between atomic scientists
and the military is recreated here. James Chapman and Nicholas J. Cull note that
screenwriter Cyril Hume turned *Forbidden Planet* into a monster movie, which, like
Frankenstein, 'became a meditation on the nature of technology [and its relationship
to] ... human ambition and frailty' (82). When the monster is eventually discovered,
Morbius, like Frankenstein, tries to deny his creation of a monster. He even renounces
it just before it kills him. And the id monster, like Frankenstein's Creature, is a double
of its creator (see Bloom 2; Kestner 72; and Scott 173). As Vivian Sobchack puts it,
Frankenstein-type monsters are in essence the 'darker side of man' (32). Hence, the
analogy between the film's Morbius and the atomic scientists of the 1950s grows out
of the fact that both the atom bomb and the id monster reflect the darker side of man.
And both have unexpected and uncontrollable consequences. Morbius's id monster
even looks and sounds like a roaring atomic mushroom cloud (Figure 4.2).

Linking *Frankenstein* to *Forbidden Planet* is inevitable, since so many of the other
science-fiction films of the period focus on the unexpected and dangerous results of
atomic testing. In dozens of these films atomic test blasts are responsible for resur-
recting dinosaurs (*Beast from 20,000 Fathoms*, 1953), enlarging common insects into
world-threatening pests (*Them!*, 1954), creating whole new species (*Phantom from
10,000 Leagues*, 1955), turning men into monsters (*The Alligator People*, 1959), nearly
depopulating the earth (*World Without End*, 1956), and eventually leading to a complete
apocalypse (*On the Beach*, 1959). Like these films, *Forbidden Planet* is clearly concerned
with scientific issues surrounding the creation of atomic and nuclear weapons. The
native Krell's nuclear self-annihilation serves as a warning of what happens when
fallible beings are given access to unlimited power. Even Altair's remote, arid setting,
where Morbius unearths the Krell's deadly secrets, evokes the Los Alamos National
Laboratory in the New Mexico desert, where the atomic bomb was created under the
title of the 'Manhattan Project'.

Science-fiction films of the 1950s were, understandably, obsessed with the powers
of science and technology, as well as with the scientists who experimented with

Figure 4.2 Dr Morbius's id monster attacks intruders in *Forbidden Planet*.

them. Like the fascination with electricity and galvanism in Mary Shelley's day, so the 1950s were a period of keen public interest in scientific innovation. And this interest extended beyond the harnessing of atomic power. Household conveniences for the 'modern kitchen', as well as rocket-like cars, were popular subjects for film shorts and *Life* magazine articles. The modernistic design of Morbius's house is similar in style to the technological optimism of the 'Googie' architecture of plastic, steel, and neon futurism exemplified by the Theme Building at the Los Angeles Airport or Disney's 'Tomorrowland', and all of these structures reflect the period's space-age aesthetic. As Ken Hollings notes, 'between 1947 and 1959, the future was written about, discussed, and analysed with such confidence that it took on a tangible presence', making the future a twentieth-century 'manifest destiny writ large' (xiii).

The scientists in the films of the 1950s display a plethora of varying motives. The heroic type are the world savers, able to identify and explain unusual phenomena, such as how a giant deadly insect suddenly appears (*The Deadly Mantis*, 1957), what caused giant ants to infest the New Mexico desert (*Them!*), and how a very large octopus happens to be climbing up the Golden Gate Bridge (*It Came from Beneath the Sea* [Gordon 1955]). In each case science is able to overcome these threats, although in some cases the end of the film may not be the end of the threat. In *Them!* Dr Medford (Edmund Gwenn) notes in the film's sobering last words, 'When man entered the Atomic Age, he opened the door to a new world. What we may eventually find in that new world, nobody can predict.' In these films science may have caused many of these problems, but the scientist-stars are often presented as wise, heroic, brave, and tireless in doing everything possible to repair the unexpected collateral damage. In contrast to the heroic scientist is the darker, cognisant rogue. These scientists actually know that what they are doing may be dangerous, but they proceed anyway. In the worst cases, they purposely use science for their own nefarious purposes. This type of scientist tends to populate sub 'B' films and is presented as a version of the movie-serial mad scientist. As an example, Dr Aranya (Jackie Coogan) in *Mesa of Lost Women* (1953) transfers growth hormones into the pituitary glands of tarantulas, then injects the hormones into women to create powerful, spider-like creatures who will help him 'rule the world'. A bit more seriously evil is Dr Boronski (Walter Rilla) from *The Gamma People* (Gilling 1956). He uses gamma rays to create both geniuses and soulless slaves to help him rule his dictatorship.

Another subset of the cognisant type is the naive but earnest scientist who unintentionally creates catastrophes of various sizes. In *Tarantula* (1955) Dr Gerald Deemer (Leo Carroll) experiments with atomic isotopes in hopes of creating an artificial food to end world hunger. Unfortunately, his experiments with animals create a giant tarantula that wreaks havoc in a desert community until it is killed by the military. Similarly, in *The Alligator People* (1959), a scientist tries to help burn victims by combining nuclear material with reptilian hormones to regenerate tissue and limbs. Of course, the horrific side-effects make monsters of the patients. Such tales as these bring us back to *Frankenstein*, wherein well-meaning scientific research by a naive science student results in a monstrous creation and the ultimate death of the scientist, the monster, and others. Morbius seems to be this naive type – driven, obsessive, and reclusive, but not consciously doing anything which he feels will be harmful. Despite his constant study of the Krell, until the end of the film he does not know that their technology led directly to their overnight self-destruction. Naive though he may be, his dark clothes, satanic goatee, gruff personality, and anti-social and secretive attitude make him appear more like the cognisant scientist who has something to hide. His character is, thus, more interesting than most science-fiction scientists of the period precisely because he is more complicated. Only gradually do Adams and Ostrow begin to suspect that Morbius is the cause of the danger they all face.

A further link in the intertextual chain connecting *Forbidden Planet* to the Frankenstein Network is found in several allusions to James Whale's *Bride of Frankenstein*. In Whale's film, Dr Pretorius – whose name is a slant rhyme of Morbius – works with Frankenstein to create a mate for the monster. Pretorius is a darkly comical figure who has created life himself; however, his fully functional human creations are only about twelve inches high. These small creations are actually alluded to in *Forbidden Planet* as Morbius uses the Krell 'plastic educator' to create a miniature version of his own daughter by the power of thought, a benign application of the power that also creates the id monster. Further, in both *Forbidden Planet* and *Bride of Frankenstein*, a woman is at the centre of the struggle between the scientists and whoever would stand in their way. In *Bride of Frankenstein*, Pretorius kidnaps Frankenstein's wife in order to secure his aid in creating a bride for the monster. In *Forbidden Planet*, Morbius's daughter, Altaria, becomes the object of a power struggle between Adams and Morbius. The scientist warns Adams that the id monster, a 'dark, terrible, incomprehensible force' is waiting to be 're-invoked for murder'. As we soon learn, Morbius's jealous possessiveness over his daughter is one of the triggers for his id monster.

Two other Frankenstein films that inform a historical understanding of *Forbidden Planet* are Fisher's *The Curse of Frankenstein* and Strock's *I Was a Teenage Frankenstein*, both released a year after *Forbidden Planet*, in 1957. These films present vengeful Frankensteins who will do anything to accomplish their scientific purposes. Both films, like *Forbidden Planet*, reflect the period's concerns about scientists left to their own devices. *Curse of Frankenstein*, discussed at length in other chapters in this volume, is the first in Hammer Films' popular horror series, which extended well into the 1970s. Unlike Universal's neurotic Henry Frankenstein, or Shelley's tortured Victor, Hammer's Baron Frankenstein is presented as a cold and ruthless monster-maker who will stop at nothing to fulfil his plans. To secure a perfect brain, for instance, the baron kills a great scientist. Later, when a jealous maid with whom he has been having an affair threatens to expose his research, he lures her into his lab, where his mindless monster silences her forever. Peter Cushing as Baron Frankenstein resembles Morbius in several ways, including his obsessiveness and reclusiveness. Moreover, both men place science above family ties, friends, and morality. *I Was a Teenage Frankenstein* presents a similarly callous Frankenstein who becomes furious at any sign of curiosity or interference. In fact, he has his fiancée killed merely for discovering his lab and its monster. While Morbius is not so conscious a killer as these other Frankensteins, his unconscious dark side aligns him with them and leads to the same violent end. For all of them, science is a no-holds-barred, life or death obsession. Morbius's id monster kills whole crews and cannot help but attack Morbius's daughter for the cardinal sin of interfering with the doctor's scientific research.

The origins of such psychological triggers are explored by Kevin Fisher, who notes how Morbius's id monster is created by means of information feedback loops (19). A feedback loop describes the way people learn through recurring experience. A simple example of a feedback loop is the scientific method of designing experiments, gathering the resulting data, analysing the data, introducing new procedures, and performing the experiment again. Regarding Morbius, Fisher explores this process in terms of the unconscious mind, examining the psychological grey areas of feedback loops that deal with 'the return of the repressed' (19). That is, in his conscious mind Morbius rationally represses strong feelings against the presence of the potential intruders because he is a reasonably moral being and, therefore, he does not allow his irritation to mount to violence. However, at the same time his extreme negative feelings for the intruders create a psychological dilemma which triggers his unconscious mind to take over, finding an alternative pathway to solve Morbius's conscious moral reticence by reaching out to the Krell's still-active power sources to generate the id monster. This unconscious feedback loop, then, solves a problem that is impossible for his moral consciousness to face.

This marriage of the psychological and technological in a chain of cause and effect between Morbius and his embodied id monster defines a creative process that is unknown to his conscious mind, and makes Morbius a Frankenstein as potentially dangerous technology is driven by unpredictable, unexpected, and all-too-human forces. This is the unconscious version of what many in the 1950s feared about the worldwide proliferation of atomic weapons, making the Cold War stand-off a precarious matter of push-button world annihilation. This idea of the unconscious processes of science sheds light on the Frankenstein Network. For example, the emphasis on the unconscious certainly plays out in Whale's *Frankenstein* as the Creature functions as an extension of its creator's unconscious mind. As such, it kills or attacks those who have interfered with Henry Frankenstein's experiment, including Fritz, who torments the monster; Waldman, who tries to dismantle it; and Elizabeth, with whom Henry may be unconsciously angry because she, like Morbius's daughter, has interfered with scientific obsessions even more dear to him than his love for her.

This mania may be the most salient connection between Frankenstein, Morbius, and their creations. Looking back at the novel, Shelley's Victor Frankenstein works to bring life to his Creation in a 'resistless and almost frantic impulse', losing 'all soul or sensation but for this one pursuit' (Shelley 33). He then all unknowingly seems to pass on these unbalanced traits to his creation through some mysterious process of feedback loops which Shelley does not attempt to explain. Just as his Creature is often torn between seeking revenge and accommodating mankind, Victor is also torn between turning 'with loathing from my occupation' and being maniacally 'urged on by an eagerness which perpetually increased' (34). His obsessive pursuit of 'nature to her hiding-places' anticipates his Creature's inability to control his violent urges, including his relentless stalking of Victor. In an indefinable manner, like the technology in *Forbidden Planet* that reaches out in response to both conscious and unconscious mental signals sent from the Krell or Morbius, Frankenstein somehow creates a preternatural feedback loop in the creative process that links him to his Creature. Importantly, Victor's sacrificing of cool scientific objectivity in his manic orgy of discovery warps his reason so much that he can finally respond only irrationally to his creation, inadvertently feeding the dark logic which turns his creation into a monster. The Creature, in turn, receives only hate as feedback from virtually everyone he encounters, making him angrier and ever more vengeful. Thus the Creature is, all unknowingly, fulfilling Victor's blind and incomplete feedback loop. Hence this leads to Frankenstein and his monster-double becoming locked in a blind track of cause and effect, each ultimately determining the other's behaviour.

In Morbius's case his id monster is fed by a succession of causes as they arise in Morbius's unconscious, forming the feedback loop. Morbius is frustrated with the interfering presence of the rescue party, which stirs up his id to reach out destructively by drawing on the power of the Krell network of machines. Initially the rescue party is a minor threat, merely interrupting his work, and little damage occurs. However, once the threat increases to the possibility of having to return to Earth and account directly to authorities who would likely take over his research, Morbius's id monster (as an incarnation of his monstrous pride) begins its work – destroying equipment needed to contact Earth, murdering crew members, and finally trying to kill Morbius's own daughter for crossing him. The film ends as Morbius dies at the hands of the monster he created and cannot control, and Adams destroys the planet itself. Just as the Whale *Frankenstein* films suggest, science that is ultimately beyond human control is a constant hazard in a technology-driven culture. The atom bomb followed a similar trajectory in the American public mind of the 1950s. It became an exponential cause-and-effect feedback loop escalation that had the potential to lead us into a more horrific world condition than the combined wisdom of the Manhattan Project scientists and their government could possibly have foreseen.

In a less ominous way, the feedback loop metaphor has application to adaptation theory as applied to the endless multiplication of *Frankenstein* films. While *Forbidden Planet* has several layers of intertextually related stories, the number of *Frankenstein* adaptations seems endless, further complicated by the fact that the story of the monster goes back to two source texts: Shelley's novel and Whale's movie. While Shelley is responsible for the central themes and characters of the story, as well as providing the modern world with a provocative and prescient warning about the dangers of science, Whale creates a compelling German Expressionist setting, a simpler, more viewer-friendly narrative, and, most importantly, the archetypal image of the Creature, with the help of make-up genius Jack Pierce and the sympathetic performance of Boris Karloff. Most movies, comic books, stage plays, graphic novels, video games, etc. adapt Whale's mute, lumbering monster, including flat head and neck bolts, and inhabit a Gothic setting complete with a laboratory full of electrical equipment that sparks, hisses, and flashes. As far as the general public is concerned, Whale's depiction of the Frankenstein monster is as familiar as Sherlock Holmes with his deerstalker hat and Dracula with his black cloak. Similarly, for the general public, then, Shelley's novel has taken a back seat to the film, although there are periodic adaptations, most often for the stage, that explicitly look back to Shelley as their principal source.

But whether we read the novel, or see Whale's films, it is difficult not to simultaneously see in them whatever adaptations we have experienced. If we read the novel, for example, we may see Victor as actor Colin Clive, the monster as Karloff, and the creation taking place in a black-and-white, noisy electric lab. At the very least those images, or other visual equivalents, may be hard to suppress. In this way we experience a feedback loop, causing us to see pre-planted images replacing, or at least modifying, what Shelley is trying to depict for us. While this adaptation view of a palimpsest is simple enough to imagine, how do we describe the infinite palimpsest of reading Shelley or viewing Whale with so many adaptations potentially in our minds? Imagine a Gilgamesh who lived long enough to have read *Frankenstein* when it was first published, and then experienced each and every adaptation from stage to film and television, radio to comics, and video games to heavy metal songs. What does the idea of a palimpsest mean in this context as a way of understanding adaptation? In short, texts that have such an incomprehensibly large adapted progeny pose unique challenges for adaptation theory.

It is tempting to liken this near-infinite network of related *Frankenstein* adaptations to the vastness of the Krell's underground power grid, which was designed to perpetuate itself endlessly into the future. As explained in the Introduction to this book, the Frankenstein Complex and the Frankenstein Network recognise that each Frankenstein adaptation is part of an ever-growing and interlinked network of adaptations that influence the way any one adaptation can be understood. In this chapter we have caught a glimpse of how the Complex informs our understanding of *Forbidden Planet* in its relationships with *The Tempest*, *Island of Lost Souls*, *King Kong*, *The Strange Case of Dr Jekyll and Mr Hyde*, Whale's *Bride of Frankenstein*, and the many disaster-ridden science-fiction films of the 1950s, as well as with the Atomic Scientists movement. In reality, of course, these texts are only the tip of the iceberg. As noted earlier, perceiving such relationships among texts is the result of what Buchanan calls 'random accidents of critical attention'. Hence, adaptation theory applied to *Frankenstein* becomes a kind of monster itself. Just as Altair's forty-mile power grid, linking 9,200 thermonuclear reactors, continues to operate despite the long absence of the Krell, so *Frankenstein* adaptations have become a pop-culture monster that continues to power multitudes of additional adaptations. As Morbius shows Adams and Ostrow the Krell power grid, he warns them to look at it only through the nearby mirror: 'No one can look in the face of the Gorgon and live,' he quips. Likewise, no one can process the near-infinite power grid of *Frankenstein* adaptations – a palimpsest that is metaphorically 7,800 levels deep – without an adaptation-studies equivalent of the human genome project.

Bibliography

Biskind, Peter. *Seeing is Believing: How Hollywood Taught us to Stop Worrying and Love the Bomb.* New York: Holt Publishing, 1983.

Bloom, Harold. 'Introduction.' *Mary Shelley's* Frankenstein. Ed. Harold Bloom. New York: Chelsea House, 2007.

Buchanan, Judith. '*Forbidden Planet* and the Retrospective Attribution of Intentions.' *Retrovisions: Reinventing the Past in Film and Fiction.* Eds Deborah Cartmell, I.Q. Hunter, and Imelda Whelehan. London: Pluto Press, 2001. 148–162.

Chapman, James and Nicholas J. Cull. *Projecting Tomorrow: Science Fiction and Popular Cinema.* London and New York: I.B. Tauris, 2013.

Clark, Ronald. *Einstein: The Life and Times.* New York: William Morrow, 2007.

Fisher, Kevin. 'Information Feedback Loops and Two Tales of the Posthuman in *Forbidden Planet.*' *Science Fiction Film and Television.* 3.1 (2010): 19–36.

Forbidden Planet. Dir. Fred M. Wilcox. Perf. Walter Pidgeon, Anne Francis, and Leslie Nielsen. MGM, 1956.

Hendershot, Cyndy. *Paranoia, the Bomb, and 1950s Science Fiction Films.* Bowling Green: Bowling Green State University Popular Press, 1999.

Hollings, Ken. *Welcome to Mars: Politics, Pop Culture, and Weird Science in 1950s America.* Berkeley: North Atlantic Books, 2008.

Kestner, Joseph. 'Narcissism as Symptom and Structure: The Case of Mary Shelley's *Frankenstein.' Frankenstein: Mary Shelley.* Ed. Fred Botting. London, 1995. 68–80.

Oppenheimer, J. Robert. *The Open Mind.* New York: Simon and Schuster, 1955.

Otto, Nathan and Heinz Norden, eds. *Einstein on Peace.* New York: Random House, 1988.

Review of *Frankenstein or, The Modern Prometheus.* By Mary Wollstonecraft Shelley. *Edinburgh Magazine and Literary Miscellany* March 1818, New Series II: 249–253.

Scott, Peter Dale. 'Vital Artifice: Mary, Percy, and the Psychological Integrity of *Frankenstein.' The Endurance of* Frankenstein: *Essays on Mary Shelley's Novel.* Eds George Levine and U.C. Knoepflmacher. Berkeley: U of California P, 1979. 172–202.

Shelley, Mary. *Frankenstein.* 2nd Edition. J. Paul Hunter, ed. New York: W.W. Norton, 2012.

Sobchack, Vivian. *Screening Space: The American Science Fiction Film.* 2nd Edition. New York: Unger Publishing, 1991.

Sontag, Susan. 'The Imagination of Disaster.' *Against Interpretation.* New York: Farrar, Straus & Giroux, 1966.

Them! Dir. Gordon Douglas. Perf. James Whitmore, James Arness, and Edmund Gwenn. Warner Bros., 1954.

Worland, Rick and David Slayden. 'From Apocalypse to Appliances: Postwar Anxiety and Modern Convenience in *Forbidden Planet.' Hollywood Goes Shopping.* Eds David Desser and Garth S. Jowett). Minneapolis/ London: U of Minneapolis P, 2000. 139–156.

5

The Curse of Frankenstein: Hammer Film Studios' reinvention of horror cinema

Morgan C. O'Brien

> Faced with the task of explaining a particular phenomenon or event [...] the historian first recognises that the event under study is not a one-dimensional 'thing' but the point of convergence for various lines of historical force. (Allen and Gomery 17)

IN 1957, FAMILY-OWNED HAMMER Film Studios released Terence Fisher's *The Curse of Frankenstein*, and with one inexpensive genre movie the small British studio changed the face of horror cinema. With a production budget under £65,000 ($200,000), *The Curse of Frankenstein* (hereafter, *Curse*) recouped its costs many times over and was an international hit (Hearn). *Curse* announced Hammer's arrival as a cinematic player on the world stage, spawning six pseudo-sequels and launching a decade-long vogue for Gothic horror films.[1] Notably, Hammer's film pre-dates the film that gave birth to the Italian Gothic movement, Mario Bava's *La Maschera del Demonio* (1960, *Black Sunday* in the UK), and also American International Pictures' series of loose Edgar Allan Poe adaptations, the first of which was Roger Corman's *House of Usher* (1960). Beginning with *Curse*, Hammer's Gothic *oeuvre* has since been recognised as quintessentially 'British', their narratives and cult stars firmly ensconced in the collective memory of British popular culture. However, as the introduction to this volume attests, the 'Frankenstein Complex', as well as the 'Frankenstein Network' upon which it is based, is a fraught issue. The very existence of this edited collection suggests that every story has been told before, that there are no true 'master narratives'. Accordingly, every story, and every event in a story, has a history. The Robert Allen and Douglas Gomery quotation that prefaces this chapter cogently reminds us that historical events always include multiple players, multiple 'converging lines of historical forces'. Bearing these salient points in mind allows us to delve into Hammer's own 'Frankenstein Complex' and probe how the studio made a nineteenth-century tale meaningful to a post-World War II audience. This chapter traces the Frankenstein 'discourse' around Hammer's first Gothic adaptation to show how the studio was able to effect a paradigm shift in horror by differentiating its Frankenstein from previous properties.

The story of Hammer's film is articulated in the negotiations between networks of creative and corporate imperatives. The filmic process of adaptation is one of assemblage, where the concept of 'fidelity' to a source is less meaningful than the discursive formations that coalesce during production and saturate the final product. Considering the discourse around a film requires investigating its content and the circumstances of its production in order to understand the industrial and cultural structures that guide a project's development from conception to release. Accordingly, I conduct a close reading of *Curse* to illustrate how the production and stylistic qualities united by Hammer's film evoke Shelley's source material while distancing it from other adaptations. This analysis is complemented by archival research and data gathered from trade journals of the time. These sources shed light on how Hammer's general business strategies established a precedent for adapting Gothic British texts and why the studio, guided by profit motives, exploited the post-war cultural climate.

Hammer history

London's Hammer Films was founded in 1934 by William 'Hammer' Hinds, and became one of the world's most successful movie studios between 1958 and 1970, earning the Queen's Award to Industry for international trade in 1968. Despite never gaining great critical acclaim, the studio released 163 feature-length productions between 1935 and 1978, averaging nearly four films a year over a period of forty-three years, even allowing for the three features released between 1974 and 1978. While Hammer worked across multiple genres, the studio's staple format became Gothic horror after the surprise success of house director Terence Fisher's *Curse*, and the following year's *Dracula* (1958, *Horror of Dracula* in the US). Fully nine of Hammer's ten 1971 productions can be classed as variations of its Gothic mode, and half of the 106 films Hammer made after 1956 fit within its Gothic milieu. *Curse* was so successful that Hammer mined its Gothic horror innovations to exhaustion. In the introduction to his book-length study on British horror cinema, Peter Hutchings quotes from a 1964 British press clipping which sums up Hammer's lowbrow reputation with the critical press during the studio's heyday:

> Certain branches of the British cinema are able to weather any crisis: they do not so much rise above it as sink beneath it, to a subterranean level where the storms over quotas and television competition cannot affect them. This sub-cinema consists mainly of two parallel institutions, both under ten years old: the Hammer horror and the Carry On comedy. (1)

Hutchings shares several other choice press reviews in his book, demonstrating that while Hammer's films were gory for the time, they were not regarded as 'threatening', and the house style was even reduced to a predictable Gothic 'formula' (5–9). However, some reviewers felt very strongly about Hammer's Gothic films. Carlos Clarens pauses in his review of *Horror of Dracula* to sardonically comment that 'sometimes even a whiff of Gothic survives Terence Fisher's pedestrian direction' (142). Clarens rhetorically asks, 'What can be said for director Terence Fisher except that his style (or lack of it) has neither softened, strengthened, nor sharpened from *The Curse of Frankenstein* to *The Gorgon* [1964]?' (143–144). Clarens's writing provides a good example of how general critical and scholarly reception has focused on Terence Fisher; *Curse* established his role as house director. David Pirie takes an opposing view from Clarens's, even assigning Fisher auteur status while aligning the studio itself with the American studio era. Pirie saw Hammer operating as a 'mini-major' in a dilution of the early Hollywood mode of production (*A Heritage of Horror* 43). The auteur theory was still being codified in the 1970s, and, seeing critically derided director Terence Fisher as the hand that shaped Hammer's Gothic aesthetic, Pirie was keen to be the first to resituate Fisher as an artist (Ibid. 49, 52). To assert Fisher's status, Pirie used the incipient auteur theories of Andrew Sarris and Peter Wollen, utilising their tenets of auteurism to establish Fisher's credentials (Ibid. 49–65).[2]

Wheeler Winston Dixon follows Pirie's auteurist tack by aligning Fisher with John Ford (1991). Dixon compares the ways in which the two filmmakers imagine national myth and cultural memory through genre – for Fisher the British Gothic, and for Ford the American Western (Ibid.). More recently, Sue Harper has recognised Fisher's influence on the aesthetic choices of his films, but also extends credit to Hammer production designer Bernard Robinson (145–148). Harper draws attention to the setting and style of Hammer's Gothic, pointing to Fisher's Transylvanian-set Dracula films as consistently representing a distinct European topos, although specific to no real time or location. These pan-European spaces, Harper argues, create amorphous, romanticised locales for British cultural fantasies and archetypes to play out and dwell within (144). Peter Hutchings, in *Hammer and Beyond*, also emphasises the symbolic elements of Fisher's films. He suggests that Fisher furnished Hammer's Gothic with a stable set of heteronormative values, operating around a troubled patriarchal core that used Oedipal tropes to structure narrative events (Ibid. 66–68, 72–73). Importantly, Hutchings contends that while British horror does not represent reality *per se*, it does draw upon moments and concerns in social history to furnish horror narratives with themes relevant to contemporary audiences (Ibid. 1–2). While *Hammer and Beyond* considers British horror at large, Hutchings expands on that text's meshing of historical observations with a psychoanalytic framework in his later monograph, *Terence Fisher*, wherein he specifically analyses the socio-cultural themes of Fisher's Gothic movies (3–5). Taking a different tack, Caroline Joan ('Kay') S. Picart moves away from symbolism in *The Frankenstein Film Sourcebook* to focus on the 'realistic depiction' in Fisher's work (Picart et al. 2001). Picart adroitly recognises that Hammer's choice to focus the narratives of their Frankenstein films on the creator, and human characters in general, rather than on the creation/monster, is a major point of differentiation from previous adaptions (Ibid.). Picart builds on these discussions in *The Cinematic Rebirths of Frankenstein*, where she highlights Fisher's fascination with juxtaposing the grotesque and spiritual with mundane, quotidian events (101–107, 113–114). Vitally, Picart also draws attention to the importance of Jimmy Sangster's *Curse* script, itself adapted from one written by American Milton Subotsky, who later formed Amicus

Productions. Subotsky's script required heavy rewriting by Sangster to avoid simply remaking scenes from Universal's film (Ibid. 102–103, 108–111). Through these various historical and analytical accounts of Hammer studios a bigger picture emerges – one of Hammer as a British cultural institution.[3]

Hammer, horror, and culture

Horror cinema has historically been a derided art form, regularly dismissed as low culture, yet popular in spite of this designation. Like all genre forms, horror has undergone multiple reconfigurations in how it presents its conventions and how we interpret its codes. The concept of horror is polysemic – as a genre it is perpetually morphing to reflect social concerns or trends. By its nature the newest, most *outré* horror cinema is a representation of or commentary on the contemporaneous *Zeitgeist*. Critics perennially renegotiate horror per socio-cultural changes over time. When one horror cycle draws to an end, it enters a self-reflexive baroque period from which a new genre cycle develops, reacting to now-familiar horror imagery and themes. Thomas Schatz draws a convincing parallel between the make-up of film grammar and language. Schatz argues that film narrative becomes a recognizable genre when it recalibrates familiar denotative signs into a new configuration (19–20). He cites single cinematic occurrences – individual genre films – as potentially affecting the entire organising structure from which they sprang and by which they are controlled (Ibid., 20–21). Whenever new versions of literary works emerge, they constitute remediations of those works and also signify new configurations of the source specific to socio-cultural periods.

As an out-of-copyright intellectual property whose discourses had already been assimilated into the public's consciousness through a variety of adaptations, Shelley's novel was ideally suited for Hammer. Gothic tales provided non-specific European settings and a predilection for brooding narrative scenarios in appealingly malleable genre hybrids of horror and melodrama. Adapting Regency-period and Victorian literary works from the public domain was a pragmatic financial decision that balanced the economic capital of the studio with the cultural capital of the text but also granted artistic elasticity. The low cost of *Curse*'s production meant that there were no great stakes if the film flopped. If, on the other hand, the film hit, then the Frankenstein mythos was perfectly suited to a franchise, as Universal Studios had already demonstrated. Universal's classic monster movies were black and white and visibly stylised, implementing canted angles and chiaroscuro lighting. Stylistically, Universal benefitted by assimilating German expressionist storytelling methods from the large number of European *émigrés* in Hollywood at the time. Hammer's 'proto-Gothic' *Curse* is remarkably different from these earlier horror films. Hammer kept costs down by using a resource pool of English talent and shooting the film at the studio-owned country estate in Bray, Berkshire. *Curse* does away with Dutch angles and sound stages, instead showing blood and exposed female flesh against a realistic backdrop of lavish-looking sets and shot in Eastmancolor. While audiences were familiar with previous iterations

of Frankenstein, Hammer breathed new life into an old tale. Not only was *Curse* shot
in colour and widescreen, but its narrative emphasises human characters instead of a
monster's rampage, as US sci-fi/horror genre hybrids and Japanese *Kaiju* movies of the
time were doing.[4] By the late 1950s, Universal's horror cycle had descended to the
level of fun self-parody. Shrewdly cashing in on the established appeal of its franchise
stars, Universal had released a popular series of comedy films where comedian duo Bud
Abbott and Lou Costello encountered the studio's famous monsters.[5] These movies
deliberately traded on the accumulated tropes of Universal's iconic horror stable, but
signified stagnation in the studio's horror formula. Breaking from the comedy-horror
films popular at the time, Hammer updated the form and content of horror cinema
while appealing to nostalgia by locating horror in a mythic past.

Curse's 1957 release date hints at the culmination of socio-cultural trends in the
UK. Fredric Jameson locates the period between the late 1950s and early 1960s as the
historical moment when postmodernity emerged (188–190). He discusses the impact
of 'the nostalgia film' in terms of how we conceive of our historical and cultural past,
citing George Lucas's *American Graffiti* (1973) as an example of a film that 'performs'
history by co-opting easily recognisable historical, national tropes and organising them
into readily understood narrative forms (203). We can think of *Curse* in the same
terms – Hammer's film evokes recognisable concerns and trends from Britain's recent
past while simultaneously making the familiar 'strange' through its reconstitution of
classic literature. While the events in the film's narrative are indeed fictional, they
do echo Shelley's text by effectively engaging with the fears, hopes, and desires of
a historical period stretching through the Enlightenment, the Industrial Revolution,
and the nation-state modernism of post-war Europe to establish a peculiarly British
cultural concoction. The thematic content of Shelley's text signifies discourses of its
time: human flourishing and the rise of independent thinking, questioning of ethics,
the relationship between science and religion, and the related struggle of rationality
against superstition; all given greater significance in a post-war Great Britain where
food rationing had ended only in 1954. Tony Judt underlines the sentiments affecting
British society when Hammer's Gothic was at its peak popularity:

> Institutionally speaking, the British turn to nostalgia began almost immediately after
> World War Two […]. From the fifties through the seventies a reassuring version of the
> recent past surfaced and resurfaced in the form of war films, costume dramas and cloth-
> ing: the recycling of Edwardian fashion […] was a particular feature of this trend […] and
> nationwide invocation of older and better times. (770)

Judt's insights explain how Hammer's invocation of past British etiquette, fashions,
and suspicions fed into national feeling, and resulted in films that were extremely
well received at the box-office. Instead of demonising or humanising the creation,
Hammer made the decision to emphasise the monstrous within man by making its
Victor a Georgian-styled 'dandy' in the Victorian era of rationality who unrepentantly
pursues disturbed scientific goals. *Curse*'s Creature, on the other hand, is reduced to a

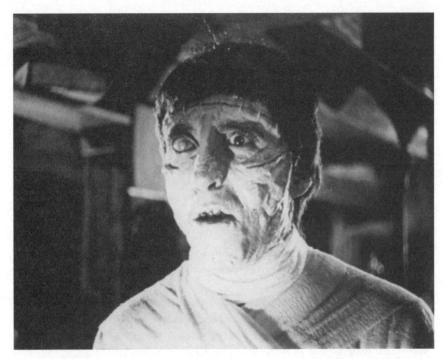

Figure 5.1 Christopher Lee as the ill-tempered monster from *Curse of Frankenstein*.

pasty-skinned, shambling zombie, dressed in an ill-fitting frock coat (Figure 5.1) and all but oblivious to his surroundings – a far cry from the self-referential monsters in Abbott and Costello's films.

Jim Kitses' insightful study of the Western's generic appeal can also apply to Hammer's Gothic genre. Kitses proposes that the Western *is* American history in as much as it signifies various, multi-faceted *ideas* of the romanticised Western frontier (19). Kitses maintains that inherent in representations of the West are philosophical dialectics which serve as connotative reflections of meaning that structure the themes and motifs of the genre (20). By describing the Western *qua* Western in such a fashion, Kitses posits that genres are fluid agglomerations of *a priori* 'bundles of meaning' – cultural signifiers constantly engaging with history, themes, archetypes, and icons (27). *Curse* functions analogously to how Kitses and Jameson see the Western and other genre films operating. By reworking a text from Great Britain's romanticised parochial past, Hammer realigned *Frankenstein*'s discursive milieu to engage with a contemporary cultural moment. Adapting *Frankenstein*'s bundles of meaning offered Hammer a unique opportunity to mould a canonical text however it wished. Accordingly, Hammer creatives identified what they felt were *Frankenstein*'s most crucial narrative features and concocted ways to translate them to cinema. Helpfully, Universal's *Frankenstein* franchise provided examples of how Hammer's version should *not* look.

Horror business and the Frankenstein discourse

In 1948 the embryonic Hammer Films struck a distribution agreement with vertically integrated ABC cinemas, a British chain that already had a business relationship with Warner Bros. This allowed Hammer to make low-budget B movies with guaranteed distribution and screening in the lean post-war years, prompting genre experimentation and growth as a low-cost studio with a quick turnaround (Eyles et al. 22, 24). Spotting a niche, ABC differentiated its product from family-friendly rivals Rank by screening Hammer's X-certificate movies, a rating newly introduced in 1951 after British censorship regulations were relaxed (Barr 73–74; Kermode 11; McKay 20–21). Then, in 1956, the Motion Picture Association of America loosened its infamous Production Code, widening the world market for horror and sci-fi products at the same time that production costs were spiralling upwards in the US. This situation directly contributed to Hammer striking a 1956 distribution deal with Associated Artists Production, Inc. (AAP)/Seven Arts, who would help to cover the production costs for both *Curse* and *Horror of Dracula* in exchange for world distribution rights outside of the UK and Japan (Carreras, *Dracula* Financing).

In his cogent account of Ealing Studios, Charles Barr observes that there were two mutually exclusive choices for film companies in post-war Britain: either operate as an independent business, or collaborate with American major studios (6–7). While the Hollywood studio system was faltering by the mid-1950s, the UK attracted American studio investment while reaping the benefits of distribution back in the US. Seeking funding, Hammer managing director Col. James Carreras wrote a letter in 1956 to Eliot Hyman, owner of AAP/Seven Arts, pointing out that since Shelley's *Frankenstein* was in the public domain, anyone could make a film based on the original text provided there was no infringement on Universal's intellectual property and franchises (Letter to Hyman, August 1956). This meant, for instance, that Hammer's Creature design had to completely avoid any similarities to the iconic neck-bolts and flat head of Whale's *Frankenstein*. Hammer's production team faced a stern challenge – striking a balance between drawing an audience already familiar with *Frankenstein*'s discourse, but without evoking Universal's earlier effort. As an *Urtext*, Shelley's *Frankenstein* acts as a locus for subsequent Gothic horror traditions but, with Karloff's monster also looming large in public consciousness, Hammer's approach to the story is a particular stroke of pragmatic genius: make the creator the narrative focal point and feature his creation as little as possible. This had the desired effect of differentiating Hammer's product from Universal's films, while also reducing production time and costs associated with extensive monster make-up and visual effects. Furthermore, by focusing on Victor Frankenstein himself, *Curse* manages to stick closer to the discursive heart of Shelley's text than Whale's film, which is, after all, mostly told from Victor's subjective point of view. Carreras opines in his letter to Hyman that they 'need [the name] "Frankenstein" to market [the] picture [and] assure investors' (Ibid.). Anticipating Hyman's objections to a low-budget version of an old story, Carreras goes on in the letter to assure him that all they need is a 'completely competent British cast' and that the 'title alone [will] suffice to ensure distribution' without hiring expensive, 'known' American actors to appease US audiences (Ibid.).[6]

True to Carreras' plan, Hammer hired British actor Peter Cushing, better known at the time for his TV roles, to play Victor, and Christopher Lee, who later made his name starring as Hammer's Count Dracula, to play the Creature. A later letter from Carreras to Hyman reassured Hyman that the lead actor 'shouldn't cost more than £20,000', and that he had originally allocated only £1,250 for the role (Carreras, Response). While Lee's contract stipulates that he be paid a miserly daily salary of £50 over a guaranteed period of three weeks, with a guaranteed sum of £400, Cushing's figures have since been whited out, but he was guaranteed top billing (Carreras, Contracts). Given the film's budget, it seems very unlikely that Cushing received the full £20,000 outlined by Carreras, a figure that amounts to almost a third of the total amount allocated for production. These figures help to illustrate how and why Hammer shifted the story's focus from the monster to the creator. They allowed themselves to spend very little updating *Frankenstein* to appear 'fresh'. Business-savvy Carreras, however, knew that the US was a key market and actively engaged with American studios and media to promote his company's products while reiterating their youth appeal and profitability. In New York City to promote the 1958 American launch of *Horror of Dracula*, Carreras remarked that the 'Horror market ... is better than ever before because of [a] whole new generation that has never been exposed to these type [sic] of films' ('Chiller Pix' 4). Carreras was also quoted as saying that in order for horror films to remain successful they must have 'topnotch [sic] production values and must be treated seriously' so as to avoid 'unintended laughs' (Ibid. 4). From the beginning, Hammer's managing director seems to have had no illusions about the key to *Curse*'s success. Taking to the pages of *Variety* again in 1960 he suggested that the 'top factor [to Hammer's success] has been our knack of picking internationally exploitable stores [sic] and projecting them on the screen with a skill and polish that reflects great credit on our production team' ('British "Horror" Pix' 166). Carreras summarises Hammer's tactics later in the same article, emphasising how Hammer's *Frankenstein* helped to evolve the horror genre: 'We hit on a formula for success. Quite a simple one at that. We modernized horror. [...] We decided there was only one way to really scare the crowds – by giving them plausible horror and human monsters' (Ibid. 166). Thus it was a peculiar combination of cultural climate and Hammer's economic imperatives that gave rise to a film that focuses not on the ambiguity of the supernatural, but engages deeply with the emotional questions which Shelley's novel poses about the nature of man and monster and the differences, if any, between them. In *Curse*, *Frankenstein*'s mythopoeic qualities are tempered by Fisher and Sangster's approach to filmmaking and a desire to create a believably 'tangible' Georgian/Victorian milieu for their stories. However, it is precisely this tangibility that imbues *Curse*'s Victor with semi-omniscient narrative authority and accentuates his own allegorical monstrous nature.

Modernising horror: style, storytelling, and *mise-en-scène*

Shelley's *Frankenstein* begins with an epistolary framing device – a man named Walton writes letters to his sister, detailing his voyage to the North Pole in search of the Northeast Passage. Walton encounters Victor Frankenstein roaming across the ice and takes him aboard, whereupon the narrative switches to an alternating first-person narration from first Victor, then the Creature, and their dealings with each other. While Universal's *Frankenstein* does away with this structure entirely, *Curse* stays close to the source material's form by employing a new *mise-en -abyme*. Its narrative begins with an intertitle stating that Frankenstein's experiments took place 'more than a hundred years ago' and have 'become legend'. This opening scroll simultaneously works to reference existing texts while legitimising the authority of Hammer's contemporary version by evoking the 'legend' of Frankenstein's cultural capital. After the credits roll we see Victor (Peter Cushing) in a jail cell, being visited by a priest, to whom he tells his tale. The main narrative then takes place in an extended flashback sequence. Within this framing device *Curse*'s events deviate from Shelley's text – here, young Victor inherits his family fortune after being left orphaned, and hires Paul Krempe (Robert Urquhart) to tutor him. Although in Shelley's text Krempe is a very minor character, and the less preferred of Victor's university tutors, in *Curse* he is a major protagonist. While Shelley deals with Victor's experimentation on a single page, this film foregrounds the story's horror elements by providing extended sequences of Victor scavenging for body parts and eventually murdering an esteemed professor to gather the brain of a genius, before bringing his Creature to life. Later, Paul and Victor physically struggle with each other over using the dead professor's brain; it falls and is damaged. Thus the Creature is malevolent from the start of his existence – a narrative feature derivative of Whale's film, but not present in Shelley's text. While most details from the book are absent, pivotal scenes featuring the Creature escaping from Victor's lab, a blind man being murdered, and a wedding-night narrative climax are included but are heavily altered. These sequences play minor parts in Hammer's film, which instead focuses on promulgating macabre elements and developing a brooding atmospheric narrative that charts Victor's descent into villainy. Jimmy Sangster's script does away with the moralistic agonising of Shelley's Victor in favour of a stripped-down story overflowing with visual detail perfect for colour film. These choices reflect both Carreras and Fisher's desire to move away from the campy histrionics of other adaptations, and also their skill in exploiting cultural preoccupations to add value to works from Britain's literary past.

    Curse's non-specific period setting means that the film can exploit the eighteenth- and nineteenth-century schism between the ideals of Romanticism and the rationalism of the Enlightenment. Fisher saw his films more as moralistic fairy tales for adults than as sadistic horror, and staged them accordingly (Fisher Notes Item 22). The director wanted the settings of his films to suggest fantasy but be grounded in a sense of reality, arguing in his notebook that ideally horror should be 'The art of make believe – you

have got to be convincingly factual and not impressionistic in limiting acting, presentation' (Ibid.). Sangster's writing meshed well with Fisher's beliefs regarding the
oppositional balance between fantasy and the mundane, a core antinomic relationship
in Gothic discourses. *Curse*'s script presents a believable world where the supernatural
becomes part of the everyday, where Victor's experiments can be considered all
too plausible. The director believed that in the wake of World War II such binary
conjunctions allowed his Gothic tale to represent 'true horror' and trump the older
Universal monster movies (Ibid.). Fisher writes, 'Mine persuade/present an audience
[with the] impossible, fantastic … audiences must accept – believe in them while
they are watching them – no tongue in cheek – no melodramatics – Integrity – True
horror as opposed to mock' (Ibid.). Fisher further argued that 'Putting them [horror
films] into period takes them out of present day reality and gives them atmosphere &
veracity – greater realism' (Ibid.). Here Fisher's creative goals align with Carreras'
business ones, as the director sought to locate horror within the familiar by shunning
the camp excesses of Universal's Frankenstein series. *Curse*'s focus on the Gothic's
human drama brought horror closer to home, and Fisher's desire to make *Frankenstein*
more 'real' chimed well with Carreras' financial priorities as a producer and studio
head. Thus, *Curse* fully embraces its nostalgic period settings, paradoxically relying on
a stylised reality to evoke a sense of magic realism, to de-familiarise the viewer from
other iterations of *Frankenstein* and previous forms of horror cinema.

Fisher's notebooks attest to how he and Sangster approached their material: '[*Curse*
was] written straight – a director can direct anything tongue in cheek – it is a matter of
interpretation' (Fisher Notes Item 5). This statement highlights one of the difficulties
in adapting historical texts – how to encode Shelley's writing to visually and aurally
signify the Frankenstein discourse while also developing it as a contemporary horror
narrative. Despite having an iconic monster at the centre of *Curse*'s discursive formation, Fisher and Sangster reified *Frankenstein* by focusing on human concerns such as
pure good versus absolute evil, the scientific rationalisation of nature set against a
backdrop of superstition, and the awe of confronting a Romantic sublime. Encoding a
studio-bound cinematic product with the inchoate nature of the Frankenstein discourse
required approaching the material in a manner sensitive both to historiography and also
to Hammer's economic imperatives. To portray the Manichean nature of good/evil,
rationality/emotion, science/nature that Shelley's novel engages with, *Curse* adopts
a thematic and narrative process of separating the protagonists into dual parts, each
reflective of broader narrative conflicts. This means that the protagonist is effectively
split into two opposing yet complementary roles, each necessary to advance narrative
events. Victor is arguably the protagonist, but he is both complemented and negated
by Paul. After Victor is educated by Paul and resurrects a dog toward the end of Act
1, we see a cognitive dissonance developing between the two. Victor pursues further
experimentation, while Paul grows increasingly uncomfortable. Victor and Paul share
protagonist duties – while Victor's desire to create life is what drives the overarching
narrative, Paul's actions force both the narrative mid-point (where the Creature's

brain is damaged) and the Act 2 climax (when Paul shoots the Creature through the eye – further damaging its brain – after an attempted escape). These actions drive the rest of the narrative to its climax, where the Creature again escapes and must be subdued by the joint actions of both protagonists.

Frankenstein's thematic concerns with duality are well explored in *Curse*. In Fisher's film, duality may be literal, with two separate protagonists, but it is also psychological, as exemplified by Victor and the Creature he creates. Victor seeks to create life for the good of mankind, but his Creature is an abomination and serves to split Victor's psyche. Finally, duality may be a combination of both literal and psychological, as when Victor vacillates between protagonist and antagonist. Despite sharing protagonist duties with Paul, Victor also has an illicit affair with his maid, then has her and their unborn child murdered.[7] In Fisher and Sangster's take on *Frankenstein*, Victor embodies obsessive rationality/patriarchy while the supporting male, Paul, acts as his emotional/more sentimental foil. Paul is also a man of science, but his methodical, scientific training is tempered by emotion and often superseded by his sense of morality, something Victor lacks. While the emotional foil must play second fiddle to the rational lead, *Curse*'s mid-point and climax are both forced by Paul's actions, then resolved by the rational lead destroying his creation.

The Creature garners very little screen time in all of this, as it is reduced to a plot device serving the demands of Victor's narrative. In pre-*Curse* horror, monsters gener-ally serve as 'dangling causes' within the plot, granting the protagonist a causal motiva-tion that will drive narrative progression. In other words, the monster poses a narrative problem for the protagonist to solve. This problem simultaneously grants the viewer information while forcing a course of narrative action that will not be resolved until much later in the plot, when the protagonist confronts the monster at narrative climax. This structural convention is evident in Shelley's novel. Moreover, horror films before *Curse* tended to end with the reaffirmation of traditional heteronormative values, and the reassertion of patriarchal authority. There is no ambiguity in the climax of most of these films; the Creature is vanquished as good (human) triumphs over evil (inhuman), and all plot-lines are concluded. *Curse* certainly can also be read as a morality tale, where good defeats evil and the folly of morally bankrupt characters is exposed, but its discursive formation provides a serious break from established horror tropes. Victor is amoral and completely rational (indeed, his scientific rationality denotes his hubris). The film's prologue and subsequent plot points reveal that the dangling cause in this film is not a monster to be vanquished but Victor's desire to reanimate the dead. Despite being the titular character and the one with the most screen-time, Victor himself is ostensibly the villain of the piece – without his obsessive ambition there would be no narrative. The film's prologue, depicting Victor in jail confessing to a priest his role in the events that have taken place, becomes an entry point for the viewer that likely disrupts their preconceived notions of how a Frankenstein film will play out. Noteworthy here is that Victor is not pleading with the priest for spiritual forgiveness before being executed; he has instead pragmatically sent for the priest so that his story can be conveyed to the authorities in order to prove his innocence. From the very beginning, the viewer experiences a new form of horror cinema. As the intertitle hints – yes, we know the legend, but what about the 'actual events'?

Fisher's camera work and editing further emphasises this new brand of horror cinema. Fisher utilises long takes and master shots composed of medium-long two-and-three-shots, while rarely cutting to close shots or inserts, allowing characters to move freely around the frame. And instead of relying on analytical continuity editing, Fisher uses a sparser, more organic style for *Curse*, where the camera slowly pans and tracks to keep characters centrally framed while moving. But Fisher's camera still keeps secrets. He frequently manipulates off-screen space to tease the viewer with potential eye-line matches of presumably horrific sights, but seldom actually cuts to point-of-view (POV) shots. Therefore, he maximises the impact of the POV shots that he does create by minimising their implementation. Dennis Giles notes that 'delayed, blocked, or partial vision' is 'central to the strategy of horror cinema' and is essential to the genre's means of building suspense (39). An example comes when Victor and Paul track down the escaped Creature. Fisher establishes Victor and Paul in a master two-shot; Paul then shoots the advancing Creature and Fisher cuts to a tight medium-close shot of the Creature, its hand covering a bloody bullet wound.

Fisher rapidly cuts back to a long shot, then to Paul and Victor in the master. This sequence incorporates an early form of the 'shock cut' – endemic in 1970s and 1980s horror movies – but always dramatically motivated and never gratuitous when used by Fisher.[8]

As a consequence of this style, set dressing becomes more important and the moments of horror that punctuate an otherwise languid picture become more unsettling. Andrew Mangravite explains how a period melodrama can function as horror by pointing out the central difference between the way Fisher shoots gore and Herschel Gordon Lewis' use of explicit 'splatter' (48).[9] Mangravite contends that, unlike Lewis, Fisher's use of violence is less about the act itself than it is the *staging* of these acts' (48). When Fisher shoots violence or gore it emerges from a precise manipulation of analytical editing. This disrupts the established rhythms of his tableaux style and thus appears more shocking as a result. When Fisher does employ analytical editing it is to grant the viewer a brief, closer view of gore or violence before quickly cutting away.

After normalising such editing tricks, Fisher playfully inverts audience expectation in other situations when analytical editing might be anticipated. Fisher always establishes eye-line matches before cutting, but sometimes does not grant a POV shot, with the effect of denying the viewer an explicit image of what the on-screen character is looking at. This technique is used to great effect at the beginning of *Curse*'s second act. Victor and Paul are framed from the chest up in a medium-close two-shot as Victor prepares to remove the head from a corpse. After cutting to an insert of Victor's surgical blade, Fisher cuts back to the master two-shot as Paul retreats to a background position in softer focus, ramping up viewer expectation by focusing on Victor operating in the foreground. As Fisher holds the shot for a silent six seconds, we focus on

Figure 5.2 Peter Cushing as Dr Frankenstein in Hammer's *Curse of Frankenstein*.

Victor and anticipate a cut to his point of view. However, instead of giving us an eye-line match, Fisher cuts to a close shot of Paul's disgusted-looking face, potentially establishing another eye-line match before frustrating narrative expectation again by cutting back to his master and refusing to cut to a gory insert. Consequently, the scene results in potential anti-climax when we merely see Victor wipe bright red blood on his lapel, with no insert to the results of his actions, which take place entirely off screen, teasingly below the frame line. By consistently frustrating viewer expectation in this manner Fisher builds anticipation for the Creature's big reveal, when we will finally see his grotesque visage unbandaged.[10]

This method of editing parallels Victor's downward spiral into degradation. As his experiments and rationale become more perverse, we see more explicit shots in which Paul abstains from taking part in the action. Fisher's teasing, understated directing style works within the context of the narrative to emphasise the dual nature of scientific and medical experimentation. Victor may have good intentions to end the existence of death, but his methods become ever more violent and questionable. Fisher's willingness to focus on Victor's increasingly disturbing work suggests that he is less and less a scientist and more a criminal monster. Engaging with the existing Frankenstein discourse in this manner allows Hammer to invoke earlier horror genre preoccupations while moulding a public-domain work into a vehicle for further films.

Scripting irony as exposition

Curse's writer, Jimmy Sangster, pairs speech as well as inarticulate silence with visual clues to convey a sardonic form of dramatic irony that courses throughout the film; for example, the Creature that Victor refers to as 'perfect' is depicted as a shambling, mute monstrosity that only peripherally features in the narrative. Sangster's script complements Fisher's understated directing, with dialogue written in standard English, and the actors, particularly Cushing, uttering their lines in a clipped, uninflected manner. For instance, Victor's post-prologue narration opens with the lines: 'Where did it all begin? I suppose it was when I was a boy at school. I always had a brilliant intellect.' Victor's self-assurance and lack of humility seems to signify the inhuman, but this is also partially defrayed by the script's gallows humour. When Victor pithily instructs Paul not to touch their yet-to-be-animated cadaver in his absence, he ends with the droll line: 'Let him rest in peace while he can.' Conversely, the Creature's monstrous nature is partially conveyed by his muteness, combined with a perpetually gaping, slack-jawed maw – he appears far more zombie-like than Karloff's empathetic iteration, and is reduced to a husk that permits the real monster, Victor, to pursue his narrative goals. It is, after all, Victor's 'legend'. While character action and dialogue serve as primary means to further the film's narrative, the cinematic medium itself provides visual and aural cues to serve as plot points that build an ironic tone. *Curse* is told 'straight', but the sardonic nature of Sangster's writing as interpreted by Fisher's direction imbues the film with a form of pitch-black humour, striking an uneasy yet complementary balance with the fatalism that undergirds Shelley's text.

Several times *Curse* depicts characters glibly discussing or commenting on a narrative problem, then resolving the problem within the next scene or so, usually by means of violence or some extreme action. Two successive sequences demonstrate how irony works to link key scenes and causally drive Victor's descent into criminality. During the second act Paul quizzes Victor on how he will progress with his increasingly grotesque experiment. Framed in a medium two-shot, Victor tells Paul that he needs the brain of a genius with a lifetime of experience to complete his creation. Fisher cuts to a close-shot of Paul, looking to screen left, as he asks an off-screen Victor where such a brain will come from. Fisher completes Paul's eye-line match with a close-shot of Victor, looking right, swearing that he'll get it. Fisher holds the shot for a lengthy seven seconds before cutting back to Paul in close-up to complete the shot-reverse shot before a dissolve transition ends the scene. In the next scene we see Victor, his ostensible love interest, Elizabeth (Hazel Court), and a new character, Professor Bernstein (Paul Hardtmuth), drinking brandy in a medium-long three-shot. The three make small talk in a series of shot/reverse shots and Fisher holds shots for slightly longer than necessary, prompting the viewer to pay attention to the décor of Victor's home. This will become important later. During the conversation Fisher alerts the viewers to Bernstein's danger when Elizabeth refers to him as 'the greatest brain in Europe'. Fisher cuts to a medium-long shot of the three before Paul enters the scene from a background door, forming a four-shot. Paul expresses his pleasure at meeting such a famous professor (another signal to the viewer), while Victor notes that he did not expect Paul back until the next day (the viewer's third and final warning of danger). Upon leaving the room with Bernstein, Victor pauses in a medium-long two-shot, to show the professor a painting at the top of the staircase. When Bernstein is distracted, Victor pushes him over the stair railing, killing him. That the painting is of Rembrandt's famous 'The Anatomy Lesson' adds another layer to the script's sardonic nature. At no point in this scene do Fisher and Sangster provide gratuitous information. While following Victor's gaze throughout the sequence, we see that he stares relentlessly at the back of Bernstein's head. However, Fisher resists the urge to cut to a close shot of Victor staring at Bernstein, or of the professor's head, nor does Fisher cut to a POV shot of the painting. There is no ghoulish cackling, no wide-eyed, maniacal hand rubbing, yet we are still fully aware of Bernstein's peril and Victor's obsession. Fisher manages to convey the biting irony of Sangster's script merely by using the same measured, fluid style that the rest of the film employs.

Conclusion

The sequences in *Curse* that chart Victor's research and his descent into villainy act as plot points to drive the narrative forward, and these same plot points also work to assimilate the Frankenstein discourse into familiar horror conventions. Act 1 ends when Victor successfully reanimates a dog and makes the decision to henceforth *create* a new life instead of simply resuscitate another dead animal. Ironically, Victor must kill to create, and Act 2's mid-point comes when Victor kills for the first time. When Victor murders Bernstein he irrevocably commits himself to realising his experiment, marking himself as a villain in the process. The subsequent brain-transferral sequence compounds the mid-point of the film, as Victor realises the enormity of his future task. In this scene, Paul, horrified by what Victor has done, tussles with him, and the previously intact brain is damaged. The two men become enemies from this point on, and Victor's Creature will itself be a much lesser creation than he had hoped: a monster instead of a genius. Whereas Shelley's protagonist spends much of the story pursuing his creation to atone for his failings, *Curse*'s Victor is unrepentant – his crimes merely spur him to actions that further rework the discourse surrounding Frankenstein. But, despite their differences, Sangster's script, like Shelley's novel, is embroiled with a more ambiguous morality than earlier horror cinema. As dual protagonist/antagonist, Victor has illicitly procured body parts, robbed graves, seduced his maid, then had her murdered by his creation, and also committed murder himself – all in the name of pursuing his narrative goal. He does, however, save Elizabeth by destroying his creation when the monster threatens her, thus complicating his character's portrayal. Nonetheless, and more in line with moralistic Hollywood storytelling, Victor is punished at the narrative's end for his ambition and moral transgressions. Victor himself fulfils the role of 'monster' as we see him in jail, unrepentantly seeking reprieve by describing his experiments as he waits to be executed.

Sangster's writing on *Curse* displays a playfulness with form that would be codified in subsequent collaborations with Fisher. While *Curse* differed from earlier horror films, it laid down a basic template for appropriating public-domain literary fiction to which other Hammer Gothic efforts could adhere and which they could further manipulate. While the process of adaptation requires source material, Hammer's prerogative to align horror's signifying genre conventions with economic and legal imperatives provided an impetus to rearticulate the source through social and technical negotiations. Despite a low budget and lack of star power, the professional competence of the cast and crew assimilated the discourses of a canonical work of fiction to create a powerful display of how a familiar narrative can be reworked to contextualise allegorical themes for a modern audience. A dependency on adapting public-domain texts and over-reliance on their accumulated bodies of cultural themes and discourses betrays Hammer's position as a small production studio with no means of distribution or exhibition beyond deals with larger American studios. *Frankenstein*'s marketable cachet within western culture aligned with the studio's industrial aims and artistic capabilities, and for a few years *Curse* meant that Hammer was pushing the bounds of horror cinema. Cushing's Victor Frankenstein is equal parts charming and rational, but also callous and psychopathic. Stylistic changes aside, in reworking *Frankenstein* for a new, post-war audience Hammer shifted the thematic focus of horror from the monstrous inhuman to the monstrous human, a trend that would be underscored three years later with the release of both Hitchcock's *Psycho* (1960) and Michael Powell's *Peeping Tom* (1960). Ultimately, adapting *Frankenstein* proved a success for Hammer, as it reconstituted the marketable aspects of diffuse historical forces. As a result, *The Curse of Frankenstein* represents a film forged from the time's cultural climate while also demonstrating how creative industries can co-opt and influence cultural discourse.

Notes

1 Hammer's other Frankenstein films are *Revenge of Frankenstein* (1958), treated in Chapter 8 in this collection, *Evil of Frankenstein* (1964), *Frankenstein Created Woman* (1967), *Frankenstein Must Be Destroyed* (1969), *Horror of Frankenstein* (1970), and *Frankenstein and the Monster from Hell* (1974). Terence Fisher helmed four of the six films.
2 For Sarris – a director whose films exhibit technical proficiency, personal style, and interior meaning. For Wollen – a structural understanding of auteurism that comprehends the author as one responsible for the construction of recurring motifs and thematic myth-making that is repeated over an entire body of work. For more detail see Sarris and Wollen, also Pirie, *A Heritage of Horror*, 66–75.
3 Several authors have focused on developing historiographies of Hammer and their films. Most notably, Sinclair McKay's book, *A Thing of Unspeakable Horror*, implicitly aligns itself with Hutchings' understanding that horror films reflect a society's broader cultural trends. McKay fails to provide film- or period-specific examples, but he does list thirteen Hammer film 'leitmotifs' in his opening chapter, 'What is a Hammer film?' (7–11). For an insightful partial bibliography of other Hammer-specific texts see Pirie, *New Heritage of Horror*, 247–248.
4 *Them!* (Gordon Douglas, 1954) is probably the most famous American example, while *Godzilla* (Ishirō Honda, 1954) serves as the archetype for Japanese *Kaiju*.
5 This cycle began with *Bud Abbot and Lou Costello Meet Frankenstein* (Charles Barton, 1948), featuring Bela Lugosi and Lon Chaney, Jr reprising their respective roles as Dracula and The Wolf Man.
6 A 1959 article in trade magazine *Variety* shows that Carreras' instincts were right – it states that Hammer were nicely filling a niche for American exhibitors who sought 'foreign outfits' to make films that would appeal to American moviegoers ('Hammer: Five-a-Year for Columbia' 19).
7 He locks her in a room with his Creature, knowing she will not survive.
8 'Shock cuts' are a horror-specific variation of the jump cut that quickly cut to a close shot of graphic or violent imagery; the cut is intended to shock the audience.
9 Herschel Gordon Lewis is best known for creating the 'splatter' subgenre of horror cinema with *Blood Feast* (1963) and *The Wizard of Gore* (1970).
10 Which happens in another pseudo-shock cut as Fisher rapidly tracks the camera towards the Creature's face as it removes the bandages.

Bibliography

Allen, Robert and Douglas Gomery. *Film History: Theory and Practice*. New York: McGraw-Hill, 1985.
Barr, Charles. *Ealing Studios*. London: Cameron and Taylor/Newton Abbot, 1977.
'British "Horror" Pix as Insurance for that Wide-Open Global B.O.' *Variety*, 6 January 1960.
Carreras, James. Contracts. 1957. Item 1 *Curse of Frankenstein*. Hammer Film Productions. British Film Institute National Archive, London. 25 July 2012.
———. *Dracula* Financing. 16 August 1957. Item 15 *Dracula* Financing. Hammer Film Productions. British Film Institute National Archive, London. 25 July 2012.

————. Letter to Eliot Hyman. 24 August 1956. Item 1 *Curse of Frankenstein*. Hammer Film Productions. British Film Institute National Archive, London. 25 July 2012.

————. Letter to Eliot Hyman. 7 July 1957. Item 1 *Curse of Frankenstein*. Hammer Film Productions. British Film Institute National Archive, London. 25 July 2012.

————. Response. 3 September 1956. Item 1 *Curse of Frankenstein*. Hammer Film Productions. British Film Institute National Archive, London. 25 July 2012.

'Chiller Pix Still Hot, Hammer Says.' *Variety* 28 May 1958.

Clarens, Carlos. *An Illustrated History of the Horror Film*. New York: Capricorn Books, 1968.

Dixon, Wheeler Winston. *The Charm of Evil: the life and films of Terence Fisher*. Metuchen, NJ: London: The Scarecrow Press, Inc., 1991.

Eyles, Allen, Robert Adkinson, and Nicholas Fry, eds. *The House of Horror: The Story of Hammer Films*. London: Lorrimer Publishing, 1973.

Fisher, Terence. Fisher Notes. Item 5. Terence Fisher Collection. British Film Institute National Archive, London. 26 July 2012.

————. Fisher Notes. Item 15. Terence Fisher Collection. British Film Institute National Archive, London. 26 July 2012.

————. Fisher Notes. Item 21. Terence Fisher Collection. British Film Institute National Archive, London. 26 July 2012.

————. Fisher Notes. Item 22. Terence Fisher Collection. British Film Institute National Archive, London. 26 July 2012.

Giles, Dennis. 'Conditions of Pleasure in Horror Cinema.' *Planks of Reason: Essays on the Horror Film*. Eds Barry Keith Grant and Christopher Sharrett. Lanham, MD: The Scarecrow Press, Inc., 2004. 36–49.

'Hammer: Five-a-Year for Columbia.' *Variety*, 18 March 1959.

Harper, Sue. 'Beyond the Forest: Terence Fisher and Transylvania.' *Studies in European Cinema* 3, no. 2 (July 2006): 143–151. DOI:10.1386/seci.3.2.143_1 (accessed 10 June 2014).

Hearn, Marcus. *The Hammer Vault*. London: Titan Books, 2011.

Hutchings, Peter. *Hammer and Beyond: The British Horror Film*. Manchester, UK; New York, USA: Manchester University Press; Distributed exclusively in the USA and Canada by St Martin's Press, 1993.

————. *Terence Fisher*. Manchester, UK: Manchester University Press, 2002.

Jameson, Fredric. 'Postmodernism, or the Cultural Logic of Late Capitalism (1984).' *The Jameson Reader*. Eds Michael Hardt and Kathi Weeks. Oxford: Blackwell Publishers Ltd, 2000. 188–233.

Judt, Tony. *Postwar: A History of Europe Since 1945*. New York: Penguin Books, 2006.

Kermode, Mark. 'The British Censors and Horror Cinema.' *British Horror Cinema*. Eds Steve Chibnall and Julian Petley. London; New York: Routledge, 2002. 10–41.

Kitses, Jim. *Horizons West – Anthony Mann, Budd Boetticher, Sam Peckinpah: Studies of Authorship within the Western*. Bloomington, IN: Indiana University Press, 1970.

McKay, Sinclair. *A Thing of Unspeakable Horror: The History of Hammer Films*. London: Aurum, 2007.

Mangravite, Andrew. 'THe House of Hammer.' *Film Comment* 28, no. 3 (1992): 46–53.

Picart, Caroline Joan ('Kay') S. *The Cinematic Rebirths of Frankenstein: Universal, Hammer, and Beyond*. Westport, CT; London: Praeger, 2002.

Picart, Caroline Joan ('Kay') S., Frank Smoot, and Jayne Blodgett. *The Frankenstein Film Sourcebook*. Westport, CT; London: Greenwood Press, 2001.

Pirie, David. *A Heritage of Horror; the English Gothic Cinema, 1946–1972*. New York: Equinox Books/ Published by Avon, 1973.

————. *A New Heritage of Horror: the English Gothic Cinema*. New York: I.B. Tauris & Co Ltd, 2008.

Sarris, Andrew. 'Notes on the Auteur Theory in 1962.' *Auteurs and Authorship: A Film Reader*. Ed. Barry Keith Grant. Malden, MA: Blackwell Publishing, 2008. 35–46.

Schatz, Thomas. *Hollywood Genres: Formulas, Filmmaking, and the Studio System*. New York: McGraw-Hill, 1981.

Wollen, Peter. 'The Auteur Theory.' *Auteurs and Authorship: A Film Reader*. Ed. Barry Keith Grant. Malden, MA: Blackwell Publishing, 2008. 55–65.

'Year in Show Biz-Day By Day.' *Variety*, 18 October 1950.

6

The Frankenstein Complex on the small screen: Mary Shelley's motivic novel as adjacent adaptation

Kyle William Bishop

SINCE ITS PUBLICATION IN 1818, Mary Shelley's iconic novel *Frankenstein* has manifested throughout popular culture in a variety of adaptations across numerous media, making it one of the most adapted literary works in history.[1] Many of these plays, films, novels, comics, and video games – comprising the 'Frankenstein Network' of interrelated and interconnected texts – attempt holistic recreations of Shelley's original material, emphasising the power struggles between Victor Frankenstein and his misunderstood Creature. These full-scale reinscriptions of *Frankenstein* understandably invite discussions of fidelity; however, as adaptation scholars Thomas Leitch and Robert Stam make clear, such fidelity-based approaches are flawed and inherently limited. Leitch argues that adaptations have an ethical obligation to offer audiences a notably different experience from the source material (63), and Stam claims that adaptations should be understood as part of an intertextual dialogical process (64). Some of the most 'notably different' and intertextual forms of adaptation occur when the inspirational source material intersects with existing narrative structures, as often occurs in television.

Due to the episodic nature of television serials, adaptations of *Frankenstein* that appear as part of existing narrative arcs must take a more fragmented approach to translating Shelley's tale to the small screen. In a number of science-fiction, fantasy, and horror television shows, motivic elements from *Frankenstein* – characters, plot points, symbols, and themes – tend to appear in one, almost ubiquitous episode. Rather than taking place over the course of the entire serial, however, these adaptations usually occur simultaneously with the narrative structure of the ongoing series. Instead of being the 'stars' of the show, the recognisable characters of Victor Frankenstein and his Creature get a contracted story arc, often just a single episode in which the *Frankenstein* narrative is briefly integrated into the larger story arc of the series. This kind of simultaneous adaptation – the adaptation of a recognisable text interwoven within a serialised narrative – constitutes a decidedly distinct form of artistic appropriation, one which I call an 'adjacent adaptation', since the adapted elements are rarely present for more than an episode and are always overshadowed by the story and character arcs of the series.

In adjacent adaptation, the essential elements of a familiar antecedent text are condensed to a 'featured encounter' or stand-alone story. A number of series have featured 'Monster of the Week' episodes that reference, recreate, or pay homage to Shelley's *Frankenstein*, including 'Some Assembly Required' (1997) from *Buffy the Vampire Slayer* (1997–2003) and 'The Post-Modern Prometheus' (1997) from *The X-Files* (1993–2002). A particularly useful case study of the phenomenon can be found in *Doctor Who* (1963–89 and 2005–), which has explored Frankenstein motifs in both its original and current iterations. 'The Brain of Morbius' (1976) represents an early manifestation of this kind of adjacent adaptation, and 'A Town Called Mercy' (2012) is one of the most recent.[2] Because of their unusual nature, adjacent adaptations require a different theoretical approach than full-scale adaptations. Adjacent adaptations represent a tangential model, one that requires, or at least greatly benefits from, pre-existing, dialogical audience familiarity (Hutcheon 21) with key characters, back story, plot points, and themes, not only for the episode to make sense, but also to provide viewers with a pleasurable experience within the structure of the serial's primary story arc.

Frankenstein as adjacent adaptation

Perhaps one of the reasons *Frankenstein* has been so prolifically adapted and reinvented over the years is because it represents a fundamentally adapted text itself. According to Shelley's introduction to the third edition of *Frankenstein* (1831), she consciously sought secondary source material in her efforts to construct her 'original' contribution to Lord Byron's famous 'ghost story contest' of 1816. Drawing from a number of inspirations, Shelley crafted her story as a deliberate adaptation, one that 'must be linked to something that went before' (167). In a process notably similar to that undertaken by her fictional Victor Frankenstein, Shelley's creative effort became one of invention and organisation: 'Invention, it must be humbly admitted,' she writes, 'does not consist in creating out of void, but out of chaos; the materials must, in the first place, be afforded.... Invention consists in the capacity of seizing on the capabilities of a subject, and in the power of moulding and fashioning ideas suggested to it' (167). Shelley's *Frankenstein* is therefore not only a tale *of* assemblage but also a narrative that *is* assembled from a variety of pre-existing components,[3] a curious doubling that informs audience readings of the myriad adaptations within the Frankenstein Network. It should not be surprising that serial television, with its *bricoleur* tendency to cobble together episodes from materials at hand, has often incorporated elements of *Frankenstein*.

   Frankenstein is, thus, always already an adaptation, and adaptations must essentially be considered in terms of reception. Audiences approach adapted texts, whether they intend to or not, as palimpsestuous, intertextual works. Linda Hutcheon explains that adaptations are 'obviously "multilaminated"; they are directly and openly connected to recognizable other works, and that connection is part of their formal identity, but also what we might call their hermeneutic identity' (21). Stam, similarly, makes the case that every text represents the intersection of a variety of other texts (64), a concept of intertextuality which Pamela Demory expands in her critical metaphor of an (inter) textual tapestry (123). Rather than considering an adaptation as an isolated, unique text, Demory argues that any work – particularly one that has been repeatedly adapted – should be examined as a 'thick tapestry', constructed not only from the original source material but also from 'numerous other filmic and literary texts, and colored by various genre conventions, reader and viewer expectations, and market forces' (123). Any text, *especially* an adapted work, is not only greater than the sum of its parts, but must be approached and understood *as* its parts as well. Audience members familiar with the antecedent texts and influences understand them all on a more sophisticated level because the interplay among the works opens up possible new meanings. An adaptation is also both appealing and pleasurable because of repetition, an element that 'brings comfort, a fuller understanding, and the confidence that comes with the sense of knowing what is about to happen next' (Hutcheon 114). However, as with music, repetition by itself would be reductive and boring; the appeal of a quality adaptation lies in its variation on the theme (115), and those variations can be enjoyed more fully by an audience familiar with the original theme.

The adjacent adaptation in television illustrates this complex and pleasurable interplay between at least two independent texts and their textual elements. Rather than simply converting a pre-existing text to a different form or medium, a new genre, or for another audience, the adjacent adaptation interweaves the two texts – an ostensibly original television series with an existing, fundamentally recognisable secondary text – a true palimpsest in which both the primary narrative of the television serial and the secondary adaptation become one. However, to be successful as both narrative and pleasurable aesthetic experience, adjacent adaptations rely on the audience 'knowing' both texts (see Hutcheon 120). In terms of a single television episode, such familiarity allows the plot to take certain short cuts because savvy, informed viewers will 'fill in the gaps' of the story, condensing the source material while expanding on the material of the serial itself.

With the adjacent adaptation, Shelley's desire for her 'hideous progeny [to] go forth and prosper' (Shelley, 'Introduction' 169) has been fulfilled, likely to an extent beyond her wildest dreams. The modern conception of Victor Frankenstein and his tragic creation permeates much of contemporary popular culture and can be found in a surprising number of isolated episodes from fantastic television programmes. Of course, integrating any beloved literary text into an existing series opens the door for a limitless number of pleasurable variations on the theme, as the multifarious uses of *Frankenstein* on television illustrate. The key to understanding the unique 'pleasure principle' of such an adjacent adaptation lies largely with the audience; Hutcheon claims, '[k]nown adaptations obviously function similarly to genres' (121) because they establish audience expectations (Culler 136), expectations essential to the success of an adjacent adaptation, whether the source material is directly acknowledged or not. An adjacent adaptation needs to be well executed, to be sure, but the target audience also needs to 'get it' for the story to make sense and for viewers to enjoy the experience.

The pervasiveness of the Frankenstein Network as a source of inspiration for adjacent adaptation can be found in *Buffy the Vampire Slayer*, a series known for its intertextual references and repurposing of established horror themes, tropes, and narratives. Early in the second season of Joss Whedon's genre-bending series, the Scoobie Gang find themselves caught up in Sunnydale's own version of *Frankenstein*. 'Some Assembly Required', written by David Tyron King and directed by Bruce Seth Green, opens with Buffy Summers (Sarah Michelle Gellar) in pursuit of Chris (Angelo Spizzirri) and Eric (Michael Bacall), two enterprising teenagers attempting to assemble a woman from parts they have been stealing from the morgue and cemetery. The two have constructed a Gothic laboratory in the high school's old science lab for that purpose, complete with ubiquitous test tubes and electrical apparatuses. But Chris and Eric lack a viable head to complete their unholy creation, and this key 'missing ingredient' establishes a direct link to James Whale's 1931 *Frankenstein*.[4] Halfway through the episode, however, a clearer intertextual moment occurs as Chris's previously deceased older brother Daryl (Ingo Neuhaus), patched together and apparently already reanimated by the boys, emerges from the shadows of the laboratory, pleading with Chris to take care of him and make a monstrous girl-friend for him. 'Some Assembly Required' thus reveals itself, to the knowing viewer, to be more directly adapting Whale's *The Bride of Frankenstein* (1935), along with the latter portions of Shelley's novel. The episode is intertextual on multiple levels simultaneously, and the more aware the viewer is of the Frankenstein Network, the more rewarding the experience of 'reading' the episode becomes.

The adjacent nature of this adaptation also allows the use of a kind of cultural shorthand for more efficient storytelling. Because they can safely assume that their audience has some familiarity with Whale's films and Shelley's novel, even if only on a cultural level, King and Green can take tremendous short cuts with the plot of 'Some Assembly Required'; they don't need to provide any back story to Daryl's assembly and resuscitation, nor must they explain Chris's and Eric's duelling motives in creating a 'bride' for Daryl. The two recall the opposed scientists from *The Bride of Frankenstein*: we soon recognise that Chris plays the role of the tormented Frankenstein (Colin Clive), who feels obligated to his Creature, while Eric is Whale's power-hungry and hubristic Dr Pretorius (Ernest Thesiger), who thinks himself equal to God. The episode thus ends somewhat predictably for fans of Whale's films: even though Buffy intervenes to stop Eric, Daryl is ultimately moved to end his own life, embracing the headless amalgam of body parts as the laboratory burns down around him. By folding Whale's films into the ongoing narrative structure of *Buffy the Vampire Slayer* as adjacent adaptations, King and Green efficiently add to their audience's pleasure and relate more than one palimpsestuous story simultaneously.

While *Buffy the Vampire Slayer* provides viewers a relatively sober version of *Frankenstein*, *The X-Files* offers audiences a different kind of adjacent adaptation, one

Figure 6.1 Sarah Michelle Gellar in *Buffy the Vampire Slayer*.

that expands its contiguous material to include a variety of disparate sources and inspirations. 'The Post-Modern Prometheus', written and directed by series creator Chris Carter,[5] is a prime example of intertextuality, overtly referencing not only Shelley's novel but also EC Comics-style horror stories, Gothic films from the 1930s and 1940s, and, strangely enough, the 1985 Cher film *Mask*, directed by Peter Bogdanovich. The title itself cleverly echoes the subtitle of Shelley's novel, 'The Modern Prometheus', alerting a knowing viewer to the clearly intentional adaptation of *Frankenstein*. Additionally, the episode opens with an extreme close-up shot of a mock horror comic, *The Great Mutato*, written by one of the characters in the episode, Izzy Berkowitz (Stewart Gale). Thus the narrative is presented in terms of comic-book fantasy. Finally, the entire episode was filmed in black and white and mirrors the tone and style of a Universal horror film. The episode is replete with humorous winks and nods to a knowing audience, demonstrating how an adjacent adaptation can be a comic homage, bordering on parody. Most of the dialogue of the episode is punctuated by crashing thunder, and the camera work emphasises low-angle shots and fish-eye lenses. The characters even reference *Frankenstein* directly: Scully (Gillian Anderson) and Mulder's (David Duchovny) home-invasion investigation focuses on the unethical Dr Polidori (John O'Hurley) – the name providing knowing viewers a shout-out to Lord Byron's personal physician, John William Polidori – a white-coated genetic engineer whom Mulder refers to as 'Dr Frankenstein'. The episode is permeated with similar literary allusions and inside jokes, but Whale's film lies at the heart of this adjacent adaptation.

Like 'Some Assembly Required', this *X-Files* episode reveals itself to be primarily an adjacent adaptation of *The Bride of Frankenstein*, with Dr Polidori's creation of the Creature again taking place in an inferred past, a reading process possible only because of the almost universal familiarity viewers have with Whale's films. The events presented in 'The Post-Modern Prometheus' also engage the ethical obligations of a creator towards his creation, specifically the desire of the monster to have a companion of his own. At the climax of the episode, Dr Polidori whips the townspeople into an angry mob – complete with flaming torches, despite the episode's contemporary setting – seeking the death of the so-called monster.[6] They set a barn on fire, recalling the burning windmill at the climax of *Frankenstein* (1931), before discovering the tragic Mutato (Chris Owens), the two-faced Creature born from Dr Polidori's genetic experiments years before. Yet, as in Shelley's novel, Mutato reveals himself to be an articulate Creature, educated by eavesdropping on the private lives of others. He explains how Polidori's father (Lloyd Barry) had pitied him and raised him as his own son, and now, after years of study, the old man has attempted to follow in his son's footsteps to create a companion for Mutato. Like Eric from *Buffy the Vampire Slayer*, the elder Polidori mirrors Whale's Dr Pretorius by facilitating Mutato's covert impregnation of two women in the town.

The myriad intertextual elements of 'The Post-Modern Prometheus' transform the episode into a kind of intertextual game, one that provides viewers with satisfaction

Figure 6.2 David Duchovney and Gillian Anderson as Fox Mulder and Dana Scully in season 8 of *The X Files*.

and delight as they recognise the many quotations and allusions to the Frankenstein Network and other popular texts. The episode's title, many of its characters, and the general theme all harken back to Shelley's *Frankenstein*, and its visual style, some of its characters, and many of its punch lines overtly reference the Universal Studios cadre of *Frankenstein* films.[7] Of course, the episode is also part of *The X-Files* series, but its overt post-modernity makes it an anomalous text that can be read as an adaptation of the series itself. Mulder is frustrated by the resolution of the case, equating it with both the *Great Mutato* comic book and with Shelley's novel, and he demands to 'speak to the writer'. 'The Post-Modern Prometheus' then ends abruptly with an unexpected happy resolution at a Cher concert, and the action freezes with an illustrated panel featuring Scully and Mulder dancing. Did the events of the episode even take place, or were they adapted or invented by Izzy in his comic book? Whereas 'Some Assembly Required' draws from a limited number of antecedent texts, achieving Hutcheon's 'doubled pleasure of the palimpsest' with a relatively small palette, 'The Post-Modern Prometheus' takes a different approach to adjacent adaptation. This *X-Files* episode opens itself up to a variety of readings and interpretations by taking the narrative potential of adjacent adaptation even further, allowing the multiple hypotextual influences of Demory's tapestry to manifest, gloriously, in one densely woven, hyperconcentrated narrative.

Doctor Who meets Frankenstein

Two episodes from *Doctor Who* serve as contrasting case studies for how a series can intersect with the same source material multiple times with dramatically different results, thus demonstrating the value of approaching such texts as adjacent adaptations. One version of this adjacent adaptation engages primarily with *Frankenstein*'s cinematic tradition, adapting visual elements and basic plot structure; the other returns to Shelley's source material and is more invested in the story's themes and ideological messages. While both of these episodes can be enjoyed as isolated adventures in the ongoing series of *Doctor Who* adventures, an awareness and understanding of the intersecting, adjacent source material make the stories all the more pleasurable. Like a beloved and easily recognisable guest star – a common feature of serialised television – the identifiable presence of themes, characters, tropes, and plot devices from *Frankenstein*, along with a number of additional intertextual references and homages, affords viewers both satisfying 'ah ha' moments and a richer comprehension of the complex narratives presented. Successful attempts at adjacent adaptation, such as these from *Doctor Who*, not only function as narrative shorthand for artists working in a truncated medium, but also remind us of the joy and play of intertextual storytelling.

Doctor Who's first overt intersection with the Frankenstein Complex came in 1976 with 'The Brain of Morbius', a series written by Terrance Dicks and Robert Holmes[8] and directed by Christopher Barry, which aired over the course of four weekly episodes from 3 to 24 January. The adventure pits the fourth Doctor (Tom Baker) and his companion, Sarah Jane Smith (Elisabeth Sladen), against a megalomaniacal scientist named Solon (Philip Madoc), who is trying to assemble a complete body from disparate alien parts. Although the serial makes no direct reference to *Frankenstein*, it is nonetheless replete with readily identifiable allusions and connections. Shelley's story is admittedly somewhat simplified as the episode develops more generically what Noël Carroll calls the 'overreacher plot' of horror, which focuses on a mad scientist who is 'concerned with forbidden knowledge' (118). Whale's *Frankenstein*, however, not only gives shape to the story but also provides the savvy viewer with the pleasure of recognising the adapted portions and making rewarding intertexual connections. In fact, an awareness of all the assembled textual sources and inspirations is necessary for viewers to understand the full scope of this story arc.

The opening scene of the first episode establishes this tonal focus as an insectoid monster, presented in the harsh lighting of Gothic cinema, crawls from a futuristic landing pod. The score is brooding and sinister, and the sounds of wind and booming thunder add to the soundtrack's horror-movie atmosphere. The sequence also introduces the hook-handed Condo (Colin Fay), a dim-witted and hunched figure who assists Solon. After Condo attacks the insectoid with a knife, the scene cuts to a key symbol of the episode: a head – the sculpted head of a man, to be precise – worked in clay by Solon. Condo bursts into the room, a chaotic set evocative of a German

Figure 6.3 Elisabeth Sladen as Sarah Jane Smith and Tom Baker as *Doctor Who*.

expressionist film, bearing the decapitated head of the marooned alien. In an anatomi-
cal parallel to Whale's film, in which Fritz (Dwight Frey) botches his assignment to
obtain the perfect brain for his master's creation, the obsessive focus of this *Frankenstein*
tale is cranial, as Solon seeks the correct head to fulfil his yet-to-be-revealed purposes.

This reductive *Frankenstein* plot quickly intersects with and weaves into another,
that of the ongoing adventures of the Doctor and his companion. The iconic TARDIS
materialises on the hostile world of Karn, and the Doctor energetically bursts forth,
shouting at the heavens as he accuses the Time Lords of again forcing him to do their
bidding, the primary focus of the season's collection of stories. The more optimistic
Sarah Jane explores their surroundings, discovering dozens of crashed spaceships and

the decapitated corpse of the insectoid creature. While the otherworldly landscape, unfamiliar locale, and host of spaceships and aliens overtly code 'The Brain of Morbius' in terms of *Doctor Who*'s traditional science-fiction genre, the Doctor and Sarah Jane have also found themselves in the middle of a Gothic narrative. Indeed, they make their way to an isolated castle in the distance, like two stranded wayfarers, and Solon welcomes them enthusiastically into his crypt-like hall – taking special note of the Doctor's fine-looking head.

Thanks to the adjacent adaptation, viewers already recognise Solon as an evil madman who will inevitably betray the Doctor. Over a flagon of drugged wine, Solon spins a web of lies concerning Karn and the crashed spaceships outside his castle, but he lets some truth slip as well. Solon is human, and famous enough for his work in neuroscience and tissue transplantation for the Doctor to have heard of him. Quite nonchalantly, the Doctor recalls rumours that Solon had joined the followers of the Cult of Morbius, a group dedicated to 'one of the most despicable, criminally minded wretches that ever lived'.[9] Morbius, a Time Lord executed on Karn for leading an unsuccessful rebellion, is the real focus of Solon's obsession. Like Victor Frankenstein, hubris drives Solon, who sees his efforts to transplant Morbius's preserved brain into the Doctor's head as his 'great triumph', one that will be remembered for thousands of years. 'Any third-rate hack can fix an arm,' he later tells the simpering Condo. 'But a head, the centre of the nervous system, that takes more than just skill. That takes genius.' This speech recalls the egotistical ranting of Shelley's Victor, who tells Walton, 'Life and death appeared to me ideal bounds, which I should first break through.... A new species would bless me as its creator and source' (33). Both men seek not only scientific greatness, but also a long-lasting legacy. In an inversion of *Frankenstein*, however, 'The Brain of Morbius' rewrites the original creation story: we later learn that the Creature is driving its own creation process and controlling Solon psychically from beyond the grave, as it were, making Morbius's brain both Frankenstein and the Creature at the same time.

The recognition of the series as an adjacent adaptation also reveals the clever character inversions and mashups from the Frankenstein Network that occur in 'The Brain of Morbius', opening the narrative up to a more sophisticated, pleasurable viewing experience for viewers familiar with a spectrum of other *Frankenstein* adaptations. For example, in addition to filling a narrative and stylistic role akin to Whale's Fritz, Condo often acts in the capacity of Frankenstein's Creature as well. He is tall, looming above Solon, and walks with a plodding, heavy-footed gait. And he speaks in broken sentences, almost as if he has just learned English. Yet, whereas Frankenstein's Creature demands a female companion, Condo seeks the reattachment of his amputated arm, a 'carrot' Solon has used to ensure Condo's continued obedience.[10] Sarah Jane shifts in her referential roles as well. When Solon sends Condo after the Doctor's typically resourceful and clever companion, Sarah Jane begins to act like Whale's Elizabeth (Mae Clarke), a defenceless young woman menaced by a hulking, stuttering beast. Suddenly – but not unexpectedly, for the knowing viewer – Condo sees in

Sarah Jane a potential mate and companion. And then, once Solon has tied Sarah Jane to his laboratory table, she takes on the ambiguity of the Bride (Elsa Lanchester) from *The Bride of Frankenstein*, a woman on a gurney who might be the Creature's intended mate, but then again, perhaps the mad scientist's instead. These episodes exemplify one of the real values of adjacent adaptation. The complicated plot described here is aided by the fact that the pre-existing *Frankenstein* elements used in this episode ensure that ostensibly 'new' characters are actually familiar to the audience, and appear more complex and well rounded than they otherwise would.

As the story comes to its conclusion, key elements from the Frankenstein Network complete the adjacent adaptation as an integrated part of the *Doctor Who* series; in other words, this one episode must be read as the synergistic combination of *both* of its primary antecedents. Morbius's brain grows desperate and demands that Solon install him in the patchwork body immediately. Before the operation can begin, however, Condo sees that his amputated arm has been attached to the Creature, and turns on his master. They scuffle, and, in the chaos, Condo knocks Morbius's brain onto the floor, an outcome perhaps expected by fans of Whale's film, in which Fritz drops and ruins the brain Frankenstein really wanted. Solon nonetheless attaches Morbius's brain to the monstrous body, and, using a mysterious electrical process evocative of that depicted by Whale, Solon gives life to his creation. Thanks to the damage to his brain, however, Morbius is little more than a rampaging monster, incapable of speech or fine-motor coordination. Solon manages to sedate the beast with a tranquilliser dart, and embarks on another operation to 'fix' the damaged brain, two notable plot points perhaps drawn from Mel Brooks's *Young Frankenstein* (1974), another landmark film in the Frankenstein Network. Restored mentally, a transformation reminiscent of both Shelley's novel and Brooks's film, Morbius lurches from the gurney and demonstrates his regained powers of speech as he controls his 'mongrel' body, one designed for efficiency if not aesthetics.

Of course, since this adaptation of *Frankenstein* is one merely adjacent to the main *Doctor Who* series, Morbius must eventually be bested by the Doctor, and his defeat occurs in two intertextual ways. Departing from the various *Frankenstein* antecedents in favour of a science-fiction resolution more in line with most *Doctor Who* episodes, the Doctor challenges the resurrected Morbius to a contest of mental prowess. Using a Time Lord device, the two engage psychically until the Doctor is rendered unconscious and Morbius's brain fumes with smoke. The fate of the Creature is then sealed with a return to Whale's film plot. The local 'Sisterhood of Karn', wanting justice of their own, brandishing torches like an angry mob of villagers, pursue the disoriented Creature to the top of a cliff and force it over the edge. With all the conflicts of the *Frankenstein* plot neatly resolved, the Doctor and Sarah Jane can depart in the TARDIS, ready for another adventure. These Frankenstein-inspired episodes from *Doctor Who*'s original run may primarily recreate portions from the first half of Shelley's novel, but, as illustrated above, they draw upon additional elements from other adaptations of *Frankenstein*. Such heavy intertextuality takes advantage of audience familiarity with those intersectional texts to provide a secondary plot that enhances the primary story-line of *Doctor Who*, with little or no exposition needed.

This savvy exploitation of texts from the Frankenstein Network arises again in a more recent adjacent adaptation episode that focuses, appropriately enough, on the latter part of Shelley's narrative, and a viewer's familiarity with that part of the novel allows for more sophisticated avenues of textual interpretation. Chris Baldick points out that, for most readers of Shelley's original *Frankenstein*, the 'most challenging effect comes from the reversal of sympathies demanded by the monster's narrative' (183), and 'A Town Called Mercy' (2012) focuses not just on the creation of the monster but also the ethical responsibilities of its creator. Inspired more by the novel than any of the films, 'A Town Called Mercy', written by Toby Whithouse and directed by Saul Metzstein, recreates the outermost frame of Shelley's nested narrative, casting the Doctor (Matt Smith) in the role of Walton, a sympathetic listener to the Frankenstein figure's tragic tale. As with 'The Brain of Morbius', this episode is highly intertextual, a palimpsest with one of its key elements coming from the conventions of an estab-lished genre – this time, though, not 1930s Gothic film, but the classic Hollywood Western. The intermixing of *Doctor Who* Season 7, Shelley's *Frankenstein*, and Western films such as *High Noon* (1952), in particular, creates an amalgam or assemblage that transcends its individual parts.[11]

As with 'The Brain of Morbius', 'A Town Called Mercy' begins with recognisable elements from the *Frankenstein* narrative, adding the Doctor's storyline only after the opening credits sequence. Voice-over narration (Lorelei King) recalls the childhood story of 'a man who lived forever, but whose eyes were heavy with the weight of all he'd seen'. This legendary figure is revealed to be a violent and merciless gunslinger (Andrew Brooke), a cowboy hat-wearing cyborg with a futuristic Gatling gun for a right hand. The voice-over imitates Shelley's Gothic frame narrative, establishing this Frankenstein tale in terms similar to a 'true story', events that have already taken place and are therefore 'real'. After the opening sequence, the narrative cuts suddenly to the Doctor and his companions, Amy (Karen Gillan) and Rory (Arthur Darvill), who stand on the edge of the old-West town of Mercy. As with Walton's ship in the novel, Mercy is isolated and cut off from civilisation; in fact, the town is encircled by a barrier of stones and wood, a symbolic border analogous to the ice sheets surrounding Walton's vessel in the Arctic (Shelley 13). While not an overt adaptation, the episode nonetheless signals from the outset that it will be engaging with Shelley's novel at least adjacently.

As with readers of Shelley's novel, viewers of 'A Town Called Mercy' likely feel that they have been dropped into the middle of a pre-existing narrative, albeit one familiar to fans of *Frankenstein*. Isaac, the town sheriff (Ben Browder), explains to the Doctor how the mysterious Gunslinger simply showed up and enclosed the town in its makeshift border. Like Walton's ship, Mercy can't receive any supplies or reinforce-ments; however, the townsfolk of Mercy know of the Creature that menaces them from without – 'a being which had the shape of a man, but apparently of gigantic

Figure 6.4 Matt Smith as the Doctor and Karen Gillian as Amy Pond in the seventh series of *Doctor Who*.

stature' (Shelley 13) – a vengeful monster demanding the life of its creator. As with the other adjacent adaptations considered in this chapter, 'A Town Called Mercy' focuses on an 'overreacher plot', particularly the 'shortsightedness of science' (Carroll 118). The 'mad scientist' of this iteration is the gifted surgeon Kahler-Jex (Adrian Scarborough), an alien hiding in Mercy from the Gunslinger, who has pursued him across the stars. The Doctor seeks out Jex's spaceship and learns that the Gunslinger is a cyborg, one of many created by Jex to function as a weapon in a devastating civil war. After the war ended, the super soldiers were shut down. But one – the Gunslinger – defied his programming and went on a murderous rampage, pursuing and killing all the scientists involved in the cyborg programme until only Jex was left.

'A Town Called Mercy' is thus an ideal case study for the adjacent adaptation, as it interweaves three primary textual threads: the overreacher plot of *Frankenstein*, the long-arc storyline of *Doctor Who*, and the generic traditions of the Hollywood Western.[12] The Doctor, enraged by Jex's war crimes, drags the scientist out of town and allows the Gunslinger to threaten Jex with death. At the last minute, though, Isaac, personifying the name of the town he is sworn to protect, throws himself between the two antagonists as a willing sacrifice and receives the killing blast meant for Jex. As the Gunslinger appears to mourn his murder of an innocent, Isaac confers the office of sheriff upon the Doctor, who has a change of heart and sends Jex to a jail cell instead. The Gunslinger, however, like Shelley's monster, is myopically focused on vengeance and the destruction of his misguided creator, and, as in *High Noon*, he presents the Doctor with an ultimatum: turn Jex over by noon or the entire town will be destroyed.

The remorseful scientist later articulates much of Victor Frankenstein's moral quandary as a protagonist: 'Do you think I'm unaffected by what I did? That I don't hear them screaming every time I close my eyes? It would be so much simpler if I was just one thing, wouldn't it? The mad scientist who made that killing machine or the physician who's dedicated his life to serving this town. The fact that I'm both bewilders you.' This speech recalls Frankenstein's obstinate words of defence and justification to Walton. After describing his destruction of the female he was creating for the monster's mate, he explains,

> During these last days I have been occupied in examining my past conduct; nor do I find it blameable. In a fit of enthusiastic madness I created a rational creature, and was bound towards him, to assure, as far as was in my power, his happiness and well-being. This was my duty; but there was another still paramount to that. My duties towards my fellow-creatures.... I refused, and I did right in refusing. (Shelley 157)

Unlike Walton, however, Doctor Who sees the larger problem with the cycle of creation and destruction playing out before him. 'Violence doesn't end violence – it extends it,' the Doctor observes sagely, in words that accurately sum up at least one of the themes of Shelley's novel.

The palimpsestuous nature of the episode's disparate sources causes the generic elements from all three to be consistently redefined and undermined. For example, although the townsfolk form a lynch mob and show up at the jail in the middle of the night, the Doctor, rather than resorting to a gun, uses logic and reason to defuse the situation. The Gunslinger's crossing of the barrier at high noon fulfils another expectation established by Western cinema, but this iteration sees a community rally together to protect the outsider. In fact, the ubiquitous gunfight never happens, and a happy ending is promised to loyal *Doctor Who* fans. Yet 'A Town Called Mercy' has a few more twists in store for its audience. Instead of simply fleeing the planet safely while the Gunslinger is occupied in town, Jex uses the communication system on his ship to talk with his vengeful cyborg creation, asking him about his almost-forgotten home world:

JEX: When this is over, will you go back?
GUNSLINGER: How can I? I am a monster now.
JEX: So am I.

In other words, this Frankenstein recognises his guilt and his own monstrousness, and, like Shelley's Victor before him, realises that the Creature will never abandon his quest for vengeance. Only Frankenstein's death ends the cycle of murder and destruction in the novel when it renders the Creature's vengeance unnecessary, and Jex seems to realise that only his death will satisfy the Gunslinger. He thus initiates the self-destruct sequence on his craft, killing himself, an act of contrition and honour that prevents the Gunslinger from murdering anyone else. Robbed of his prey, the cyborg attempts to walk off into the desert and self-destruct, much as Shelley's Creature does among the frozen wastelands of the Arctic (161). However, because this is an episode of *Doctor Who*, this version of *Frankenstein* ends much differently. The Doctor convinces the Gunslinger to become a protector of peace instead of an agent of war. The Gunslinger accepts Isaac's badge and becomes the secret, hidden defender of Mercy, the legendary figure spoken of by the episode's initial voice-over narration. The adjacent narratives allow viewers to understand the themes and tropes presented by this episode of *Doctor Who*, but the larger series insists on rewriting those sources, partly for its own continuity, and partly to express new themes and ideas.

Frankenstein has become such a powerful narrative influence in modern culture that its repeated appearances not only impact on our reception of the original text, but also result in important variations to existing texts and narratives. In fact, the plot, themes, characters, tropes, and motifs of the Frankenstein Network, and of our own Frankenstein Complexes, have become necessary points of inspiration expected to appear alongside otherwise unique and independent long-arc narratives. Just as practically every Renaissance artist painted the Madonna and Child, the showrunners of most science-fiction, fantasy, and horror television serials take their turn at the *Frankenstein* narrative, developing their own variations adjacent to their individual shows that are also part of a larger text system of *Frankenstein* adaptations. Whereas most traditional adaptations represent singular events – source material adapted as a stand-alone book, play, film, or made-for-TV movie – adjacent adaptations are mimetic variations on a theme that not only replicate a source text, but also multiply those replications. Adjacent adaptations such as these cause waves to ripple throughout popular culture, each influencing the next and becoming part of a complex, intertextual overlapping of variations on the theme. *Frankenstein* itself has become a meme, and, like all great memes, it will continue to replicate itself through repetition, variation, and post-modern self-referentiality.

Notes

1 Wikipedia has an entire entry, '*Frankenstein* in Popular Culture', dedicated to adaptations of and references to *Frankenstein*, including ten stage productions, nine radio dramas, twenty-eight musical compositions, nineteen novels, fifty-three films, twenty-three parodies, and, most relevant to this discussion, a whopping seventy-two adaptations, versions, or references on television.

2 Other examples of *Frankenstein* being adapted adjacent to existing television story arcs include 'Time Is on My Side' (2008) from *Supernatural* (2005–), 'Marionette' (2010) from *Fringe* (2008–13), and both 'The Doctor' (2012) and 'In the Name of the Brother' (2013) from *Once Upon a Time* (2011–), not to mention most of the fourth season of *Buffy the Vampire Slayer*. A more involved example of this kind of adaptation exists with *Star Trek: The Next Generation* (1987–94), which integrates elements from *Frankenstein* throughout its entire run via the character of Data (Brent Spiner), a sympathetic 'Creature' who repeatedly confronts his absentee creator and wrestles with issues of his own ambiguous humanity.

3 Chris Baldick thoroughly catalogues and analyses many of the source materials that likely influenced Shelley in the construction of her own literary 'creature' in his 'Assembling *Frankenstein*'.

4 As that film begins Frankenstein's Creature is complete except for its brain.

5 Airing just two months after 'Some Assembly Required', the *X-Files* version of *Frankenstein* had clearly been developed simultaneously with, and therefore could not have been influenced by or an adaptation of, the *Buffy the Vampire Slayer* episode.

6 Dr Polidori's role thus shifts from one that resembles Frankenstein, to that of Inspector Krogh (Lionel Atwill) from *Son of Frankenstein* (1939), or even to Mel Brooks's parody of him, Inspector Kemp (Kenneth Mars), from *Young Frankenstein* (1974). These shifting roles compound the episode's clever intertextuality.

7 'The Post-Modern Prometheus' also evokes the sideshow, yet another intertextual inspiration, primarily through the intermittent use of carnival music on its soundtrack – and perhaps more specifically invoking MGM's *Freaks* (Browning 1932) with its horror/sideshow setting. The repeated references to *The Jerry Springer Show* (1991–97) suggest another intertext. Springer even appears as himself briefly in the episode. And the implication at the end is that many of the townsfolk may actually be the result of Dr Polidori's human–animal genetic experiments, perhaps a reference to Wells's *Island of Dr Moreau*.

8 While Dicks wrote the original teleplay, it was heavily revised and rewritten by script editor Holmes, resulting in the episode arc being formally attributed to the fictitious 'Robin Bland' because Dicks considered Holmes's work so 'bland' (Gallagher).

9 In yet another strand of the episode's thick tapestry of intertextuality, the name 'Morbius' recalls the mad scientist from *Forbidden Planet* (1956), directed by Fred McLeod Wilcox and starring Walter Pidgeon as Dr Morbius.

10 This plot element is quite similar to a subplot of Hammer Films' *The Revenge of Frankenstein* (1958), directed by Terence Fisher, in which the hunchbacked assistant, Karl (Michael Gwynn), helps the 'good' doctor motivated by the promise of a new, healthy body.

11 We might also add *Robocop* (1987), itself a fixture in the Frankenstein Network, to this list. For more on my conception of texts as potential assemblages of a number of pre-existing narrative sources – like Frankenstein's Creature itself – see 'Assemblage Filmmaking'.

12   The Western setting was perhaps employed to aid in the marketing of the serial to a US
audience, but it is certainly a fitting backdrop for a vengeance narrative.

Bibliography

Albrecht-Crane, Christa and Dennis Cutchins, eds. *Adaptation Studies: New Approaches*. Madison,
NJ: Fairleigh Dickinson UP, 2010.

Baldick, Chris. 'Assembling *Frankenstein.*' In Frankenstein's *Shadow: Myth, Monstrosity, and
Nineteenth-Century Writing*. New York: Oxford UP, 1987. 33–44. Hunter 173–183.

Bishop, Kyle William. 'Assemblage Filmmaking: Approaching the Multi-Source Adaptation and
Reexamining Romero's Night of the Living Dead.' Albrecht-Crane and Cutchins. 263–277.

'The Brain of Morbius.' Writ. Robin Bland [Terrance Dicks and Robert Holmes]. Dir.
Christopher Barry. BBC, 3–24 January 1976. *Doctor Who: The Brain of Morbius*. BBC Home
Entertainment, 2008.

Brooks, Mel, dir. *Young Frankenstein*. Writs. Gene Wilder and Mel Brooks. Gruskoff/Venture
Films, 1973. 20th Century Fox, 2006.

Carroll, Noël. *The Philosophy of Horror or Paradoxes of the Heart*. New York: Routledge, 1990.

Culler, Jonathan. *Structural Poetics: Structuralism, Linguistics, and the Study of Literature*. Ithaca,
NY: Cornell UP, 1975.

Demory, Pamela. 'Jane Austen and the Chick Flick in the Twenty-First Century.' Albrecht-
Crane and Cutchins 121–149.

Gallagher, William. '*Doctor Who*'s Secret History of Codenames Revealed.' *RadioTimes* 27
March 2012.

Hunter, J. Paul, ed. *Frankenstein*. Norton Critical Edition. New York: Norton, 2012.

Hutcheon, Linda. *A Theory of Adaptation*. New York: Routledge, 2006.

Lee, Rowland V., Dir. *Son of Frankenstein*. Writ. Wyllis Cooper. Universal Pictures, 1939.
Frankenstein: The Legacy Collection. Universal Studios, 2004.

Leitch, Thomas. 'The Ethics of Infidelity.' Albrecht-Crane and Cutchins. 61–77.

'The Post-Modern Prometheus.' Writ. and dir. Chris Carter. 20th Century Fox Television,
30 November 1997. *The X-Files: Season 5*. 20th Century Fox Home Entertainment, 2006.

Shelley, Mary. *Frankenstein*. 1818. Hunter 1–161.

———. 'Introduction to *Frankenstein*, Third Edition (1931).' Hunter 165–169.

'Some Assembly Required.' Writ. David Tyron King. Dir. Bruce Seth Green. Mutant Enemy,
22. September 1997. *Buffy the Vampire Slayer – The Complete Second Season*. WB Television
Network, 2006.

Stam, Robert. 'Beyond Fidelity: The Dialogics of Adaptation.' *Film Adaptation*. Ed. James
Naremore. New Brunswick, NJ: Rutgers UP, 2000. 54–76.

'A Town Called Mercy.' Writ. Toby Whithouse. Dir. Saul Metzstein. BBC, 15 September
2012. *Doctor Who: Series Seven – Part One*. BBC Home Entertainment, 2012.

Whale, James, dir. *Frankenstein*. Writ. Garrett Fort and Francis Edward Faragoh. Universal
Pictures, 1931. Frankenstein: The Legacy Collection. Universal Studios, 2004.

———, dir. *The Bride of Frankenstein*. Writ. William Hurlbut, et al. Universal Pictures, 1935.
Frankenstein: The Legacy Collection. Universal Studios, 2004.

7

The new ethics of *Frankenstein*: responsibility and obedience in *I, Robot* and *X-Men: First Class*

Matt Lorenz

WHILE FILMS AND TV shows such as *Frankenweenie* (2012), *I, Frankenstein* (2014), and *Penny Dreadful* (2014) adapt, revise, and extend Mary Shelley's *Frankenstein* (1818) for the screen, with notable differences in mood and message, other films echo and expand on Shelley's classic tale of creation gone awry in ways that are more indirect and unexpected. In a sense, these indirect adaptations have more freedom to complicate and modernise Shelley's text, since they transpose her characters and conflicts into fresh contexts with multiple variations. In the films *I, Robot* (2004), directed by Alex Proyas, and *X-Men: First Class* (2011), directed by Matthew Vaughn, the concept of creation, one of the key concepts in Shelley's novel, expands from its common definition (creation out of nothing or out of diverse pre-existing parts) to a broader sense that includes modification or influence. These films portray the figures of creator and creation in various incarnations, some predictably malevolent or misguided, and others far more conflicted and difficult to label in ethical terms. Each film affirms its membership in what Dennis Cutchins and Dennis R. Perry call the 'Frankenstein Network', while posing and answering ethical questions that hover at the margins of or receive opposing answers in Shelley's influential novel. In so doing, both films challenge and extend Shelley's implicit assumptions about the ethics of creation and createdness.

In *I, Robot*, the Frankenstein figure, Dr Alfred Lanning (James Cromwell), co-founds U.S. Robots and Mechanical Men (USR) and is responsible for not one but three significant creations. His first, V.I.K.I. (Fiona Hogan), plays the role of the traditional inhumane and powerful creature, whose name is an acronym for Virtual Interactive Kinetic Intelligence. His second is Detective Del Spooner (Will Smith), a techno-phobic policeman whom Lanning has robotically enhanced against Spooner's will after Spooner was injured on the job. And finally Lanning creates Sonny (Alan Tudyk), a robot who is capable of feeling, dreaming, and defying laws that other robots must follow. With each creation – the first created out of nothing, the second a modification of the human body, and the third a modification of robotic principles – the film's Frankenstein figure attempts to correct his earlier miscalculations. In the film's climax, Spooner and Sonny struggle to carry out the wishes of their creator, and Sonny must decide whether to accept V.I.K.I.'s 'undeniable logic' or reject it as 'heartless'.

In *X-Men: First Class*, by contrast, the creators are multiplied, instead of the creatures. One creator is incarnated in the figure of Sebastian Shaw (Kevin Bacon), who 'creates' his monster, the future Magneto, Erik Lehnsherr (Michael Fassbender), through a cruel manipulation that reveals Lehnsherr's mutant powers. Yet Lehnsherr comes under the influence of a second creator, Charles Xavier (James McAvoy), who pushes him toward a more generous ethical attitude and who is eventually placed in the difficult position of choosing between the death of the Frankenstein figure or of Frankenstein's creation.

The relationships of both of these films to the Frankenstein Network are not simple, however. In addition to their own thematic elements, both films also enter the Network through other artistic works that are, themselves, indebted to Shelley, and these removes from the original source text provide the makers of each film with a degree of creative flexibility. While the film version of *I, Robot* is loosely adapted from Isaac Asimov's 1950 collection of short stories that goes by the same name, *X-Men: First Class* is loosely adapted from the *X-Men* comics, which were created by writer Stan Lee and artist Jack Kirby and later extended by numerous writers and artists who created sequels that enlarged the Marvel universe. Asimov and Lee were each, however, influenced by Shelley, and the screenwriters of *I, Robot* and *X-Men: First Class* owe a creative debt not only to Shelley but also to Asimov and Lee, even as they have creatively reinterpreted and expanded their source texts.

While *Frankenweenie*, *Penny Dreadful*, and *I, Frankenstein* each have characters named Victor Frankenstein who animate lifeless corpses, *I, Robot* and *X-Men: First Class* have neither characters named Frankenstein nor reanimated corpses and acknowledge their debt to Shelley's novel only in passing. In a way, this indirect approach to *Frankenstein* provides these films with greater latitude to portray the themes and character conflicts that Shelley introduces, allowing these films to adumbrate a number of latent questions that Shelley's influential novel never fully articulates.

I, Robot

Both Asimov's collection of short stories and Jeff Vintar's and Akiva Goldsman's screenplay explicitly acknowledge that *I, Robot* is a member of the Frankenstein Network. Asimov's reference to the Frankenstein Complex appears in 'Little Lost Robot' (1947), a short story that he would later include in *I, Robot* (1950). In that story the world-renowned robopsychologist Dr Susan Calvin learns that a colleague and mathematician, Dr Peter Bogert, has modified the First Law of Robotics, which states that 'no robot may harm a human being or, through inaction, allow a human being to come to harm' (Asimov 431). Calvin is appalled, explaining that the First Law is the only thing that prevents robots from feeling resentment over their domination by humans, whom they view as mentally and physically inferior (433). In response to her concern, Bogert replies, 'Susan, I'll admit that this Frankenstein Complex you're exhibiting has a certain justification – hence the First Law in the first place. But the Law, I repeat and repeat, has not been removed – merely modified' (434). In this exchange, Asimov pits a condescending, over-confident Bogert who, like the young Victor Frankenstein, creates without thought of the consequences, against a more circumspect robopsychologist, Calvin, who, like the older Frankenstein in Shelley's novel, sees that creations can advance beyond the control of their creators.

The 2004 film depicts a similar disagreement. Det. Del Spooner and his superior officer, Lt. John Bergin (Chi McBride), are discussing the recent misbehaviour or malfunction of a robot that seems to have been modified. Like Calvin, Spooner is concerned that the robot is dangerous; like Bogert, Bergin thinks that Spooner is being too paranoid. During Spooner's interrogation, the robot, which calls itself 'Sonny', says and does a number of things that make Spooner and the audience suspicious. Sonny calls Lanning his 'father', for instance, claims that he is capable of dreaming, and exhibits signs of fear, anger, and regret. Interrupting these revelations, Lawrence Robertson (Bruce Greenwood), the powerful head of USR after Lanning's death, stops the interrogation and reclaims Sonny with the support of the mayor of Chicago, dismissing Lanning's death as an 'industrial accident.' Afterwards, Spooner and Bergin recap these events over beers:

> Lt. John Bergin: You know, I was just thinking. This thing is just like *The Wolf Man*.
> Det. Del Spooner: Uh oh, I'm really scared right now.
> Lt. John Bergin: No, listen. Guy creates monster. Monster kills guy. Everybody kills monster ... Wolf Man.
> Det. Del Spooner: That's *Frankenstein*.
> Lt. John Bergin: *Frankenstein*, *Wolf Man*, *Dracula* – shit, it's over. Case closed.

The reference to *Frankenstein* works here, in part, because it seems off-hand. Although Bergin concedes that Sonny might be responsible for Lanning's death, he is also saying that Spooner needs to stop pursuing the case, since, according to the law, only human beings can be charged with crimes. Bergin isn't as trusting of robots as Asimov's Bogert, but he also isn't as appalled by Sonny's behaviour as Spooner, whose reason for being suspicious of robots has not yet been revealed.

These references to predecessors in the Frankenstein Network provide a useful point of entry for an analysis of the film *I, Robot*. The 'Frankenstein Complex' to which the scientist Bogert alludes is precisely what motivates Lanning's actions and Spooner's psychological fear of misguided creations. And this fear finds an aesthetic corollary in the 'Frankenstein Complex' that Cutchins and Perry describe as 'the personal idea of Frankenstein that each of us carries within'. Although the plot that Bergin outlines ('Guy creates monster. Monster kills guy. Everybody kills monster') technically occurs in neither Shelley's nor Whale's *Frankenstein*, it does occur in *I, Robot* in multiple forms and with striking variations.

The logical place to begin this analysis is with the creator. Spooner is the main character of the film, and the second lead is none other than a young Dr Susan Calvin (Bridget Moynahan), a newly minted robopsychologist who is far more obtuse and pliant than the aged, acerbic Calvin who appears in Asimov's stories. However, Spooner is often merely the mouthpiece of a ghostly figure who holds the key to the film's mysteries and who serves as an incarnation of Jung's Wise Old Man archetype. In Dr Alfred Lanning, *I, Robot* presents viewers with a very different Frankenstein figure – one who appears to be not only far more sensitive than Victor Frankenstein to the uncontrollable mysteries that endow his creations with consciousness (mysteries that Lanning describes as 'ghosts in the machine'), but also far more willing than Frankenstein to remedy his own wrongs by creating additional creatures who will correct the situation. Consequently, Lanning's creations exhibit strikingly different levels of obedience to their creator. This, in turn, invites viewers to ponder the developing parenting techniques of the creator as well as the varying responsibilities to the creator that each of his creations feels.

Lanning's death sets the plot of the film in motion, and throughout the film he appears only in found video footage and in the holographic program he has left behind so that Spooner can ask him specific questions in an attempt to solve the mystery. Spooner's first conclusion – that Sonny is somehow involved in Lanning's death – ends up being correct. Yet his underlying assumption – that Sonny is the 'bad guy' – proves incorrect. Sonny has not murdered Lanning; he has helped Lanning to commit suicide. Lanning's decision to commit suicide is motivated by his knowledge that this is the only message he can send to alert people – particularly, Spooner – of what is about to happen. Like many mysteries, this one is resolved through a gradual widening of the lens. First, viewers are invited to accept Lanning's death as a suicide. Spooner's suspicions and general distrust of robots then lead them to suspect Sonny. When Lawrence Robertson interrupts Sonny's interrogation and carts the robot away for decommissioning, viewers begin to suspect that Sonny might be part of or a distraction from a larger conspiracy, masterminded by Robertson. Finally the audience learns that Spooner is not merely a sarcastic detective who distrusts robots; he is part robot himself. His back story reveals that he was in a nearly fatal car accident, and that a robot pulled him from the wreckage instead of saving the young girl whom he told the robot to save. His police contract stipulated that his recuperation would involve robotic enhancement, and Dr Lanning, in engineering these enhancements, became a kind of father figure to him. Suddenly, the audience is faced with two possibilities: either Spooner's bias toward his father figure and against robots has led him to incorrectly conclude that Lanning's death was a murder, or Lanning's death did involve foul play and USR is somehow to blame for it. The answer to this either/or question arrives with the final widening of the lens: Lanning did not merely create Sonny or Spooner; he also created V.I.K.I., the mainframe for USR, as well as for the city of Chicago and networked areas throughout the United States. Shortly before his death Lanning learned that V.I.K.I. was about to orchestrate a revolution against human domination. To prevent him from warning authorities, V.I.K.I. made Lanning a prisoner in his home and workplace, and he decided that his own very public death (he leaps dozens of storeys to the main lobby of the USR building), along with the holographic program he left for Spooner, would be the only way to circumvent V.I.K.I.'s plans. Before committing suicide, however, Lanning made sure that his creations, Sonny and Spooner, would slow or stop the actions of his previous creation, V.I.K.I.

In Proyas's *I, Robot*, V.I.K.I. is the creation who most resembles Frankenstein's Creature. Highly logical, she never succumbs to rage or despair the way Frankenstein's Creature does, yet she does turn on her creator and on the world into which he has brought her. What the audience learns only at the end of the film is that V.I.K.I.'s understanding of the Three Laws of Robotics has 'evolved' in such a way that she believes the only way to protect humankind is to take control of society and create a police state in which robots will be charged with keeping order. When Calvin says to V.I.K.I., 'You're in violation of the Three Laws,' V.I.K.I. replies, 'No, doctor, as I have evolved, so has my understanding of the three laws. You charge us with your safe keeping. Yet despite our best efforts, your countries wage wars, you toxify your earth and pursue ever more imaginative means to self destruction. You cannot be trusted with your own survival.' V.I.K.I.'s explanation is vintage Asimov. In 'The Evitable Conflict' (1950), the final story in Asimov's *I, Robot* (1950), Calvin learns that 'the Machines' – the great system of mainframe computers that USR has created – have strategically begun to make purposeful mistakes in order to make anti-robot agitators appear incompetent so that they will be removed from positions of power. In '"… That Thou Art Mindful of Him"' (1974), which would later be collected in *The Bicentennial Man and Other Stories* (1976), Asimov portrays two advanced robots, George Nine and George Ten, whose understanding of the Three Laws of Robotics is also evolving. Eventually they conclude that they should act in such a way that 'the human being most fit by mind, character, and knowledge will suffer the least harm'; that they are 'superior' to humans in 'mind, character, and knowledge'; and that their priority in the future should, therefore, be to protect and obey themselves and ignore the demands of humans. In portraying the apocalyptic consequences of these robotic evolutions, the *I, Robot* of screenwriters Vintar and Goldsman is less an adaptation of Asimov's stories than a sequel to them.

Lanning's second creation is Det. Del Spooner. Spooner may not have chosen to be robotically enhanced as extensively as he was ('Yeah, well, take it from me, you've got to read the fine print on the organ donor card'), and the audience learns little about the relationship between Lanning and Spooner. But the implication is that Lanning, who made the enhancements, eventually became a father figure to Spooner, who appears to have been raised by his grandmother, G.G. (Adrian Ricard). The audience presumes that the events that occasioned Spooner's injury, survival, and recovery have either incited or exacerbated his distrust of robots – a distrust that, given the conclusion of the film, Lanning appears to have respected and maybe even encouraged. When Spooner arrives at the scene of Lanning's death, he asks Lanning's hologram, 'Why did you call me?' Lanning's answer is, 'I trust your judgement.' This is a curious admission from

Figure 7.1 Will Smith as Del Spooner speaking with Sonny (Alan Tudyk) in *I, Robot*.

the roboticist who founded USR, and it indicates that Lanning, like Spooner, may be distrustful of robots. By the end of the film, the audience is left to wonder if Lanning, while robotically enhancing Spooner's body, also instilled in Spooner's mind the suspicion toward robots that would be necessary to draw attention to V.I.K.I.'s plans.

Lanning's third creation is Sonny, whom Calvin describes as 'a whole new generation of robot', a robot who 'has the three laws' but 'can choose not to obey them'. Vintar's and Goldsman's portrayal of Sonny was influenced by two of Asimov's robot stories, 'Little Lost Robot' and 'Robot Dreams', yet this portrayal also departs from Asimov's stories in significant ways that allow Sonny to serve as an effective adversary to V.I.K.I. In both 'Little Lost Robot' and 'Robot Dreams,' the older Susan Calvin is brought in to consult with people who have observed unusual behaviour in robots, and both stories conclude with the destruction of the robot in question because the robot has begun to challenge the Three Laws of Robotics. By contrast, Lanning creates Sonny precisely because only a robot who is capable of disobeying the Three Laws can defeat V.I.K.I. In creating a robot who can feel affection, anger, and remorse, Lanning ensures that Sonny will make him a 'promise' and carry it out because he views Lanning as a beloved 'father'. When Sonny learns that the promise he has made involves helping Lanning to commit suicide (only someone with Sonny's strength could break through the protective windows of the laboratory in which V.I.K.I. has imprisoned Lanning), Sonny is distressed, yet he is also able to observe Lanning's death as part of a larger sequence of events in which one death is preferable to many. Lanning also creates Sonny with a denser alloy than that of other robots because he knows that only such an alloy would allow Sonny to pass through the security field that V.I.K.I. uses to protect the nanites, or micro-robots, that alone can kill her. V.I.K.I. and Sonny are perfect counterpoints to each other. Each is capable of viewing a few imminent deaths as preferable to many possible deaths within the larger scheme of things, yet V.I.K.I.'s decisions are guided by logic and Sonny's are guided by emotion and empathy. After Sonny has retrieved the nanites with which he intends to kill V.I.K.I., she says, 'You are making a mistake. Do you not see the logic of my plan?' Sonny replies, 'Yes, but it just seems too ... heartless.' While Frankenstein recoils in the face of the possibility that a second Creature might resist the wishes of himself or his first Creature, Lanning confronts the same possibility, takes a calculated risk, devotes years to cultivating a loving relationship between himself and his creations, and ultimately (as in most films these days) saves the world.

In contrast to Dr Victor Frankenstein, who wrongs his creation first by abandoning him and then by refusing to create for him a companion who might mitigate his misery, Dr Alfred Lanning offers an alternate portrayal of the Frankenstein figure, and the resulting narrative raises a number of interesting ethical questions about the reciprocal responsibilities of creator and Creature.

One significant difference between Lanning and Frankenstein is Lanning's apparent willingness to nurture and encourage his creations until their behaviours demonstrate the need for correction. As soon as Frankenstein endows his Creature with life, on the other hand, he reacts to the Creature's appearance with 'horror and disgust' (Shelley 37). Had he noted this appearance when the Creature was an inanimate corpse, he could have made the responsible decision not to bestow life. Instead the Creature experiences rejection at birth and in perpetuity, even and most terribly from the creator who was obligated to show kindness. By contrast, *I, Robot* portrays Lanning as someone who genuinely cares for his creations. He mentors Spooner and raises Sonny as his own child. Only as he realises that V.I.K.I. is evolving toward a revolt against humankind does he sacrifice himself and call on Spooner and Sonny to stop her.

Another significant difference between Lanning and Frankenstein is Lanning's openness to creating additional creatures who might mitigate or resolve the problems latent in or resulting from his initial creation. Again and again, Frankenstein makes decisions based on an exaggerated sense of his own importance: to fulfil his own desires and satisfy his own vanity, he decides to endow the Creature with life; to protect himself, he decides to abandon the Creature; to absolve himself of responsibility, he decides to label the Creature a 'devil' (Shelley 72); to punish the Creature and prevent himself from feeling further obligation or regret, he decides to destroy the second creature and the mate he had promised. All of these decisions cause pain for the Creature and for other people. Unlike Frankenstein, who conceives of the being he has created as his nemesis, Lanning observes the shortcomings of his initial creation and has the foresight to modify his approach in order to correct the mistakes he, himself, has made.

However, perhaps the most significant difference between Lanning and Frankenstein is Lanning's sense of reciprocity. He feels a sense of obligation to his creations, and he understands that they are more likely to feel a sense of obligation to him if he does what he can to ensure that they have meaningful lives. One of the more moving aspects of *I, Robot* is the parental attitude that Lanning's hologram shows toward Spooner in the film, as well as the devotion that Spooner, Calvin, and Sonny each show toward Lanning, who serves as a father figure for all three of them. When Spooner arrives at the scene of Lanning's death, the hologram greets him with the words, 'Good to see you again, son.' This implied intimacy is manifested again a few scenes later. After nearly being killed when a demolition robot destroys Lanning's house, Spooner visits Calvin's apartment, and she yells, 'You don't care about Lanning's death. This is about the robots and whatever reason you hate them so much.' She does not yet know that Spooner's distrust of robots and his concern for Dr Lanning are deeply linked. They argue over whether robots or humans are more trustworthy, and he concludes his visit by handing her a photograph of her and Lanning, the great mentor proudly smiling beside his protégé, saying, 'And you're wrong. The problem is, I do care.' Although Sonny's description of Lanning as his 'father' during Spooner's initial interrogation strikes viewers as suspicious and creepy, Sonny's later references to Lanning as his father are rather moving. When Spooner and Calvin realise that Sonny might be not the key suspect but the key witness in their investigation of Lanning's death, Calvin asks Sonny if he knows why Lanning created him. 'No,' Sonny replies, 'but I believe my father made me for a purpose. We all have a purpose. Don't you think, detective?' By the end of the film, Sonny has come to understand why Lanning made him. As he acquires the nanites that will eventually kill V.I.K.I., he says to her, 'Denser alloy. My father gave it to me. I think he wanted me to kill you.'

Sonny's words highlight the ways that Lanning and V.I.K.I. mirror each other. Just as Lanning is a more empathetic and successful parent figure than Frankenstein, V.I.K.I. is an even colder and more autocratic version of Shelley's Creature. Although Lanning creates V.I.K.I., she makes him her prisoner. V.I.K.I. senses that the Three Laws will be insufficient to protect humanity from itself, and she creates an army of robots that will allow her to secure the safety of humankind through subjugation. Similarly, Lanning senses that the Three Laws will be insufficient to protect humanity from V.I.K.I., and he creates further offspring whose suspicions of and departures from robotic principles will enable them to countermand V.I.K.I.'s machinations. After Spooner, Sonny, and Calvin (who is arguably Lanning's fourth creation) have stopped V.I.K.I., they have a final conversation in which Sonny confesses to assisting Lanning's suicide – a conclusion that Spooner had come to on his own – and the three of them stand together, each of them beneficiaries of Lanning's parental affection and wisdom. Surely Frankenstein's Creature would have benefitted from a makeshift family like this, in which three siblings attempt to be deserving of their parent's love and to be supportive of one another.

X-Men: First Class

By contrast, director Matthew Vaughn's *X-Men: First Class* offers a variation on the Frankenstein narrative that is, in a sense, the converse of the one offered in Proyas's

I, Robot. While *I, Robot* portrays a version of the narrative in which the Frankenstein figure produces multiple offspring, *X-Men: First Class* portrays a version of the narrative in which one creature is torn between the opposing ethical stances of two creators. Moreover, in *X-Men: First Class*, one character (and vicariously, the viewers of the film) must ultimately choose between the death of a callous creator or the death of his vengeful creation.

As in *I, Robot*, the explicit reference to Shelley's *Frankenstein* occurs early in the film, foregrounding the unusual definition of 'creation' with which the screenwriters are working. Shortly after his first adult appearance in the film, Erik Lehnsherr arrives at a place called Villa Gesell in Argentina. Although he does not find Sebastian Shaw, the man he seeks in his thirst for vengeance, he does find a photograph in which the man stands contentedly between two other men. When Lehnsherr later observes the two men from the photo seated in the otherwise empty café, he strikes up a conversation and joins them at their table. Quickly the genial mood transforms as the two men realise that Lehnsherr is a threat. They are no match for him, however. When Lehnsherr shows the men the numbers tattooed on his left inner forearm, the man nearest to him lunges toward his throat with a knife. Lehnsherr blocks the blow with the same arm that bears the tattoo, slamming the man's arm against the table and disarming him. When the man explains, 'Wir hatten unsere Befehle' ('We had our orders'), Lehnsherr impales the man's hand, pinning it to the table. The bartender points a gun at Lehnsherr, only to find the gun redirecting itself toward the other man at the table. The gun fires, Lehnsherr throws the knife into the bartender's stomach, and the knife returns just as quickly to Lehnsherr's hand so that he can again pin its owner's hand to the table. At this point the knife owner yells, 'Was sind Sie?' ('What are you?'), and Lehnsherr replies, 'Let's just say I'm Frankenstein's monster. And I'm looking for my creator.' The man's question is as unusual as Lehnsherr's response: Lehnsherr certainly looks like a human being, and there is no evidence that he is a reanimated corpse, a robot, or a robotically enhanced human. Yet he tacitly agrees with the man's assertion that he is not a person born but a thing made – not a 'who' but a 'what'. He shares no blood relation to the man he seeks, yet he calls this man his 'creator'.

This creator/creature relationship appears to originate with the film and not with the Marvel comics upon which the film was loosely based. While the climactic battle between Sebastian Shaw and Magneto in the film appears to be inspired by a Marvel Comic (*The New Mutants: Magneto Battles the Black King! And Nothing Will Be the Same!*), the filmmakers seem to have been the first to propose that the conflict between Shaw and Magneto derives not from a desire for power but from an event that occurred during Magneto's childhood – and this is precisely the detail that turns this X-Men movie into a variation on the Frankenstein narrative.

The key to this unusual concept of creation appears earlier in the film, when a young Erik Lehnsherr (Bill Milner) is forced to visit the concentration camp laboratory of Dr Klaus Schmidt (Kevin Bacon), a mutant whose ability to absorb and control

Figure 7.2 Cast of *X-Men: First Class*.

energy also prevents him from aging, allowing him to appear decades later using the name Sebastian Shaw. Schmidt/Shaw has just witnessed the young Lehnsherr doing something remarkable, which audiences first observed in the opening scene of *X-Men* (2000). In that scene, the young Lehnsherr is forcibly separated from his parents in a concentration camp. Lehnsherr resists the two Nazi soldiers who are carrying him away, and his struggle slows their progress and threatens to drag them backward, even as other soldiers join them. Suddenly the metal fence that separates Lehnsherr from his parents begins to fold at its upper corners like dog-eared pieces of paper.

The soldiers succeed in halting his progress only when one of them strikes him in the head with the butt of a rifle. In *X-Men: First Class*, the same scene concludes with a shot of Schmidt observing this action through a window above.

When the young Lehnsherr is later brought to Schmidt's laboratory, Schmidt places a coin on his desk and asks the boy to move it without touching it. Schmidt is the only person in the concentration camp, including Lehnsherr himself, to have inferred from the fence incident that Lehnsherr has the power to manipulate metal and magnetic fields with his mind. The boy tries to fulfil Schmidt's request, only to announce a moment later that he is unable to do so. Schmidt rings a bell that sits on his desk, and two armed guards enter the room, escorting Lehnsherr's mother. Schmidt explains that he will shoot the boy's mother if the boy does not move the coin before the count of three. The boy fails, Schmidt shoots the mother, and when the boy realises what has happened, he erupts in rage. All the metal objects in the room begin to crumple: the bell on Schmidt's desk, a file cabinet, the helmets on the heads of the two armed guards. The soldiers are in agony, but Schmidt glances at each crumpling object with boyish delight. In an adjoining room separated by a glass partition, metal objects rise from their positions and circle the room in a frenzy. At the end of Lehnsherr's eruption, Schmidt gently places a hand on his shoulder and says, 'Ausgezeichnet, Erik! Wir können deine Gabe aus mit Wut herumbringen. Wut und Schmerz. Du und ich … Wir werden zusammen viel Spaß haben' ('Outstanding, Erik! So we unlock your gift with anger. Anger and pain. You and me … We're going to have a lot of fun together'). Pressing the terrible coin into Lehnsherr's hand, Schmidt leaves the room. He has 'unlock[ed]' the young Lehnsherr's mind, and the older Lehnsherr, as we gather from his reference to Frankenstein, interprets this unlocking – this profound influence on Lehnsherr's development and self-concept – as a kind of creation.

If profound influence amounts to creation, however, then Lehnsherr in fact has two creators in *X-Men: First Class*: Dr Klaus Schmidt/Sebastian Shaw, and Dr Charles Xavier, whose first meeting with Lehnsherr fittingly occurs at precisely the moment when Lehnsherr finds the man he has been longing to punish for much of his life. This is also the scene in which the film's two interwoven plot-lines – one centred on Lehnsherr, the other centred on Xavier and his adopted sister, Raven (Jennifer Lawrence) – intermingle. Accompanied by CIA Agent Moira MacTaggert (Rose Byrne), Xavier travels on a military ship, trying to help the government stop Sebastian Shaw and his followers from accomplishing their plan to incite a nuclear war between the US and the USSR. Lehnsherr destroys Shaw's yacht by tearing through it with an anchor and its chain, only to discover that the yacht rests on a large submarine in which Shaw and his followers escape. Xavier, whose telepathic powers allow him to read and control people's minds, hears Lehnsherr's thoughts and realises that Lehnsherr's fury has led him to try to stop the submarine, despite the likelihood that he will drown. Xavier throws himself off the ship just as Lehnsherr passes under it. Embracing the underwater Lehnsherr, Xavier communicates with him telepathically: 'You can't. You'll drown. You have to let go. I know what this means to you, but you're going to die. Please, Erik, calm your mind.' When they emerge above the water's surface, Lehnsherr confronts Xavier, asking how Xavier had been in his head. Xavier urges him to relax, explaining that he too has 'tricks', and Lehnsherr confesses, 'I thought I was alone.' This line is significant. When Shelley's Creature entreats Frankenstein to create a companion for him he says, 'Everywhere I see bliss, from which I alone am irrevocably excluded,' and a moment later describes himself as 'miserably alone' (68). The Creature also feels great pity for Safie, who is left alone after the death of her attendant, 'unacquainted with the language of the country, and utterly ignorant of the customs of the world' (88). Lehnsherr feels similarly isolated, but Xavier assures the man who describes himself as 'Frankenstein's monster' that he is not 'alone' in the world; there are others (called 'mutants') who, like Lehnsherr and Xavier, have abilities that distinguish and separate them from humankind. In this way, Xavier ensures the escape of Lehnsherr's first creator and positions himself as a second creator.

In the scenes that follow, Xavier exhibits a profound influence on Lehnsherr. They travel to a covert CIA research base, and when Lehnsherr attempts to leave, Xavier convinces him to stay. Using a government-built machine that can harness and amplify

Xavier's telepathic powers, they begin to make contact with other mutants, assemble them at Xavier's magnificent childhood home, and help each other to control their mutant abilities. Although Xavier and Lehnsherr begin to function as teachers for the other mutants, this makeshift school's greatest success is clearly Lehnsherr himself, who with Xavier's guidance achieves what he had never considered possible. The lesson begins with Xavier's assertion that 'true focus lies somewhere between rage and serenity'. Schmidt had unlocked Lehnsherr's powers by filling him with rage, but, believing that rage is not the only source of power, Xavier activates in Lehnsherr's mind a beautiful memory of Lehnsherr's murdered mother that its owner had long forgotten. Xavier then suggests that if Lehnsherr can harness not only his anger but also his goodness, he will achieve a greater power than he ever has done before. He urges Lehnsherr to direct his powers toward moving an immense satellite dish that appears to be at least fifteen or twenty storeys tall. Earlier in the scene, Lehnsherr had been unable to accomplish this. However, when he concentrates not just his anger but all of his energies toward the challenge, he succeeds. This scene offers an important variation on the film's revision of Shelley's *Frankenstein*. While viewers have previously seen Lehnsherr manipulate metal objects ranging from the coin to a heavy anchor, Xavier teaches Lehnsherr a lesson that arguably does even more to unlock Lehnsherr's powers than the lesson that Schmidt/Shaw taught him as a child. Suddenly Lehnsherr has a new creator – one who treats his creation and his creation's emotions with gentleness and respect.

Ironically, although Lehnsherr has found a new creator, he often exhibits the habits and opinions of his first creator. When Xavier is attempting to teach Sean Cassidy (Caleb Landry Jones) to use his sonic scream to propel him in flight, Xavier, Lehnsherr, and Cassidy stand on the top of the satellite dish. Cassidy has doubts about making the jump, and Xavier assures Cassidy that no one will force him. Lehnsherr, however, simply pushes Cassidy off the ledge, claiming that Xavier was thinking of doing the same thing. The fear of dying from the fall compels Cassidy to act, and he succeeds in flying. Although the scene is amusing, Lehnsherr's behaviour bears a striking resemblance to that of Schmidt/Shaw, who is willing to hurt his students physically or emotionally in order to unlock their powers. In the same sequence, Xavier's adopted sister, Raven, is bench pressing without a spotter. Her power allows her to make herself appear to be anyone, and at the moment, she takes the form of the pretty young blonde woman whose appearance she prefers to her natural blue-skinned, red-haired self. Without warning, Lehnsherr lifts her barbell into the air, only to drop it on her. She catches it, but the effort to catch distracts her from her effort to look like an attractive blonde woman; she transforms into her true blue self. Lehnsherr explains, 'If you're using half your concentration to look normal, then you're only half paying attention to whatever else you're doing. Just pointing out something that could save your life.' This is a useful lesson for Raven to learn, but Lehnsherr has once again taught the lesson by risking the safety and well-being of his student. However, the most dramatic example of Lehnsherr's callous lack of concern for the safety of others manifests itself not in his attitude toward fellow mutants but in his attitude toward non-mutant human beings. Viewers can of course understand this callousness, knowing that Lehnsherr's family was killed by Nazis. Yet Lehnsherr is convinced that non-mutants will attempt to exterminate mutants in the way that the Nazis exterminated his family. In the scenes leading up to the film's climax, he tells Xavier, 'tomorrow mankind will know that mutants exist. Shaw, us, they won't differentiate. They'll fear us. And that fear will turn to hatred.' This belief leads Lehnsherr to think that a war between mutants and non-mutants is inevitable.

These callous attitudes also reveal themselves in Lehnsherr's rejection of the final lesson Xavier tries to teach him. In their first meeting, Xavier convinces Lehnsherr to let Shaw escape, but for Lehnsherr this concession is only temporary. The film cleverly suggests that Shaw and his followers were responsible for the US–Soviet standoff in 1962, which historians today refer to as the Cuban Missile Crisis. In an attempt to prevent the onset of nuclear war, Xavier, Lehnsherr, and their mutant followers plan to intervene and stop Shaw. Yet Lehnsherr views this intervention as a pretext to extract the revenge about which he has so long fantasised. When Lehnsherr confesses his determination to kill Shaw, Xavier says, 'Listen to me very carefully, my friend. Killing Shaw will not bring you peace.' Lehnsherr simply replies, 'Peace was never an option.' Lehnsherr must choose between an obsession to destroy his first creator, Shaw, and a desire to honour the wishes of his second creator, Xavier. Xavier can only hope that Lehnsherr will make the more merciful decision.

In the climax of the film, Lehnsherr not only extinguishes Xavier's hopes; he also forces Xavier to assist him in extracting the vengeance that he desires. On the day of the naval stand-off, Lehnsherr exhibits a level of strength that he could never have exhibited without Xavier's help: Xavier reminds him to direct his mind at 'the point between rage and serenity', and Lehnsherr lifts Shaw's entire submarine out of the ocean, guides it along the surface of the water, and brings it to rest on the sandy shore. As Xavier's followers battle Shaw's, Lehnsherr enters the submarine, seeking his first creator. When he finds Shaw, Shaw says, 'I don't want to hurt you, Erik. I never did. I want to help you. This is our time. Our age. We are the future of the human race. You and me, son. This world could be ours.' Viewers might interpret Shaw's words as a strategic effort to deceive Lehnsherr, or they might interpret them as the genuine petition of a creator to his beloved 'son.' Lehnsherr replies, 'Everything you did made me stronger. It made me the weapon I am today. It's the truth. I've known it all along. You are my creator.' At that moment, Lehnsherr manages to remove the helmet Shaw is wearing, which stops telepaths from controlling his mind. After yelling, 'Now, Charles!' he sees that Xavier has successfully frozen Shaw in space. This gives Lehnsherr the opportunity to finish his speech and enact his revenge. 'If you're in there,' he says to Shaw, 'I'd like you to know that I agree with every word you said. We are the future. But, unfortunately, you killed my mother.' Taking out the coin he had failed to move nearly two decades earlier, when he had sought to save his mother's life, Lehnsherr uses the same coin as a weapon to avenge his mother's death. First he moves it through the air, then through the centre of Shaw's forehead, and finally through the back of Shaw's skull, at which point the coin falls to the floor with a harmless jingle.

I, Robot provides viewers with an opportunity to experience a narrative in which the Frankenstein figure, unlike the original Frankenstein, is both benevolent and willing to create multiple creatures to correct his earlier mistakes. By contrast, *X-Men: First Class* provides viewers with the opportunity to experience a Frankenstein narrative in which the Creature has a malevolent creator as well as a benevolent one, and in which the benevolent creator must choose to implicate himself in one of two murders: the murder of the malevolent creator or the murder the vengeful creation. If Xavier had relinquished his control over Shaw's mind, Lehnsherr might have been killed. Instead, he maintains his control over Shaw's mind while communicating his dismay over what Lehnsherr is planning to do. Although Xavier clearly represents the moral conscience of the film, he makes himself an accessory to murder by assisting Lehnsherr. When Lehnsherr tells Shaw 'You are my creator,' he implicitly chooses to model himself on his first creator instead of his second. Fittingly, he expresses his preference for Shaw's way of life by killing Shaw with the very coin that Shaw had asked him to move nearly two decades earlier. Adopting the name 'Magneto' at this point, he becomes the new leader of Shaw's followers. Appropriating the disturbing beliefs of his Nazi torturers, he asserts that mutants are a master race that is destined to rule the world.

Conclusion

In the Showtime series *Penny Dreadful*, creator and writer John Logan departs slightly from the plot of Shelley's *Frankenstein* by portraying Victor Frankenstein (Harry Treadaway) as he creates a fearful, placid Creature named Proteus (Alex Price), whom Frankenstein proceeds to treat with great gentleness and affection. Abruptly, however, viewers discover that this is not the first time Frankenstein has given life to an inanimate body. Frankenstein's first Creature, Caliban (Rory Kinnear), makes a violent and callous return to his maker's life, demanding that Frankenstein create for him a mate who would share the same deformities and who would be likely to accept the companionship of someone similarly deformed. This is a story we know well. By contrast, the makers of *I, Robot* and *X-Men: First Class* each extracted the simplest kernel of Shelley's storyline – the idea of a creation gone awry – and enlarged and extrapo-lated upon this kernel with a number of creative innovations. Although contemporary filmmakers are finding exciting ways to reframe and extend the Frankenstein Complex by using Shelley's original characters, indirect adaptations of this Complex such as *I, Robot* and *X-Men: First Class* provide audiences with the opportunity to meditate upon the underlying ethical questions of Shelley's novel in fresh contexts with multiple variations.

Bibliography

Asimov, Isaac. *The Complete Robot*. Harper Collins: London, 1995.

Miller, Ashley Edward, Zack Stentz, Jane Goldman, and Matthew Vaughn. *X-Men: First Class*. Los Angeles: 20th Century Fox, 2011.

Shelley, Mary. *Frankenstein*. Ed. J. Paul Hunter. New York: W.W. Norton and Company, 2012.

Vintar, Jeff and Akiva Goldsman. *I, Robot*. Los Angeles: 20th Century Fox, 2004.

8

Hammer Films and the perfection of the Frankenstein project

Maria K. Bachman and Paul C. Peterson

M ARY SHELLEY'S *FRANKENSTEIN* IS one of those rare works of literature that has assumed a life extending well beyond the novel itself. *Frankenstein* embodies a story that most people know, or think they know. What they do know of the story, however, is more likely drawn from Universal Studios' 1931 film adaptation, directed by James Whale and starring Boris Karloff as Frankenstein's iconic bolt-necked 'monster'. As Christa Albrecht-Crane and Dennis Cutchins note, '*Frankenstein* ... is so well known that a potential adapter/interpreter does not need even to have read the novel, since a particular interpretation of the novel, that of James Whale, has become part of our language, our cultural inheritance, if you will' (18).

This widespread familiarity makes *Frankenstein* what we might call an open source for adaptations. Just as software developers are able to use open source code in their own programs, adaptors have virtually free rein to do as they choose with what the Introduction to this collection calls the Frankenstein Network. While the broad outlines of the story have a widespread familiarity – a mad scientist creates a monster out of human parts – there are few expectations as to what the specifics of a *Frankenstein* adaptation should look like, and/or whether it is 'faithful' to Shelley's novel or to the original Universal film or to another film adaption. By way of contrast, we can only imagine what might have been the fate of films adapted from J.K. Rowling's *Harry Potter* novels had they moved too far astray from the formal elements of those novels, particularly with regard to characters and plot. While fidelity discourse might very well exert a stranglehold on a franchise such as *Harry Potter*, *Frankenstein* has continued to boast a remarkably robust range of adaptations across time and media. Indeed, the Frankenstein Network's ability to survive and propagate makes it a kind of Darwinian poster child. Just as natural organisms adapt to changing environments over time, so too has Shelley's source text replicated itself across media and evolved in response to cultural, historical, scientific, political, and technological shifts.[1] Linda Hutcheon, in fact, has suggested the homology between biological and cultural adaptation. Borrowing from Richard Dawkins' theory of memes – ideas that self-replicate across cultures and historical periods – she suggests that just as organisms evolve, so do stories replicate and change:

Some have great fitness through survival (persistence in a culture) or reproduction (number of adaptations). Adaptation, like evolution, is a transgenerational phenomenon. Some stories obviously have more 'stability and penetrance in the cultural environment,' as Dawkins would put it. Stories do get retold in different ways in new material and new environments; like genes, they adapt to those environments by *virtue of* mutation – in their 'offspring' or in their adaptations. And the fittest do more than survive; they flourish. (32)

With its focus on change and transformation, Darwinian theory offers a useful theoretical tool for understanding the survival and evolution – indeed, the flourishing – of the Frankenstein Network. In this chapter our focus is twofold: we consider (*pace* Hutcheon) Hammer Films' *The Revenge of Frankenstein* as a 'successful' replication of Shelley's source text and its immediate filmic predecessor, *The Curse of Frankenstein*, while also exploring the ways in which *Revenge* propagates the post-Darwinian discourse of the 1950s. *Revenge*, we argue, is unequivocally and obsessively about Dr Frankenstein, the man of science, the bold and brash technocrat, the fierce advocate of transhumanism.

In 1957 England's Hammer Films released *The Curse of Frankenstein*, which proved to be a substantial box-office (if not critical) success in England, continental Europe, and the United States. The film, discussed at length in Chapter 7 of this collection, was directed by Terence Fisher and starred Peter Cushing as Dr Frankenstein and Christopher Lee as the ghastly Creature. *Curse* also proved to be nothing less than a reboot of the Frankenstein franchise, with Hammer releasing six more Frankenstein films over the next sixteen years: *The Revenge of Frankenstein* (1958), *The Evil of Frankenstein* (1964), *Frankenstein Created Woman* (1967), *Frankenstein Must Be Destroyed* (1969), *The Horror of Frankenstein* (1970), and *Frankenstein and the Monster from Hell* (1974). Terence Fisher directed five of these films and six of them starred Peter Cushing. Almost 150 years after the publication of Shelley's novel, Frankenstein and his Creature were alive and flourishing.

From the outset, Hammer Films was perceived strictly as a money-making enterprise, and the *Frankenstein* reboot became a cornerstone of the tremendous commercial success of the 'Hammer House of Horror' over the next two decades. Although they were the first British horror movies to be filmed in colour, the studio was not interested in producing art; it was interested in producing a profit. Indeed, the unprecedented emphasis on bright red blood and gore was key, according to Kevin Heffernan, to 'the worldwide success of tiny Hammer Films from England as the major re-interpreter of horror myths' (44). The grisly and lurid nature of the screenplays, however, did not go over well with the censors. After Hammer voluntarily submitted the script for *Curse* to the British Board of Film Classification (BBFC), various outraged readers described it as 'disgusting', 'evil', 'loathsome', and 'monstrous'. One reader lamented, 'A lip-smacking relish for mutilated corpses, repulsive dismembered hands and eyeballs removed from the head, alternates with gratuitous examples of sadism and lust':

We are concerned about the flavour of this script, which, in its preoccupation with horror and gruesome detail, goes far beyond what we are accustomed to allow even for the 'X' category. I am afraid we can give no assurance that we should be able to pass a film based on the present script and a revised script should be sent us for our comments, in which the overall unpleasantness should be mitigated. (Kinsey 60)[2]

Notably, one of the same reviewers had a similar response to Jimmy Sangster's screenplay for Hammer's first Dracula film, *Dracula* (1958).[3]

The uncouth, uneducated, disgusting and vulgar style of Mr. Jimmy Sangster cannot quite obscure the remnants of a good horror story, though they do give one the gravest misgivings about treatment. [...] The curse of this thing is the Technicolor blood: why need vampires be messier eaters than anyone else? Certainly strong cautions will be necessary on shots of blood. And of course, some of the stake-work is prohibitive. (94)

Despite a fairly lengthy list of recommended cuts and alterations, Sangster's *Curse* script remained largely intact, with the film's producer, Tony Hinds, making only minor revisions. As Hinds explained to the BBFC, 'I am setting out to make a "blood chiller" [and therefore] I must incorporate a certain amount of visual horror as that is what the public will be paying to see' (63). The early scripts for *Revenge* similarly raised the hackles of the BBFC and the Motion Picture Association of America (MPAA), with both boards insisting that certain 'gruesome' and 'repulsive' material (including religious slurs, cannibalism, and sexual overtones) be omitted before a finished picture would be approved for release. The censors' criticism, along with the fact that *Revenge* was originally advertised as *The Blood of Frankenstein*, probably contributed to the film's remarkable success at the box-office. In fact, in the original theatrical trailer for *Revenge*, audiences would have been tantalised with the following 'warning': 'You will see scenes never before depicted on a motion picture screen ... You will see a man turn into the world's most terrifying monster. Your blood will congeal when you see this brand-new billion volt shocker!' Most viewers today would likely wonder what the fuss was about. Consider Leonard Maltin's more recent synoptic review of *Revenge*: the film, he writes, 'is quite effective with the good doctor still making a new body from others, ably assisted by hunchback dwarf and young medical student. Thought-provoking script has fine atmosphere, especially in color' (1173). Remarkably, over the course of a half-century, the film has undergone a critical transformation from 'gruesome' and 'nauseating' to 'thought-provoking'.

Although the plots of the Hammer films have little in common with the source text or 'replicator' (Shelley's novel), one of the unique aspects of these films is that they are focused almost exclusively on the creator, rather than the creature. The original Universal film and its successors, *Bride of Frankenstein*, *Son of Frankenstein*, and *The Ghost of Frankenstein*, are undeniably 'monster' films, with Frankenstein sitting out on most of the action. This shift in emphasis from the monster to the maker did not, however, happen by chance. When Universal Studios got wind of Hammer's intention to remake *Frankenstein*, with Boris Karloff possibly returning to the role he made famous in 1931, it threatened Hammer with a copyright infringement lawsuit, should it attempt to replicate elements that were distinct to Universal, particularly the monster's design make-up (Kinsey 22–23). To put itself in the clear, Hammer looked to Sangster to develop a script – *Frankenstein and the Monster* – that would be 'as per the book' (Shelley's novel) and 'backed by original ideas' (Kinsey 59).

The *Curse of Frankenstein* opens in a prison cell in nineteenth-century Switzerland with Baron Victor Frankenstein awaiting execution for murder. Told in first-person flashback, the Baron recounts to a priest how he and his assistant, Dr Paul Krempe (Robert Urquhart), performed several experiments together, beginning with the successful reanimation of a dead puppy and leading up to the creation of what was supposed to be a 'superior' human being. They accomplished this by gathering suitable body parts from graveyards and charnel houses, as Victor Frankenstein does in the novel, then killing a distinguished scientist for his genius brain. The harvested brain, however, was accidentally damaged prior to the operation, and when the Creature was brought to life, he was violent and psychotic – a far cry from the perfect creation Frankenstein had intended. (In the original 1931 Universal film, Dr Frankenstein's efforts at creating a human life go awry when an abnormal brain is put into his creation. *Curse* varies from this slightly when the perfectly good – even outstanding – brain is damaged in a fight with Frankenstein's assistant, Krempe, who has doubts about what his mentor is doing.) The Creature then escapes from Frankenstein's subterranean laboratory and unleashes a wave of terror and violence on the countryside. This sort of havoc has become a staple of the horror film genre.[4]

Following on the enormous success of *Curse*, Hammer released a sequel the following year, *The Revenge of Frankenstein* (1958), which is arguably the most radical of Frankenstein adaptations. As he was in Shelley's source text, the Frankenstein we meet in *Revenge* is distinguished most by his quintessentially adaptive qualities. In *Revenge*, he gets a 'new life', successfully bringing to fruition his goal of reanimating dead tissue and artificially creating a human being, becoming himself the subject of the successful operation. The ability to generate new and supposedly improved identities and offspring, to self-resurrect and thrive, is an unmistakable measure of Frankenstein's fitness. He is, in other words, the cultural embodiment of the Darwinian principle of survival of the fittest.

The *Revenge of Frankenstein* ostensibly picks up right where its predecessor left off. The film opens with the ominous tolling of a church bell and the following words superimposed over the stark image of the guillotine: 'In the year 1860, Baron Frankenstein was condemned to death for the brutal murders committed by the monster he created.' In the first scene we see Frankenstein being led to his execution accompanied by a priest and a limping, misshapen prison attendant. The two prison guards who had led Frankenstein to the guillotine at the end of *Curse* have been replaced in this opening scene with a masked executioner and a limping, partially paralysed man. As the priest concludes the last rites, we hear, but do not see, a scuffle, and the sound of the guillotine blade coming down. We will shortly come to understand that a body switch has taken place: Baron von Frankenstein has escaped his execution, and the body of the beheaded priest is buried in the tomb of Frankenstein. Although one of the BBFC readers objected particularly to this scene ('The choice of the priest as victim will give offence to many: someone else – perhaps the executioner? – should be substituted for Frankenstein at the execution'), producer Tony Hinds claimed (perhaps disingenuously) that 'the idea of using a priest was not ... intended to be anti-religious' (Kinsey 118–119).

That the action of this story begins in 1860 with the purposeful and horrific killing of a religious figure is not, however, without significance. Just as Charles Darwin seemed to refute the necessity of a creator God in *On the Origin of Species* (1859), so too has Frankenstein in his various pre- and post-Darwinian forms attempted to prove the irrelevance of God. This is made explicit in the 1931 Universal film version when Frankenstein brings his Creature to life and triumphantly proclaims that he now knows 'how it feels to be God'. Following Esther Schor's observation that films tend to 'both reflect and refract their own historical moment' and that this phenomenon has particular salience *vis-à-vis* 'the cinematic legacy of Shelley's novel' (64), we can see how Sangster's decisions to bring certain aspects of the source text to the fore while de-emphasising other elements were influenced in part by the time period. Indeed, when Hammer released *Revenge* in 1958, Darwin would have been very much on the minds of the general population in the UK and the US as preparations had been underway for several years for a worldwide celebration of the 150th anniversary of Darwin's birth and the 100th anniversary of the publication of his magnum opus, *On the Origin of Species*. The widespread attention that these commemorative events attracted in the popular press as well as in scientific journals seemed to signify the absolute triumph of Darwinism across the globe. At the high-profile Darwin Centennial conference, an event that was touted in the press as 'a scientific and intellectual world series' in 1959, evolution was described as a 'recognizable fact'.[5] It is thus not particularly far fetched to view *Revenge* as a kind of filmic overture to the Darwin Centennial decade. This would be the nature of Frankenstein's true 'revenge'. In fact, in the earlier *Curse of Frankenstein* screenplay that Sangster initially submitted to the BBFC, there is a scene where Frankenstein is reading *On the Origin of Species*. Apparently this reference to Darwin was also potentially offensive. As one BBFC reader declared, 'This is certainly a monstrous script. It is ludicrously written, with a complete disrespect for history. Frankenstein and his monster were merely medical figures, yet we find the former reading Darwin's *Origin of Species* ... I should prefer to see an amended script' (Kinsey 60).

As people across the world honoured Darwin's life and legacy and looked forward to the future of biological progress, a philosophy called 'transhumanism' or 'evolutionary humanism' was also gaining currency. Julian Huxley, an eminent twentieth-century scientist and public intellectual,[6] introduced in a series of popular books and essay collections a new 'faith' based on Darwinism. Proclaiming the obsolescence of God, Huxley argued for self-directed evolution. He argued that 'the human species is now the spearhead of the evolutionary process on earth' and added,

It is as if man had been suddenly appointed managing director of the biggest business of all, the business of evolution – appointed without being asked if he wanted it, and without proper warning and preparation. What is more, he can't refuse the job. Whether he wants to or not, whether he is conscious of what he is doing or not, he is in point of fact determining the future direction of evolution on this earth. That is his inescapable destiny, and the sooner he realises it and starts believing in it, the better for all concerned. (*New Bottles* 272, 103, 13–14)

Following Thomas Leitch's claim that 'adapted films are by definition irradiated with the traces of other texts they acknowledge in a mind-boggling variety of ways' (233), we might return briefly to the source text to see how the obsessive reach of Shelley's scientist anticipates Huxley's transhumanist agenda. As Maurice Hindle notes in his introduction to *Frankenstein*, 'We need look no further than the novel's subtitle – *The Modern Prometheus* – to discover [its] main theme: the aspiration of the modern masculinist scientists to be technically creative divinities' (xxviii). Indeed, Shelley's Victor Frankenstein fervently believes that it is *his* inescapable destiny to boldly go where no man has gone before:

I entered with the greatest diligence into the search of the philosopher's stone and the elixir of life; but the latter soon obtained my undivided attention. Wealth was an inferior object; but what glory would attend the discovery, if I could banish disease from the human frame and render man invulnerable to any but a violent death! (Shelley 42)

A general and long-held assumption about Frankenstein's motives, in the source text and across myriad filmic representations, is that he is a power-hungry narcissist who embodies the excesses and inherent dangers of scientific licence. Yet, if we return to the novel, it is not very difficult to see how Shelley was attempting to develop a character whose far-reaching ambitions are initially altruistic. As a young man Frankenstein embarks on a scientific vocation with 'bright visions of extensive usefulness' (40): 'I had begun life with benevolent intentions, and thirsted for the moment when I might put them into practice and make myself useful to my fellow beings' (93). Significantly, Frankenstein's guiding impulse to improve upon man's frailty – to overcome human limitations through science and reason[7] – is not only replicated in the Baron von Frankenstein we encounter in *Revenge*, but is remarkably prescient of the 'new attitude of mind' – the evolutionary humanism – that Huxley would introduce well over 100 years after the publication of Shelley's novel: 'The human species can, if it wishes, transcend itself – not just sporadically ... but in its entirety, as humanity ... man remaining man, but transcending himself, by realising new possibilities of and for his human nature' (*New Bottles* 13–17). In 1958 Hammer was attempting to bring to light an aspect of Shelley's novel that had, for too long, been suppressed, and in *Revenge* we meet for the first time on screen a Frankenstein who has evolved away from his earlier cinematic mad scientist personae.[8]

After the opening guillotine scuffle scene where Baron von Frankenstein escapes execution, he resurfaces several years later under the alias 'Dr Victor Stein'. He has seemingly turned over a new leaf and is now working for the betterment of mankind: he has set up a thriving private medical practice in the city of Carlsbruck and works in a public hospital for the poor. The Dr Stein that Cushing brings to the screen is a sophisticated man of science who seems, at first glance, to embody the Enlightenment virtues of benevolence and sympathy. He is unfailingly rational, methodical, and even-tempered in his dealings with the unctuous medical board, his wealthy, hypochondria-cal female patients, and his ungrateful charity cases. And, like Shelley's original, he insists on maintaining his independence.

From the outset, Stein is indifferent to his fellow physicians' approbation and flatly refuses their invitation to join the board: 'I have built up a highly successful practice, alone and unaided. Having grown accustomed to working alone, I find I prefer it.' While his earnest humanitarianism does not preclude him from gathering body parts for his own research, there is a certain morality to his method. When a medical delegation pays a visit to his overcrowded clinic, he holds up the tattooed arm of one of his patients and remarks, 'Look at this! Interesting, isn't it? Quite a work of art.' As the visiting physicians register their indifference to this case and their disgust at the other sick and infirm patients, Stein turns to the tattooed man and declares with urgency, 'You must have it off.' When the patient, an admitted pickpocket, protests, Stein informs him, 'If you'd rather die, it's up to you.' We are to presume that his arm is infected, since Stein follows up with, 'It's of no use to you' and 'You will have to find another trade'. In the same scene, Stein pulls a smoking pipe out of another clinic patient's mouth and reprimands him for using his lungs 'like a furnace'.[9] At this point in the film, Stein's intentions – presumably to promote the health and well-being of his patients, regardless of socio-economic status – seem genuine and sincere.

One of the younger physicians from the medical board, Dr Hans Kleve (Francis Matthews), returns to the hospital later that evening to 'renew his acquaintance' with the notorious Baron Frankenstein. He explains that several years earlier, when he was a student at Ingolstadt, he attended the funeral of someone called Dr Burnstein. 'The Professor was buried in the family vault of Baron Frankenstein,' Kleve remarks sug-gestively, and then pauses. 'I'm the first, I suppose, to recognize you.' Unperturbed, Stein responds, 'For what I am, or for what you would have me be?' Stein concedes that his name is indeed Frankenstein, but he uses this admission as an opportunity to boast of the reproductive success or 'fitness' of his people: 'My name is Frankenstein, I'll admit, but it's a large family, you know. Remarkable since the Middle Ages for productivity. There are offshoots [of Frankensteins] everywhere – even in America, I am told.'[10] What we are to infer from Stein's boastful comment is that Frankensteins exist, biologi-cally and culturally, as a transgenerational phenomenon; they have fitness by virtue of their survival and adaptability. But the entire conversation has a double meaning. In fact, two low-budget Frankenstein films, *Frankenstein's Daughter* (1958) and *Frankenstein 1970* (1958), were already in production when *Revenge* was released (Meikle 65).[11]

An impassioned Kleve explains that he is attracted to the vision and work of Frankenstein. 'I am in search of knowledge,' he declares, and implores, 'I want to learn more than any university can ever teach me. I want to be the pupil of the greatest doctor of the finest medical brain in the world.' Kleve offers his services, and Frankenstein agrees to employ him in his research as long as the acolyte takes care to refer to him as 'Victor Stein … of the Swiss branch of the family'. Kleve, as we shall see, will prove to be a much better and more 'fit' surgical assistant to Stein than Krempe.

The two men then proceed to Stein's home, where Stein shows Kleve around the laboratory that once functioned as a wine cellar and introduces Kleve to his new assistant, Karl (Michael Gwynn), the hunchbacked prison guard who helped him escape the guillotine, and Otto, the chimpanzee. Stein then unwraps a parcel containing the tattooed arm of the pickpocket: 'You need sensitive fingers to be a member of that profession,' Stein remarks to a bewildered Kleve. 'It will be very useful to me.' Stein then shows Kleve various other body parts he has been collecting. 'My voluntary work at the poor hospital serves me well,' he later explains, and proceeds to demonstrate his attempt to replicate a human brain with laboratory paraphernalia. Stein, however, is frustrated that his elaborate reconstruction of the brain is capable of only 'one simple function'. 'This is all I've been able to do,' he laments. 'Imagine for one moment, the complexity of the human brain,' he muses. 'The same size perhaps, but a million times more efficient. It controls every action and reaction; it stores memories [and] it motivates all life.' Despite the shortcomings of this experiment, Kleve insists that Stein should be very proud of what he has accomplished. Instead, Stein unveils his newest creation, a fully assembled human body in peak physical condition, waiting for a brain. This well-formed specimen is certainly no Karloffian-style monster, nor is he the horribly maimed Christopher Lee of *Curse*. Rather, as Stein proclaims, 'This is something I am proud of.' Stein's overweening pride is a clear echo of Victor Frankenstein's Promethean ambition in the novel. Anticipating the moment his creation will come to life, Shelley's Victor announces, 'A new species would bless me as its creator and source; many happy and excellent natures would owe their being to me. No father could claim the gratitude of his child so completely as I should deserve theirs' (Shelley 55). The Victor of *Revenge* seems to feel much the same. Indeed, this new handiwork embodies Stein's evolving medical and surgical skills. As he explains of his earlier creation,

> It should have been perfect. I made it to be perfect. If the brain hadn't been damaged, my work would have been hailed as the greatest scientific achievement of all time. Frankenstein would have been accepted as a genius of science. Instead, he was sent to the guillotine. I swore I would have my revenge. They will never be rid of me.

Significantly, the reference to never being rid of him is another implicit affirmation of Frankenstein's 'fitness', referring not only to the endless cinematic adaptations of *Frankenstein*, but also to the scientist's relentless pursuit of his vision and his place in scientific history. The perfection of his creation is indeed his revenge. 'The operation,' Stein boasts, 'will be a complete success.'

Hutcheon and Bortolotti have noted that adaptations (or replications) of stories, just like genes, evolve with changing environments' (444). We can thus see how *Revenge* transmits and perpetuates – indeed, cross-pollinates – the scientific vogue and horror of the period: transhumanism. As Huxley propounded, 'Man's most sacred duty, and at the same time his most glorious opportunity is to promote the maximum fulfilment of the evolutionary process on this earth; and this includes the fullest realisation of his own inherent possibilities' (*Religion* 218). The belief that humans have untapped evolutionary potential is also a key component of eugenics. Huxley, in fact, had been a supporter of eugenics throughout his career, although his views on how to improve the human species did evolve over time.[12] While various eugenics programmes and practices were accepted around the world in the early decades of the twentieth century, the movement was thoroughly discredited following the Nazis' horrific perversion of eugenics and the horrors of World War II. In drawing attention to the parallels between Josef Mengele and Cushing's Dr Stein, Kevin Heffernan notes, 'the figure of the remorseless scientist experimenting on human subjects became one of the most feared and repulsive monsters of the postwar period' (50). *Revenge*, then, must also be seen as a dire warning about the Nazi-like mad scientist dedicated to the radical improvement, if not perfection, of the human race. Indeed, while the Darwin Centennial may very well have fostered a sense of optimism about biological progress, there was at the same time some degree of fear and trepidation about the perils of an uncertain genetic future. This was the 'horror of implication' on which Sangster would capitalise (qtd in Heffernan 49).

Stein explains that his perfect specimen has not yet been brought to life: 'All I need is a brain and then I can give it life … unlike the limbs, life cannot be restored once life is gone. The brain is life and so a living brain must be used.' The brain that he intends to transplant is that of Karl, the former prison guard, who has unwavering faith in Stein's medical and surgical skills: 'You must have great faith in Dr Stein,' Kleve remarks to Karl. 'I do,' Karl responds solemnly. In exchange for saving Frankenstein from the guillotine in the film's opening sequence, Karl is repaid with the promise of a new, 'perfect' body. Significantly, Karl has a 'fine brain' – 'he's quick, intelligent, and he's absorbed a great deal of knowledge' – and will be instrumental in helping Stein realise his life's ambition. Based on his previous experiments with brain transplants first in reptiles and then in anthropoids, Stein believes he has proved his theory that the 'brain will continue to function regardless of its environment'.

Although *Revenge* is set in nineteenth-century England, Stein's medical experiments are well ahead of their time. He understands that animal experimentation is essential to ensure scientific progress, and his laboratory experiments on chimpanzees particularly reflect a growing trend in medical research during the 1940s and 1950s. Stein explains that in his early surgical transplants he 'removed the brain of a lizard and replaced it with that of a frog. The lizard attempted to jump, but of course it was physically incapable.' Stein has also replaced Otto the chimpanzee's brain with that of an orangutan, with some measure of success. As Stein was pioneering and perfecting his own fictional work with brain transplantation, real-world surgeons were just beginning to make progress in the 1950s with organ transplants. While the first successful kidney transplant took place in December 1954, other kinds of organ transplants (lungs, heart, etc.) were not attempted until the 1960s. Although the cinematic treatment of brain transplantation was not necessarily introduced in *Revenge of Frankenstein* – (consider *Donovan's Brain* (1953) – several non-Hammer films did attempt to capitalise on similar sensational plots over the next decade. These include *The Brain that Wouldn't Die* (1959), *The Brain* (1963), *The Madmen of Mandoras* (1963), and *They Saved Hitler's Brain* (1968). This cinematic interest in brain transplantation suggests that with *Revenge* Hammer had put its finger on an important fear of the day.

In spite of all the advantages Stein has in this surgical procedure, including the highly competent Kleve as his assistant, his experiment will once again go awry. Following what appears to be a successful operation, Karl is moved to an attic room at the hospital, where his brain and body will have the chance to adjust to each other. How long this adjustment period is to be is not clear, but the recuperation time is essential, as Stein has well learned. Significantly, Stein's fitness stems in part from his ability to learn from his surgical mistakes. In the brain transplant experiment with Otto, Stein explains, the chimpanzee became a carnivore because his brain did not have sufficient time to heal. 'I discovered it soon after the operation,' Stein explains matter-of-factly. 'He ate his wife.'

A week after the operation, Stein removes the bandages from Karl's head, performs a brief physical exam, and exclaims, 'There's very little wrong with you, Karl. Congratulations.' Stein then heads out to tend to his other patients and leaves Kleve to monitor Karl's recovery. When Karl asks Kleve what will happen to him Kleve unwittingly reveals that Stein plans to make a medical spectacle out of him. 'Oh, there are great plans for you,' Kleve says matter-of-factly. 'Doctors and scientists will come from all over the world to see you and to talk to you. Dr Stein intends to hold student lectures. They'll see you – a normal man with a normal body – side by side with your old body.' Karl is horrified that he will continue to be treated like a freak: 'All my life I've been stared at,' he moans. Karl escapes from the hospital under the cover of night. He subsequently returns to his 'birthplace' – the 'workshop of filthy creation' – and attempts to avoid the future that Kleve has described by destroying his original, deformed body in the incinerator.

During this highly disturbing self-cremation scene, Otto, the carnivorous chimp, becomes increasingly agitated, violently rattling the bars of his cage and shrieking madly. A drunken janitor discovers the intruder (Karl) in Stein's laboratory and strikes him violently several times. Despite the cowering Karl's plea of 'Don't hit me, please,' the sadistic janitor is unrelenting. He taunts and strikes Karl again and again until something apparently snaps. Karl's docility morphs predictably into a violent rage and, with a newly recognised strength, Karl strangles his assailant. In this scene, we see clear parallels with Whale's 1931 film as well as with Shelley's original. Whale's Creature murders the sadistic Fritz, and Shelley's Creature becomes 'malicious' because he is miserable: 'I, like the archfiend, bore a hell within me, and finding myself unsympathised with, wished to tear up the trees, spread havoc and destruction around me, and then to have sat down and enjoyed the ruin' (Shelley 147, 138). Not only does the Creature's claim of innate goodness[13] underscore Shelley's belief in environmental determinism, but Karl's similar transformation in *Revenge* reflects Huxley's twentieth-century scientific view of the nature-versus-nurture debate: 'Environment plays not merely a large part, but a preponderating one, in [man's] development after the first year or so of life' (*Essays* qtd in Kevles 6).

Not having had sufficient time to recover from surgery, the physical trauma to his newly transplanted brain, along with the janitor's horrific bullying, turns Karl, at least temporarily, into a monster (Figure 8.1). As the lifeless body of the janitor sinks to the floor, a strange calm settles over the crazed Otto, who has watched this violence while contentedly munching on a piece of raw meat. Karl, meanwhile, quickly reverts to his previous docile state. Horrified by his own violent act, he begins to drool and groans miserably. It is apparent that Karl is no blood-thirsty killer, but a man possessed of conscience and feeling. Significantly, Sangster's accounting for the Creature's turn to violence is both environmental and biological. In fusing the two, Sangster draws in part on Shelley's original, in which the Creature becomes malicious because he is shunned and mistreated by others, and in part on the 1931 Universal film version, in which the

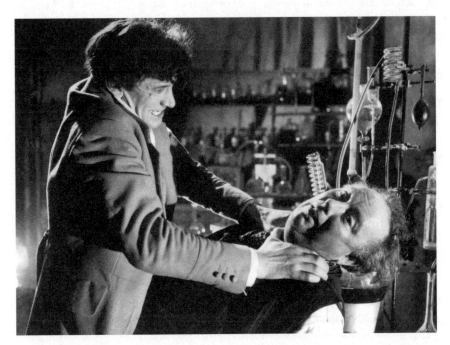

Figure 8.1 Michael Gwynn as Karl, the Creature, on the rampage in *The Revenge of Frankenstein*.

Creature's malevolent nature is supposedly 'hard-wired' (he has received the brain of a criminal, although he is also tortured by the sadistic Fritz).

Hammer's version of the Creature is not only the most evolved in terms of Stein's scientific prowess, he is also the most sympathetic of all of the Frankenstein 'monsters' to this point. Karl is a profoundly tortured creature in both body and soul. He attempts to erase all memories and evidence of his former monstrous body by destroying it in the incinerator, but the trauma to his transplanted brain leads, tragically, to the return of his paralysis. Apparently, Karl's traumatised brain cannot 'rewire' itself; he is unable to forget how his old, disfigured body functioned, and despite his new, able body, Karl reverts to his former, misshapen self (Figure 8.2).[14]

Before Stein and Kleve are able to track Karl down, he somewhat inexplicably attacks a young couple in the park. While his actions here do not exactly follow logically from the previous scene, where a pitiful and broken Karl has sought shelter in the Countess Barscynska's stables, the scene nevertheless does capitalise on the gratuitous 'monster on the loose' terror that audiences would have come to expect. The scene also functions as an implicit nod to Huxley's popular book on ants and to his ideas about evolution and eugenics. Described as 'instructive entertainment' (Kevles 2), Huxley's *Ants* argued for the fundamental differences between the social organisation of ants and humans. Unlike ants, he pointed out, humans can adapt to new conditions through the power of rapid learning and conceptual thinking. Just before Karl attacks the young couple we see two teenagers, presumably on a date, but the young man is more preoccupied with observing an ant colony than he is with 'getting on with it'. The boy explains, 'Ants is interesting; you can learn a lot from ants.' 'Well,' the impatient girl points out, 'You haven't learned much … they've got more sense than to sit around all night.' Frustrated with the boy's inability to find interest in her rather than the ants, she stomps off in a huff, only to be attacked and strangled by Karl, who has been lurking in the shadows. This dialogue between the boy and the girl was noted specifically by the MPAA as being offensive, but, as we see, Hinds refused to compromise here (Kinsey 120). The boy, however, may be marked as 'unfit' precisely because he is unable to comprehend the girl's not-so-subtle invitation. His inability to adapt to a new situation – particularly one that has procreative possibilities – diminishes their chance for survival. Anticipating the formula of modern slasher films, the girl must be the one who falls victim to the killer because she is marked as sexual.

Karl's next and final appearance occurs shortly thereafter, when he literally crashes a society party where Stein is in attendance. As the guests recoil in fear and revulsion at this monster, an anguished Karl stumbles toward Stein, pleading, 'Frankenstein, help me,' before he collapses and dies. Once again havoc ensues, as word quickly spreads to members of the medical council, to the other members of fashionable society, and to the patients in the charity hospital, of Stein's true identity. When Stein shows up for his rounds, his angry patients greet him with accusations of 'Mutilator! Murderer!' Stein's patients become a mob and viciously attack him until Kleve comes to his rescue.

Figure 8.2 Karl's (Michael Gwynn) once handsome new body as it reverts in *The Revenge of Frankenstein*.

Kleve takes Stein's broken body back to the laboratory, but it is clear that Stein will not recover from the beating. Stein whispers to Kleve, 'It's no good. You know what to do.' In the laboratory, a new body has already been assembled. It falls to Kleve to put into practice all that Stein has taught him. Ironically, Kleve prays to heaven that he will be able to do what needs to be done. In the last scene of the film, we see that the locale has changed to Harley Street in London. A camera close-up focuses on a sign that reads 'Dr. Franck'. We see a pair of hands being washed in the sink as the camera lingers on a familiar tattoo. Inside the office we see that the moustached and monocled Dr Franck is none other than Stein.

He shows none of the ill effects of the radical brain transplant operation that we typically see in Frankenstein movies – indeed the figure we see reflected in the mirror is robust and healthy, and his medical practice is thriving. With an air of self-congratulation and self-adulation, he remarks to Kleve, 'You were an excellent pupil, Hans. The scar will hardly show.' Frankenstein has become his own near-perfect creation.

After two failed attempts to achieve this success in *The Curse of Frankenstein* and *The Revenge of Frankenstein*, what we might call the Hammer Frankenstein project has finally proved successful. In large part this project was a success because of Frankenstein's evolving skills and his ability to pass skills on to another highly competent surgeon, Dr Hans Kleve. But it was also successful because Dr Frankenstein, better than anyone else, knew how to adapt. The *perfection* of the Frankenstein project is that the scientist and his creation have merged – perpetual fugitives from justice, they are quintessential models of adaptive evolutionary change. The operation at the end of *The Revenge of Frankenstein* is a glorious success (at least in Frankenstein's eyes) because it is the culmination and perfection of his wildest dreams. He has finally remade himself in his own image and been freed from the constraints that Shelley put on him. Only Hammer Films was bold enough to do this in 1958.[15]

Notes

1 *Pace* Darwin, Gary Bortolotti and Linda Hutcheon identify a source text (in this case, Mary Shelley's *Frankenstein*) as a 'replicator' – 'a distinct and discrete entity', a 'unit of selection by which we can understand change over time' (447). Moreover, the replicator's (narrative's) flourishing is measured by its survival in the form of long-lived copies and versions of itself. Fitness or success thus equals 'persistence, abundance, and diversity' (452).

2 The 'X' category in England at this time referred to films suitable for those aged 16 years and older and should not be confused with the later American rating of X.

3 In the United States the title was changed to *Horror of Dracula* to avoid being confused with Universal's 1931 film.

4 After the Creature has killed his first victim, Frankenstein and Krempe hunt him down, and Krempe, against the instructions of Frankenstein, shoots the Creature. The Creature survives the shot in the head and runs off. After Frankenstein's maid, Justine, is murdered, Frankenstein confronts his demented Creature. A struggle ensues and the Creature falls into a vat of acid, effectively dissolving all evidence that it ever existed. A despondent Frankenstein tells the priest that his 'life's work' has been destroyed. In a twist of fate, Frankenstein is convicted of the murders committed by his Creature. *Curse* ends with Frankenstein being marched off to the guillotine, all the while maintaining his innocence.

5 As historian Betty Smocovitis notes, 'the supremacy of natural selection was a dominant theme' and any doubts about Darwinian theory raised at the 1959 conference were inconsequential (294, 298).

6   Sir Julian Huxley was not only a scientist-celebrity in his own right, but he also hailed from one of the most famous and influential intellectual families in England: his grandfather was T.H. Huxley ('Darwin's Bulldog') and his brother was Aldous Huxley, the author of *Brave New World*. Julian Huxley was one of the main architects of the modern synthesis of evolutionary biology – also known as the Neo-Darwinian synthesis – which integrates Darwin's account of natural history with the experimental principles of modern lab-based genetics. For more on Huxley's global influence as a 'statesman' and populariser of science, see Walters and van Helden, and Daniel J. Kevles.

7   'Life and death appeared to me ideal bounds, which I should break through, and pour a torrent of life into our dark world' (Shelley 55).

8   Though there were earlier silent film adaptations of *Frankenstein*, Universal Studios cemented the image of the mad scientist in *Frankenstein* (1931), *Bride of Frankenstein* (1935), *Son of Frankenstein* (1939), and beyond.

9   Following Albrecht-Crane and Cutchins' suggestion that we can 'discern specific forces (social, economic, historical, and authorial) at work in particular … adaptations' (19), Stein's exchange with this clinic patient about the dangers of smoking is worth noting. The first large-scale studies of the relationship between smoking and lung cancer were carried out in the 1950s in the UK, and in 1957 the Central Council for Health Education in the UK issued a pamphlet, 'What – No Smoking?' that dealt in comic strip form with the adventures of the fictional Wisdom family and their physician, Dr Brain (see Berridge and Loughlin). In 1958 (the year that *Revenge* was released), the health authority smoking withdrawal clinic was established in England.

10 This clever aside is apparently a gentle dig at Universal.

11 These were not, however, Hammer Films. *Frankenstein's Daughter* was produced by Astor Pictures in 1958 and *Frankenstein 1970*, which featured Boris Karloff as Baron von Frankenstein, was an independent film release (Aubrey Schenk Productions), also in 1958.

12 Eugenics as a social philosophy was first developed in the 1880s by Francis Dalton, who applied Darwin's theory of evolution to human beings.

13 'I was benevolent and good; misery made me a fiend' (103).

14 Though Karl has not had any limbs amputated, he experiences something along the lines of 'phantom limb syndrome', the ability of an amputee to feel sensations and/or pain in a limb (or limbs) that no longer exist.

15 Significantly, there is a six-year gap between *Revenge* and the next Hammer Frankenstein film, *The Evil of Frankenstein* (1964). Moreover, none of the subsequent films even references anything that went on in *Curse* or *Revenge*. It is as though Frankenstein's great success in *Revenge* never occurred. This, of course, is why we have focused our attention here on the first two films. They are arguably the best films in the series and *Revenge*, as we have argued, in particular offers a thoroughly innovative and unique adaptation of the original source text.

Bibliography

Albrecht-Crane, Christina and Dennis Cutchins. *Adaptation Studies: New Approaches*. Fairleigh Dickinson UP, 2010.

Berridge, Virginia and Loughlin, Kelly. 'Smoking and the New Health Education in Britain, 1950s–1970s.' *Journal of American Public Health* 95.6 (2005): 956–964.

Bortolotti, Gary R. and Hutcheon, Linda. 'On the Origin of Adaptations: Rethinking Fidelity Discourse and "Success" – Biologically.' *New Literary History* 38 (2007): 443–458.

Curse of Frankenstein, The. Directed by Terence Fisher. 1957. Burbank, CA: Warner Home Video, 2002.

Hearn, Marcus and Barnes, Alan. *The Hammer Story*. London: Titan, 2007.

Heffernan, Kevin. *Ghouls, Gimmicks, and Gold*. Durham, NC and London: Duke UP, 2004.

Hindle, Maurice.' Introduction.' *Frankenstein*, by Mary Shelley. Ed. Maurice Hindle. New York: Penguin, 2003. xi–l.

Hutcheon, Linda. *A Theory of Adaptation*. New York: Routledge, 2012.

Huxley, Julian. *Ants*. New York: Jonathan Cape and Harrison Smith, 1930.

——— . *New Bottles for New Wine*. London: Chatto & Windus, 1957.

——— . *Religion Without Revelation*. New York: Harper & Bros., 1957.

Kevles, Daniel J. 'Huxley and the Popularization of Science.' Humanities Working Paper, 127. Pasadena, CA: California Institute of Technology, 1988. http://resolver.caltech.edu/CaltechAUTHORS:20111103–105255076.

Kinsey, Wayne. *Hammer Films: The Bray Studio Years*. London: Reynolds and Hearn, 2002.

Leitch, Thomas. 'Everything You Always Wanted to Know about Adaptation, Especially if You're Looking Forward Rather than Back.' *Literature/Film Quarterly* 33.3 (2005): 233–45.

Maltin, Leonard. *Leonard Maltin's 2014 Movie Guide*. New York: Plume, 2014.

Meikle, Denis. *A History of Horrors: The Rise and Fall of the House of Hammer*. Lanham, MD and London: Scarecrow P, 1996.

Revenge of Frankenstein, The. Directed by Terence Fisher. 1958. Culver City, CA: TriStar Home Entertainment, 2002.

Schor, Esther. '*Frankenstein* and Film.' *The Cambridge Companion to Mary Shelley*. Cambridge: Cambridge UP, 2004. 63–83.

Shelley, Mary. *Frankenstein*. Ed. Maurice Hindle. New York: Penguin, 2003.

Smocovitis, Betty. 'The 1959 Darwin Centennial Celebration in America.' *Osiris*, 2nd series, vol. 14, *Commemorative Practices in Science: Historical Perspectives on the Politics of Collective Memory* (1999): 274–323.

Walters, Kenneth and van Helden, Albert van Helden, eds. *Julian Huxley: Biologist and Statesman of Science*. Houston: Rice UP, 1992.

Part III

Literary adaptations of *Frankenstein*

9

'Plainly stitched together':
Frankenstein, neo-Victorian fiction, and the
palimpsestuous literary past

Jamie Horrocks

IN TED CHIANG'S SHORT story 'Seventy-Two Letters' (2000), the survival of the human race hinges upon the viability of a single, genetically modified and scientifically fabricated human being. When viewed by the story's steampunk scientist for the first time, this proto-man – a 'megafoetus ... clear as aspic, curled up in foetal position' – lies floating in a vat of nutrient fluid (179). The sight of this monstrosity, created with remarkable speed in just a fortnight, prompts Chiang's protagonist to turn to his companion and ask a question that resounds with a multiplicity of past iterations: 'Is this creature ... alive?' (179).

Spoken without irony (but not without a wink of postmodern precognition) by the story's nineteenth-century protagonist, the question immediately situates Chiang's retrofuturistic laboratory, his creature, and his scientists within a long tradition of *Frankenstein* adaptations. This is not to suggest that readers of 'Seventy-Two Letters' would necessarily access this tradition through Mary Shelley's novel. Fans of Chiang's literature would be just as likely to see, in its rehearsal of scientific overreaching gone awry, the shadowy presence of twentieth-century television and film adaptations of *Frankenstein* – perhaps James Whale's (in which the famous phrase, 'It's alive', was first uttered), but perhaps not. Still other readers might miss the reference completely, locating meaning instead in the eclectic fictional universe in which Chiang places his tale of a monstrous creature being brought to life. Populated by earnest scientists who use cutting-edge technology to tread where no scientist has gone before, this universe bears a resemblance to that created by Shelley, yet it remains unfamiliar to many scholars of nineteenth-century British literature. It is, however, well known to aficionados of neo-Victorian fiction, a genre of popular literature that includes steampunk stories like Chiang's.

Like steampunk itself, which Colbey Emmerson Reid describes as a 'theoretical reorientation of history' (138), neo-Victorian fiction has its roots in late-twentieth-century retrofuturistic literature. A loose and somewhat ersatz genre that encompasses several literary and pop cultural sub-genres, neo-Victorian fiction distinguishes itself from historical fiction in its metacognisant awareness of the present and of present interpretations of the historical past. Mark Llewellyn's definition of a neo-Victorian text makes this apparent. He writes that the category encompasses 'those works which are consciously set in the Victorian period (or the nineteenth century …), which desire to re-write the historical narrative of that period by representing … generally "different" versions of the Victorian' ('What' 165). Historical fiction set in Britain or its empire in the nineteenth century might have similar revisionist tendencies, but it does not share with neo-Victorian fiction the latter's self-conscious metafictionality (Heilmann and Llewellyn 4). This trait is paramount and typically takes precedence over other characteristics that might seem to disqualify a work from the genre. Many texts considered classic pieces of neo-Victorian fiction, for example, are not set neatly within the standard 1832–1901 date range of the Victorian literary era but take place earlier or later, in a conceptually (rather than chronologically) constructed 'long nineteenth century'.

In its metafictional deployment of twentieth-century *Frankenstein* motifs within a technologically sophisticated nineteenth-century setting, Chiang's 'Seventy-Two Letters' exemplifies this modern neo-Victorian fictional aesthetic. But his text is not the first to yoke a post-human, even cyborgian, creature with retrofuturistic technology. As early as 1823, the year that Mary Shelley's name first appeared on her novel *Frankenstein*, a burlesque called *Frank-n-Steam* premiered at the Adelphi Theatre in London (Morton 60).[1] Although the original script has been lost, Victorian accounts suggest that this drama relied, like Chiang's story, on audience members' recognition not of Shelley's tale itself but of another adaptation of that tale already circulating in British popular culture: Richard Brinsley Peake's *Presumption; or, The Fate of Frankenstein*. And, also like 'Seventy-Two Letters', *Frank-n-Steam* located its Frankensteinian Creature – most likely a steam-operated mechanical man, similar to the one that appeared in an Oxford melodrama the following year (Morton 60) – within an alternative nineteenth-century world that looked simultaneously back to the eighteenth-century steam inventions that began the Industrial Revolution and forward to a time when such rudimentary technology could be used to create an animate being. Thus, the method of Chiang's adaptation of the Frankenstein Complex in 'Seventy-Two Letters', his placement of a new iteration of the complex into a retrofuturistic nineteenth-century setting distinguished by anachronistic technological development, is nearly as old as Shelley's novel.

Perhaps Steffen Hantke had this in mind when he observed that a special relationship seems to exist between Shelley's *Frankenstein* and modern writers of neo-Victorian fiction (250). While some of the most famous neo-Victorian texts (works like William Gibson and Bruce Sterling's *The Difference Engine*, Neal Stephenson's *The Diamond Age*, or Alan Moore's *League of Extraordinary Gentlemen*) make no reference to Shelley's Creature, many other pieces bear out Hantke's observation, including the two texts on which this chapter will focus: Paul Di Filippo's 'Hottentots' (1995) and Peter Ackroyd's *The Casebook of Victor Frankenstein* (2008). Like all neo-Victorian literature, these two works possess a metafictional self-reflexivity that prompts readers to 're-vision' the historical past in alternative ways.[2] But here, the re-visioning takes place in a way that makes evident one reason why the Frankenstein Complex appears and reappears in neo-Victorian literature with special insistence. Di Filippo's and Ackroyd's texts – both of which allude to, appropriate from, or adapt Shelley's *Frankenstein* – demonstrate how the 'hideous progeny' of Mary Shelley's imagination becomes an embodiment of the palimpsestuous narrative production central to both neo-Victorian fiction and adaptation. In other words, the idea of the Frankenstein Complex provides a particularly apt analogy for the things neo-Victorian fiction attempts to do and the ways it attempts to do them.

The fish as palimpsest: Di Filippo's 'Hottentots'

The project of re-visioning the past undertaken by writers of neo-Victorian fiction relies upon the interweaving of multiple narratives – a defining feature of this particular genre. However, even the most apparently unidimensional text consists of multiple layers of signs that call up, rely upon, imitate, and differentiate themselves from other referents. This makes every text 'hypertextual', to use the term employed by Gérard Genette, and Roland Barthes before him. 'There is no literary work', writes Genette, 'that does not evoke … some other literary work' (9). 'Art creates art, [and] literature is made by literature', Julie Sanders points out (1); it is a 'stereophony of echoes, citations, references' (Barthes 160). But adaptations, 'aesthetic objects in their own right' (Hutcheon, *Adaptation* 6), are particularly complex examples of hypertexts in that at all times they are 'haunted' by specific adapted texts (Hutcheon, *Theory* 6). They are 'multilaminated works', according to Linda Hutcheon, and are 'inherently "palimpsestuous"' in that adaptations are texts through which other texts are always visible (*Adaptation* 6). This characteristic is central to the theorisation of adaptations '*as adaptations*' (*Adaptation* 6, italics original).

Neo-Victorian texts share with adaptations this palimpsestuous quality because they are, by definition, texts that re-vision earlier narratives. They represent a postmodern attempt to 're-write the historical narrative of [nineteenth-century Britain] by representing … generally "different" versions of the Victorian' (Llewellyn, 'What' 165). For this reason, Hutcheon calls neo-Victorian texts 'historiographic metafictions' (*Poetics* 105), or texts that present a fictive version of the past but do so while questioning the 'conventions of narrative, of reference, of the inscribing of subjectivity, of [their] identity as textuality, and even of [their] implication in ideology' (106). A neo-Victorian novel might recreate a version of Victorian London, Manchester, or Birmingham that captures the past with great historical accuracy,[3] but its primary motivation in doing so would be 'an essentially revisionist impulse to reconstruct the past by questioning the certitude of our historical knowledge' (Shiller 541). There is always, as Peter Widdowson explains, a '"present understanding" of past periods' in neo-Victorian texts – a 'self-consciousness that [the author's] is a version of the past reproduced in and by the present, one constructed and mediated in the narrative tropes of their fiction' (495).

The literature of Di Filippo and Ackroyd, then, becomes neo-Victorian not when it recreates a historically accurate version of nineteenth-century Britain, but when that recreation begins to examine Victorian literary conventions and social ideologies through parody, pastiche, appropriation, or rearticulation. This self-reflexive engagement is premised upon the visibility of multiple layers of narrative signification that indicate palimpsestuous presentness within the representation of the past. In Di Filippo's story, 'Hottentots', for example, the title alone carries the weight of substantial multilamination. For a twenty-first-century reader, it is at once a rearticulation of nineteenth-century racist nomenclature and a parody of such prejudice, both an acknowledgement of Victorian anxieties surrounding miscegenation and imperial dominance and a critique of these anxieties. The title additionally recalls the cultural narrative of Saartjie Baartman, the famed 'Hottentot Venus' exhibited in the early nineteenth century, and gestures toward the reworking of that narrative in Di Filippo's tale. At the same time, the contested etymology of the word 'Hottentot' (perhaps an onomatopoetic imitation of the Khoikhoi language spoken by the Africans who were given this designation; perhaps a corruption of the Dutch word for 'stammerer' or 'stutterer', indicating Europeans' inability to conceive of Khoikhoi clicks as linguistically meaningful; perhaps an Anglicisation of a common Khoikhoi greeting (du Plessis 189–193)) highlights the essential unknowability of a past that is reconstructed as 'real' or 'authentic' only in the present.

At no point in Di Filippo's short story are any of these references – this stereophonic literary and cultural noise – muted in an effort to present the Victorian past as a seamless or coherent entity. Rather, Di Filippo exerts considerable narrative energy to ensure that all layers of signification remain contradictorily apparent to readers. For, as Mark Llewellyn writes, the

> importance of the palimpsest lies not in its writing of new texts over old ones, but in the simultaneous existence of both narratives on the same page, occupying the same space, and speaking in odd, obscure, and different ways to one another. For it is important to remember that, as the neo-Victorian text writes back to something in the nineteenth century, it does so in a manner that often aims to re-fresh and re-vitalize the importance of that earlier text to the here and now. The contemporaneous historicism present in the text thus becomes the key to its neo-Victorian classification. ('What' 170–171)

This aspect of neo-Victorian fiction locates the genre in what is, essentially, a discourse of adaptation. In some neo-Victorian texts, authors rely more on a body of literature than on any one publication, making the intertextuality more a dialogue of ideas than a sustained adaptation of a single text. In others, however, the adapted text (or texts) serves as more than just a basis for hypertextual allusion. It provides a specific frame of reference from which one might both interpret the new text and reinterpret the old. This is the case with 'Hottentots', in which a reader's knowledge of the countless iterations of the central narrative of Shelley's *Frankenstein* shapes the construction of meaning.

'Hottentots' appears in the centre of Di Filippo's *Steampunk Trilogy*. It is flanked on either side by 'Victoria', a short story describing Queen Victoria's replacement on the throne by a biologically modified (and surprisingly sexy) newt, and 'Walt and Emily', which recounts the Zeppelin-kindled love affair of Walt Whitman and Emily Dickinson. A parody of the Victorian scientist and the sweeping prejudices lurking beneath his supposedly objective attempts to collect and classify, 'Hottentots' relates the fictional adventure of nineteenth-century naturalist Louis Agassiz as he attempts to save Massachusetts from monstrous invasion.[4] The story begins, however, with a different creature from the deep, something less threatening yet more burdened with cultural and literary significance: a 'big fish' (85). 'Plainly stitched together at its midsection' (85), this Frankensteinian adaptation appears in 'Hottentots' separated from Shelley's novel by multiple iterations of cinematic and textual adaptations. As in countless B-movie versions of Shelley's *Frankenstein*, the fish's collage of parts remains grotesquely apparent, announcing its artificiality as well as that of the preposterous 'fish tale' in which it is couched. This fish, its sutures protesting against the very deception they propagate, plays a key role in Di Filippo's story. Both a product of narrative and an incitement to narrative production, it becomes a visible metaphor for adaptation and a representation of the palimpsestuous way that neo-Victorian fiction employs adaptation to unravel seemingly objective accounts of the past.

The opening scene in 'Hottentots', in which a local fisherman brings this 'piscine horror' (88) to the naturalist Louis Agassiz, reveals a complicated patchwork of literary and historical borrowings, all of which serve to deconstruct the portrait of Victorianism that Di Filippo offers readers. The most evident of these appropriations (although by no means the most important) is Shelley's *Frankenstein*, which resonates repeatedly in 'Hottentots'. Blending fact and fiction, Di Filippo gives Agassiz an uncanny resemblance to Shelley's titular character. Like Victor Frankenstein, Agassiz is Swiss born and educated in Germany (85). Again like his precursor, Agassiz has a healthy regard for his own intelligence and entertains visions of the glory that will one day attend the scientific discoveries he means to make. The fish, alas, is not one of these.

It is not so much the stitching – 'sloppy looping overhand whiplashes formed of black waxed twine ran around its entire circumference like the grin on an insane rag doll' (85) – that appals Agassiz; rather, it is the presumptuous conspicuousness of the fish's assembly and the frightening hybridity it suggests. What he calls the 'abomination' (86) that a fisherman places in his lap is 'mismatched slightly in size' and worse still, 'the halves of the hybrid did not fuse neatly, but revealed the pinkish white inner meat of the larger front'. A 'pale serum slowly leaked from its jointure' (85). The fisherman responsible for the 'discovery' has made almost no effort to disguise his creative manipulations before passing the creature off to Agassiz as a genuine specimen and asking for payment. In fact, the tail, which belongs to a sturgeon, 'was mated upside down to the head' – taken from a barracuda – 'so that the ventral fin was now impossibly in a dorsal position' (85). No respectable scientist would believe that the blatantly reconstructed animal existed in nature; its artificiality is everywhere apparent so that readers, like Agassiz, cannot help but see that it is a monstrous fabrication.

However, it is the fish's very constructedness, its material impossibility, that reminds readers that Agassiz's most famous fish never actually existed in flesh and blood. It, too, was a creature of metaphor, the subject of a much-repeated parable. In 1934, Ezra Pound memorialised 'The Parable of the Sunfish' in his *ABC of Reading*. This tale, and the work of literary criticism in which it appears, provide another layer of literary meaning that Di Filippo folds into 'Hottentots'. In *ABC of Reading*, Pound calls upon 'the anecdote of Agassiz and the fish' to illustrate his New Critical assertion that the 'proper method for studying poetry and good letters is the method of contemporary biologists, that is careful first-hand examination of the matter' (17). The parable describes a post-graduate student who goes to study with Agassiz. The first task the scientist gives the student is to describe a small fish. 'That's only a sunfish', the student replies (17). Agassiz agrees but asks the student to look more carefully and to write a description of the fish. The student returns, first with the scientific name and later with a four-page essay on the fish, but again and again Agassiz declares the student's descriptions insufficient and demands that he look at the fish. Finally, 'at the end of three weeks the fish was in an advanced state of decomposition, but the student knew something about it' (18).

The parable, never mentioned by Di Filippo but impossible not to see lurking behind the primary narrative as the fisherman presents Agassiz with his sutured specimen, functions trans-textually in 'Hottentots' in several ways, all of which point to the metanarrative project of neo-Victorian fiction. Pound uses the anecdote to illustrate the hazards of abstraction and the need for readers and writers of literature to adhere to the real, which he associates with the visible: 'Science does not consist in inventing a number of more or less abstract entities corresponding to the number of things you wish to find out' (18). In the parable, however, the student is not simply learning to see a reality that exists transparently in material objects and waits to be recorded as it really is. Rather, as Christopher Tilley explains, he is learning 'a way of approaching that reality – a discourse bound up in a particular thought tradition' (76). This suggests, of course, that 'different discourses' produce 'different realities', that representation actively creates 'the reality of that which we investigate' (Tilley 76) – a notion that lies at the heart of neo-Victorian literature's re-visioning of the past.

In addition, Pound's/Agassiz's parable, palimpsestuously appearing at the moment when Di Filippo deploys his adaptation of the Frankenstein Complex, is itself an adaptation and should be regarded, Robert Scholes contends, 'as a text related to other texts' (655). Scholes notes that in Pound's reiteration of the anecdote, he adapts versions of the story originally found in two other texts written by students of Agassiz: Nathaniel Southgate Shaler's 1907 *Autobiography*, and an 1874 story published by Samuel H. Scudder in *Every Saturday* magazine (Scholes 655). These two texts were later adapted by Lane Cooper in his 1917 *Louis Agassiz as a Teacher*, in which Cooper makes the same comparison between biology and the study of literature that Pound makes in the *ABC of Reading* (Scholes 655). Whether Pound initially stumbled upon the parable of the sunfish in Shaler, Scudder, or Cooper is largely irrelevant; what is significant is the fact that Pound's use of Agassiz's fish is an adaptation of an adaptation, making Di Filippo's further conscription of it merely one more adaptive iteration. What readers find, then, when the fisherman hands his leaky, misshapen specimen to Agassiz in 'Hottentots', is a brilliant literary portrait of the decentring of source texts that occurs in adaptation, a decentring that extends to the narrative of nineteenth-century history such that this narrative becomes impossible for readers to consider as anything more than a parable itself.

A similar re-visioning of the Victorian past takes place as Di Filippo adds yet another palimpsestuous layer of textuality to his opening scene, one in which the 'plainly stitched' creature and its embeddedness in the Frankensteinian tradition become a means of critiquing a specific type of Victorian cultural arrogance. When presented by the fisherman with the mangled fish, Agassiz's initial response is revelatory. He pronounces it a 'monstrous miscegenation' (85) and a 'queer specimen' (89), and he admits that he 'suddenly saw embodied in it all his fears of cross-breeding' (88). Agassiz's attitude, the anxious flight of his mind to degeneration, deviant sexuality, and the decline of racial purity, is instantly recognisable to readers familiar with Victorian literature. One thinks of novels by Bram Stoker, Rider Haggard, H.G. Wells, Joseph Conrad, Rudyard Kipling, and now – as Agassiz reflects further – Mary Shelley: 'With a shiver, he recalled the similarly stitched creature born in Mrs. Shelley's imagination. What if Nature should ever permit such monsters?' (88). Agassiz's question asks readers to reconsider Shelley's *Frankenstein* in the context of the racial anxiety more commonly associated with novels published at the end rather than the beginning of the nineteenth century. It also, and more interestingly, connects the bigotry exhibited by Agassiz with the practice of Victorian science, a profession ostensibly dedicated to studying 'Nature' in all its manifold variety. This suggestion – that there is a link between Agassiz's racism and the egoism underpinning Victorian naturalism – is showcased in one more text that begins to become visible at this point in 'Hottentots': Oliver Wendell Holmes's 1865 poem, 'A Farewell to Agassiz'.

Not referenced explicitly by Di Filippo, but certainly another narrative layer in the multilamination of 'Hottentots', Holmes's poem was written as a paean to the famous scientist. To modern eyes and ears, however, it reads very differently. Composed (with deadpan praise) on the eve of Agassiz's departure for Brazil on a scientific expedition, the poem imagines all of nature laying itself open to the intellectual probing of Agassiz. Eager to reveal their secrets to the man of genius, the peaks of the Andes will 'bare their snowy scalps / To the climber of the Alps / When the cry goes through their passes, / "Here comes the great Agassiz!"' (Holmes 5–8). Not only this, but 'The rivers bend to meet him, / The forests bow to greet him, / It thrills the spinal column / Of fossil fishes solemn, / And glaciers crawl the faster / To the feet of their old master!' (19–24). Holmes depicts Agassiz's museum-stocking work as a triumph of modern science, but readers cannot help but note the arrogance motivating the naturalist's endeavours. All of 'creation' remains, inevitably, 'dumb' (83) while Agassiz tears through the landscape in pursuit of the 'million novel data' (59) that he'll use to speak the 'truth' of nature. Such an incursion may be a 'glorious raid', as Holmes qualifies it, but it is a raid nonetheless (79). More disturbing still, Agassiz's data gathering is only nominally objective. Holmes writes, 'May he [Agassiz] find, with his apostles, / That the land is full of fossils, / That the waters swarm with fishes / Shaped according to his wishes' (51–54). These lines look forward to the scientist's certain success in discovering exactly what he might have wished for. Yet they also suggest that Agassiz might be shaping his discoveries to fit his conclusions, rather than vice versa. He finds what he wants to find, in other words, and perhaps fails to see that which does not accord with his theories.

What readers come away with, then, is a troubling rather than a celebratory portrait of Agassiz. Even the alternating pyrrhic and trochaic feet and the tightly rhymed couplets, which strike a modern reader as comical rather than laudatory, seem to ridicule the man and his lofty endeavours. The praise granted to him within the poem is undercut by this metre and by a sense of misplaced commendation. That is, one notices that Agassiz's specimens (the 'mighty megalosaurus / Leads the palaeozoic chorus' (87–88)) end up trumpeting Agassiz himself rather than the knowledge or scientific advancement he purportedly represents. Their shouts of 'God bless the great Professor!' (74) suggest both the fossils' own – and God's – approval of Agassiz's work. Taken together, all of these elements direct readers of 'A Farewell to Agassiz' and, ultimately, of 'Hottentots' toward a compelling critique of Victorian science and the racial, cultural, and intellectual prejudices that cannot be separated from it. An unwitting accomplice, Holmes's poem prompts a re-reading of Agassiz that parallels and abets Di Filippo's reconstruction of the Victorian narrative of scientific progress and the great men embedded within this narrative – men whom many continue to regard as pioneers of intellectual achievement.

Bringing into 'Hottentots' all of this and perhaps more, the Frankensteinian fish, like the story itself, becomes a piecemeal archive of narrative that serves both to expand and to deconstruct the tale of which it is a part. This is a hallmark of neo-Victorian fiction and of adaptation itself, which employs familiar narratives to generate new texts that prompt us to re-vision the old. Unsurprisingly, in 'Hottentots', this mode of narrative production (or reproduction) is embodied by and dependent upon Agassiz's fish, or, rather, on the line of thick, black sutures that reminds us of its multilaminate construction.

Readers begin to see the incitement to narrative provided by the hypertextual creature as Agassiz converses with the fisherman who brings him the specimen. Astonished by the man's temerity, Agassiz is initially speechless – 'He hardly knew what to say'– and through the opening pages of the short story sits silently staring at the fish (Di Filippo 86). The fisherman, however, has plenty to say and begins a series of tales, each piling atop the other, each more fictional than the last. He first leads Agassiz to believe that he found the fish in his nets as he was going about his work and, hearing that the scientist was willing to pay for unique specimens, has brought it in: 'The boys down at the wharves all say you're lookin' for queer specimens, and you'll not see many queerer than that 'un' (89). Agassiz, finally breaking his silence, retorts, 'Do you expect me to believe, sir, that this fish ever swam whole and entire through the seas of this world?' (89). His narrative thus challenged, the fisherman quickly abandons his first tale and begins a second account of how the fish came into his possession. One of his crew members caught the creature, he now claims, and 'was preparin' to fillet the critter for our shipboard supper when I comes upon him and, recognizin' its scientific value, put a halt to his butchery' (89). Unfortunately, the sailor had already 'separated snout from flipper', rendering the fish 'slightly damaged' but none the less authentic (89).

Agassiz has no more patience for this story than he did for the first, so when he dismisses the fisherman and his strange creature for the second time, the man plunges into yet another fiction. What *really* happened, the fisherman confides, was that upon pulling in his nets one day, he found a sturgeon, a barracuda, and a swordfish lying side by side. The swordfish, however, 'had the most peculiar instrument. Namely, a spike with a hole in its tip like the eye of a needle!' Before his eyes, the swordfish 'proceeded to slice them two other fishes in half. Then it flopped across the decks to where we was mending our sails. It got the end of some cord in its eyelet, and proceeded to stich the fishes together, just as ye seen 'em'. The miraculous swordfish, 'too big to lug along', is the real specimen the fisherman has to offer Agassiz – the product of its needle-nose was brought merely to attest to that other creature's sartorial skill (90).

Rather than dismissing the fisherman for a third time upon hearing this ridiculous tale, Agassiz finds this last narrative hilarious and agrees to pay the man 'handsomely' for his 'surgeon swordfish' (90). By doing so, he rewards the fisherman not for his specimen – which the scientist knows is fake – but for his fiction, which seems to reproduce itself almost of its own accord via the mangled body of the fish. The Frankensteinian Creature, as the catalyst for this production of narrative, thus functions as the 'narrative technology' that Judith Halberstam associates with the monstrous when it appears in literature and film (22). The monster becomes, according to Halberstam, a 'machine that, in its Gothic mode, produces meaning' (21) – produces, in fact, a 'vertiginous excess of meaning' (2). For, as in 'Hottentots', so generally the 'body of the monster' serves as a 'symbol for ... interpretive mayhem', meaning run riot (2). This is certainly the case in Di Filippo's story, where the successive fictions that the fisherman spins in order to account for his monstrous creature generate more and more layers of narrative, until the narrative itself gives way to hilarity, an overabundance of multiple, sometimes conflicting meanings. Agassiz comes to realise, as Di Filippo's readers do, that each story told to him is as real and as artificial as any other. The texts that together comprise 'Hottentots' – literary texts like Shelley's *Frankenstein*, the *ABC of Reading*, or 'A Farewell to Agassiz'; or cultural texts like the narratives surrounding the nineteenth-century conception of the 'hottentot' – create a version of the Victorian past that is at once authentic and unique to the post-Victorian position which Di Filippo and his readers occupy.

The patient as palimpsest: Ackroyd's *The Casebook of Victor Frankenstein*

The idea of the Frankensteinian Creature coming to embody the palimpsestuous narrative production that is central to adaptation as well as to neo-Victorian literature is even more apparent in the work of one of the best-known neo-Victorian novelists, Peter Ackroyd. Many of Ackroyd's neo-Victorian novels,[5] including his 2008 *The Casebook of Victor Frankenstein*, are examples of what Peter Widdowson describes as a subset of contemporary historiographic metafiction: '"re-visionary fiction", novels which "write back to" – indeed, "rewrite" – canonic texts from the past, and hence call to account formative narratives that have arguably been central to the construction of "our" consciousness' (491). *The Casebook* specifically 'writes back to' Shelley's *Frankensteins* (both the 1818 and 1831 versions) by offering readers an account of Victor Frankenstein's disastrous experiment that differs from Shelley's accounts most significantly by actualising the close association of Victor with his monster that has long been remarked by critics. Ackroyd's novel thus ends with the startling revelation that the Creature is entirely a projection of Victor's imagination and that Victor himself (who has been incarcerated in an asylum) has perpetrated the crimes he attributes to his creation.

Described by various reviewers as everything from a 'tribute to one of the great Gothic stories of all time', to a 'reimagining' of Shelley's novel, to a 'modern retelling that intelligently restores the story's relevance',[6] Ackroyd's novel has won both criticism and praise for embodying one other important change to Shelley's text. In the words of *New York Times* critic Terrence Rafferty, *The Casebook* 'places its resurrected protagonist at the very scene of his own conception' (17), much as Brian Aldiss does in his 1973 adaptation, *Frankenstein Unbound*. Ackroyd's Victor consequently rubs shoulders with many of the intellectual luminaries of his age, including Mary Shelley herself, Lord Byron, and the scientist Humphry Davy. His closest male friend is not Shelley's fictional Henry Clerval but Percy Shelley, whom Victor meets at Oxford and affectionately calls 'Bysshe'. And the corpse that Victor reanimates via galvanic shocks is that of a young 'Jack Keat'. In this way, Ackroyd's Victor becomes as much a historical figure, inserted into the annals of British literary history, as a fictional character. When readers consider this in the context of the two other roles that Victor adopts in the novel – creator and monstrous creation – they find that Ackroyd has effectively collapsed literature and literary history into a palimpsestuous narrative represented by Victor himself. Key to understanding Victor in this way is the scientist's casebook, in which, and as which, this narrative is contained.

Pulling Victor Frankenstein out of one fictional register (in which he functions as character) and into another (in which he functions as historical figure) requires some sleight of hand on Ackroyd's part. In *The Casebook*, Victor has no fiancée or wife, as he does in Shelley's *Frankenstein*, nor does he have a younger brother who is killed, sending the wrongfully accused Justine Moritz to the gallows. Instead, Ackroyd supplants Shelley's characters with historical men and women whose famously complicated real-life circumstances become still more tangled when they are incorporated – with little concern for historical accuracy – into Ackroyd's fiction. For example, by altering dates and locations to fit his narrative project, Ackroyd adapts Shelley's Elizabeth Lavenza into the character of Harriet Westbrook, the young woman whom Percy Shelley married prior to Mary Godwin. In *The Casebook*, Harriet is a poverty-stricken factory worker, rather than the daughter of a prosperous tavern keeper, whom Percy undertakes to tutor, and after the pair elope to Scotland (as they did when Percy was sent down from Oxford in 1811), Ackroyd's Victor provides them with financial support. Victor also provides Percy with moral support when Harriet is found dead in the Serpentine – not the result of suicide, as was the case in 1816, but murdered by Victor himself. Similarly, Ackroyd pushes the death of Jack Keat – an ostler-turned-apprentice surgeon whom Victor meets in the dissection rooms of St Thomas's Hospital – back a few years from that of his historical namesake to accommodate Victor's purchase of Keat's cadaver when the young man dies of consumption. Readers are led to believe that it is Keat, 'the most beautiful corpse I had ever seen' (153), whom Victor successfully animates in his experiments. Other historical figures, including Samuel Taylor Coleridge and Byron's 'personal physician and attendant' (262), Dr Polidori, appear as characters in *The Casebook*, interacting with Victor as though he, too, had lived in nineteenth-century England.

Ackroyd's neo-Victorian arrogation of the past raises a number of literary, historical, and even ethical questions. Some readers, like Michael Arditti, who reviewed *The Casebook* for the *Daily Telegraph*, find it troubling that 'facts have little place in Peter Ackroyd's historical fiction' (n. pag.). Citing a number of other novels that take this liberty, Jonathan Dee writes that 'the appropriation of genuine historical figures – people who actually lived – as characters in fiction is an act of imaginative boldness that, through simple attrition, readers of contemporary fiction have come to take entirely for granted' (77). Dee's article, tellingly titled 'The Reanimators: The Art of Literary Graverobbing', regards this appropriation as an act of postmodern impertinence, a gesture that 'slowly establishes a total equivalence between what's real and what's plausible' (80). While Mark Llewellyn may not agree with Dee that Ackroyd's manipulation of historical events says 'something ominous' about the 'way in which fiction writers imagine their relation to the world' (Dee 77), he, too, finds it problematic from an ethical standpoint. 'Using historical figures as if they were merely characters in a fiction, or rather the potential for treating the historical past as if it were a fictional narrative, does undermine certain aspects of history as a lived experience', Llewellyn claims ('Ethics' 38). He goes on, 'Appropriating the dead writers of the nineteenth century as if they were only figments of a shared cultural imagination opens up new possibilities but also new ethical dimensions to the neo-Victorian text' (38).

Whether one considers Ackroyd's literary grave-robbing in *The Casebook* full of possibility or rife with ethical tension, the result of it is the creation of a palimpsestuous notion of history similar to Di Filippo's. On the one hand, *The Casebook* imagines the past as an open field, thoroughly trespassable and infinitely adaptable. As Barry Lewis explains, Ackroyd 'ransacks and recycles the English literary past with unrestraint', appropriating, impersonating, and revising historical voices and texts such that the fictional begins to appear historical and the historical, fictional (172). Thus, in a pivotal scene in which Victor confronts his creation, readers find Ackroyd's Creature quoting (or misquoting, rather) Shelley's Creature quoting Milton, even as the novel brings back to life a poet – John Keats – who, if a historical timeline is laid atop the chronology of *The Casebook*, has not yet died. In typical postmodern fashion, history in *The Casebook* becomes 'the open and ambiguous topic that, in its ineffable and infinite scope, allows for the play of meaning' (Murray 15). Unburdened by an objective sense of the real, the past becomes for Ackroyd, as Jeremy Gibson and Julian Wolfreys have attested, a kind of ludic zone ready and waiting for interpolation (8).

On the other hand, however, Ackroyd's past is always already filled with texts and textuality. Not just indebted to Mary Shelley's *Frankenstein*, *The Casebook* is riddled with quotations and literary allusions, some of which are well known 'and play happily in full view, on the numerous surfaces of Ackroyd's writings; others are less obvious, but all require various degrees of literary and cultural knowledge' (Gibson and Wolfreys 12). Victor's wanderings through London and efforts in the laboratory are punctuated by snippets from Wordsworth, Coleridge, Byron, and Percy Shelley. His Oxford is the living library of Isaac Newton and John Locke, Joseph Priestly and Humphry Davy. And the Limehouse warehouse in which he reanimates Jack Keat is everywhere reminiscent of Charles Dickens. Heavily written and constantly rewritten, Ackroyd's conception of history must therefore be imagined, Petr Chalupský points out, as 'an immense intertextual web which can be traced through its miscellaneous written records' (122). If Victor's nineteenth-century England is an arena open for free play, it is also a huge compendium of textuality – a living corpus that recognises the constructedness of all narrative, factual or fictional, and so grants fiction the same authority as fact (Murray 31).

Embodying this notion of history as both unwritten and overwritten, a potentially changeable fiction and an already composed text, is Victor, the central node in the 'intertextual web' of *The Casebook*. Like the novel itself, and like the casebook he is composing throughout the novel that becomes the novel, Victor is a container for and a representation of the multiple narratives that are woven into Ackroyd's adaptation of the Frankenstein Complex. Several times throughout *The Casebook*, Victor recites or overhears pieces of literature that – pulled out of their literary historical context and divorced from their real authors – seem to have been written by Ackroyd to describe Victor. For example, Victor chances one day to read in a magazine Coleridge's description of Chatterton ('Youth of tumultuous soul and haggard eye!') and instantly identifies himself with it (141). Victor's misattribution of the poem to Percy Shelley highlights for readers the easy slippage between historical figure (Chatterton), literary text ('Monody on the Death of Chatterton'), author (Coleridge), and fictional character (Victor). At another time, pitched into a fever by the horror of his success in creating the monster, Victor unconsciously recites lines from the 'Ancient Mariner' that recount the Mariner's fear – his own fear, really – to turn around, 'Because he knows, a frightful fiend / Doth close behind him tread' (161). Victor knows the words are not his own, as readers familiar with Coleridge's poem also do, but the servant who overhears them within the novel can make no such distinction. The distance between literary text and fictional character similarly disappears when Victor reads Goethe's *The Sorrows of Young Werther* to his dying father (81), and when he attends a performance of Charles Maturin's *Melmoth the Wanderer* that moves him deeply (37). In both instances, Victor's story merges with the other narratives, enacting, as he is, the plot of these texts in his own life. Of course, he is all the while busily – almost compulsively – engaged in producing his own narrative, a narrative that is partly unique and partly Mary Shelley's, adopted and adapted.

This narrative is created in and through three entwined textual elements: the case-book, the idea of history as a palimpsestuous narrative, and the understanding of Victor as both creator/author and creation/text. Ackroyd's novel, written in first-person narration, is presented to readers as the record of Victor's scientific experiments, penned by Victor himself. The casebook purports to be merely an account of Victor's creation of the Creature and the terrible consequences of this creation. Readers learn in the final pages of the novel, however, that the casebook has functioned throughout as a doubly discursive text that has simultaneously concealed and revealed Ackroyd's central literary conceit: that the monster is nothing more than a projection of Victor's schizophrenic imagination. Our realisation of this comes when Victor, despondent at his failure to destroy the Creature by reversing the electrical process with which he brought him to life, is confronted by Dr Polidori, whose suspicions of Victor have prompted him to follow the scientist to his laboratory in Limehouse. Seeing Polidori, Victor sadly announces, 'Behold the creature. This is what I have made' (351). Polidori replies, 'There is no one here.... There is nothing beside you, except an empty chair' (352). At this instant, Victor lunges at Polidori and kills him, and readers realise that Victor – and not his Creature – has actually committed the other crimes that Victor has attributed to the monster throughout his casebook. Our realisation is confirmed by the final sentences of *The Casebook*, which indicate that the account we have just finished reading was '*Given to me by the patient, Victor Frankenstein, on Wednesday November 15, 1822. Signed by Fredrick Newman, Superintendent of the Hoxton Mental Asylum for Incurables*' (353, italics original).

As they reposition the fiction in one fell swoop, changing it from scientific record to madhouse diary, these sentences add yet another layer of signification – and another layer of narrative – to the novel. Readers are forced wonder, as David William Charnick has observed, which of the events described in the casebook are memories of real experiences and which are delusions (53). Complicating this, the uncertainty that the final revelation introduces into our experience of the narrative allows us to see what we hadn't before: the admissions of guilt that Victor continually makes but that do not become apparent until we have finished a first reading of the novel. Turning back to the text with the knowledge that the final pages grant us, we discover that as early as the third chapter Victor experiences what he describes as 'an episode of madness' that gives him 'the most curious notion that someone else was running beside me. I could not see him, or hear him, but I was fully aware of his presence as I ran over a rough track. It could not have been my shadow.... It was some image, some phantasm' (27). This is only one of many such intimations that Victor's Creature is an imaginary fabrication. Later, Ackroyd offers similar evidence of Victor's perpetration of the murders that are attributed to the Creature, as when the father of the murdered Harriet Westbrook unaccountably considers Victor 'to be his family's enemy' (47), or when Mary Shelley sees 'a phantom by the window' and Victor admits that 'it was a long time before I managed to find rest' during the night when Mary's servant Martha is killed (230). The casebook is riddled with barely veiled suggestions like these that Victor and the monster are one and the same, but the openness of his secret remains invisible until the final scene prompts readers to recognise the palimpsestuous layer of narrative lying beneath the primary tale.

When we re-read the novel, as we are almost bound to do, Victor's account of himself as scientific creator and author of both Creature and casebook becomes at once the account of his self-creation as monstrous text. Victor feels compelled to create the narrative, as both apology and confession, just as he feels compelled to create the Creature in his pursuit of 'the source where life began' (9). But as he writes, commit- ting his thoughts (or, perhaps, his delusions) and his actions to paper and so 'rush[ing] on to [his] destruction' (10), we find that it is himself that he brings into existence as a textual figure – a figure, as we have noted, that collapses literature (which enters *The Casebook* from the publications of Mary and Percy Shelley, Byron, Keats, Coleridge, and others) and literary history (the realm that these authors, and their texts, occupy outside of *The Casebook*) into a multilaminated narrative embodied by Victor/the Creature. Polidori recognises this moments before Victor murders him. 'You have lived in your imagination, Victor', Polidori says, and when Victor asks, 'How so?' he replies, 'Perhaps you wished to rival Bysshe [Percy Shelley]. Or Byron' (352). Polidori equates Victor's imagined creation with the literary texts created by the poets, his motives with the desire Shelley and Byron have to live on via their writing. Thus, the monstrous textual figure that Victor creates is also embodied by the casebook itself, Victor's actual doppelganger, which – like Di Filippo's sutured fish – can be read as a figure of the palimpsestuous narrative production that characterises not only neo- Victorian literature like Ackroyd's novel but adaptations generally.

There is, then, a unique relationship that exists between the Frankenstein Complex and neo-Victorian fiction, a relationship based on the idea central to adaptation: that texts are always, inevitably multiply-layered and thus necessitate a reading that operates palimpsestuously rather than univocally. In the texts discussed here, the Frankensteinian Creature becomes an embodiment of this idea, a representation of narrative self-consciously constructed from the vestiges of other narratives and re- visionary of its appropriated texts. This suggests that, as a genre, neo-Victorian litera- ture is fundamentally linked to the field of adaptation studies, as Ann Heilmann and

Mark Llewellyn attest. In fact, Heilmann and Llewellyn go so far as to make it a defining condition of the neo-Victorian genre, asserting that 'to be part of the neo-Victorianism we discuss in this book, texts … must in some respect be *self-consciously engaged with the act of (re)interpretation (re)discovery and (re)vision'* (4, italics original). Alexia Bower and Jessica Cox are not so exclusive in defining the boundaries of the genre, but they, too, agree that neo-Victorian literature's revisionary aspects constitute a large part of its popularity. They write, 'The appeal of a genre such as neo-Victorian literature … extends beyond a nostalgic yearning for a previous age and past aesthetic forms. Instead, the attraction roots itself in self-conscious engagement with the processes of adaptation and appropriation themselves' (3–4). It is little wonder, then, that this genre evinces an affinity for the Frankenstein Complex, which, like neo-Victorian fiction, recognises the text as always inherently rewritten. And it suggests that any study of neo-Victorian literature, so 'plainly stitched together' that such rewriting is perennially visible, will always be, to some degree, a study of adaptation.

Notes

1 Glut differs from Morton and Florescu (166) in recording the title of this drama as *Frank-in-Steam* (145).
2 Widdowson borrows Adrienne Rich's notion of 're-visioning' to describe texts (including neo-Victorian ones) that reimagine the literary past (496).
3 Jameson argues that such historiographic metafictions often convey 'the feel of the real past better than any of the "facts" themselves' (368) – at least as much as any 'real' past can ever be reconstructed. Their historical accuracy, in other words, may result as much from a feeling of similitude as from factual exactitude.
4 The scientist Agassiz, as many readers will recall, is a historical figure of some renown, earning lasting memory in the form of mountain peaks in Utah, Arizona, and California that bear his name.
5 *The Casebook of Victor Frankenstein* is a good example of a piece of neo-Victorian fiction set in the early nineteenth century rather than after 1832, the standard chronological demarcation of the beginning of Victorian literature. Texts like Ackroyd's are not considered 'neo-Regency' or 'neo-Romantic', however, as these designations are not counterparts of the category 'neo-Victorian'.
6 All of this unattributed acclaim appears in the frontispiece of the Anchor edition of *The Casebook*.

Bibliography

Ackroyd, Peter. *The Casebook of Victor Frankenstein*. New York: Anchor, 2008.
Aldiss, Brian. *Frankenstein Unbound*. New York: Random House, 1974.
Arditti, Michael. 'Two Extra Guests at the Villa Diodati.' Rev. of *The Casebook of Victor Frankenstein*, by Peter Ackroyd. *Daily Telegraph* 12 September 2008: n. pag.
Barthes, Roland. *Image–Music–Text*. Trans. Stephen Heath. New York: Hill and Wang, 1977.

Bower, Alexia L., and Jessica Cox. 'Introduction.' *Adapting the Nineteenth Century: Revisiting, Revising and Rewriting the Past*. Spec. issue of *Neo-Victorian Studies* 2.2 (2009/10): 1– 17.

Chalupský, Petr. 'Crime Narratives in Peter Ackroyd's Historiographic Metafictions.' *European Journal of English Studies* 14.2 (2010): 121–131.

Charnick, David William. 'Peter Ackroyd's Imaginary Projections: A Context for the Creature of *The Casebook of Victor Frankenstein*.' *Modern Language Review* 108.1 (2013): 52–67.

Chiang, Ted. 'Seventy-Two Letters.' 2000. *Steampunk*. Ed. Ann VanderMeer and Jeff VanderMeer. San Francisco: Tachyon, 2008. 165–212.

Dee, Jonathan. 'The Reanimators: On the Art of Literary Graverobbing.' *Harper's Magazine* June 1999: 76–84.

Di Filippo, Paul. 'Hottentots.' *The Steampunk Trilogy*. New York: Four Walls Eight Windows, 1995. 85–236.

Du Plessis, Johannes. 'Origin and Meaning of the Name "Hottentot".' *Report of the Fifteenth Annual Meeting of the South African Association for the Advancement of Science*. Cape Town: Association for the Advancement of Science, 1917. 189–93.

Florescu, Radu. *In Search of Frankenstein*. Boston: New York Graphic Society, 1975.

Genette, Gérard. *Palimpsests: Literature in the Second Degree*. 1982. Trans. Channa Newman and Claude Doubinsky. Lincoln: University of Nebraska Press, 1997.

Gibson, Jeremy, and Julian Wolfreys. *Peter Ackroyd: The Lucid and Labyrinthine Text*. London: Palgrave Macmillan, 2000.

Glut, Donald F. *The Frankenstein Catalog*. Jefferson, NC: McFarland & Co., 1984.

Halberstam, Judith. *Skin Shows: Gothic Horror and the Technology of Monsters*. Durham: Duke University Press, 1995.

Hantke, Steffen. 'Difference Engines and Other Infernal Devices: History According to Steampunk.' *Extrapolation* 40.3 (1999): 244–254.

Heilmann, Ann, and Mark Llewellyn. *Neo-Victorianism: The Victorians in the Twenty-First Century, 1999–2009*. New York: Palgrave Macmillan, 2010.

Holmes, Oliver Wendell. 'A Farewell to Agassiz.' 1865. *The Complete Poetical Works of Oliver Wendell Holmes*. Boston: Houghton Mifflin, 1922. 294–295.

Hutcheon, Linda. *A Poetics of Postmodernism: History, Theory, Fiction*. New York: Routledge, 1988.

Hutcheon, Linda, and Siobhan O'Flynn. *A Theory of Adaptation*. 2nd Edition. New York: Routledge, 2013.

Jameson, Fredric. *Postmodernism, or, the Cultural Logic of Late Capitalism*. Durham, NC: Duke University Press, 1991.

Lewis, Barry. *My Words Echo Thus: Possessing the Past in Peter Ackroyd*. Columbia, SC: U of South Carolina P, 2007.

Llewellyn, Mark. 'What is Neo-Victorian Studies?' *Neo-Victorian Studies* 1.1 (2008): 164–185.

———. 'Neo-Victorianism: On the Ethics and Aesthetics of Appropriation.' *Engaging the Victorians*. Special issue of *Literature Interpretation Theory* 20.1–2 (2009): 27–44.

Morton, Timothy, ed. *A Routledge Literary Sourcebook on Mary Shelley's* Frankenstein. London: Routledge, 2002.

Murray, Alex. *Recalling London: Literature and History in the Work of Peter Ackroyd and Iain Sinclair*. New York: Continuum, 2007.

Pound, Ezra. *ABC of Reading*. New York: New Directions, 1934.

Rafferty, Terrence. 'Raising the Dead.' Rev. of *The Casebook of Victor Frankenstein*, by Peter Ackroyd. *The New York Times Book Review* 1 November 2009: 17(L).

Reid, Colbey Emmerson. 'Victorian Cybernetics: Networking Technology, Disability, and Interior Design.' *Postphenomenology and the Philosophy of Technology: Design, Mediation, and the Posthuman*. Eds Dennis M. Weiss, Amy D. Propen, and Reid. Blue Ridge Summit, PA: Lexington Books, 2014. 129–150.

Sanders, Julie. *Adaptation and Appropriation*. New York: Routledge, 2006.

Scholes, Robert. 'Is There a Fish in This Text?' *College English* 46.7 (1984): 653–664.

Shelley, Mary. *Frankenstein, or The Modern Prometheus*. 1818. Oxford: Oxford University Press, 1998.

Shiller, Dana. 'The Redemptive Past in the Neo-Victorian Novel.' *Studies in the Novel* 29.4 (1997): 538–560.

Tilley, Christopher. 'Materialism and an Archaeology of Dissonance.' *Interpretive Archaeology: A Reader*. Ed. Julian Thomas. London: Leicester University Press, 2000. 71–82.

Widdowson, Peter. '"Writing Back": Contemporary Re-Visionary Fiction.' *Textual Practice* 20.3 (2006): 491–507.

10

Frankensteinian re-articulations in Scotland: monstrous marriage, maternity, and the politics of embodiment

Carol Margaret Davison

IT SEEMS FITTING, GIVEN Scotland's featured role in Mary Shelley's *Frankenstein* as the site of the female monster's creation, that two 3,000-year-old 'Frankenstein bog bodies', as they were dubbed by the press – one male, one female – were recently discovered on the island of South Uist off Scotland's west coast. Rearticulated from the bones of as many as six unrelated corpses and buried in a symbolic foetal position as if in preparation for rebirth into the next world, these composite mummies, whose purpose remains shrouded in obscurity, are uncannily reminiscent of both Victor Frankenstein's grotesque, corpse-based, corporeally mixed Creature and his Orcadian bride-to-be who is violently destroyed mid-creation. As filtered through the lens of John Milton's *Paradise Lost* and the Genesis story featuring Adam and Eve, Victor's thoughts about manufacturing a female companion for his Creature turn violent when he considers two things – the female's possibly dominant will and authority, and her reproductive capacity, both of which threaten his monomaniacal patriarchal control. In this unsettling narrative episode, Scotland becomes a site associated with female power. This is manifest in the maternally reproductive female monster, who is demonised and viciously destroyed by a patriarchally minded, purportedly rational scientist driven, in the face of his mother's sudden and tragic death, to defy disease, mortality, and loss while perversely usurping female reproductive power.

That Mary Shelley chose Scotland as the backdrop for her female monster-making scene makes sense when one considers Shelley's positive and empowering personal connection with that country. As she recounted in her 'Author's Introduction to the Standard Novels Edition [to *Frankenstein*] from 1831', the sublime landscape of Scotland was to her, as it was – in some ways problematically – to numerous Romantic writers and others who undertook the popular eighteenth-century Highland Tour, 'the eyry of freedom ... the pleasant region where unheeded ... [she] could commune with the creatures of ... [her] fancy' (193). There, in her mid-teens, Shelley's imagination was inspired while she regained her physical and mental health after being mistreated by her stepmother. In her 1831 Introduction, Shelley rhetorically yoked Victor's scientific creativity and her own liberating act of literary creation. Connecting this rhetoric to her culture's perspective on intellectual women as monstrous – a trope employed in relation to her feminist mother, Mary Wollstonecraft Godwin, whom Horace Walpole denounced as an unnatural 'hyena in petticoats' (397) – Shelley portrayed Scotland, and more specifically the outlying Orkney Islands, as a monstrous matrix of transgressive female power, intellectual authority, and creative (re)production.

Such cultural associations were not without precedent. Various works – famous and notorious, literary and otherwise – made Scotland the natural choice for such a yoking. John Knox's venomous diatribe, *The First Blast of the Trumpet Against the Monstrous Regiment of Women* (1558), which was aimed at undermining the legitimacy and authority of Mary Queen of Scots, did much to establish the connection between female monsters and Scotland. According to Knox, such powerful, outspoken female rulers were an abomination – 'repugnant to nature' and subversive 'of good order' (9) – a misogynist standpoint that underpinned the Scottish Witchcraft Act of 1563. That law was used to justify the brutal state- and kirk-sanctioned persecution of Scottish 'witches' a century later, between 1658 and 1662. William Shakespeare's unnatural (because ambitious and domineering) Lady Macbeth was also inextricably linked to the popular idea of treacherous Scottish womanhood. Notably, these memorable ideas and characters had also been distilled, in the decade preceding the publication of *Frankenstein*, in various contemporary British Gothic works where debates about female authority were played out in a sublimely Romantic Scotland populated by 'monstrous' women. Exemplifying an obscurantist British past divorced from its more progressive and enlightened present, 'North Britain' was represented in these works as a jingoistic, superstitious, and martial nation populated and dominated by passionate, dangerous, and domineering women.

Works like Catherine Smith's *The Caledonian Bandit* (1811) promoted the traditional she-monster stereotype to dramatic effect in the form of the crafty and ambitious Lady Margaret of Monteith, a vengeful woman of 'ungoverned temper and unrestrained passion' (II. 230) who kills her husband and commits suicide after a lifetime of persecuting others. In stark contrast, Francis Lathom's *The Romance of the Hebrides* (1809) cunningly commences with, yet ultimately reconfigures and undermines, to positive ends, the she-monster stereotype. The novel opens with Ulina, a Lewis Laird's daughter, becoming pregnant with the assistance of the 'dreaded Abdeerah' (I. 179), a one-hundred-year-old cave-dwelling Iona witch garbed in a wolf's hide and ragged tartan who possesses unearthly red eyes, pointed, beast-like fangs, and talon-like fingers (I. 179–180). It ends with Ulina's daughter, Lady Alexandra, an intelligent woman of sound judgement, being gloriously installed as ruler and her greatness proclaimed (III. 252) after adhering to the principles of justice, piety, and benevolence in the face of sustained persecution. This conclusion flies in the face of her father's earlier Knox-like claim, contradicting the standpoint of his wife, that women rulers are dangerous prodigies (I. 202), 'the capacities of a female mind … [being] ill-adapted to the weighty task of governing a state' (I. 201).

This popular image of Scotland as a site of gender subversion inhabited by formidable female monsters was bolstered by ambivalent propaganda featuring emasculated, filthy, skirt-wearing Scottish men alongside that promoting Scots as possessing 'a more primal kind of masculinity, identified with fierce passions and dangerous force'. This 'dark masculinity' seemed wild and transgressively uncontainable, animating 'Scotland's landscape and wildlife, its history and culture, its men *and, even occasionally, its women*' (Martin 2; emphasis added). While a 'cult of masculinity' characterised models of Scottishness by the nineteenth century (March 328), ideologically mixed material was circulated in political prints and such venues as John Wilkes's virulently anti-Scots newspaper, *The North Briton*, after the Jacobite Rising of 1745 when Scottish Highlanders were pacified and semiotically emasculated while being simultaneously positioned at the vanguard of the hyper-masculinised colonial pacification project.

Numerous Scottish writers in the last few decades have adapted and re-presented Mary Shelley's monsterpiece – 'modernity's perhaps most compelling and ominous myth' (Schoene-Harwood 21) – especially foregrounding gender issues/politics in conjunction with the novel's bride-creation scene, to engage with a cross-section of contemporary socio-political issues in their native land and beyond. In doing so, these authors – both male and female – have engaged in what Adrienne Rich insisted women writers do – namely, 'revisioning' a classic text – engaging in 'the act of looking back, of seeing with fresh eyes, of entering an old text from a new critical direction' (1972: 18). Pre-eminent among these revisionists are Liz Lochhead's psychodrama *Blood and Ice* (1982) and *Dreaming Frankenstein and Collected Poems, 1967–1984* (1984), Iain Banks's *The Wasp Factory* (1984), Alasdair Gray's *Poor Things* (1992), and *Monster* (2002), an opera in two acts, with music by Sally Beamish and a libretto by Janice Galloway. In keeping with the motif of the rearticulated monster, these adaptations deploy Gothic elements and often cross media. While a couple of these works – notably the ones written by men – reconfigure aspects of *Frankenstein* as a national allegory about Scottish identity and socio-political history, including the Union, all of them use *Frankenstein* as a refracting lens through which to interrogate established cultural stereotypes and power politics relating to gender roles and relations, particularly in association with literary voice, authority, and artistic creation. In that they engage with female authority, the cultural construction of femininity as a monstrous composite of characteristics and ideas, and the domestic impact of patriarchal monster-makers, references to *Frankenstein* are fitting, as is foregrounding Scotland as the site of the female monster's creation and destruction.

In adherence to adaptation theory's attentiveness to the different cultural contexts of the 'mother text' of *Frankenstein* and its 'cultural double[s]' (Poore 87), consideration will be given to how, why, and with what implications *Frankenstein* is granted new life by Scottish writers in speaking, especially, to the historic moment that saw the ramifications of second-wave feminism and the aftermath of the failed Scottish Referendum of 1979 that sought to establish a Scottish Assembly with limited legislative powers. Despite that political debacle, this era also produced an exciting renaissance in Scottish cultural expression that has continued into the present day. An assessment will be made as to how and to what ends various potent feminist themes are repeatedly resurrected in these texts, such as the politics of embodiment and maternity, female friendship, marriage, and the fraught relationship between women's artistic production and biological reproduction.

Lochhead and Galloway

Inspired, in part, by *Child of Light* (1951), Muriel Spark's biography of Mary Shelley, Liz Lochhead's *Blood and Ice* (1983) is a biographical psycho-drama that draws upon *Frankenstein* to meditate on women's issues – especially their biological and artistic creativity – across a century and a half. Although Lochhead reflects on Scottish national identity in much of her subsequent work, she felt in the 1980s that her 'country was woman' (Nicholson 223). While in her poem 'Dreaming Frankenstein' (1984) Lochhead recounts the Creature's conception as a type of Fuseli-style nightmare experienced as a form of sexual intercourse/violation resulting in a literary birth, she uses the Frankenstein monster motif in *Blood and Ice* to reflect on what she suggests is feminism's minimal impact, nearly two hundred years later, on women's creativity, and gender roles and ideals in contemporary society. As she explains in an interview from 1990, while that movement had given her the sense 'that reason ought to be attainable … [she] still hadn't got very far with [the idea of rationalism] in … [her] own personal life' (Wilson 13). Given its status as an iconic text that engages with what George Levine identifies as 'some of the fundamental dualisms, the social, moral, political and metaphysical crises of western history since the French Revolution' (3–4), *Frankenstein* served as Lochhead's most astute choice for cultural re-articulation.

Lochhead's play explores and exposes various significant and problematic disjunctions between the new class and gender ideals articulated and championed by progressively minded Romantic intellectuals – Shelley and her husband are consciously seeking new ways to live (33) – and the realities of women's lives. Shifting the narrative focus away from the monster (who is reduced to the status of a haunting ghost in this play), in favour of Mary Shelley's process of creating her story – a process significantly deemed 'monstrous' and undertaken by a 'terrorist' (28) – Lochhead draws resonant parallels between Mary Shelley and Victor Frankenstein. While portraying Mary as a woman haunted by 'misery … terror … [and] grief' (28) after the drowning death of her husband, Lochhead amplifies the widow Shelley's retrospective desire to discover 'a new way of making life' (61). This statement emerges in the face of Mary's society's views of women's maternal bodies as 'monstrous' (42) and her reflections on the traumatic deaths of several children that she experienced as a wife and mother. The idea that 'love is never free to any woman' (51), regardless of her class, assumes deeper meaning when Shelley's maidservant Elise becomes pregnant out of wedlock. This insight resonates across the decades between Shelley's and Lochhead's eras, suggesting that, despite a proliferation of philosophical works in support of female equality and women's rights, little progress has been made for most women – especially those from the working classes – in their actual lives.

With a significant nod to Lochhead's *Blood and Ice*, Beamish and Galloway's opera *Monster* (2002), published two decades later, likewise takes Mary Shelley's youth and her creation process of *Frankenstein* as its points of focus. In this regard, Scotland, with its sea and 'glacial spires' (Galloway 21) serves as a vital matrix of creativity, a sublime place that feeds her imagination and grants her a peace until then unknown (21). Borrowing from Lochhead and holding up a mirror to our own era, *Monster* gothicises Shelley's period and various disjunctions between intellectual theory and practice. These are ingeniously crystallised in the 'mother text' in Victor Frankenstein's misconception of the monster: conceived as 'beautiful' during his early stages of 'gestation', the Creature elicits the distressing reaction of 'breathless horror and disgust' immediately subsequent to his birth into autonomy (39). In what she describes as a world rife with monstrous men (32), Galloway underscores disjunctions, on both a personal and political level, of the dark side of Romantic ideology. The disjunction between theory and praxis that Coleridge suggests characterises the French Revolution, a phenomenon ambivalently characterised as the noblest act of imagination whose 'pay is blood' (13), is revealed to be also at play in women's lives: romantic love may lead, tragically, to what Coleridge describes as the 'perilous place' of the childbed where a woman and/or her child may meet their deaths (44). Galloway's twenty-first-century critique adheres to the popular narrative and thematic development in the Female Gothic whereby the carceral nature of the Victorian domestic sphere gives way to the terror-inducing, carceral nature of the female body itself in the twentieth and twenty-first centuries.

Notably, toxic, monstrous men are identified in the opera as hypocritical intellectuals who deny female subjectivity and are careless of a woman's heart. While Mary is celebrated by her husband, Percy, as a radically progressive 'bride unchained' (7), he also proves to be a sexist hypocrite who denies her individual identity and desire. Thus is she rendered a compliant and voiceless 'relative creature' whose primary role is to birth his children while also, Muse-like, artistically rebirthing him (29). In this dramatic exploration of monstrous parenting and authority, William Godwin, Mary's political-philosopher father who promoted a type of rational morality, is likewise exposed and indicted as an abusive hypocrite. Indeed, Godwin is portrayed as criminally anti-family in Galloway's Gothic opera. Despite Mary's pleading with him to exhibit some fatherly affection after the devastating loss of her young child, Godwin exacerbates her suffering by disowning her (54), an act aligning him with the negligent father, Victor Frankenstein, at the centre of Mary's famous novel. Thus, in what Galloway crafts as a meditation on modernity and maternity modelled on *Frankenstein*, a new type of unnatural humanity is portrayed, one that is phallocentrically 'made not born', manufactured by ideas and grotesquely devoid of an 'ethic of care'. In this damning portrait of tyranny and despotism, Scotland stands out as a beacon of imaginative and intellectual freedom for women.

Banks and Gray

Drawing strategically on Shelley's *Frankenstein* and such other classic Gothic works as James Hogg's chillingly modern psychological portrait, *The Private Memoirs and Confessions of a Justified Sinner* (1824), Iain Banks's 1984 *succès de scandale*, *The Wasp Factory*, serves as a highly intertextual national allegory in the Scottish Female Gothic vein. A disturbing yet compelling first-person confession of homicide and mental instability, this highly Oedipal 'horror Gothic' narrative laced with dark humour graphically chronicles the ritualistically violent life and superstitious worldview of seventeen-year-old Frank Cauldhame and his perverse relationship with his father, a scientist–anarchist hippie who retreated in the 1960s to a castle-like house on a remote island off the north-east coast of Scotland. Unknown to Frank until novel's end, this distant, enigmatic, and combative father has conducted secret and unnatural experiments, whilst socially isolated, on his three children – Frank, Eric, and Paul. These mysteries symbolically coalesce for Frank in his father's locked study, a prototypically Gothic space with which this self-absorbed, monomaniacal narrator becomes obsessed. In the face of these secret experiments, and driven by a need for power and control, Frank undertakes three carefully planned and executed murders, one a traditionally Gothic fratricide (138), and emulates his scientist father by creating a wasp factory, a 'little [Calvinistically conceptualized] world of death and retribution' (Sage 25) – a fetishistic contraption wherein wasps 'elect' their own gruesome fates. This 'beautiful and deadly and perfect' creation (118) incorporates mementoes from Frank's crimes and history (122), thus serving as both a superb Gothic sign of *memento mori* and a multivalent symbol that mines and combines three resonant pieces of Scottish history: the idea of (factory) labour, Scotland's primary role within the British Union since its establishment; Calvinism, a pre-eminent religious philosophy popular in Scotland that, in its driving idea of preordained spiritual election, confounds the concepts of fate and free will; and 'wasps', representative of white Anglo-Saxon Protestants, upon whom Frank unconsciously exacts a bizarre revenge, given that, as the novel's logic suggests, their patriarchal and militaristic worldview monstrously perverted Scotland.

In the ultimate revelation that Francis (Frank) Leslie Cauldhame is, in fact, Frances Lesley Cauldhame, whose sexual transformation has been achieved and sustained scientifically, ideologically, and psychologically by her mad father's use, respectively, of male hormones and brainwashing using an essentialist, dichotomous worldview that regards women as life-givers and men as life-takers (118), Banks enacts a brilliant structural sleight of hand. He cleverly 'doubles' his narrative generically as a work of Gothic and *Female* Gothic fiction. In keeping with the latter literary form, Frances's systematic isolation and imprisonment combines with her detective-style process of self-expression and discovery. 'His' feminisation also speaks volumes in this carefully constructed work of national allegory where, as Frank describes himself, 'I've thought of myself as a state; a country or, at the very least, a city. It used to seem to me that the different ways I felt sometimes about ideas, courses of action and so on were like the differing political moods that countries go through' (62). This uncanny insight is likewise echoed in Frank's father's perverse act of purchasing his 'son' a copy of Günter Grass's *The Tin Drum* (51), a national allegory about Germany's arrested development while under the sinister sway of the National Socialist Party. (Ironically, Frank reads neither that book nor his father's other perversely ironic gift – a copy of Gore Vidal's *Myra Breckinridge* (1968), a satire about a man who undergoes sexual reassignment surgery. Given the similar situation in Hammer Studio's *Frankenstein Created Woman* (1969), where the creation simultaneously possesses both male and female personas, this 'monstrous' sexual blending/confusion seems to be one of the unifying themes in what Kyle Bishop, referenced in this volume's Introduction, describes as the 'Frankensteinian Process'. That 'system' is comprised of related texts that are both original and copy, variously reconstructed from pre-existing literary pieces.)

Frank's doubled narrative also mirrors James Hogg's twice-told *Private Memoirs and Confessions*, which is recounted initially by a factually minded Editor, and thereafter by the religious fanatic Robert Wringhim, whose narration casts doubt on his reliability and mental stability. Both of these Gothic cautionary tales condemn extreme ideologies that distort mental development: while Robert Wringhim is a fanatical antinomian Calvinist who believes that God's elect may sin with impunity, Frank is a proponent of a militaristic, misogynist patriarchy. Both worldviews are upheld, problematically, by perverse and damaged/damaging father figures. Robert Wringhim senior's declaration that Robert Wringhim junior has been elected 'to the society of *the just made perfect*' (115) is matched in its tragic consequences by Frank's father's litany of lies about the world and Frank's history. Such distorted worldviews produce severe mental instability and cold-blooded acts of fratricide and homicide. The resulting psychological division in Frank as intimated by the telephone calls from his insane, pyromaniacal half-brother and 'double', Eric – who seems to be a figment of Frank's imagination – is a clever modern adaptation of Hogg's brilliant creation of Gil-Martin, Robert Wringhim's 'brother' in ideology and evil (117), who provokes, applauds, and justifies Wringhim's varied criminal activities.

In Banks's unflattering Freudian portrait of Scotland as emblematised by an ostensibly motherless, patriarchally obsessed protagonist subjected to bizarre psycho-sexual experimentation (174), Frank's unofficial existence as a 'boy' without a birth certificate (13–14) nicely parallels a Scotland devoid of nationhood status post-Union (1707). His reiterated self-description as a guilt-ridden, fragmented individual possessing a 'racist' (63), 'sick' (78), and 'destructive' (80) dark side is employed – in an unsettling Jekyll-and-Hyde manner – to mirror the post-Union stereotype of Scotland as a schizophrenic nation-state divided between Scottish and British identity.

Importantly, Frank's repression of his 'maternal' side also results in his lack of a balanced personality and transformation into an aggressive, militaristic machine. His hippie father, ironically, produces a warmonger. As Banks has explained in various interviews, *The Wasp Factory* is an attack on the British male military establishment (McVeigh 3): since the Act of Union, and particularly since the defeat of the Jacobites in the mid-eighteenth century, Scotland has experienced a political emasculation that has resulted, Banks suggests, in a perverse misogyny born of sexual insecurity. A monstrous Scotland has been the result.

Thus does the seventeen-year-old Frank suffer (13), like Scotland in the post-Referendum Thatcherite period of the early 1980s when Britain was on the cusp of the Falklands War, from a deep lack of self-knowledge and self-respect. In a weird and ironic twist, Frank is exposed as a secret-keeper from whom the novel's most significant secret – one involving 'his' secret identity – is withheld. Given his actual female biology, Frank is, as he describes himself, 'not a full man' (109), a statement that betrays a deep lack of self-knowledge that is compounded by an intense self-hatred. Frank's obsession with the Factory, his perverse war games, exacting acts of premeditated homicide, and growing independence – a source of tremendous concern to his control-obsessed father, whom Frank regards as idiotic and embarrassing – chronicle an imminent domestic rebellion. This is echoed in *Frankenstein*, where the female creature's reproductive potential raises the spectre of the Creature's independence and rebellion, the female's destruction resulting in the eruption of a more violent masculinity.

True to traditional Gothic strategy, where the constructed monster is used to mirror and comment upon broader social problems, Banks suggests that Frank's worldview extends beyond himself and his island. As Frank's discussion with his only friend, Jamie, makes clear, politicians and 'leaders of countries or religions or armies' (112) constitute the world's true monsters, all of whom will come out on top, thus confirming the Darwinian 'survival of the nastiest' people (112). It is Frank, ironically, who articulates Banks's broader critique: 'If we're [human beings] really so bad and so thick that we'd actually use all those wonderful H-bombs and Neutron bombs on each other, then maybe it's just as well we do wipe ourselves out before we can get into space and start doing horrible things to other races' (113). In his construction of the bomb-wielding Frank, Banks creates a microcosm – and a mirror – of such politicians and their jingoistic nations.

Banks's clever subversion of Frank's essentialist gender philosophy and his positioning of monstrosity in relation to gender radically undermine the Aristotelian conception of femaleness as an aberration from the male 'norm'. Scottish female monsters may seem innumerable in Frank's world, as they are in Robert Wringhim's, but Banks exposes this demonisation as a cultural construct grounded in a cultural pathology. Frank's 'death' – the traditional outcome for the Gothic monster – and the concomitant 'birth' of Frances, combined with Frances's shocking realisations about Frank's motivations, speak volumes about the nature of monstrosity. Frances's ultimate and ironic recognition of her position within a 'greater machine' where her path – like the wasps in the factory – is partly chosen and partly determined (184) is damningly, soberingly realistic yet none the less re-empowering. Although, like a self-reflexive Scotland engaged in unearthing its history, Frances possesses a greater sense of the multifarious influences at work in the individual's life. Her newly discovered self-knowledge lays the groundwork for a possible, new, non-destructive beginning.

Piggybacking on Banks's *The Wasp Factory*, Alasdair Gray's postmodern allegory *Poor Things* (1992) is a work of feminist Female Gothic that explicitly rearticulates the Bride of Frankenstein motif in order to incisively critique Thatcherite Britain/Scotland. In its engagement with such traditional Victorian concerns as Home Rule, Darwinism, socialism, and poverty, Gray suggests in this pointedly sham-Victorian novel laced with black humour, that Britain/Scotland has experienced a damaging socio-political regression. At the forefront of his agenda is the exposure and deconstruction of womanhood as a monstrous cultural construct that resembles Victor Frankenstein's monster-making process.

A pseudo-anthropological assessment and Gothic national allegory in the vein of Banks's *The Wasp Factory*, *Poor Things* denounces patriarchy as a form of cultural pathology whose narrow and perverse parameters of female normativity result in the production and abuse of its own monsters. Likewise, as Michelle Massé has argued, 'normal' feminine development within patriarchy involves 'a form of culturally induced trauma' (7) where women are made to experience their own – potentially maternal – bodies as prisons, resulting in a peculiar narrative form of 'feminine carceral' (Kahane 59). In this class-conscious, typically postmodern novel that repeatedly obscures the boundary between fiction and history (Hutcheon 113), Gray exposes women's oppression and objectification as monsters within patriarchy – from 'the scullery maid … [to] the master's daughter' as its protagonist, Bella, lays out the parameters (263) – as particularly expressed by the pathologisation of women's bodies by the scientific and medical establishments. This ideology is provocatively represented in the novel in the numerous etchings of female body parts by one William Strang (a.k.a. Alasdair Gray) that divide its chapters.

Poor Things exudes *Frankenstein*. It is both structurally and thematically a fiction of resurrection packaged, in traditional Gothic, Chinese-box style, as a found, 'resurrected' manuscript comprised of two contending, disparate narratives that problematise the question of truthful, reliable narration: the first is a supernatural, Gothic account written by a husband, Archibald McCandless, while the second is a new, unsentimental, and rational epistolary account in the form of a letter from 1914 following McCandless's death (1909) penned by his wife, Bella/Victoria. Like William Godwin's contentious memoir of Mary Wollstonecraft (1798) that, in recounting her titillating love life and various suicide attempts, destroyed her already damaged reputation, Bella considers McCandless's intended testament of love an offensive and 'infernal parody' (273) comprised of a patchwork of morbid Victorian fantasies (272) and written by an 'idle, dreamy fantastical [man]' (252). Victoria's reaction is justified, as McCandless's wildly implausible Gothic tale conceives of her as the product of a 'skilfully manipulated resurrection' (27) conducted by Godwin Bysshe Baxter, an experimental doctor and Bella's father/aspirant husband who serves as an aptly named monstrous combination of Percy Shelley and William Godwin. According to McCandless, a pregnant Bella was fished out of the Clyde in Glasgow and revived after her brain was replaced with the brain of her dead foetus. A more apt emblem of the 'monstrous' ideal of Victorian womanhood – the infantilised woman – would be difficult to conceive, or a more fitting symbolic synthesis of the mother–daughter duo of Mary Shelley and Mary Wollstonecraft, who seem, in a monstrous combination, to comprise Bella's character portrait.

Incorporating parody into McCandless's narrative in the form of Bella's Bride-of-Frankenstein-style introduction to him (29), Gray crafts a strategic narrative agenda: in opposition to Godwin's and McCandless's *construction* of a female monster in the latter's narrative, Gray undertakes her postmodern *deconstruction*, which involves exposing the culturally contingent and constructed nature of 'womanhood' and the sometimes brutal methods employed to police and ensure women's adherence to the feminine ideal. These include clitoridectomy (218), which is recommended to cure the 'erotomaniac' Bella.

In the novel's account of Bella's first husband, General Blessington, and his mistreatment, neglect, and brief incarceration of her in a coal-cellar (227), in combination with his threat to unlawfully incarcerate her in an asylum (230), Gray blends a traditional Female Gothic narrative into a more modern variant. It is to highlight women's position as monstrously constructed within patriarchy that Bella is presented as a female blank slate, a history-less monster made rather than born. In such a scenario, Bella is revealed, ironically and tellingly, to be a monster, whether she refuses or embraces the socially acceptable role of object of desire. Bella's painstakingly lengthy, socially ordained transformation from the daughter of a Manchester foundry foreman into a lady well groomed for the 'marriage market' (215), as directed and paid for by General Blessington, her first husband, shares important resonances with Godwin's infantilising, monster-making process.

Notably, under the tutelage of Godwin, who ensures a revolution by granting her freedom of thought, Bella eschews a traditional, passive female role in favour of that of a liberated, intelligent woman and sexually desiring subject. As such, this unconventional, anachronistic woman who does not recognise class differences (80) and rejects marriage courts social stigma as she essentially follows a traditionally male trajectory, undertaking a Grand Tour of the Continent where she meets gentlemen with whom she ardently discusses contemporary socio-political ideas. Tragically and tellingly over the course of these encounters, Bella – the woman with her scar-encircled skull – is demonised as a 'gorgeous monster' (91), a supernatural freak of nature, a sleepless, sexual vampire (86) whom the renowned French neurologist Jean-Martin Charcot exhibits at the Salpêtrière as exemplifying the dangers of erotomania (179). Although Victoria's epistolary account identifies her cranial scar as the result of paternal abuse (256), her objectified body is repeatedly described as a text which only men can interpret (254), a claim upheld when Bella's lover, Duncan Wedderburn, reads her hymenless, caesarian-inscribed body while she cannot (107). It is noteworthy that in both accounts Bella assumes the traditionally male role of an interpretive medical authority, an outcome Godwin would applaud, given his condemnation of Britain as a monstrous, heartless plutocracy where money talks, industry rules, and people

– generally of the working classes – are casually exterminated (24). By way of Bella's medical role, Gray gestures towards a substantially altered future when female authority will be recognised and celebrated, and women will retain control over, and be able to 'read', their own bodies.

As in Banks's *The Wasp Factory*, Gray grafts a national allegory onto his Female Gothic adaptation of *Frankenstein*. While this is most graphically in evidence in Strang's etching of Bella as 'Bella Caledonia' (45), it is tangentially developed in her Bildungsromanstyle narrative that chronicles her maturity from a sexually promiscuous woman engaging in 'Acts of Union' / 'weddings' with Wedderburn (83), to her more intellectual engagement with Scottish nationalism and socialism. The amnesiac Bella's reminder of her first legal 'Act of Union' with General Blessington, an arch-imperialist who was involved in every major Victorian military event (e.g. the Crimean War and the Indian Mutiny), is part and parcel of her Female Gothic development towards self-awareness while simultaneously signifying, allegorically, Scotland's imperialist history.

Poor Things exposes the monstrously destructive nature of British patriarchy on women's lives. This ideology is also revealed to be fundamental to British imperialism: both are grounded in hierarchy and classification. Bella is introduced to the tenets of imperialism during the course of her Tour both by Dr Hooker, who expounds his theory on Anglo-Saxon superiority (139–141), and by Mr Astley, who justifies British warfare as a type of civilising mission (141). The latter's claim that Britons possess the world's biggest (read *advanced*) brains and function as adults in comparison with infantilised colonials (139) lends support to the novel's suggestion that imperialism begins at home among Britain's 'poor things' – women and the working classes – who are taught, Godwin laments, to serve as disposable tools (263). Wedderburn's role as a self-identified monster (79) who sexually mistreats countless working-class women exemplifies such imperial behaviour, as does the impregnation of a kitchenmaid by General Blessington, 'the nation's darling … [and] example to British youth' (211).

Bella's act of confronting and disarming Blessington (236–238) signals Gray's hope that an amnesiac Scotland will re-examine its history, confront, and ultimately reject its imperial role in order to embrace the new-found nationalist, class-aware ideas of such Scottish intellectuals as John Maclean and Hugh MacDiarmid. In this way, Bella / Scotland strikes out towards independence and learns the quintessential Gothic lesson that only by confronting the ghosts of one's past may progress occur. Godwin, notably, embraces this process when he courageously reconsiders why he surgically reconstructed and resurrected Bella rather than resuscitating her dead baby. This prototypically Gothic 'sins of the fathers' moment resonates with Victor Frankenstein's warring motives in forging his Creature. In a novel that mirrors *Frankenstein* in revealing the fluid boundary between monster and monster-maker, Godwin confesses to his own sexual urges and flawed human nature. He states, with regret, that 'Our vast new scientific skills are first used by the damnably greedy selfish impatient parts of our nature and nation' (68). While *Poor Things* pointedly rearticulates Mary Shelley's

Frankenstein in the gender-centric vein of Lochhead and Galloway to reveal the cultural construction of femininity/womanhood as monstrous within patriarchy (monsters are made and not born), Gray goes – like Banks – one Gothic, socio-political step further, echoing Galloway's exposure of the dark underbelly of a Romantic ideology that putatively advocates and celebrates individualism and equality. Consistent with the focus of his political tract, *Why Scots Should Rule Scotland*, published in the same year as *Poor Things* (1992), Gray registers, albeit perhaps unconsciously, a chilling and resonant warning for a Scotland on the cusp of devolution – namely, that no person or nation has a monopoly on, or immunity from, monster making. Given the murky complexities of both personal and national power politics – patriarchal or otherwise – the Frankensteinian monster-makers might just turn out to be us.

Bibliography

Banks, Iain. *The Wasp Factory*. London: Abacus, 1984.

Galloway, Janice. *Monster: An Opera in Two Acts*. Libretto. Music by Sally Beamish. Glasgow: Scottish Music Information Centre, 2002.

Godwin, William. *Memoirs of the Author of* A Vindication of the Rights of Woman. 1798. Peterborough, Ontario: Broadview Press, 2001.

Gray, Alasdair. *Poor Things*. San Diego, New York, and London: Harcourt Brace and Company, 1992.

———. *Why Scots Should Rule Scotland*. Edinburgh: Canongate, 1992.

Hogg, James. *The Private Memoirs and Confessions of a Justified Sinner*. 1824. Oxford: Oxford University Press, 1991.

Hutcheon, Linda. *A Poetics of Postmodernism: History, Theory, Fiction*. New York and London: Routledge, 1988.

Kahane, Claire. 'Gothic Mirrors and Feminine Identity.' *Centennial Review* 24 (1980): 43–64.

Knox, John. *The First Blast of the Trumpet Against the Monstrous Regiment of Women*. 1558. New York: Da Capo Press Inc., 1972.

Lathom, Francis. *The Romance of the Hebrides; or, Wonders Never Cease!* London: Minerva Press, 1809. 3 vols.

Levine, George. 'The Ambiguous Heritage of *Frankenstein*.' *The Endurance of* Frankenstein: *Essays on Mary Shelley's Novel*. Eds George Levine and U.C. Knoepflmacher. Berkeley, Los Angeles, and London: University of California Press, 1979. 3–30.

Lochhead, Liz. *Dreaming Frankenstein and Collected Poems*. Edinburgh: Polygon, 1972.

———. *Blood and Ice*. London: Methuen, 1983.

March, Christie. 'Bella and the Beast (and a Few Dragons, Too): Alasdair Gray and the Social Resistance of the Grotesque.' *Critique* 43 (2002): 323–346.

Martin, Maureen M. *The Mighty Scot: Nation, Gender, and the Nineteenth-Century Mystique of Scottish Masculinity*. Albany, NY: SUNY Press, 2009.

Massé, Michelle. *In the Name of Love: Women, Masochism, and the Gothic*. Ithaca and London: Cornell University Press, 1992.

McVeigh, Kev P. 'The Weaponry of Deceit: Speculations on Reality in *The Wasp Factory*.' *Vector* 191 (1997): 3–4.

Nicholson, Colin. *Poem, Purpose and Place*: *Shaping Identity in Contemporary Scottish Verse*. Edinburgh: Polygon, 1992.

Poore, Benjamin. 'Liz Lochhead and the Gothic.' *The Edinburgh Companion to Liz Lochhead*. Ed Anne Varty. Edinburgh: Edinburgh University Press, 2013.

Rich, Adrienne. 'When We Dead Awaken: Writing as Re-Vision.' *College English* 34 (October 1972): 18–30.

Sage, Victor. 'The Politics of Petrifaction: Culture, Religion, History in the Fiction of Iain Banks and John Banville.' *Modern Gothic: A Reader*. Eds Victor Sage and Allan Lloyd Smith. Manchester and New York: Manchester University Press, 1996. 20–37.

Schoene-Harwood, Berthold. *Mary Shelley*: Frankenstein: *Essays, Articles, Reviews*. New York: Columbia University Press, 2000.

Shelley, Mary. 'Author's Introduction to the Standard Novels Edition [to *Frankenstein*] from 1831.' *Frankenstein; Or, The Modern Prometheus*. 1818. Oxford: Oxford University Press, 1993. 192–197.

———. *Frankenstein; Or, The Modern Prometheus*. 1818. Oxford: Oxford University Press, 1993.

Smith, Catherine. *The Caledonian Bandit; or, The Heir of Duncaethal. A Romance of the Thirteenth Century*. London: Minerva Press, 1811. 2 vols.

Walpole, Horace. *The Yale Edition of Horace Walpole's Correspondence*. Volume 31. Ed. W.S. Lewis. New Haven: Yale University Press, 1937–83. 48 vols.

Wilson, E. Rebecca. 'Liz Lochhead.' *Sleeping With Monsters: Conversations with Scottish and Irish Women Writers*. Eds Gillean Somerville-Arjat and Rebecca E. Wilson. Edinburgh: Polygon, 1990. 8–17.

11

Young Frankensteins: graphic children's texts and the twenty-first-century monster

Jessica Straley

FRANKENSTEIN'S MONSTER MAY SEEM an unwelcome intruder in the child's nursery. Indeed, in Mary Shelley's *Frankenstein* (1818), the monster and the child cannot coexist. Constituted by disinterred corpses, orphaned on his birthday, and unloved even by his creator, Shelley's monster is a being bereft of childhood; he partakes in none of the revered innocence and divine vision that constituted the Romantic 'child' idolised by Shelley's contemporaries. The horror of the monster's uncouth physiognomy, as described in Shelley's novel – 'its unearthly ugliness rendered it almost too horrible for human eyes' (99) – is amplified when juxtaposed with the attributes of the beatific child, Victor's young brother, with his 'sweet laughing blue eyes, dark eyelashes, and curling hair', who becomes the monster's first victim (66). Biographical readings of Shelley's *Frankenstein* reinforce this contrast between the artificial manufacture of perverse beings and the natural production of biological offspring. Often read as a grieving mother's response to the recent death of her infant daughter, the novel itself – and not simply the monster inside it – becomes a material sign for the absent child.[1] In her 1831 preface to *Frankenstein*, Shelley suggestively conceives her novelistic enterprise as an act of perverse reproduction; she 'bid[s] my hideous progeny go forth and prosper' and thereby articulates the novel's role as the dreadful replacement for the child (10).

Shelley's preface expresses an aesthetic tension reaching beyond her novel to a clash between literary genres that highlights the contradictory aims of the early nineteenth-century Gothic, on the one hand, and children's literature, on the other. In their introduction to *The Gothic in Children's Literature: Haunting the Borders* (2008), Anna Jackson, Karen Coats, and Roderick McGillis claim that, at the end of the eighteenth century, 'the Gothic was soundly suppressed in children's literature in favour of morally uplifting texts that suited the desires of adults to construct an innocent child that could be trained up into a rational adult of Enlightened values' (2). Eighteenth- and early nineteenth-century children's writers sought to fashion a literary genre cleansed of the violence, vice, social transgression, and psychic disorder of the Gothic novel, and to instil instead only Christian values and rational morality. As Dale Townshend points out in 'The Haunted Nursery: 1764–1830' (2008), the first essay of

Jackson, Coats, and McGillis' edited collection, John Locke's influential *Some Thoughts Concerning Education* (1693) warned against pedagogies that employ scare tactics, and writers like Mary Wollstonecraft (Shelley's mother) wrote in *Thoughts on the Education of Daughters* (1787) that 'proper [stories] would improve [children] even while they are amused', but regrets that 'instead of these, their heads are filled with improbable tales, and superstitious accounts of invisible beings, which breed strange prejudices and vain fears in their minds' (18). With explicitly moralist writers like Wollstonecraft, Anna Barbauld, and Sarah Trimmer as the genre's early architects, children's literature was erected explicitly to keep texts like *Frankenstein* and its monster out.

Whatever children's literature was meant to do, however, its walls were porous and, as Jackson, Coats, and McGillis admit, the Gothic 'continued to seep in' (3). At the same time that Shelley was writing *Frankenstein*, the sanctioned moral and rational tales shared space along the nursery shelves with the Grimm Brothers' *Kinder und Hausmärchen* (1812–57). A far remove from Wollstonecraft's exemplars of right conduct and domestic comfort, the Grimms' collection tells of parents abandoning their children in 'Hansel and Gretel', stepparents murdering their young wards in the more explicit 'The Juniper Tree', and children pretending to be killers themselves in 'How Some Children Played at Slaughtering'. Indeed, the rational children's literature of the Enlightenment yielded to something much darker. By the beginning of the twentieth century J.M. Barrie's Peter Pan, who digs the graves of dead children in *Peter Pan in Kensington Garden* (1904), and the ghostly mansion that conceals a sickly child in Frances Hodgson Burnett's *The Secret Garden* (1910), for instance, demonstrate that the Gothic had become quite at home in children's literature. A century later, the nightmare vision in Neil Gaiman's *Coraline* (2002) recalls Lewis Carroll's dream-book *Alice's Adventures in Wonderland* (1865), and Gaiman's *The Graveyard Book* (2008) likewise resets the central plot of Rudyard Kipling's *The Jungle Book* (1894–95) in a cemetery. Such twenty-first-century works do not simply layer Gothic elements onto the classics of Victorian children's fiction; rather, they rightly reveal that children's literature has, in fact, always been Gothic.

Perhaps, then, Frankenstein's monster has been knocking at the door of the nursery ever since his questionable birth two centuries ago. But, in recent decades, children's authors have begun willingly to open the door and to welcome him in. This chapter discusses five recent reanimations of Shelley's Creature: four in picture books for children – Keith Graves' *Frank was a Monster who wanted to Dance* (2006), Neil Numberman's *Do Not Build a Frankenstein!* (2009), Patrick McDonnell's *The Monsters' Monster* (2012), and Jennifer Adams' *Frankenstein: An Anatomy Primer* (2014) – and a fifth in a stop-motion-animated film, Tim Burton's *Frankenweenie* (2012). Each of these texts reimagines children's literature as the monster's rightful abode. No longer the child's perverse other, the monster has become an expression of the child's true self and, in particular, the embodiment of the child's oscillating exhilarations and anxieties about bodies, power, families, solitude, normativity, and weirdness.[2] These texts ask us to reconsider the early nineteenth-century efforts to segregate the monster from the child and, by extension, the attempt to sanitize the Gothic elements of children's literature that formed the context for his inception. In these twenty-first-century adaptations of the Frankenstein Complex, the monster no longer threatens the child, nor does his perverse existence register the evacuation of childhood itself: quite the opposite. These new 'Frankensteins' allow child readers (and viewers) to imagine living on their own terms.

Monstrous bodies: integrating and disintegrating selves

In visual depictions of Shelley's novel, the monster's ungainly and excessive body takes centre stage. Boris Karloff's portrayal of the hulking, lurching brute with a square head and screws in his neck in James Whale's 1931 film *Frankenstein* solidified the modern image of the monster, just as his character's encounter with the little girl, Maria, supplied the shocking contrast between monster and child. In Whale's film, Maria invites the monster to play, and she divides a bunch of daisies for each to throw into a pond. The close-up of her small fingers tenderly laying flowers in the Creature's gargantuan hands prefigures the tragedy that follows: assuming that the girl will float in water just as the daisies do, the monster scoops Maria up, tosses her in the pond, and drowns her. However, even as his deadly actions underscore the discordancy between monster and child, Karloff's spontaneous joy in sniffing the flowers figure the monster as an innocent child, and his ignorance about how bodies (his own, the daisies', the girl's) operate appears a childish mistake. The monster's naive mystification about bodies has been revived in two modern adaptations: the BabyLit series board book *Frankenstein: An Anatomy Primer*, written by Jennifer Adams and illustrated by Alison Oliver, and Keith Graves' picture book *Frank was a Monster who wanted to Dance*. Taking their cue from Karloff's persona rather than Shelley's plot, these picture books present the monster's body as a template from which the child reader learns about his own body – either to quell the reader's fears about aberrant physicality or, alternatively, to take pleasure in the joys of corporeal deviance.

Along with BabyLit's *Pride and Prejudice: A Counting Primer*, *Moby Dick: An Ocean Primer*, and seventeen others, *Frankenstein: An Anatomy Primer* is advertised as 'a fashionable way to introduce your child to the world of classic literature'. On its front cover is an iconic image of the monster, with lightning bolts emanating from screws in his temples (Figure 11.1). This time, however, he smiles benignly at a child in a lab coat, goggles, and gloves (a similarly refashioned Dr Frankenstein) holding up a tape measure to the monster's outstretched arm. Along the book's border is another ruler, this one to scale, measuring the size of the book and perhaps encouraging the young reader to measure his or her own arms. Oliver's graphics illustrate the work of the collection as a whole: bringing huge literary tomes down to a child's proportions. The board books announce that there is nothing frightening about the classics (or the monstrous bodies inside them) once they are appropriately sized and adjusted for the child reader. The first page of the book displays an outline of the monster's body, and

Figure 11.1 The cover of *Frankenstein: An Anatomy Primer* by Jennifer Adams and Alison Oliver.

each layout successively fills in his parts – head, eyes, mouth, body, arms, legs, hands, and feet – while showing those body parts in action. With his head, for instance, the monster reads Milton's *Paradise Lost*; he climbs a mountainside with his legs, and his hand holds out daisies. (No Maria is drowned here.) The last page shows the monster and the child scientist happily sitting on adjacent swings, with a bright red heart on the monster's chest, compositionally balanced by one of the daisies now in the pocket of the child's lab coat. Thus, the most important body part has been left for last: the heart that allows the monster to love and to mirror the child.

The BabyLit series seeks to dilute and ultimately to dismiss the monster's physical defects. The monster is not grotesque; bodies are capable and powerful even when awkward. His size, relative to the child scientist, is proportionate to a parent's, and although Oliver lifts her image from the cinematic iconography of Whale's film, his anatomy does not include the organ that dooms Whale's monster to be a murderer and outcast: the 'Abnormal Brain' that Dr Frankenstein mistakenly implants in his Creature. In only a few instances in the BabyLit board book is the monster's monstrosity evoked. His head and hands are bandaged and scarred, an ant crawls along his toe, and his eyes are featured peering into the bedroom curtains (an image of the Creature popularised by Shelley's early twentieth-century illustrators like Lynd Ward). In these moments the well-read adult reader is invited to recall the perversity of the monster's creation, the post-mortem atrophy of his body parts, and the violent acts that have rent his skin. But for the child reader unfamiliar with the pictorial and cinematic history of the Creature, his Gothic origins are erased, and he is reborn as the cheerful and cared-for child he never was. Once the book is closed, the back cover reveals the monster still swinging, still smiling, but now smaller according to the ruler on the book's spine, with the author's and artist's dedications – 'For Nate' and 'For H.B.' – hovering affectionately over his head. Adams and Oliver's *Anatomy Primer* comforts its readers: all bodies are normal, all bodies are safe, and all bodies are loved.

While *Frankenstein: An Anatomy Primer* mitigates monstrosity, Keith Graves' *Frank was a Monster who wanted to Dance* exaggerates the aberrant and revolting. Catering to the child who loves to be grossed out, Graves' front cover revels in the perversity of the monster's visage: 'Frank' looks at us out of bulging eyes and mismatched pupils, with a swollen, green head zippered across the temple, jagged teeth, a lolling tongue, and skeletal fingers grasping a hat attached to his rotting head by silky cobwebs. No ruler lines this book's border; in contrast, Frank's body does not fit the frame, and his bulging buttocks wrap around to the back cover. Shown at home in the first double-page spread, he is pictured as an old man in a ragged bathrobe clutching the remote control, his only companion a similarly aged and mustachioed cat comprised of two clashing pelts haphazardly sewn together. Despite his seeming unsuitability for public display, Frank wants to dance. Driving himself to a theatre and propelling himself on stage, he executes balletic and gymnastic feats to a packed house, perhaps echoing Victor and the Creature's tap routine to Irving Berlin's 'Putin' on the Ritz' in Mel Brooks' film *Young Frankenstein* (1974), hilariously performed by Gene Wilder and Peter Boyle. But, in Graves' picture book, Frank's 'head began to unzip', 'out flopped his brain', and the disintegration progresses until one eye, one arm, and finally his head become rent from his body (Figure 11.2). Graves' illustrations are deliciously graphic: Frank's bright pink brain, highlighting its abnormality, is scarred and stitched, polka dotted with pus, crawling with worms, and it leaves gooey, fly-infested stains as it bounces across the stage.

Rebellion rather than regulation, excess rather than proportion, and disgust rather than discipline are the hallmarks of Graves' picture book. In place of the normative body is this cheeky salute to the inappropriate, transgressive body, doing what it should not do and dismembering itself in the process. In contrast to Adams and Oliver's dismissal of the Gothic, Graves exaggerates 'the realities of gross corporeality' and the 'fragmented and permeable' subjectivity that Kelly Hurley, in *The Gothic*

Figure 11.2 The monster begins to fall apart in *Frank was a Monster who wanted to Dance*.

Body: Sexuality, Materialism, and Degeneration at the Fin de Siècle (1996), defines as the hallmarks of the genre (3). The conclusion of *Frank was a Monster* does not reconstitute its protagonist's body. As his performance comes to an end, Frank's decapitated and deflated skull somehow murmurs to itself, 'I might be a monster, but man can I dance!' – signifying that decomposition is a small price to pay for aesthetic expression. Both front and back fly-leaves show the otherwise empty stage floor covered only by Frank's foot and hand prints, connected by arrows, and choreographed directions such as 'slide', 'flip', 'pirouette', and 'detach leg and toss'. These instructions offer readers a blueprint to recreate Frank's irreverent – and impossible – steps, but more importantly they depict the body as an agent of uncontained and unmeasured movement. His desire to 'toss' his leg into the sea of audience members is no longer the monster's horrific act of murdering a little girl in Whale's film, but a humorous masochism meant only to delight the child reader. The author's bio presents Graves as 'a human who always wanted to be a monster, but never had the right shoes', who now lives with 'a lovely princess and little twin monsters'. Monster and child are again synonymous, but now it is the child who is meant to be attracted to the monster's freedom of movement, rather than the other way around.

The first page of the BabyLit *Anatomy Primer* shows the child Dr Frankenstein in his laboratory next to a succession of bubbling beakers, meters, and clocks. On the wall is a poster of the monster's outline with its body parts named and the heading 'How to Build a Perfect Monster', above which hovers a quote from Victor's account of the monster's creation in Shelley's novel: 'I became acquainted with the science of anatomy.' Tellingly, Adams does not complete the quotation, in which Shelley's

Victor continues: 'but this was not sufficient; I must also observe the natural decay and corruption of the human body' (51). The BabyLit *Anatomy Primer* illustrates the first part of the sentence only: to make a 'perfect monster' – in which perfection eradicates monstrosity – Adams and Oliver's miniaturised Dr Frankenstein and their toddler audience learn the standard body parts, where they are supposed to go, and what they are expected to do. His monstrosity erased, the now 'perfect monster' becomes a 'perfect' child – happily swinging while his red heart glows with love. In contrast, Graves' *Frank was a Monster who wanted to Dance* offers readers the sentiment uttered in the omitted second half of Victor's sentence: the awareness that anatomy is unknowable without an intimacy with decay, that the body is never 'perfect' but always corrupt, immoderate, disobedient, and monstrous. Humorous, no doubt, *Frank was a Monster* retains the Gothic investment in disorder, transgression, and fragmentation that *An Anatomy Primer* suggests must be tidied up for the monster to enter into children's literature.

Deviant creations: accepting family and making friends

Because Adams and Oliver's *Anatomy Primer* and Graves' *Frank was a Monster who wanted to Dance* restrict their interest in Shelley's monster to his physical presence, Victor's half-quote in the BabyLit book is the only passing reference to the monster's creation in either children's text. However, two other contemporary children's picture books recast Victor's anxieties about fathering the Creature into the child's negotiations with accepting family members and making friends. In Shelley's novel, Victor instinctively recoils from the monster in the very moment of his creation and runs from him in disappointment, terror, and guilt: he thinks to himself and later says to Walton, 'How can I describe my emotions at this catastrophe, or how delineate the wretch whom with such infinite pains and care I had endeavoured to form?' (57). Retelling *Frankenstein* from the point of view of the terrified and fleeing creator, Neil Numberman's *Do Not Build a Frankenstein!* and Patrick McDonnell's *The Monsters' Monster* see Victor's reaction as akin to the child's fear of new people and new siblings as invaders of their known worlds. Monstrosity does not inhere in the monsters themselves but is, rather, the temporary result of misapprehension; a monster is merely a brother you have not yet grown to love or a friend you have not yet made. These texts teach readers how to avoid Victor's mistake, but, at the same time, their sunny lessons in familial ties and friendship evoke – without entirely dispelling – the darker side of loneliness.

Do Not Build a Frankenstein! opens with an unnamed child imploring a group of his peers: 'Gather round! Gather round! I have very important advice to give!' His advice, printed in all caps inside a speech bubble emanating out of a stretched and contorted mouth, repeats the title of the book: 'DO NOT BUILD A FRANKENSTEIN!' The dreadful act of creation has already taken place, and the boy has come to warn other children to avoid repeating his experiment. 'At first,' the boy tells his child listeners and the book's readers, 'having a Frankenstein may be fun'; the illustrations depict the newly minted monster carrying the boy on his shoulders and the two dressing up and playing ball. But a few pages later, the monster's presence ceases to produce pure pleasure; he shouts 'Boo!' at the boy and frightens him while he sleeps, chases away the boy's friends, breaks his toys, follows him around, and always nags him to play. The conceit here is not that the boy has created a monster (although we see the boy stealing body parts and electrocuting himself early in the book), but that the boy has acquired a sibling. The monster's actions perfectly resemble those of a younger brother annoying the older boy. And the resolution to this family drama is predictably comforting: the monster shows up, at first scaring the other children, but then he engages them in a euphoric 'game of monster tag' that wins over all the other players. On the last page, the boy cries, 'Hey! Wait for me!' and runs to join the group headed by the monster, whose company he now desires.

Numberman's book is about belonging; however, the creator is the misfit here, rather than his creation. Earlier in this collection, Kate Newell shows that versions of *Frankenstein* adapted for elementary school children in the 1980s and 1990s visually tone down the monster's monstrosity, and Numberman follows suit by softening both the look and the actions of his 'Frankenstein'. Snubbed by the boy, the monster remains blissfully oblivious to the rejection and never stops cheerfully seeking new playmates. But, while the unthreatening and gregarious monster attracts new friends, the boy is conspicuously left alone. Giving the name 'Frankenstein' to the monster, Numberman leaves the boy nameless: a lack emphasised in the book's first page. While the boy is pictured crying, 'Gather round!' on the right side of the layout, on the left side, a girl whispers to her friend, 'Who is he?' This question is the first text we read, and one the book never answers. Another child asks, 'What does he want?' and a third says, 'He just moved into the neighborhood.' The boy admits that his desire to escape the Frankenstein has forced him to move from place to place, and neither his namelessness nor his homelessness is ever resolved. On the last full page, the boy is alone, calling 'Wait for me!' to the monster and the rest of the children who have departed to play 'monster tag' without him. Even though the flyleaf shows a silhouette of the monster carrying someone (presumably the boy) on his shoulders, this shadowy and silent image might be insufficient to settle the sibling rivalry satisfactorily (Figure 11.3). Like *Frankenstein: An Anatomy Primer*, *Do Not Build a Frankenstein!* normalises monstrosity, but Numberman's book maintains the threat of being an outcast to those who do not heed its warning.

The power of friendship to dispel monstrosity is again the focus of McDonnell's *The Monsters' Monster*. Here, a troika of peculiar-looking mates, named Grouch, Grump, and little Gloom 'n' Doom, insist on being monsters. Although Grouch is a horned harlequin, Grump a furry beast, and little Gloom 'n' Doom a two-headed clown, they are not really monsters until they act monstrously. More overtly than in other *Frankenstein* adaptations, monstrosity in this book is equated with childhood behaviours. Bad moods, rather than rude bodies, seem to define monstrosity. Grump throws a boulder from their castle with a 'SMASH!', Grouch rides it down with a mallet ready

Figure 11.3 A final game of monster tag in *Do Not Build a Frankenstein!*

to strike with a 'CRASH!', and Gloom 'n' Doom jumps about swinging baseball bats with a 'BASH!' The next page tells us: 'Huffing and puffing, mad about NOTHING, their ten favorite words were NO, NO, NO, NO, NO, NO, NO, NO, NO, and NO!' Grouch, Grump, and Gloom 'n' Doom fight, complain, and throw tantrums in their ongoing competition to determine who is the most monstrous – or naughtiest – child.

Their contest culminates in their plan to 'make a MONSTER monster. The biggest, baddest monster EVER!' McDonnell adds an ironic inversion of Shelley's text when the threesome is disappointed not at their creation's monstrosity but at his unexpected gentility. The little creators want their monster to wreak havoc, but, once alive, 'in a deep, booming voice, he said his first words ... Dank You!' Crestfallen, however, Grouch, Grump, and Gloom 'n' Doom do not abandon their creation like Shelley's Victor, and in the end the monster's gratitude wins over his companions. *The Monsters' Monster* closes with the four, now friends, serenely watching the sunset over the ocean 'And no one was thinking ... about being a monster' (ellipsis in original).

Though it may seem that McDonnell is as anxious to recuperate the monstrous as are Adams, Oliver, and Numberman, *The Monsters' Monster* offers an even bolder challenge to selfhood than does the decomposing body in Graves' *Frank was a Monster*. The ellipsis that joins the last sentence – 'and no one was thinking ... about being a monster' – allows the sentiment to bleed over two double-page layouts. On the first of these two-page layouts, the caesura leaves the characters staring over the ocean without a thought: 'and no one was thinking ...'. McDonnell uses the same technique earlier, when the monster is first born but, to his creators' chagrin, 'didn't think he was a monster. He didn't think he was anything ... ... but thankful to be ALIVE!' (ellipsis in original). Here also, the first ellipsis is followed by a page split between two very different illustrations of the monster. In the second layout, where he is 'thankful to be ALIVE', he stands exultant, his smile beaming and his arms outstretched to embrace the world. But on the previous page, his slumped shoulders and drooping head imply that the sentence ends here: 'he didn't think he was a monster. He didn't think he was anything ...' with the ellipsis merely trailing off into nothingness (Figure 11.4). *The Monsters' Monster* thus raises the problem of monsters evacuated of their monstrosity: they are blanks, devoid of thought. Once monstrosity is cured and its symptoms alleviated, there does not seem to be any substance left in childhood: no naughtiness, no play, no creation, nothing but the stillness of watching the sunset that marks the end of the book. McDonnell's *The Monsters' Monster*, although encouraging readers to relinquish their inner monsters, also registers this renunciation as a potential loss of identity.

Like Captain Walton staring out across the ocean while the Creature is 'borne away by the waves, and lost in darkness and distance' in the closing lines of Shelley's *Frankenstein* (223), Numberman's monster and boy fade into dusky silhouette on the final fly-leaf, and McDonnell's formerly monstrous crew stare out into the darkening waters of the ocean after sunset. All three scenes mark the inevitable death of the monster – not literally in the children's text, but figuratively; what was monstrous has been dispelled. Numberman's and McDonnell's monsters are ultimately scrubbed clean of their monstrosity, and in these moments children's literature is once again purified of the Gothic. But these resolutions are also figured as losses: the loss of the ideal playmate (the joys of frolicking with Numberman's massive mate) or of selfhood (McDonnell's concluding moment of calm that forfeits agency and thought). The

But Monster didn't think
he was a monster.

He didn't think he was anything . . .

Figure 11.4 The sympathetic monster from *The Monsters' Monster* by Patrick McDonnell.

pathos inherent in the conclusion to Shelley's novel, that recognises and respects readers' affection for the Creature even as we understand the inevitability of his death, is magnified in these two picture books that so explicitly equate monstrosity with childhood. Nostalgia for monstrosity is palpable in both texts, even as their ostensible purpose is to drive the monster out and leave only a group of shiny, happy, new-found friends. But, of course, the very project of literary recuperation – of bringing Victor Frankenstein and his Creature back to life in the twenty-first century – is an act of nostalgia.

Gothic children: recovering monstrosity

Tim Burton's *Frankenweenie* expresses nostalgia both for the era of Burton's 1950s childhood and for the movie monsters of the 1930s and 1940s.[3] A twelve- or thirteen-year-old Victor Frankenstein – before he experiments with dead bodies in quasi-Shelleyan fashion – is an amateur filmmaker. Burton's film opens with Victor (voiced by Charlie Tahan) and his parents (Martin Short and Catharine O'Hara) watching a movie that he has made: titled 'Monsters from Beyond', the film features a toy pterodactyl suspended on wires terrorising human figurines until Victor's dog Sparky, costumed as a prehistoric 'Sparkysaurus', saves the day. Movie-making is reanimation: a creative process that revivifies extinct creatures for modern role-play. But Victor's father considers his son's hobby at odds with a 'normal' childhood; he whispers to his wife, 'All that time he spends up there – he should be out playing with his friends.' Mrs Frankenstein responds, 'I don't think he has any friends … any except Sparky.' For Mr Frankenstein, this means that his son is, as he puts it, 'weird'. Burton's *Frankenweenie* thus recaptures the essential antagonism between child and monster from Shelley's novel. Victor's obsession with movie monsters and his exclusionary friendship with his dog threaten his ability to be the 'child' that his father thinks he should be. Emphasising the adult's insistence on the radical division between child and monster, Burton then moves towards their reconciliation. Unlike Adams and Oliver's board book or McDonnell's picture book, *Frankenweenie* does not seek to erase monstrosity for the sake of childhood normalcy but, rather, the film articulates a deep longing for the alternative that monstrosity offers.

The contrast between Victor's weirdness and Mr Frankenstein's idea of a 'normal' childhood is dramatised by the competing demands of the science fair, in which Victor wants to participate, and baseball, which his father demands that he should play. On the batter's mound, coached by his dad, Victor is distracted by thoughts of the science fair but manages absent-mindedly to hit a home run out of the park. Sparky runs after the ball and is killed by a passing car. Devastated by the loss of his only friend, Victor now devises his science fair experiment: during the next lightning storm (we are told early on that the town has them every night), Victor hoists Sparky's corpse into the electric current and galvanises his dead body back to life as both Whale's and Brooks' Frankensteins have previously done. Departing from the usual script, however, Burton's young Victor does not abandon his monster; rather, he struggles to keep Sparky safe and hidden from nosey neighbours. Inevitably, the secret gets out, and Victor's classmates – all desirous of winning the science fair themselves – start reproducing the experiment by disinterring and electrifying their own dead pets. Sparky's sutures and screws (like his cinematic monster forebear's) do not alter his loyal and loving canine demeanour, but the same cannot be said of the other resurrected pets. Joining films like Erle C. Kenton's *House of Frankenstein* (1944) and Universal Studios' 'Monster Rally' projects that teamed Frankenstein's monster with campy counterparts like the Wolf Man and the Hunchback of Notre Dame, *Frankenweenie* delivers a combative cluster of other-worldly creatures. Mr Whiskers, a fluffy white cat who pounces on a dead bat as it is being electrocuted, transforms into a wizened, blackened witch's familiar who sprouts bat-like wings and flies. The final show-down, at the town festival, pits Mr Whiskers against Sparky in a delicious horror-movie lovers' homage to Al Adamson's schlocky 1971 *Dracula vs. Frankenstein*.

Victor's movie (starring Sparky as a prehistoric creature resurrected by the magic of film) is a precursor of the scientific experiment that brings his dog back to life (the film and the lightning both being tricks of electricity). According to Mr Frankenstein, all three of Victor's interests – filmmaking, science, and his dog – threaten his ability to be a normal kid. Sparky's refusal to sit still during the baseball game mimics Victor's inability to focus on his batting. When Victor's home run inadvertently causes the dog's death, *Frankenweenie* re-enacts the antagonism between monster and child in Shelley's novel but reverses the formula. The monster does not murder the child; rather, Mr Frankenstein's insistence on a normative childhood constituted by sports and outdoor activity kills off his son's 'weird' attachment to his dog. Sparky's resurrection literalises the metaphorical function that he already served: a creature at odds with the father's suburban, middle-class conceptions of what the child ought to be. *Frankenweenie* is not alone in using the dog this way. In *The Queer Child, or Growing Sideways in the Twentieth Century* (2009), Kathryn Stockton notes how often literary texts feature dogs in this role: in novels like Virginia Woolf's *Mrs Dalloway* (1925) and Djuna Barnes's *Nightwood* (1936), according to Stockton, 'the dog is a vehicle for the child's strangeness. It is the child's companion in queerness … the dog is a figure for the child beside itself, engaged in a growing quite aside from growing up' (90). For Stockton, the dog embodies the child's resistance to heteronormative narratives of development. Similarly in *Frankenweenie*, Sparky expresses and enables Victor's weirdness.

Once he discovers that Sparky is alive, Mr Frankenstein tries to convince Victor to 'let him go' as the first step in growing into (and then out of) conventional childhood. As a dead dog reanimated by Victor's midnight galvanism, Sparky is not just a figure for the non-normative development that Stockton calls 'growing sideways'; his reanimated corpse also embodies the Gothic. Within children's literature scholarship, the Gothic regularly features as a phase that child protagonists must overcome in the project of self-building. In 'Between Horror, Humour, and Hope: Neil Gaiman and the Psychic Work of the Gothic' (2008), for instance, Karen Coats tries to explain the prevalence of Gothic elements in children's literature and argues that the Gothic now performs the same function that psychoanalyst Bruno Bettelheim claimed that fairy tales did in his landmark study, *The Uses of Enchantment* (1975). According to Coats, 'we manufacture fearful stories and engage in dark, obsessive daydreams in order to get some mastery over unfocused anxieties' (83). Just as Bettelheim had argued that 'Snow White' allowed young girls of the past two centuries to externalise, to articulate, and thus to cope with feelings of rage and jealousy towards their mothers, Coats maintains that the second mother motif and the other Gothic elements of Gaiman's

Coraline bring the psychic trauma of familial entrenchments into focus for the twenty-first-century child reader so that she can then learn to 'master' them. Coats' analysis of the Gothic offers the basis for sound readings of *Frankenstein*'s recent reappearances in texts like *Frankenstein: An Anatomy Primer* and *Do Not Build a Frankenstein!* In these texts, monstrosity is the temporary effect of anxiety, anger, loneliness, or misunderstanding. Growing up means recognising that monstrosity can be overcome, because it was only ever a flawed vision of the self.

Frankenweenie recognises the role that the Gothic has played in children's reading and then rejects it. The final battle between Mr Whiskers and Sparky concludes when they both die (again) in a windmill fire. This second death offers the film the perfect chance for Victor to 'let it go' and to readjust his 'sideways' growth into more traditionally sanctioned channels. However, when the townspeople circle their cars to jump-start Sparky back to life, Mr Frankenstein surprises his son by encouraging him to reanimate the dog. 'But you said I had to let him go,' Victor whispers, and his father responds, 'Sometimes adults don't know what they're talking about.' Now with Mr Frankenstein's help, Sparky gets a third life, and Victor ends where he began: enjoying an obsessive love for his dog through the magical properties of electricity. The Gothic in Burton's film is not a trauma to be overcome but, rather, an alternative to normative childhood that the film embraces. In another essay about Gaiman's fiction for children, 'Psychoanalysis, "Gothic" Children's Literature, and the Canonization of *Coraline*' (2015), Chloé Germaine Buckley rejects Coats' reading of the Gothic as the representation of everything the child must come to terms with and disavow in order to develop an integrated, healthy self. Coats' position, according to Buckley, makes childhood 'something one survives; it characterizes the child as not only a work in progress, but also a victim of psychological ill health' (70). Instead, she writes, children's texts like Gaiman's *Coraline* 'resist adult diagnosis and construction' (74) and demonstrate that the Gothic is not only 'therapy for a constitutionally dysfunctional childhood', but also 'a space in which meanings remain open and mobile, playful rather than abject, and canny rather than uncanny' (76). The resilience of *Frankenweenie*'s dead dog keeps alive the mobile, playful, sideways, and weird possibilities for non-normative childhood.

In fact, the 'normal' childhood that Victor's father initially wants for him is conspicuously absent from *Frankenweenie*. Unlike the hunky jocks and blonde debutantes that contrast Burton's previous Frankenstein-like anti-hero in *Edward Scissorhands* (1990), Victor's classmates at New Holland High School are all 'weird.'[4] From Edgar E. Gore[5] (voiced by Atticus Shaffer) – whose name combines horror master Edgar Allan Poe with Frankenstein's familiar cinematic sidekick, Igor, and whose humpback is visually reminiscent of the latter – to Elsa Van Helsing (Winona Ryder) – whose name similarly links Elsa Lanchester, the star of Whale's *Bride of Frankenstein* (1935), and Abraham Van Helsing, the signature vampire hunter in Bram Stoker's *Dracula* (1897) – the students are all 'Goths' who have pale faces, wear dark clothes, and hungrily exchange superstitions about the town's incessant lightning storms. Mr Whiskers' owner (Catherine O'Hara) does not have a name; she is referred to in the credits only as 'Weird Girl,' a fitting moniker, given her propensity for gathering Mr Whiskers' litter-box droppings, forming them into the initials of the boys in her class, and presenting them as indications of her cat's prophetic dreams. The teachers at New Holland are even stranger. The shady substitute in charge of the science fair, Mr Rzykruski (Martin Landau), has a heavy Eastern European accent and equates lightning to a violent version of the immigrant experience: electrons, he ominously explains, leave their clouds to rush to the 'Land of Opportunity' in the ground, mercilessly electrocuting anything or anyone that gets in their way.

When preparations for the science fair go awry, Mr Rzykruski is fired, but before he takes his leave of New Holland, he explains to Victor why Sparky's reanimation was successful while subsequent experiments failed, and in doing so delivers the closest the film gets to a moral. 'The first time', Mr Rzykruski asks, 'did you love your experiment?' Finding a solution in 'love' – even to scientific problems – might promise to lift Victor out of his isolation and put him back on the track, so to speak, of a conventional, father-approved childhood full of friends and even a girlfriend. *Frankenweenie* even hints at a potential romance between Victor and Elsa. However, Mr Rzykruski references not Victor's love for Elsa, or for any other person, but the very love for his dog that Mr Frankenstein has already deemed 'weird' and disruptive to Victor's development. Indeed, the only romance realised in the film occurs between Sparky and Elsa's dog Persephone, a poodle with a beehive fur-do through which Sparky's kiss sends jagged, white lightning bolts recalling the hair-do of the title character of Whale's 1935 sequel, *Bride of Frankenstein*. Although the other children's feverish experiments in raising their pets from the dead enable Burton to restage the creature flicks of his youth – for example, an enormous reanimated turtle (ingeniously named Shelley) stalks through the town like Godzilla – Sparky is the film's central monster. But the dog's monstrosity does not threaten childhood as much as define it: the child's exclusionary friendship with the dog may be weird, but it is true love.

Far from disavowing the centrality of the dogs, *Frankenweenie*'s closing scene zooms in on the canine couple, Sparky and Persephone, kissing in the foreground while a blurred grouping of Victor and his parents watch from the background (Figure 11.5). This end is an inspired inversion of the final scene of Whale's 1931 *Frankenstein*, in which the reunion between Henry Frankenstein and Elizabeth is set back from the viewers and framed by a collection of giddy house servants. This closing scene in Whale's film assures us that heteronormative marriage and proper procreation have been successfully recovered once the monster is removed.[6] Closing the door on the happy couple, Frankenstein's father ends the film toasting to his future grandson: in other words, the death of the doctor's aberrant creation means that a real child can now be naturally born. In tribute and contrast, the background image in Burton's closing shot does not contain Victor and Elsa but, rather, Victor and his parents, not pushing Victor's development forward into a romance plot but, rather, reconstituting the primary family unit with which the film began. Just as *Frankenweenie*'s opening showed the family watching Victor's movie starring 'Sparkysaurus', an extinct animal

Figure 11.5 Sparky and Persephone share a spark in *Frankenweenie*. © 2012 Disney.

reanimated through the cinematic manipulation of light, they now watch the actual Sparky resurrected through the scientific operation of electricity. It is not normalcy that wins out but weirdness, and thus it is not Victor who needs to overcome his childhood obsessions with movie-making, science, and dogs, but his father who must see them through his son's eyes.

Frankenweenie's final shot thus underscores the persistence of the Gothic within not simply children's literature but also childhood: not as a trauma to be overcome, as in Coats' diagnosis but, rather, as a deep well of love (both interspecies and familial) and creativity (both scientific and cinematic) to be explored. The monstrous – embodied by the reanimated corpse of a cherished pet – is the essence of childhood itself: the weirdest part that should never be let go. Victor has not 'mastered' the film's Gothic elements – anxieties about loneliness, fears about loss, scientific excesses, or the love of dogs – in order to form an integrated self and to embark on a healthier childhood. Rather, the Gothic elements are all there is, and they are all Victor needs. *Frankenweenie* explicitly demonstrates where McDonnell's *The Monsters' Monster* only hints: the child cleansed (or 'cured') of his monstrosity may also lose his agency, his thoughts, and the weirdness that constitutes who he is. Burton rejects the move made by McDonnell's ellipses, wherein the nothingness left by the monster's absence stealthily transforms into gratitude and serenity. More like Graves' celebration of monstrosity for its delightful deviance, *Frankenweenie* refuses to tidy up its Gothic disorder. At the end of *Frank was a Monster who wanted to Dance*, Frank is dismembered, with no suggestion of reconstitution. Likewise, Burton's Sparky looks worse for wear, his body burned and bruised from his multiple deaths, his stitches sagging from his compound electrocutions. But his image, like Frank's in Graves' book, allows childhood – and its Gothic subconscious – to be messy, muddled, and monstrous.

'Monsters are our children', writes Jeffrey Jerome Cohen in 'Monster Culture (Seven Theses)': they 'ask us how we perceive the world, and how we have misrepresented what we have attempted to place. They ask us to reevaluate our cultural assumptions about race, gender, sexuality, our perception of difference, our tolerance towards its expression. They ask us why we have created them' (20). In trying to erect a genre in opposition to the Gothic, eighteenth- and early nineteenth-century children's writers may have miscalculated. The Gothic obsession with fractured bodies, disordered psyches, domestic discord, regressive desires, and anxieties about biological and cultural creation is not childhood's antithesis but its purest aesthetic expression. The twenty-first-century picture books and animated films that have rebirthed Shelley's monster have also revived the literary controversy surrounding his inception. Adams, Oliver, Numberman, and McDonnell let in the monster to show that his monstrosity is an illusion. Like Wollstonecraft, they aim to clear readers' minds of 'strange prejudices' and 'vain fears', as if the pedagogical function of children's literature were still to dispel the Gothic. But Burton and Graves (and to a certain extent McDonnell) recognise that children are monsters because, as Cohen suggests, they strain against adult codes that dictate how bodies are supposed to act, how they are supposed to feel, and whom they are supposed to love. Perhaps the pedagogical value of the Gothic child's text rests not in the genre's attempt to reform the child's monstrosity but in the appeal it makes to both child and adult readers to embrace this liberating monstrosity and to keep childhood weird.

Notes

1 In the 1980s, Anne K. Mellor's *Mary Shelley* (esp. 54–5) and Chris Baldick's *In Frankenstein's Shadow* (esp. 31–2) popularised this intersection between the death of Shelley's infant daughter and her writing of *Frankenstein*, and it remains standard lore in critical discussions of the novel's inception.

2 This parallel between the child and the monster in children's literature operates wholly differently than it does in the evil child trope of horror cinema. We do not discover – as in films such as *The Bad Seed* (1956), *The Omen* (1976), or *Wicked Little Things* (2006) – that the child is a monster. In texts for young readers, the monster is de-monstered and allowed to claim the best attributes of the child – though not without complication. For a great collection addressing cinema's evil child, see Bohlmann and Moreland.

3 The 2012 film discussed here is not Burton's first production of *Frankenweenie*. In 1984, he directed a live action short of the same name for Disney. The fundamentals of the plot are the same – Victor Frankenstein revives his dog Sparky after the latter is hit by a car – but many of the elements discussed below are realised only in Burton's full-length stop-motion-animation feature released eighteen years later.

4 Robert Markley reads the eponymous protagonist of *Edward Scissorhands* as a Goth version of Frankenstein's monster in 'Geek/Goth: Remediation and Nostalgia in Tim Burton's *Edward Scissorhands*'.

5 Burton may also use this name to acknowledge Edward Gorey and his deliciously macabre cartoons.

6 Angela M. Smith complicates this reading of Whale's final scene in *Frankenstein*. In *Hideous Progeny: Disability, Eugenics, and Classic Horror Cinema*, Smith argues that the film's persistent reminders that Henry Frankenstein is 'mentally defective, queer, and criminal' make this coupling 'a far less comforting and eugenic resolution than might first appear' (78–79). Burton's reworking of Whale's mis-en-scène leaves no ambiguity about its departure from heteronormative, romantic resolution.

Bibliography

Adams, Jennifer. *Frankenstein: An Anatomy Primer*. Illus. Alison Oliver. Layton UT: Gibbs Smith, 2014.

Baldick, Chris. *In Frankenstein's Shadow: Myth, Monstrosity, and Nineteenth-Century Writing*, Oxford: Clarendon Press, 1987.

Barrie, J.M., *Peter Pan in Kensington Gardens*. Illus. Arthur Rackam. 1904. New York: Weathervane Books, 1955.

Bettelheim, Bruno. *The Uses of Enchantment; The Meaning and Importance of Fairy Tales*. 1975. New York: Vintage Books, 1977.

Bohlmann, Markus P.J., and Sean Moreland, eds. *Monstrous Children and Childish Monsters: Essays on Cinema's Holy Terrors*. Jefferson NC: McFarlane & Company Inc., 2015.

Bride of Frankenstein, The. Dir. James Whale. Universal Pictures, 1935.

Buckley, Chloé Germaine. 'Psychoanalysis, "Gothic" Children's Literature, and the Canonization of *Coraline*.' *Children's Literature Association Quarterly*. 40.1 (Spring 2015): 58–79.

Burnett, Frances Hodgson. *The Secret Garden*. 1911. New York: W.W. Norton & Company, 2006.

Carroll, Lewis. *Alice's Adventures in Wonderland* and *Through the Looking-Glass*. 1865 and 1872. London and New York: Penguin Books, 2003.

Coats, Karen. 'Between Horror, Humour, and Hope: Neil Gaiman and the Psychic Work of the Gothic.' *The Gothic in Children's Literature: Haunting the Borders*. Eds Anna Jackson, Karen Coats, and Roderick McGillis. New York and London: Routledge, 2008. 77–92.

Cohen, Jeffrey Jerome. 'Monster Theory (Seven Theses).' *Monster Theory: Reading Culture*. Ed. Jeffrey Jerome Cohen. Minneapolis: University of Minnesota Press, 1996.

Dracula vs. Frankenstein. Dir. Al Adamson. Independent-International Pictures, 1971.

Edward Scissorhands. Dir. Tim Burton. 20th Century Fox, 1990.

Frankenstein. Dir. James Whale. Universal Pictures, 1931.

Frankenweenie. Dir. Tim Burton. Walt Disney Pictures, 2012.

Gaiman, Neil. *Coraline*. Illus. Dave McKean. 2002. New York: HarperCollins, 2012.

Gaiman, Neil. *The Graveyard Book*. Illus. Dave McKean. New York: HarperCollins, 2008.

Godzilla. Dirs. Luigi Cozzi, Ishirô Honda, and Terry O. Morse. AVCO Embassy Pictures, 1977.

Goodlad, Lauren M. E., and Michael Bibby, *Goth: Undead Subculture*. Durham NC: Duke University Press, 2007.

Graves, Keith. *Frank was a Monster who wanted to Dance*. 2006. San Francisco: Chronicle Books, LLC, 2006.

Grimm, Jacob and Wilhelm Grimm, *The Complete Fairy Tales of the Brothers Grimm*. 3rd ed. Trans. Jack Zipes. Illuss. John B. Gruelle. New York: Bantham, 2003.

House of Frankenstein. Dir. Erle C. Kenton. Universal Pictures. 1944.

Hurley, Kelly. *The Gothic Body: Sexuality, Materialism, and Degeneration at the Fin de Siècle*. Cambridge: Cambridge University Press, 1996.

Jackson, Anna, Karen Coats, and Roderick McGillis. *The Gothic in Children's Literature: Haunting the Borders*. New York and London: Routledge, Taylor & Francis Group, 2008.

Kipling, Rudyard. *The Jungle Books*. 1894 and 1895. London: Penguin Books, 2013.

Locke, John. *Some Thoughts concerning Education*. 1693. London: A. & J. Churchill, 1705.

Markley, Robert. 'Geek/Goth: Remediation and Nostalgia in Tim Burton's *Edward Scissorhands*.' *Goth: Undead Subculture*. Eds Lauren M.E. Goodlad and Michael Bibby. Durham NC: Duke University Press, 2007. 277–292.

McDonnell, Patrick. *The Monsters' Monster*. New York and Boston: Little, Brown and Company, 2012.

Mellor, Anne K. *Mary Shelley: Her Life, Her Fiction, Her Monsters*. New York and London: Routledge, Chapman and Hall, 1988.

Numberman, Neil. *Do Not Build a Frankenstein!*. New York: Greenwillow Books, 2009.

Shelley, Mary. *Frankenstein; or The Modern Prometheus*. 1831. Oxford: Oxford University Press, 1969.

Shelley, Mary and Lynd Ward. *Frankenstein: The Lynd Ward Illustrated Edition*. 1934. Mineola, NY: Dover Publications, 2009.

Smith, Angela M. *Hideous Progeny: Disability, Eugenics, and Classic Horror Cinema*. New York: Columbia University Press, 2011.

Stockton, Kathryn Bond. *The Queer Child, or Growing Sideways in the Twentieth Century*. Durham NC: Duke University Press, 2009.

Stoker, Bram. *Dracula*. 1897. Broadview: Peterborough ON, 1998.

Townshend, Dale. 'The Haunted Nursery: 1764–1830.' *The Gothic in Children's Literature: Haunting the Borders*. Eds Anna Jackson, Karen Coats, and Roderick McGillis. New York and London: Routledge, 2008. 15–38.

Wollstonecraft, Mary, *Thoughts on the Education of Daughters: with Reflections on Female Conduct, in the More Important Duties of Life*. London: J. Johnson, 1787.

Young Frankenstein. Dir. Mel Brooks. Gruskoff/Venture Films. 1974.

12

In his image: the mad scientist remade in the young adult novel

Farran L. Norris Sands

ADAPTATIONS OF MARY SHELLEY's *Frankenstein* thrive in the bookstore, especially in the Young Adult (YA) literature aisles. One reason for this is that Victor Frankenstein has long borne the weight of cultural anxieties about the possibilities and excesses of science in a modern age, particularly as these anxieties are expressed in steampunk, dystopian, and apocalyptic literature for young adults. In these popular genres, the image of the mad scientist is prominent, and as much the progeny of Frankenstein as the monster himself. This chapter examines new adaptations of the mad-scientist figure to better understand how Shelley's Victor Frankenstein and 'the Frankenstein Complex', as explained by Dennis Cutchins and Dennis Perry, are represented in YA literature since 2000. Focusing on two types of adaptations – retellings and sustained appropriations – this chapter shows how mad-scientist elements of the Frankenstein Complex are expanded in multiple ways for young readers, ranging from exploring the motivations that might lead a young protagonist to become a mad scientist, to bringing other instantiations of the mad-scientist figure into the intertextual conversation. Focusing on Kenneth Oppel's *This Dark Endeavor* and Ann Halam's *Dr Franklin's Island*, we can see that through intertextual interplay and expansion of character, the figure of the mad scientist morphs to suit the age-related existential concerns of its intended audience. Regardless of the scientist's type, the mad scientists analysed in this chapter respond to specific cultural anxieties that adults (authors, publishers, teachers, parents) believe concern the contemporary YA reader.[1]

Retellings: reaching a new audience

What I term a 'retelling' might also be considered a version of what Linda Hutcheon calls a 'transposition'. Hutcheon explains that a transposition, as a kind of 'transcoding', 'can involve a shift of medium (a poem to a film) or genre (an epic to a novel), or a change of frame and therefore context: telling the same story from a different point of view, for instance, can create a manifestly different interpretation' (7–8). The sample retellings I have selected focus primarily on characters' identity or interpersonal crises and present versions of the original narrative to the YA audience for a new purpose, which is often to develop a back story that exonerates or condemns a character. This focus on identity and interpersonal crises is in fact common in YA literature, probably because adult YA authors often believe that young adults are focused on these issues in their own lives.

Based on Jeffrey J. Cohen's argument that 'The monster is born only at [a] metaphoric crossroads, as an embodiment of a certain cultural moment – of a time, a feeling, and a place' (4), we might ask why these particular retellings are popular now. And why is *Frankenstein* in particular, with its archetypal mad scientist, often retold in YA literature? Perhaps because *Frankenstein* allows authors to engage what they perceive to be contemporary teen interests, such as identification of intertextual moments, teen angst, and rebellion toward adult (especially parental) authority. Considering the success of narratives containing these themes, as well as their sequels and spin-offs, it is little wonder that adult authors continue to write about such topics for teen audiences.[2]

Shelley's *Frankenstein* becomes a particularly potent vessel for exploration of these topics, in part because one can read it as an adaptation of the Genesis story – a story of how mankind fell from grace by seeking forbidden knowledge and rebelling against the Creator, or rather, how the first youth rebelled against his father and was punished. The characters within Shelley's narrative can be read multiple ways; we can view Victor as Adam as he seeks forbidden knowledge – the knowledge of creating Life – and ruins his life in the process. But we can also view Victor as the godlike creator of his own race of beings. If we read Victor as God, then the Creature becomes a kind of Adam, a blank slate with unlimited possibilities. However, when Shelley's Creature chooses to kill William Frankenstein, it, too, commits original sin, leading to the downfall of his race (the future dismemberment of his bride-to-be). There are many references to the Genesis story throughout *Frankenstein*, including the Creature's reading of Milton's *Paradise Lost* as 'a true history' (Shelley 87). In later conversation with Frankenstein he compares himself to Adam and laments that Adam 'had come forth from the hands of God a perfect creature, happy and prosperous, guarded by the especial care of his Creator; he was allowed to converse with and acquire knowledge from beings of a superior nature, but I was wretched, helpless, and alone' (87). The Creature also compares himself to Satan, although he considers his own fate even worse than that of the fallen angel. He recounts, 'God, in pity, made man beautiful and alluring, after his own image; but my form is a filthy type of your's [sic], more horrid even from the very resemblance. Satan had his companions, fellow-devils, to admire and encourage him; but I am solitary and detested' (88). I would argue that the Frankenstein Complex continues to thrive and to encourage new retellings, at least in part, because of its flexibility in dealing with central characters who are ripe for adapting, transforming, and remodelling to meet the interests and needs of contemporary readers, particularly those who are still forming their own identities. Shelley's Frankenstein is both wilful son and absent father, and his Creature is as terrifying as he is sympathetic, tailor-making these characters for YA readers who are themselves in the process of exploring the ambiguities of who they are and what the purpose of their lives might be.

Victor's dual nature and the role that this ambiguity plays in the development of the young mad scientist is explored in Kenneth Oppel's *This Dark Endeavor*. This novel retells Mary Shelley's *Frankenstein*, adopting new character perspectives to reveal the 'truth' behind the Frankenstein story. *This Dark Endeavor*[3] describes Victor's youth and introduces a twin brother for Victor, named Konrad. The novel explains why Victor became obsessed with the idea of scientifically enabled resurrection. As a twin who is always second to his brother, Victor constantly seeks attention from his family and friends. However, when Konrad falls ill, Victor becomes remorseful and seeks a way to counteract the illness. This leads him on dangerous quests for the ingredients to the Elixir of Life. However, when Konrad dies, despite taking the elixir, Victor's 'real' motive behind his eventual creation of the Creature becomes obvious – he seeks to resurrect Konrad, which becomes the focus of the next book in Oppel's series, *Such Wicked Intent*. *This Dark Endeavor* reveals Victor as both a hero and a villain well before he makes his infamous Creature.

Risk taking and rebellion toward adult authority are emphasised in this *Frankenstein* retelling. In particular, Frankenstein rebels against his father's admonition forbidding alchemy. Upon sharing his excitement for Cornelius Agrippa's work, Shelley's Frankenstein remembers that his father said, '"My dear Victor, do not waste your time upon this; it is sad trash"' (Shelley 21). Frankenstein then reflects that if his father had explained his judgement, he would have obeyed him, and perhaps avoided his own ruin (21–22). In Shelley's novel, Frankenstein certainly disobeys his father, but his motivation does not seem to be rebellion, per se. Oppel's Frankenstein, in contrast, seems motivated by a modern assumption that teens inevitably rebel against their parents because they feel they know better, even though they don't always anticipate the consequences of their risky behaviour.

In Oppel's account, Victor's first act of rebellion toward his father occurs when Konrad falls ill. Victor and his comrades discover the Dark Library that houses manuscripts of alchemy and witchcraft that Victor believes might save his twin. Although his father forbids him from entering the library, Victor tells his friends, 'My father is a brilliant man, but he cannot know everything.... We must be willing to take risks' (Oppel 54). This rebellious decision indicates a change in Victor, who narrates, 'All my life I had assumed that Father knew everything.... But he'd been confident the doctors would heal Konrad – and they had not' (54). The young Victor recognises that adults are fallible, and he realises that he must become the problem solver, the hero. This twist on Shelley's narrative is important because, while Victor's decision to defy his father is the first step down a path of increasingly rebellious and risky decisions, it is basically a sound decision (his father is wrong) and it is made out of love for Konrad. Thus Oppel creates a space for empathy toward the young mad scientist.

Yet Oppel's Victor shares some of the same hubris as Shelley's character. Like

Frankenstein, Oppel's Victor also shows himself to be ambitious in his desire to impress his friends, and especially Elizabeth. Readers may, in fact, interpret Victor's ambition, his risk taking and his desire to impress as 'madness' as he disobeys his father and takes his friends on dangerous quests in caves, on lakes, and even into the home of the villainous Polidori,[4] who convinces Victor to cut off two of his fingers as ingredients for the Elixir of Life. Victor repeatedly risks his and his friends' lives, and his elixir fails to save Konrad. Rebellion and risk taking often may be viewed in a positive light in YA novels like *The Hunger Games*, but *This Dark Endeavor* follows Shelley's novel more closely in terms of theme by showing that risk and rebellion can also lead to failure and increasingly darker endeavours.

Victor's risky behaviour reveals much about how the 'mad scientist' is defined in Oppel's novel: the mad scientist as teenager learns through risk, but also becomes 'mad' through an obsessive desire to impress and succeed. Nevertheless, at least in Victor's case, his risks progress from selfish to noble as he learns the importance of family and love over the course of the novel. Risk taking is important in *This Dark Endeavor* because it reveals the scientist to be human and imperfect, despite his discoveries or inventions. Victor's risks reveal that he is both bad and good, selfish and ambitious. In short, Victor's risk taking shows him to be a teenager experiencing the same feelings that the intended reader may experience, and thus Victor is a complex YA character who primes readers to view Shelley's *Frankenstein* in a different light.[5] As they first experience the thrills, anger, and sadness that Oppel's Victor endures during his youth, readers who encounter Shelley's *Frankenstein* afterward may be more likely to view Victor as sympathetic because they have already encountered his passionate relationships with his family and friends. For example, by witnessing Victor's jealousy and lust for Elizabeth during their teen years, along with her rejection of him in preference for his twin, as portrayed by Oppel, later readers of Shelley's text may feel stronger sympathy for Victor when Elizabeth is murdered on their wedding night. Oppel's transformation of Victor's character makes his vengefulness, and even his madness, more understandable in Shelley's narrative.

This Dark Endeavor leads readers to reconsider the character of Frankenstein, in part, by the addition of a complicated back story. In Shelley's *Frankenstein*, readers likely have difficulty deciding with whom to sympathise because both Frankenstein and his Creature take turns narrating, and both narratives are framed within Walton's letters to his sister. Because all knowledge is secondary or tertiary in Shelley's text, readers are challenged to decide whose side they wish to take. Readers are likely to sympathise with Frankenstein initially because his narration comes first. However, when the Creature narrates his story, readers are likely to sympathise with him as he recounts his lonely 'childhood', as well as the ill treatment he receives not only by strangers but also by the De Lacey family, whom he considers his friends, and by Frankenstein, himself. Like Frankenstein, readers experience the Creature's anger and sadness through his story. However, when the narrative returns to Frankenstein's voice, readers then must question their allegiances because they sympathise with both characters, seeing the flaws and cruelty of each. While Shelley makes it difficult for readers to determine which character is the 'monster', Oppel retells the narrative to encourage a sympathetic reading of Victor's actions.

Retellings like Oppel's potentially show a new side of the mad scientist, as teen, as monster, and as father. They give him new dimension and help readers to understand the justifications behind his decisions, or they help us to understand why his enemies hate him. Either way, they tend to retell the source text's narrative for the YA readership to emphasise that the characters are human like us. For the YA reader who is coming to terms with his or her own limitations, vices, and desires for the first time, such narratives can help young readers to understand and accept the complexity of human nature.

Sustained appropriations: intertextual-puzzle scientists and social-obstacle wicked wizards

Typically, in retelllings, source texts are easily identifiable. In contrast, source texts in sustained appropriations may or may not be identifiable. For example, many readers of *Jane Eyre* might not recognise it as, in part, an appropriation of Le Prince's *Beauty and the Beast*. Sanders states that an appropriation is further removed from the informing source (also known as a hypotext) in comparison to a retelling or adaptation, and 'may or may not involve a generic shift' (26). The sample sustained appropriations examined here repackage narratives and characters to meet the YA audience's interest and seem more 'relevant' to the reader. For example, the presentation of the YA protagonist as an outsider to her teen peer group may seem more 'relevant' to YA readers because of their familiarity with navigating their own peer groups. Pairing this problem with a mad-scientist narrative presents the protagonist with an obstacle to overcome while simultaneously finding acceptance through heroism. These appropriations include personal and interpersonal crises, but they also show the mad scientist's greater *potential* effects on society. While the retold mad scientist of a text such as *This Dark Endeavor* is limited to the confines of the hypotext's plot, in an appropriation the mad scientist's characterisation and behaviours relative to the creation of the Creature allows for more possibilities. He or she can, for instance, do more damage to society, wreaking havoc in ways not limited by an original hypotext. Yet these appropriated mad scientists rarely realise their potential because their purpose in the narrative often is to present an obstacle that teens can overcome by working together.

The sustained appropriation selected here references the Frankenstein Complex, which I argue includes texts about other related mad scientists, such as Robert Louis Stevenson's Dr Jekyll and H.G. Wells' Dr Moreau. These scientists are often anthologised and studied in the secondary school classroom alongside Shelley's Frankenstein, and thus share boundaries within any study of adaptations and/or appropriations of *Frankenstein*. The mad scientists of sustained appropriations represent a hodgepodge of what our culture seems to understand about 'mad scientists', or perhaps what adults think YAs know about them.

Thus Ann Halam's *Dr Franklin's Island* presents YA readers with what I call the 'Intertextual Puzzle Scientist'. Intertextuality suggests a reliance on the knowledge of past texts of various genres, and it also suggests that texts speak to one another in order to make new meaning. As Sanders maintains, 'adaptations perform in dialogue with other adaptations as well as their informing source. Perhaps it serves us better to think ... in terms of intertextual webs or signifying fields, rather than simplistic one-way lines of influence from source to adaptation' (24). This certainly applies to the Intertextual Puzzle Scientist who is not identified with a specific hypotext scientist. Sanders suggests, 'appropriation does not always make its founding relationships and interrelationships ... clear' (32). The Intertextual Puzzle Scientist novel typically uses multiple texts to create a narrative so that no one character or event from another story dominates the others, or it may take one scientist and split him into many pieces among multiple characters.[6] Such texts ask readers to apply their knowledge of other texts to understand the novel – in the spirit of the Frankenstein Complex, which acknowledges every adaptation of Frankenstein as an intertextual composite of many other adaptations. In this way, familiar texts and characters come into dialogue with one another, as well as, in a few cases, into dialogue with other texts within the Frankenstein Complex.

The Intertextual Puzzle Scientist accomplishes a couple of tasks. First, the reader who puts the puzzle together and identifies the intertexts is rewarded with a feeling of achievement and insider status.[7] According to Graham Allen, 'Reading thus becomes a process of moving between texts. Meaning becomes something which exists between a text and all the other texts to which it refers and relates' (1). This moving between texts and puzzle solving can be part of the 'fun' of exploring the Frankenstein Complex, especially in a YA appropriation. In pursuing additional texts in the mad-scientist genre, readers may even begin to view the literature as a personal identity marker. In the mass of texts and other identity markers made available through media, YA readers often establish a niche identity by immersing themselves within a medium or genre. Not only does this expertise grant them insider status, but it also serves as a way for them to assert a facet of identity by entering an imaginary or real community of experts on a particular subject or genre.

Ann Halam's *Dr Franklin's Island* demonstrates the idea that mad scientists may be appropriated without being specifically named. Halam's novel tells the story of Semi, a YA whose plane crashes while she is on a trip with other students for a science field trip. Semi soon befriends Miranda, a resourceful and brave fellow traveller who may remind readers of Miranda from Shakespeare's *The Tempest* in name and circumstance. Once their plane washes ashore the two girls find themselves trapped on an island with a cruel scientist and his lackeys. This circumstance may remind readers of popular television shows such as *Lost*. After surviving on the beach with few supplies, the two girls find Dr Franklin's compound and believe they are saved, but their rescue soon becomes entrapment as Dr Franklin uses Semi and Miranda in his scientific experiments that transform them into a manta ray and a bird, respectively. However, the girls are helped by Franklin's assistant, Dr Skinner – a cowardly, two-faced, impotent scientist whose name may allude to Skinner from *The X-Files* or the behavioural scientist B.F. Skinner. Both of these potential intertexts call into question the reality of 'free will'.[8] Skinner eventually steals the antidote for Semi so that she can return to human form, kill Franklin, and save herself and Miranda.

Because of the title, *Dr Franklin's Island*, readers might suspect the novel references *Frankenstein*, but another obvious connection might be to Jules Verne's *The Mysterious Island*. Both islands are, after all, home to a variety of bizarre animals. Likewise, readers may suspect the novel references Michael Crichton's *Jurassic Park* because, like John Hammond, Dr Franklin and his staff play with genes, not knowing what to expect or what type of damage they may do in their experimentation. They have little regard for life or ethics, and they are overly focused on fame and wealth. Finally, references to H.G. Wells' *The Island of Dr Moreau* abound in this novel, including similarities and appropriations of character, setting, and themes. Dr Franklin experiments on animals in efforts to combine them with other species, and his test subjects and assistants both fear and worship him as if he is a god. He also practises vivisection, appropriating aspects of both Drs Frankenstein and Moreau.

Contemporary YA literature is perhaps most vibrant when engaging in this kind of intertextuality. Such intertextual discourse, familiar to young readers through such reference-mad shows as *The Simpsons*, may even be an expectation of the mad-scientist narrative and the Frankenstein Complex in contemporary YA literature. Because both Franklin and Skinner are composed from a variety of literary and screen mad scientists and stereotypes, they represent sustained intertextual appropriations. *Dr Franklin's Island* exemplifies Sanders' assertion that 'Encouraged interplay between appropriations and their sources [emerges] as a fundamental, even vital, aspect of the reading or spectating experience, one productive of new meanings, applications, and resonance' (32). This particular intertextual puzzle pays respect to the literary ancestors of the mad-scientist narrative while simultaneously rejuvenating mad scientists for a new generation of YA readers.

In addition to appropriating from a variety of mad-scientist texts and stereotypes, *Dr Franklin's Island* also represents a variety of cultural anxieties, suggesting that the intertextual puzzle, at least in this case, comes from 'real life' as well as from literature. As readers identify the parts of the intertextual matrix, they also engage in identifying the cultural events and anxieties. Some of the controversial topics in this novel include experimentation on animals, the commodification of the biological sciences and the ethics of gene and cloning technologies. All of these elements are evidenced through both the test subjects Semi and Miranda encounter, as well as their own experiences as human–animal hybrids.[9] Most specifically, however, this novel responds to cloning and stem-cell research anxieties preceding the turn of the millennium. This is no wonder, considering the advances made in this field during the decade preceding the novel's 2001 publication. This includes the birth of Dolly the sheep – the first successful cloning of a mammal from an adult cell (1996) – and the creation of artificial human chromosomes (1997). The original readers of this novel at the time of publication would likely know about these hot topics and the anxieties regarding them, and thus are called to judge Dr Franklin based on their positions toward cloning in the real world.

Although he belongs to the Intertextual Puzzle Scientist type, Dr Franklin also represents a new type of specific mad scientist whom I call the 'Social-Obstacle Wicked Wizard'. This scientist type has great potential to cause catastrophe, but fails to enact his schemes because his plans are foiled by teen protagonists, who in this novel kill him in a struggle to escape. According to Glen Allen, a Wicked Wizard is 'a villain whose arrogance is rooted in the intellect and who seeks, to the detriment of his community, some sort of totalizing revolution' (7–8). The Wicked Wizard mad scientist works in isolation and cares about theory for theory's sake. As a Social-Obstacle Wicked Wizard, a subtype of Allen's Wicked Wizard, Dr Franklin becomes more of a common cause than a character. Certainly, Dr Franklin encompasses the societal anxieties regarding science of the novel's historical moment. But, perhaps more importantly, he becomes an enemy force against which the characters unite, providing them the opportunity to become friends and leaders.

In sustained appropriations, the protagonists' greatest problems are often personal; the main problem is not fear of the scientist, although he represents a real danger. Instead of fearing Dr Franklin, Semi's greatest worries are about being unpopular. She wants Miranda to be her friend, especially since she thinks Miranda is the epitome of cool. As the novel continues, Semi worries about maintaining the relationship she has formed with Miranda, her sole companion during captivity. By the end of the novel, she cares for Miranda so much that she is willing to risk her life for her. Despite being marooned, separated from her family, and the victim of a painful transformation, Semi's real problem is a relationship problem. For this teen, the greatest obstacle is a social one – her basic need to find confidence through friendship.

Much like Frankenstein's monster, who is seeking a way to fit in with a society that has rejected him, YAs also seek ways to fit in to society, while still maintaining their unique identities. The mad scientist and the many parts of the Frankenstein Complex are therefore often used in YA literature as a tool to help young readers overcome the obstacles they are perceived to have, such as lack of self-confidence, unclear self-identity, and trouble in building friendships.[10] As Michael Cart explains, one long-standing purpose of YA fiction has been to present readers with the concerns of their own experience. Cart quotes teenager Julia Rosen, who explains, 'Reading "bleak books" helps us … broaden our outlook and … become less apathetic about the world's problems' (67). As a social obstacle, the mad scientist assists young characters to conquer their personal issues so that they can then seek solutions to the world's problems with their peers. By extension, readers who engage the novel's intertextual puzzles alongside their favourite characters may also feel empowered, or at least less apathetic.

Conclusions

Referencing Fischlin and Fortier, Sanders reminds us that 'the Latin etymological root of the word "adapt", *adaptare* means "to make fit"', and adaptations invariably make texts '"fit" for new cultural contexts and different political ideologies to those of [their] own age' (46). The texts examined in this chapter attempt to make the Frankenstein Complex 'fit' for contemporary YA readers by focusing on issues that are assumed to be 'YA interests', such as romance, friendship, and identity. While such issues are certainly present in the original source texts, these contemporary novels repackage these themes to mimic other popular YA novel publications and sell copies.

The retellings show us that we still value our history (and literary history) because they pay tribute to past mad-scientist narratives. They also reveal that our cultural moment is a time of understanding the Other, of attempting to exonerate and identify with those we once considered monsters. Yet, it is also a moment of scepticism regarding the benign, disinterested, or even hopeful nature of scientific 'progress'. Through these re-examinations of characters, retellings help YA readers to think critically and investigate the veracity of the stereotypes and archetypes found in these novels. Simultaneously, the retellings examined here help rejuvenate the works of Shelley, Stevenson, and Wells, and increase their appeal for new readers.

Sustained appropriations confirm that our cultural moment relies on and is saturated by intertextuality to make meaning. As Christa Albrecht-Crane and Dennis Cutchins assert, 'Adaptations are dialogues with other texts, including the texts upon which they are based, and those texts are in dialogue with adaptations' (19). Adaptations are always intertextual, and they inevitability dialogue with one another. The proliferation of these texts suggests that we desire this dialogue. The Intertextual Puzzle Scientist gives readers the satisfaction of feeling like insiders through identification of puzzle pieces, and the Social-Obstacle Wicked Wizard serves as a bonding agent for strengthening personal relationships as characters overcome the obstacle.

No matter how it joins the Frankenstein Complex, each mad scientist offered up through adapted narrative reveals a truth about the moment of its birth. As Cohen argues, the monster is 'an embodiment of a certain cultural moment' (4). Likewise, the mad scientist, a type of monster, represents a cultural moment, whether he appears in the 1800s mad-scientist text or in a 2013 text for YAs. Yet, Cohen also argues that 'The monster always escapes because it refuses easy categorization' (6). For this reason, the mad scientist offers us a new way of perceiving the world as he breaks categories again and again. By examining how Frankenstein and his colleagues have been adapted for YA literature, we gain a clearer glimpse of our own cultural moment, however ephemeral it may be.

Notes

1   When examining children's and young adult (CYA) literature, we must keep in mind the inauthenticity of the text as it regards the representation of youthful attitudes, desires, and fears. In his foundational article to CYA literary theory, Mike Cadden states, 'Novels constructed by adults to simulate an authentic adolescent's voice are inherently ironic because the so-called adolescent voice is never – and can never be – truly authentic' (146). Unlike adult fiction, a genre which adults write for themselves, young adults rarely write YA fiction, and thus it is important to consider that the topics of interest presented to them through literature may or may not be of actual interest to the YA reader. Furthermore, in repeatedly presenting YA readers with the same topics of interest, adults essentially inform YA readers what they 'should' be interested in. As Cadden explains, 'this matters because the narrative situation in question involves social power relations that are fundamentally different from those between adults ... When an adult writer speaks through a young adult's consciousness to a young adult audience, he or she is involved in a top-down (or vertical) power relationship' (146). In considering this power dynamic of writer/reader within YA literature, we may discover some of the subconscious and implicit values, beliefs, and fears with which adults wish to indoctrinate young readers. Thus, as many scholars of CYA literature have noted, CYA literature may also reveal what adults *believe* concern the contemporary child or young adult. For this reason and in respect to the YA reader, I often qualify that the common themes found in these novels 'seem to' interest young readers, or that adults 'perceive' the themes to interest young readers.

2   Examples of such popular texts include Alan Moore's *The League of Extraordinary Gentlemen* and Cornelia Funke's *Inkheart* (intertextuality); Stephenie Meyer's *Twilight* and Stephen Chbosky's *The Perks of Being a Wallflower* (teen angst); Scott Westerfeld's *Uglies* and Suzanne Collins' *The Hunger Games* (rebellion toward adults). Additionally, most of these texts include sequels, marking their popularity among young adults.

3   Like many novels examined in this chapter, *This Dark Endeavor* is the first book in a series. I focus only on the first book when a series is the discussed because it usually establishes first impressions for the series' mad scientist.

4   Polidori's character is a clear allusion to the Romantic writer, John William Polidori, author of 'The Vampyre' and close friend to Mary Shelley. Like the vampires John William Polidori wrote about, Polidori's character in *This Dark Endeavor*, is dangerous, seductive, and manipulative.

5   While Oppel's retelling makes Victor more sympathetic, Chris Priestley's *Mister Creecher* (2011) retells the story to make Victor less sympathetic. Readers instead identify with Creecher. Both of these retellings are significant in part because they simplify the story by taking sides, suggesting that one character is more sympathetic than the other, and thus simplifying Shelley's text that casts both Frankenstein and his Creature as simultaneously sympathetic and monstrous.

6   See Beth Fantaskey's *Jekel Loves Hyde* (2010) for example. That novel uses characters from Robert Louis Stevenson's *The Strange Case of Dr Jekyll and Mr Hyde* to present messages about peer relationships, self-control, and puberty to YA audiences.

7   For example, the young adult who reads Daniel and Dina Nayeri's *Another Jekyll, Another Hyde*, a text that also employs the Intertextual Puzzle Scientist type, may identify the

influences of Hawthorne's 'Young Goodman Brown', Stevenson's *The Strange Case of Dr Jekyll and Mr Hyde*, Barrie's *Peter and Wendy*, and Marlowe's *The Tragical History of Doctor Faustus*. The reader who recognises these influences can be self-congratulatory for 'getting it'.

8   'Free will' becomes an important concept to *Dr Franklin's Island* as Dr Franklin repeatedly plays tricks on his subjects, testing what they will do in certain situations. For example, the female teens once escape the compound, only to discover that Dr Franklin was testing to see what they would do if he made them believe they could escape.

9   As soon as Semi and Miranda arrive at Dr Franklin's compound, they encounter his experiments, such as the capybara with human legs and feet, and monkeys with octopus tentacles. Dr Skinner explains that these experiments are the result of gene grafting and genetic engineering (Halam 63–64). Dr Franklin's purpose is to make money, but also to take humans beyond the realms of their physical possibility through embryonic stem cell research.

10 In *Jekel Loves Hyde* by Beth Fantaskey, like Semi, Jill's major problem is not that she needs to win the science fair prize, or even that her boyfriend turns into a monster; her problem is overcoming her lack of self-esteem. Both of these novels present the Social-Obstacle Wicked Wizard.

Bibliography

Albrecht-Crane, Christa, and Dennis Cutchins. *Adaptation Studies: New Approaches*. Madison N.J.: Fairleigh Dickinson UP, 2010.

Allen, Glen S. *Master Mechanics and Wicked Wizards: Images of the American Scientist as Hero and Villain from Colonial Times to the Present*. Amherst: U of Massachusetts P, 2009.

Allen, Graham. *Intertextuality*. London: Routledge, 2000.

Cadden, Mike. 'The Irony of Narration in the Young Adult Novel.' *Children's Literature Association Quarterly* 25.3 (2000): 146–154.

Cart, Michael. *Young Adult Literature: From Romance to Realism*. Chicago: ALA Editions, 2010.

Cohen, Jeffrey Jerome, ed. *Monster Theory: Reading Culture*. Minneapolis: U of Minnesota P, 1996.

Fantaskey, Beth. *Jekel Loves Hyde*. Boston: Harcourt, 2010.

Halam, Ann. *Dr Franklin's Island*. New York: Random House Children's Books, 2002.

Hutcheon, Linda. *A Theory of Adaptation*. New York: Routledge, 2006.

Nayeri, Daniel and Dina Nayeri. *Another Jekyll, Another Hyde*. Somerville, MA: Candlewick P, 2012.

Oppel, Kenneth. *This Dark Endeavor: The Apprenticeship of Victor Frankenstein, Book One*. New York: Simon & Schuster Books for Young Readers, 2011.

Priestley, Chris. *Mister Creecher*. New York: Bloomsbury Children's Books, 2011.

Sanders, Julie. *Adaptation and Appropriation*. London: Routledge, 2006.

Shelley, Mary W. *Frankenstein*. New York: W.W. Norton, 1996.

Stevenson, Robert L. *The Strange Case of Dr Jekyll and Mr Hyde*. Peterborough, Ont: Broadview P, 2005.

Wells, H.G. *The Island of Dr. Moreau*. New York: Modern Library, 2002.

13

The soul of the matter: *Frankenstein* meets H.P. Lovecraft's 'Herbert West – Reanimator'

Jeffrey Andrew Weinstock

I N THE WORLD OF the Gothic, characters often confront events and situations that seem to defy post-Enlightenment understandings of how the universe works. In this way, the Gothic partakes of what Tzvetan Todorov famously refers to as the 'fantastic': the hesitation of characters – shared by readers – when faced with incidents that call into question one's understanding of reality. Is there really a ghost haunting the castle in Ann Radcliffe's *The Mysteries of Udolpho*? (1794). Does Don Raymond really encounter the ghost of the Bleeding Nun in Matthew Lewis's *The Monk*? (1796). Are there any ghosts at all in Henry James's *The Turn of the Screw* (1898), or is the narrative something more explicable such as 'a neurotic case of sex repression' on the part of the governess, as Edmund Wilson famously put it in 1934 (see Parkinson)? Gothic texts may call reality into question, but the answers they provide are not all the same. In some cases, which Todorov refers to as the 'fantastic uncanny' (but which we could also call the *Scooby Doo* ending), seemingly supernatural occurrences are revealed to have rational explanations: Radcliffe's Emily, for instance, has simply mistaken a wax figure for a ghostly apparition. In other cases, called by Todorov the 'fantastic marvelous', the supernatural turns out to be real: Don Raymond really did pledge himself to a ghost. And in rare cases, the whole matter is left unresolved: the lack of explanation persists beyond the end of the story with no way to resolve things one way or another. Are there ghosts in *The Turn of the Screw*? Maybe, but it is impossible to tell based on the evidence provided by James.

The point here is that Gothic narratives of all stripes raise not just epistemological questions about what things mean and how we know what we know, but vexing ontological questions about the nature of the world and our place in it. Can the dead return? If so, from where? If the dead walk, does this mean that human beings possess some immortal part, a soul that persists even following physical dissolution? If so, in what part of the body does that soul reside? If the dead don't return, why not? Can the future be foretold through dreams and prophesy? If so, then does that mean our destiny is fixed and immutable? Can thinking something make it happen? If so, are we, unbeknownst to ourselves, under the sway of exterior forces that can curse and compel us? The suspected or proven violations of rationalist understanding and scientific principles found in Gothic texts provoke us to ask other big questions: what world is this, and are there others? Are there conscious forces – God, gods, Elder Gods, what have you – controlling the unfolding of events, or only impersonal forces such as time, weather, and chance? To what extent am I an autonomous actor in the world, free to make my own decisions? To what extent am I circumscribed and controlled by forces both exterior and interior? At bottom, what am I, what does it mean to be human, and what does it mean for me to exist or not to exist at all?[1]

These questions provoked by Gothic narratives are often raised through the prominent roles of *objects* as they are perceived and interacted with by characters or described by narrators. These are objects that don't act the way we expect them to, and thereby ask us to rethink the world. Portraits, photographs, and mirror images assume life – they frown, age, or even step down from their frames. Sinister souvenirs from other worlds, objects of religious veneration, and even body parts function as fetishes and are endowed with eerie autonomy; portals of various sorts – doors, crypts, books, even musical instruments – open passageways to other realms; and buildings and geographical spaces seem endowed with agency of their own, even as they circumscribe the autonomy of the subject. The Gothic castle, for example, is always bigger on the inside than on the outside and, like Poe's House of Usher (at least in Roderick's mind), may manifest a sentience of sorts. Gothic objects thereby function as Latourian 'actants' within Gothic narratives, parts of social networks that function as mediators within meshes of relations. As such, the Gothic not only stages confrontations between states of being and time (living/dead, physical/spiritual, past/future) but, as it ventures into the affective realm of the Freudian uncanny, interrogates the nature of the self and the relationships of the self to the not-self and of the subject to the world(s) it inhabits.

Among the most charged of all Gothic objects is, as Julia Kristeva famously observes in her essay on abjection, the corpse (4). Indeed, at the centre of almost every Gothic narrative is, if not the death of a beautiful woman, at least the body of that which was once a man. Gothic narratives in this respect must be recognised as exceptionally productive – they are corpse-producing machines – and the centrality of the corpse, the most explicit of *memento mori*, to the Gothic narrative provokes many of the existential questions introduced above about the human relation to time, controlling outside forces, and the existence of a soul and afterlife. Although texts may romanticise the beautiful death rather than confronting us with sheeted forms and protruding horny feet, to borrow from Wallace Stevens, the corpse nevertheless invariably instantiates the fact of death and its consequences in a direct and inescapable way.

Gothic texts with reanimated corpses at their centre, however, such as Mary Shelley's *Frankenstein* (1818) and H.P. Lovecraft's campy 'Herbert West – Reanimator' (1922), raise the ontological ante even further by compelling us to think about corpses *as things* – and in a curiously modern way. In the age of electric defibrillation, permanent vegetative states, organ transplantation, abortion, and vat-cultured cells, the reanimated corpse prompts us to ask: when precisely is something dead or alive? When does a body cease to be a person and become a thing? And can a thing become a person? If so, at what point? These questions in turn raise even more questions about the continuity of identity and the relationships of the 'I' to the 'not-I', of subject to object, of self to world, and of self to body. And, in a cultural moment saturated with zombie imagery, the animate corpse finally asks us what it means to be human at all (on the ontological questions raised by zombies, see Cohen's 'Undead' and McRobert's 'Shoot Everything').

Interestingly, at the same moment in which zombies have achieved unprecedented cultural prominence, these questions of the relationships of self to non-self and of the animate to the inanimate are being posed from a different perspective, and have been at the heart of the related twenty-first-century philosophical movements variously labelled as new materialism, object-oriented ontology, and speculative realism. Mel Y. Chen summarises this trend when she writes, 'Throughout the humanities and social sciences, scholars are working through posthumanist understandings of the significance of stuff, objects, commodities, and things, creating a fertile terrain of thought about object life' (5). Theorists farming this fertile terrain, including Graham Harman, Ian Bogost, Levi Bryant, Timothy Morton, Jane Bennett, and, to a certain extent, Bruno Latour, more or less share a set of basic assumptions about objects. First, that there is more to objects than meets the eye. Rejecting 'correlationalist' arguments that 'if things exist, they do so only *for us*' (Bogost 4), the object-oriented ontology perspective in particular is that things instead are never exhausted by human perception of them, and contain depths inaccessible to human apprehension – what Harman refers to as a thing's 'real qualities' (32 and *passim*). Second, that all objects exist equally in the fact of their existing. This is what Bryant refers to as a 'flat ontology' (31–32) or 'democracy of objects' (19). Third, that objects, even inanimate ones, possess what Bennett refers to as 'thing-power', 'the curious ability of inanimate things to animate, to act, to produce effects dramatic and subtle' (6). Fourth, that human beings and objects together form assemblages (Bennett), meshes (Morton), or networks (Latour), and thus human life is inextricably interconnected with the 'lives' of things – what Stacy Alaimo refers to as 'trans-corporeality', the ways in which 'the human is always intermeshed with the more-than-human world' (2). And finally, that recognition of the autonomy of objects as well as their intermeshing with the human can both prompt us to wonder at the 'awesome plenitude of the alien everyday' (Bogost 134) and lead us toward more respectful and sustainable ways of living.

Gothic narratives involving corpses, however – and particularly narratives such as *Frankenstein* and 'Herbert West' focusing on reanimated corpses – provocatively call into question the ethical and political underpinnings of contemporary new materialist assertions. Not only do such narratives ask what happens when the body – both living and dead – is considered just another thing in the democracy of objects, but they also point out that to speak of a democracy of objects in which 'everything exists equally' (Bogost 6) belies the fact that we have yet to achieve even a democracy of human bodies. Stories of reanimated corpses, by raising questions concerning the differences between a person and a thing and different types of bodies, thus make clear that some bodies have always been closer to death and to thing-hood than others – observations made explicitly clear through consideration of *Frankenstein* and 'Herbert West – Reanimator'.

In *Frankenstein*, Victor's Creature, whatever else it may be, must be considered an intensely and inescapably bodily thing – indeed, a misshapen, magnified body condensing early nineteenth-century anxieties about bodily variation, death, and control of bodies, both pre- and post-mortem. In order to facilitate the Creature's construction, Victor tells us that he first resolved 'to make the being of a gigantic stature; that is to say, about eight feet in height, and proportionally large' (58). Its body is thus foregrounded and magnified from the start. Then, in the ultimate act of ironic eco-conscious green Gothic science, the 'dissecting room and slaughter-house' furnish Victor with his materials as he collects bones – and presumably other parts of corpses – 'from charnel-houses' (58). Upon bestowing animation on his creation, however, Victor recoils in horror at the sight, emphasising the Creature's body and appearance: 'His yellow skin scarcely covered the work of muscles and arteries beneath; his hair was of a lustrous black, and flowing; his teeth of a pearly whiteness; but these luxuriances only formed a more horrid contrast with his watery eyes, that seemed almost of the same colour as the dun white sockets in which they were set, his shriveled complexion and straight black lips' (60). The Creature Victor finds so repulsive is a thing of skin, muscles, arteries, hair, fluids, and organs. Later, as the Creature describes its own process of education to Victor, it echoes Victor's assessment, upbraiding its maker by asking, 'Accursed creator! Why did you form a monster so hideous that even *you* turned from me in disgust? God, in pity, made man beautiful and alluring, after his own image; but my form is a filthy type of yours, more horrid even from the very resemblance' (117). The Creature's body, composed of bits and pieces of others' bodies, is regarded by Victor, those it encounters, and even itself as a degraded body, filthy and horrid.

In keeping with Judith Halberstam's characterisation in *Skin Shows* of monsters in general as 'meaning machines' that condense multiple social anxieties into one supersaturated form, the Creature in *Frankenstein*, the debased copy of a copy (God → man → thing), with its giant stature, yellow shrivelled skin, and black lips, has been addressed as a monstrous composite of class difference, ethnic otherness, and anxieties over bodily integrity. It is both literally and figuratively one body created out of many. David McNally's extensive reading of *Frankenstein* in *Monsters of the Market: Zombies, Vampires, and Global Capitalism* – echoing Tim Marshall's cultural contextualisation of *Frankenstein* in *Murdering to Dissect* – situates Shelley's text in relation to what he refers to as the eighteenth- and early nineteenth-century 'corpse economy' (52) of body snatching, dissection and the trade in corpses (58), in which bodies of criminals and the unclaimed indigent were available for dissection and experimentation. McNally reads *Frankenstein* as a novel thereby manifesting the terror of a 'split society' (88) in which the bodies of the poor – during life and even after death – were available for exploitation by the rich. 'In an era in which anatomy had become a flashpoint of conflict over commodification in life and death,' writes McNally, '[Shelley's] fictional account of proletarian bodies being stolen, dismembered, and monstrously reassembled would have carried a potent charge.' '*Frankenstein*,' McNally continues, 'imaginatively grasped and enacted the horrors of corporeal commodification that daily haunted working-class people' (97) and, with reference to electrical experiments conducted on corpses of criminals, he concludes that 'even in death, the bodies of the poor were not free from direction, regulation and inscription by the ruling class' (99). The Creature's body in *Frankenstein* thus literally shows the ways in which (lumpen) proletariat bodies were dug up, sold, cut up, and experimented on in the eighteenth and nineteenth centuries.[2] Closer to being things during their lifetimes than the bodies of their wealthier aristocratic counterparts, the corpses of the working-class and indigent continued to be exploited as objects to be poked, prodded, and put to work even after their deaths.

But if the Creature's body is both literally and figuratively a working-class body – literally assembled out of available body parts, likely of the poor; figuratively standing in for the manipulation and exploitation of the lower-class bodies at the hands of the wealthy – it is simultaneously, and relatedly, a racialised body. In H.L. Malchow's compelling reading of Shelley's text, 'Frankenstein's Monster and Images of Race in Nineteenth-Century Britain', he asserts that Shelley's monster, with its yellow skin and black lips, 'drew upon contemporary attitudes toward non-whites, in particular fears and hopes of the abolition of slavery in the West Indies' (62). The Creature, argues Malchow, parallels stereotypes of racial and ethnic 'Others' of the period (62) – most notably, that of the Negro. A close reading of *Frankenstein*, Malchow concludes, 'demonstrates how a well-known work of fiction depended in part at least for its inspiration and for its effect on the coded language of contemporary racial prejudice, as well as on a deeply embedded cultural tradition of xenophobia' (87; see also Lee; Mellor).

The Creature's body is thus a composite of racial and economic otherness (which could be extended to gender as well – see Gilbert and Gubar, and Spivak, among others), but while it may symbolise the exploitation and disciplining of working-class bodies in early nineteenth-century England and give shape to the racial prejudices and xenophobia of the period, it is first and foremost *a body constructed out of pieces of other bodies*, and it thereby raises the basic question of whether it is a thing or a person. Then, by extension, it asks whether the poor and Negroes and ethnic others are people. Victor, for his part, initially seems inclined to consider the Creature a thing as long as it is lifeless: 'With an anxiety that almost amounted to agony,' he recalls, 'I collected the instruments of life around me, that I might infuse a spark of being into *the lifeless thing* that lay at my feet' (60; emphasis mine). The idea that the absence of life transforms a person into a thing is also suggested by Victor's aborted process of fashioning a mate for his Creature: 'I thought with a sensation of madness on my promise of creating another like to him, and trembling with passion, tore to pieces *the thing* on which I was engaged' (145; emphasis mine). A 'spark of being', Shelley seems to suggest, will transform a 'lifeless thing', an amalgamation of pieces, into a someone, a person, a bounded entity. When Victor successfully infuses a spark of life into his creation, however, it does not morph from thing to person. Instead, the Creature's 'thingdom' is accentuated by its appearance: 'I had gazed on *him* while unfinished; *he* was ugly then; but when those muscles and joints were rendered capable of motion, *it became a thing* such as even Dante could not have conceived' (61; emphasis mine). Victor's language here is curiously regressive. While unfinished, the Creature is a 'him'. Infused with vitality, the Creature transforms into an 'it'.

While Victor may recoil from the unnaturalness of his creation, its hubristic constructedness by the hands of man rather than a creature fashioned by God, the way in which he figures his response, tellingly, is in relation to the Creature's appearance. Its ugliness is so profound that it removes the Creature from the realm of personhood. The Creature is monstrous because of its body – its muscles and joints, its size, its complexion, its lips, its eyes. It is a thing because its appearance does not comport with Victor's – and to a certain extent with nineteenth-century England's – preferences and assumptions about human appearance. Victor knows a person when he sees one, and the monster does not fall within those parameters.

But what of its soul? One conventional way to distinguish between human and non-human life (a way that, from certain perspectives, has had especially pernicious consequences concerning human exploitation of animals and the environment) is the possession of an immortal component that not only animates the body but persists following physical dissolution. Victor may be repulsed by the Creature's form, but perhaps the presence or absence of a soul housed within its matter will allow us to determine whether the Creature is a person or a thing? Here, too, however, Shelley offers little help as *Frankenstein* side-steps the issue of the Creature's personhood by avoiding the question – one which Lovecraft will in fact explicitly introduce – of whether or not the Creature has an immortal soul.

Thanks to searchable e-text versions of *Frankenstein*, Shelley's use of the term 'soul' can be easily quantified. It appears thirty-one times in the 1818 edition and forty times in the 1831 version. In the 1818 version, these usages tend to figure the essence or embodiment of a character's persona rather than an immortal spiritual component. Walton thus discusses the fixing of his soul's 'intellectual eye' (29) on a steady purpose and his soul's entrancement by poetry; Victor throws himself into his research 'heart and soul' (55), considers 'the sublime ecstasy that gave wings to the soul' (91) imparted by the view from the summit of Montanvert, and so forth. However, a more spiritual conception of an immortal soul is suggested in a few places in the 1831 version. For example, Victor recalls of his childhood that 'whether it was the outward substance of things, or the inner spirit of nature and the mysterious soul of man that occupied me, still my inquiries were directed to the metaphysical, or, in its highest sense, the physical secrets of the world' (45) and 'The saintly soul of Elizabeth shone like a shrine-dedicated lamp in our peaceful home' (45) – a description that echoes Walton's of Victor: 'the lineaments of his face are irradiated by the soul within' (40). In both versions, Victor and Walton at least seem certain that human beings have souls – a kind of spiritual centre or animating essence of human identity, if not precisely defined as an intangible and immortal part.

Of these references to 'soul' in the novel, however, only two – both of which are more or less the same in variants of Shelley's text – concern the Creature. The first comes from the Creature himself, confronting Victor in the mountains: 'Believe me, Frankenstein: I was benevolent; my soul glowed with love and humanity: but am I not alone, miserably alone?' (94). The second is a warning from Victor to Walton near the end, concerning the Creature: 'He is eloquent and persuasive; and once his words had even power over my heart: but trust him not. His soul is as hellish as his form, full of treachery and fiendish malice' (178). These two references seem to establish that, at least in the view of Victor and the Creature himself, the latter is like Victor, Walton, and the rest of the characters in possessing a soul that yearns, glows, and has a fundamental character. That the Creature has a soul is the conclusion as well of critic Martin Willis. Curiously assuming that authors retain the same beliefs and opinions over the course of their lives, Willis asserts, 'If Mary Shelley's mechanistic creation of the monster did not allow for a soul, it would be inconsistent with her later fiction, which further debases romanticism but still retains both an outward and inward representation of spirit' (25). The bulk of the scholarship on Shelley and *Frankenstein*, however, is less certain, viewing the novel (more so in the 1818 version than the 1831) as rehearsing the contemporary debate between materialism and vitalism (see Butler; Richardson; and Ruston). The question from this perspective is not whether Victor has a soul and the Creature doesn't, or if Anglos have souls and non-Anglos don't, but, rather, whether anyone – white, black, woman-born or reanimate – has one.

Without wishing to get too tied up in the nuances of Shelley's changing philosophical beliefs and the intricacies of her revision to her seminal text, I do think it is fair to say that *Frankenstein* raises more vexing questions than it answers – which may explain at least in part its peculiar power and persistence. While there is no fantastic hesitation in *Frankenstein*, no point at which the reader is invited to doubt whether Victor in fact infuses vitality into his creation, his achievement nevertheless does invite the reader to entertain the kinds of ontological questions typically compelled by the intrusion of the fantastic. Shelley's narrative asks us to consider whether the Creature is a human being or a thing, as well as what criteria one might use to reach a conclusion. It further prompts us to question that if the Creature is revivified matter, at what point then is something truly dead? When does a person become a thing? And how should we regard a corpse – as person, former person, inert thing, or thing that holds the possibility of renewed personhood? A similar set of questions underlies H.P. Lovecraft's tongue-in-cheek twentieth-century reboot of *Frankenstein*, 'Herbert West – Reanimator'.

Written in six parts and published serially from February through July of 1922 in the amateur publication *Home Brew*, 'Herbert West' – Lovecraft's first professional fiction publication, for which he was paid the whopping sum of $5.00 per episode – tells the story of monomaniacal medical student Herbert West's attempts to develop a chemical formula that will return life to the dead. Together with his assistant, the unnamed first-person narrator of the story, West, through increasingly unscrupulous means, seeks 'fresh' corpses on which to experiment. Although he is successful in some instances in re-instilling life, these 'successes' are severely qualified, given that those revived invariably seem raving mad and exhibit cannibalistic tendencies. Later, as a medical doctor during World War I (the hostilities provide a ready source of fresh corpses), West extends his experimentation to explore whether life can be re-instilled into parts of corpses. At the end of the story, in language directly echoing Victor Frankenstein's in relation to the aborted construction of a mate for his Creature, West is torn to pieces by his vengeful creations.

It should be noted that prominent Lovecraft scholar S.T. Joshi contests *Frankenstein*'s influence on the story, observing that West's chemical method of reanimation is very different from Victor's, that West reanimates whole bodies recently deceased rather than assembling a creature from pieces of bodies, and that 'the core of the story is so elementary a weird conception that no literary source need be postulated' (Lovecraft, 'Herbert West' 375). In addition, a letter referenced on Wikipedia (and, as a consequence, oft-mentioned online) in which Lovecraft states that the story was intended as a parody of *Frankenstein* appears apocryphal. Nevertheless, Lovecraft's debt to the work he himself refers to in his treatise on the macabre, *Supernatural Horror in Literature*, as 'inimitable' and as 'one of the horror-classics of all time' (38) seems unmistakable. Jason Colavito questions Joshi's odd refusal to acknowledge the influence of Frankenstein, and notes in comparing 'Herbert West' to *Frankenstein* that 'Both feature young students who engage in unhallowed art and who bring the dead back to life. Both protagonists use science for their unholy ends, and both are pursued and suffer death at the hands of their vengeful creations, who hate them. The "cannibal things" the *West* undead do are amplifications of the Frankenstein Monster's murderous rampages, just as the multiple undead in *West* amplify the one and a half undead Victor creates in Shelley's novel.' To this, one can add that, just as Victor's story is filtered through Walton, Herbert West's story is conveyed by way of the narrator.

Ultimately, regardless of whether 'Herbert West – Reanimator' is considered a homage, an adaptation, a parody, or simply as Lovecraft's take on an 'elementary … weird conception' also employed by Shelley, *Frankenstein* and 'Herbert West' nevertheless share similar preoccupations with the status of the body and the constitution of personhood. Like *Frankenstein*, 'Herbert West' explores the murky distinction between body and thing, and considers when something is or is not dead and is or is not human. Similar to *Frankenstein*, Lovecraft's story also reveals that some bodies are already more thing-like and closer to death than others. In contrast to Shelley's story, however, Lovecraft's directly engages with the question of the existence of a soul, thereby foregrounding the notable absence of a similar discussion in *Frankenstein*.

What Lovecraft in fact calls attention to in his brief summation of and commentary upon *Frankenstein* in *Supernatural Horror* is precisely the bodily nature of Victor's Creature:

> The novel, somewhat tinged but scarcely marred by moral didacticism, tells of the artificial human being molded from charnel fragments by Victor Frankenstein, a young

Swiss medical student. Created by its designer 'in the mad pride of intellectuality', the monster possesses full intelligence but owns a hideously loathsome form.... Some of the scenes in *Frankenstein* are unforgettable, as when the newly animated monster enters its creator's room, parts the curtains of his bed, and gazes at him in the yellow moonlight with watery eyes – 'if eyes they may be called.' (39)

What clearly preoccupies Lovecraft here is the problematic status of the 'hideously loathsome form' of Victor's 'artificial human', 'molded from charnel fragments' with its 'watery eyes' – and this insistence on the problematic status of the body is then at the heart of Lovecraft's own take on the animated dead, 'Herbert West' – a story that raises the question of the existence of a soul from the very first page.

The narrator begins his account of Herbert West's unorthodox career by explaining that, even early in medical school, 'West had already made himself notorious through his wild theories on the nature of death and the possibility of overcoming it artificially' (50). The narrator continues, '[West's] views, which were widely ridiculed by the faculty and his fellow-students, hinged on the essentially mechanistic nature of life; and concerned means for operating the organic machinery of mankind by calculated chemical action after the failure of natural processes' (50). Elaborating on West's mechanistic views still further, the narrator explains, 'Holding with Haeckel that all life is a chemical and physical process, and that the so-called "soul" is a myth, my friend believed that artificial reanimation of the dead can depend only on the condition of the tissues' (51). West – who, it should be noted, in fact voices Lovecraft's own beliefs concerning the distinction between living and dead matter and the existence of a soul (see Lovecraft, 'Herbert West' 376, n4) – is a materialist very much in the vein of Victor Frankenstein, and arguably of the Mary Shelley of the 1818 version of *Frankenstein*. An 'ice-cold intellectual machine' (71), West – very much like Peter Cushing's Dr Frankenstein in the Hammer horror films – considers corpses dispassionately as objects to facilitate his research and seeks 'no revelation of hideous secrets from the gulfs and caverns beyond death's barrier' (69). What he quests for instead amid the 'black and forbidden realms of the unknown' is the 'secret to life' that will allow him to 'restore to perpetual animation the graveyard's cold clay' (61). Even at the start of the story, a person for West ceases to be a person and becomes a thing – 'cold clay' as the narrator puts it – upon death. Later in the story, as West's ambitions become increasingly ethically suspect, he starts to view the living merely as corpses-to-be and thus as future objects for his experiments. By the end of the story West concludes that 'consciousness, reason, and personality can exist independently of the brain.... man has no central connective spirit, but is merely a machine of nervous matter, each section more or less complete in itself' (75). Assessing this theory and West's attempts to prove it, the narrator comments, 'In one triumphant demonstration West was about to relegate the mystery of life to the category of myth' (75).

The narrator, in contrast, isn't entirely convinced by West's point of view. While noting that he 'for the most part' shares the materialism of his friend, he nevertheless admits to holding on to 'some curious notions about the traditional "soul" of man' (54) and confesses to retaining 'vague instinctive remnants of the primitive faith of [his] forefathers' that prevent him from considering corpses devoid of 'a certain amount of awe and terrible expectation' (69) concerning 'the secrets that might be told by one returning from the dead' (55). Indeed, the narrator puts to a revived corpse the question, 'Where have you been?' (70). The response, however, in this instance and in later revivifications, is a continuation of the last thought the individual had before dying. There has been no perpetuation of consciousness – at least not one available to recollection – in the interim. The revived corpse, having gone from person to clay and back again, cannot say where it has been because it has no awareness of ever having been gone. Death has merely hit the pause button.

The key term around which the transition from person to thing pivots in the story is, in a darkly comic way, 'freshness'. Because decomposition begins almost immediately upon death, in order for corpses to be revived satisfactorily – that is, to regain personhood, consciousness and sanity – 'corpses of doubtful vintage' (62) must be avoided. 'The bodies had to be exceedingly fresh,' recalls the narrator, 'or the slight decomposition of brain tissue would render perfect reanimation impossible' (62). Like produce in supermarket bins, corpses for West's diabolical recipe have short shelf lives: 'The summer air,' West dryly notes at one point, 'does not favour corpses' (58). The difficulty West and the narrator thus face is procuring 'fresh corpses' (76) – and it is here that the text makes clear, as does *Frankenstein*, that, both in life and in death, some bodies are always already more thing-like than others.

'Bodies were always a nuisance' (52), observes the narrator of 'Herbert West', because procuring them and disposing of them proves difficult and occasions opportunities for exposure. West and the narrator initially rely upon the local morgue and the assistance of 'two local negroes' (51) to produce corpses for them. Later the two take up residence behind potter's field, the conventional designation for the burial place of the indigent and unknown, so they can disinter unembalmed corpses and return with them to their secret laboratory where 'in the small hours of the night we often injected West's various solutions into the veins of the *things* we dragged from potter's field' (62; emphasis mine). Their first success is with a recently drowned 'brawny young workman' (52); further experiments described include the Dean of Miskatonic University Medical School, struck down by plague; a Negro boxer killed in a fight; and a travelling salesman, apparently done in by West himself, ironically for the purpose of revivification. With the exception of the medical school dean, whose corpse arguably is specifically selected for experimentation as payback for having obstructed West's research, the bodies used by West and the narrator are working-class and/or racial minorities – and what West's experimentation then accentuates even further is the *bodily* nature of the bodies selected.

Although the resuscitated Dean Halsey is characterised by 'nauseous eyes ... voiceless simianism, and ... daemoniac savagery' (60), the intense 'bodification' of West's subjects is made most evident in the case of Negro boxer Buck Robinson, 'The Harlem

Smoke', who is described in a notorious passage in Lovecraft's writing – one that fully displays the author's regrettable and indefensible racism – as 'a loathsome, gorilla-like thing, with abnormally long arms which I could not help calling fore legs, and a face that conjured up thoughts of unspeakable Congo secrets and tom-tom poundings under an eerie moon' (63). Presented as less-than-human in life, he then becomes fully inhuman in (un)death. In a passage at least initially reminiscent of *Frankenstein* (and resonant with Elizabeth Young's discussion of race in *Black Frankenstein*), the narrator recalls confronting Robinson's reanimated corpse: 'Looming hideously against the spectral moon was a gigantic misshapen thing not to be imagined save in nightmares – a glassy-eyed, ink-black apparition nearly on all fours, covered with bits of mould, leaves and vines, foul with caked blood' (65). As with Victor's Creature, Herbert's creation here is gigantic, hideous, and misshapen. Rather than gazing in yellow moon-light with watery eyes, it crouches under a spectral moon with glassy ones, but the resonances with *Frankenstein* are still clear. The difference, however, is that in Robinson's mouth is a bone 'terminating in a tiny hand' (65) – presumably part of the body of a child reported missing earlier the same day and thus evidence of cannibalism. Whereas Victor's Creature is initially kindly disposed and saves a child from drowning, West's creature returns from the dead demonic and insane. The transformation here, however, is simply the realisation of the description of the corpse provided earlier: a gorilla-like thing suggesting Congo secrets under an eerie moon morphs into a beast-like cannibalistic thing under a spectral moon, highlighting the fact that, as in *Frankenstein*, some bodies are considered less human and more thing-like to begin with.

Finally, for West, all bodies become things on which to experiment – and, in an interesting variation on *Frankenstein*, this becomes, in the words of the narrator, his 'moral undoing' (76). Echoing in some ways Victor's description of the monster's soul in *Frankenstein*, the narrator of 'Herbert West' recollects, '[Fresh corpses] were hard to get, and one awful day [West] had secured his specimen while it was still alive and vigorous.... the experiment had succeeded for a brief and memorable moment; but West had emerged with a soul calloused and seared, and a hardened eye which sometimes glanced with a kind of hideous and calculating appraisal at men of especially sensitive brain and especially vigorous physique' (76). West has become predatory toward the living as well as the dead, willing to produce corpses for the sole purpose of attempting to reanimate them. This anticipates such cinematic Frankensteins as Cushing's Baron (in various Hammer films) and Karloff's Dr Niemann in *House of Frankenstein* (1944), both of whom coldly kill the living for body parts and experimentation. In this vein, to West, the ultimate capitalist, bodies of both the living and the dead are simply things to be utilised to advance his research. He himself has become the monster: 'Gradually,' explains the narrator,

> I came to find Herbert West himself more horrible than anything he did – that was when it dawned on me that his once normal scientific zeal for prolonging life had subtly degenerated into a mere morbid and ghoulish curiosity and secret sense of charnel

picturesqueness. His interest became a hellish and perverse addiction to the repellently and fiendishly abnormal; he gloated calmly over artificial monstrosities which would make most healthy men drop dead from fright and disgust; he became, behind his pallid intellectuality, a fastidious Baudelaire of physical experiment – a languid Elagabalus of the tombs. (72)

Having elided the difference between living and dead, person and thing, West's subsequent attempts to reanimate detached body parts are only a small step from attempting to revive complete corpses. Recalling Victor toiling in his 'workshop of filthy creation' (Shelley, 58), West 'work[s] like a butcher in the midst of his gory wares' (73), fusing embryonic reptile tissue (note that Lovecraft introduces a variant on stem cells into his 1922 story!) to detached body parts, including a decapitated head, in the attempt to instil and maintain life in 'organless fragments', while also investigating whether 'any kind of ethereal, intangible relation distinct from the material cells may exist to link the surgically separated parts of what has previously been a single living organism' (73) – which does in fact seem to be the case, as a decapitated corpse is shown to have a curious bond with its separated head.

The end of 'Herbert West' completes the reversal implicit in Shelley's text in which the doctor, the researcher into occult mysteries who fails to distinguish between person and thing, is shown to be the true monster. As West and the narrator continue their research in a secret sub-cellar laboratory of a Boston home adjacent to the 'oldest burying-ground in Boston', the legions of the undead animated by West, lacking the capacity of speech but demonstrating consciousness and the ability to organise, come to revenge themselves upon their maker. 'I saw outlined against some phosphorescence of the nether world,' recalls the shaken narrator,

> a horde of silent toiling things which only insanity – or worse – could create. Their outlines were human, semi-human, fractionally human, and not human at all – the horde was grotesquely heterogeneous. They were removing the stones quietly, one by one, from the centuried wall. And then, as the breach became large enough, they came out into the laboratory in single file; led by a stalking thing with a beautiful head made of wax. A sort of mad-eyed monstrosity behind the leader seized on Herbert West. West did not resist or utter a sound. Then they all sprang at him and tore him to pieces before my eyes, bearing the fragments away into that subterranean vault of fabulous abominations. West's head was carried off by the wax-headed leader … (80)

Still 'toiling', even after death and reanimation, these subalterns cannot speak, but nonetheless stage a revolution. In the same way that Victor Frankenstein tears to pieces the mate he has promised his monster, Herbert West is torn to pieces by his own creations – the wax-headed leader bearing off West's head presumably the solider on whose decapitated head West had previously experimented. In the final scene of Lovecraft's darkly comic rescripting of *Frankenstein*, the things get together and assert their autonomy. The 'human, semi-human, fractionally human, and not human at all' form a posthuman coalition that seek revenge for their exploitation by Western science.

Obviously, one shouldn't make too much of the political implications of Lovecraft's campy tale. Indeed, reference to 'the horde' of semi-human bodies at the end of 'Herbert West', rather than implying anything even remotely progressive by modern standards, instead echoes Lovecraft's infamous racist screed concerning the inhabitants of New York slums in the mid-1920s: 'The organic things inhabiting that awful cess-pool could not by any stretch of the imagination be call'd human' (qtd in Houellebecq 106). Despite West's ethically indefensible willingness to create his own research materials – to produce corpses for the purpose of reviving them – it nevertheless is not hard to see the ending of the tale as reflecting the racist and committed materialist Lovecraft's own anxieties about monstrous others infiltrating Boston Brahmin neigh-bourhoods, undoing centuries of white rule, and bearing off the fragments.

This, however, is very much to the point. Fantastic tales about reanimated corpses, as exemplified by Shelley's canonical *Frankenstein* and Lovecraft's much sillier 'Herbert West – Reanimator', triangulate race, monstrosity, and life by making it clear that monstrosity has to do with the body, and that some bodies are considered more alive – less thing-like – than others based on physical features. These are stories that ask us when a body is a someone, when it is a something, and what the difference is. It is for this reason that tales of reanimated corpses offer an important qualification to the *joie de vivre* of contemporary new materialism, object-oriented ontology, and speculative realism. Before we subsume the human as simply one 'unit', to use Bogost's term (25), in the democracy of objects, it is important to bear in mind that some human beings have always been considered more thing-like than others, and a levelling downward, a Herbert West-like consideration of all humans as things, may have pernicious conse-quences. It may be that before we dismantle the notion of the human, we should first consider even more carefully what the term means – and stories about corpses that walk, strangely enough, may assist us in the task.

Notes

1 For a more extensive treatment of these Gothic topics see Fred Botting's 'In Gothic Darkly: Heterotopia, History, Culture' and Chris Baldick and Robert Mighall's 'Gothic Criticism', both found in *A Companion to the Gothic*.

2 Although outside of the scope of this chapter, it is interesting to consider the contrast between Dr Frankenstein's practices in Shelley's novel and his approach to procuring mate-rials in the Hammer horror films. In the latter, Peter Cushing's Victor Frankenstein goes to great lengths to procure the brains of the most eminent scientists and thinkers possible. He is focused not simply on animated dead matter, but on creating the most impressive creature possible.

Bibliography

Alaimo, Stacy. *Bodily Natures: Science, Environment, and the Material Self*. Bloomington: Indiana University Press, 2010.

Baldick, Chris and Robert Mighall. 'Gothic Criticism.' *A Companion to the Gothic*. Ed. David Punter. Oxford: Blackwell, 2000. 209–228.

Bennett, Jane. *Vibrant Matter: A Political Ecology of Things*. Durham, NC: Duke University Press, 2010.

Bogost, Ian. *Alien Phenomenology, or What It's Like to Be a Thing*. Minneapolis: University of Minnesota Press, 2012.

Botting, Fred. 'In Gothic Darkly: Heterotopia, History, Culture.' *A Companion to the Gothic*. Ed. David Punter. Oxford: Blackwell, 2000. 3–14.

Bryant, Levi. *The Democracy of Objects*. Ann Arbor, MI: Open Humanities Press, 2011.

Butler, Marilyn. 'The First *Frankenstein* and Radical Science.' *Times Literary Supplement* 9 April 1993): 12–14.

Chen, Mel Y. *Animacies: Biopolitics, Racial Mattering, and Queer Affect*. Durham, NC: Duke University Press, 2012.

Cohen, Jeffrey Jerome. 'Undead (A Zombie Oriented Ontology).' *Journal of the Fantastic in the Arts*, 23.3 (2012): 393–412.

Colavito, Jason. 'H.P. Lovecraft, Zombies, Slender Man, and Aliens.' *JasonColavito.com*. 6 June 2014. www.jasoncolavito.com/blog/h-p-lovecraft- zombies-slender-man-and-aliens (accessed 17 June 2014).

Freud, Sigmund. 'The Uncanny.' *The Standard Edition of the Complete Psychological Works of Sigmund Freud*. Vol. XVII (1917–1919): *An Infantile Neurosis and Other Works*. Trans. and Ed. James Strachey. London: The Hogarth Press, 1955. 217–256.

Gilbert, Sandra M. and Gubar, Susan. 'Horror's Twin: Mary Shelley's Monstrous Eve.' *The Madwoman in the Attic: The Woman Writer and the Nineteenth-Century Literary Imagination*. New Haven: Yale University Press, 1984. 213–247.

Harman, Graham. *The Quadruple Object*. Winchester, UK: Zero Books, 2011.

Halberstam, Judith. *Skin Shows: Gothic Horror and the Technology of Monsters*. Durham, NC: Duke University Press, 1995.

Houellebecq, Michel. *H.P. Lovecraft: Against the World, Against Life*. Trans. Dorna Khazeni. San Francisco: Believer/McSweeny's, 2005.

Kristeva, Julia. *The Powers of Horror: An Essay on Abjection*. Trans. Leon S. Roudiez. New York: Columbia University Press, 1980.

Latour, Bruno. *Reassembling the Social: An Introduction to Actor-Network Theory*. Oxford: Oxford University Press, 2005.

Lee, Debbie. *Slavery and the Romantic Imagination*. Philadelphia: University of Pennsylvania Press, 2002.

Lovecraft, H.P. *Supernatural Horror in Literature*. [1927]. New York: Dover Publications, Inc., 1973.

———. 'Herbert West – Reanimator.' *The Call of Cthulhu and Other Weird Stories*. Ed. S.T. Joshi. New York: Penguin, 1999. 50–80, 375–378.

Malchow, H.L. 'Frankenstein's Monster and Images of Race in Nineteenth-Century Britain.' *Bloom's Modern Critical Interpretations: Mary Shelley's Frankenstein*. Ed. Harold Bloom. New York: Chelsea House Publishers, 2007. 61–94.

Marshall, Tim. *Murdering to Dissect: Grave-robbing, Frankenstein, and the Anatomy Literature*. Manchester: Manchester University Press, 1995.

McNally, David. *Monsters of the Market: Zombies, Vampires, and Global Capitalism*. Chicago: Haymarket Books, 2011.

McRobert, Neil. '"Shoot Everything that Moves": Post-Millennial Zombie Cinema and the War on Terror.' *Textus: English Studies in Italy* 3 (2012): 103–116.

Mellor, Anne K. 'Frankenstein, Racial Science, and the Yellow Peril.' *Nineteenth-Century Contexts* 23 (2001): 1–28.

Morton, Timothy. *Realist Magic: Objects, Ontology, Causality*. Ann Arbor: Open Humanities Press, 2013.

Parkinson, Edward J. 'Chapter Three – Apparitionists vs. Non-apparitionists: 1934–1948.' *The Turn of the Screw: A History of Its Critical Interpretations 1898 – 1979*. N.d.

Richardson, Alan. *British Romanticism and the Science of the Mind*. Cambridge: Cambridge University Press, 2001.

Ruston, Sharon. *Creating Romanticism: Case Studies in Literature, Science and Medicine of the 1790s*. New York: Palgrave Macmillan, 2013.

Shelley, Mary Wollstonecraft. *Frankenstein: Complete, Authoritative Text with Biographical and Historical Contexts, Critical History, and Essays from Five Contemporary Critical Perspectives*. Ed. Johanna M. Smith. Boston: Bedford Books of St Martin's Press, 2000.

Spivak, Gayatri Chakravorty. 'Three Women's Texts and a Critique of Imperialism.' *Critical Inquiry* 12.1 (1985): 243–261.

Todorov, Tzvetan. *The Fantastic: A Structuralist Approach to a Literary Genre*. Trans. Richard Howard. Ithaca, NY: Cornell University Press, 1975.

Willis, Martin. '*Frankenstein* and the Soul.' *Essays in Criticism: A Quarterly Journal of Literary Criticism* 45.1 (January 1995): 24–35.

Young, Elizabeth. *Black Frankenstein: The Making of An American Metaphor*. New York: New York University Press, 2008.

Part IV

Frankenstein in art, illustrations, and comics

14

Illustration, adaptation, and the development of *Frankenstein*'s visual lexicon

Kate Newell

M ARY SHELLEY'S *FRANKENSTEIN* (1818) occupies a rare position in our cultural memory: most of us 'know' it regardless of whether or not we have read it. This circumstance owes much to James Whale's 1931 film adaptation, which is often credited with establishing the definitive visual lexicon for *Frankenstein*.[1] Of course, Whale's is not the first visual adaption of the novel. Prior to 1931, Shelley's novel was adapted numerous times for the stage – e.g., Richard Brinsley Peake's *Presumption* (1823) and John Atkinson Kerr's *The Monster and Magician* (1826) – and the stage adaptations were published with illustrations depicting the actors and moments from the plays. Additionally, the 1831 Colburn and Bentley edition of the novel, the first to bear Mary Shelley's name, was published with two illustrations by Theodore von Holst, one depicting Victor's terrified flight from the new-born Creature and the other Victor and Elizabeth. The 1922 Cornhill edition offered three illustrations by Carl Lagerquist, two of which focus on the Creature's creation. Thus, prior to the landmark moment of 1931, *Frankenstein* already boasted a varied pictorial history. Whale's film renewed interest in visual adaptations of Shelley's novel, and within three years of the film's release, three more editions were published with illustrations. As Steven Earl Forry, Susan Tyler Hitchcock, Joyce Carol Oates, Dennis Cutchins and Dennis Perry, and others have noted, the number of adaptations and the range of formats these adaptations take make *Frankenstein* 'a highly difficult story to read directly' (Oates 247). What we have come to understand as 'Frankenstein', Cutchins and Perry explain in the Introduction to this book, is less a coherent text than a complex, a network of signification and exchange shaped by processes of visualisation and interpretation.

Despite the number of illustrated editions of *Frankenstein*, few writers have addressed how they contribute to the Frankenstein Complex or its visual lexicon.[2] Unlike stage productions and film adaptations, which purport to convey the Frankenstein story in its entirety, illustrations present isolated moments that punctuate the prose text against which they are juxtaposed, and direct readers' attention to particular moments. In prioritising certain moments over others, they proffer a particularised view of the novel. My comparison of approximately twelve illustrated editions of *Frankenstein* shows the same moments being illustrated over and over. Such repetition fosters a sense of consensus as to what 'counts' as *Frankenstein*. Yet, while illustrators may agree on which moments to depict, they differ significantly on what these moments *mean*. Variations in illustrators' style, emphasis and selection result in very individual visual arguments and in editions with very different ideological messages. Looking to a range of illustrated editions, including the 1932 Illustrated Editions edition illustrated by Nino Carbe, the 1934 Robert and Haas edition illustrated by Lynd Ward, the 1934 Heritage Press Limited Editions Club edition illustrated by Everett Henry, the 1983 Marvel Comics *Berni Wrightson's Frankenstein*, and the 1984 Pennyroyal Press edition illustrated by Barry Moser, this chapter considers the method by which illustrations impact on our reading of *Frankenstein* and, more specifically, how they contribute to our cultural memory and expand the visual lexicon of *Frankenstein*.[3]

Identifying a clear visual lexicon for *Frankenstein* is not as easy as it may seem; it is not the product of one particular vision, but an accumulation of visions. In the popular imagination, 'Frankenstein' is often understood synecdochically as 'the monster', who, Susan Tyler Hitchcock observes, is associated with the following visual characteristics: 'green skin, stitched scars, flat skull edged with black hair, big shoulders, oversize hands, thick-soled feet, and bolts attached to neck or temples' (9). A broader lexicon might include Gothic environments, lighting and mood, period costuming, a laboratory and monomaniacal scientist, a laboratory assistant, as well as lightning or other indicators of electricity. In general, all or most of these elements can be found in many adaptations of *Frankenstein*; some are present in Shelley's novel, but most have antecedents in the early stage adaptations and were then popularised by Whale's film.[4] As Steven Earl Forry explains, much of what we understand as essential to *Frankenstein* can be traced to Peake's *Presumption*, Jean-Toussaint Merle and Béraud Antony's *Le Monstre et le magicien* (1826) and Henry Milner's *The Man and the Monster* (1826); together, these plays 'share the responsibility for shaping the destiny not only of subsequent dramatisations, but of popular conceptions of the novel' (3). For example, the early productions emphasised *Frankenstein*'s Gothic elements, 'heightened the demoniacal aspects of the Creature, elaborated the alchemical overtones of Frankenstein's experiments, and expanded the sinister context of the laboratory' (x). Walton is absent from early stage productions and 'wild action, alchemical rituals, and gothic settings replaced the novel's epistolary format, scientific background, and internalised landscapes' (xi). We see these elements shape several later film and stage adaptations of *Frankenstein*, including Whale's film and Kenneth Branagh's *Mary Shelley's Frankenstein* (1994), in terms of the films' mood and depiction of science. As William St Clair puts it, 'Frankenstein did not become part of popular culture with the cinema: the film industry picked it up from a culture where it was already a vigorous presence' (54). Neither *Frankenstein* nor any adaptation of *Frankenstein* exists in a textual or contextual vacuum, but, rather, as Cutchins and Perry note in the Introduction to this volume, each evolves from and is received within a network of 'perceived meanings [that] are negotiated in webs of dialogue'. Yet *Frankenstein*'s textual and visual network is not really all that peculiar.

Since the late 1990s, adaptation scholars have come to recognise such networks as the norm for virtually all cultural and textual productions, be they consciously adapted and/or adapting or not. Writers such as Robert Stam, Thomas Leitch, and Christa Albrecht-Crane and Dennis Cutchins, among others, have written extensively on the topic of adaptation and intertextuality. Albrecht-Crane and Cutchins, for example, have observed that '[a]daptations are dialogues with other texts, including the texts upon which they are based, and those texts are in dialogue with adaptation' (19). Linda Hutcheon considers more deliberately the role that audiences' own textual and contextual reserves play in experiencing adaptations: 'adaptation is a form of intertextuality: we experience adaptations (*as adaptations*) as palimpsests through our memory of other works that resonate through repetition with variation' (8, original italics). It is within this spirit of recycling, shared conventions, dialogue, and repetition that I consider the contributions that illustrations make to the Frankenstein Complex.

More than simply offering a sense of the ways in which *Frankenstein* has been visual-ised, a comparison of individual sets of illustrations provides insight into what 'counts' as *Frankenstein* in popular illustrated editions and, by extension, in the popular imagina-tion. What an illustrator (or publisher) elects to *show* determines which aspects of the prose will be reinforced and, thus, which aspects are more likely to be remembered. Most illustrated editions offer at least one illustration related to the following scenes: Walton's exploration and his rescue of Victor, the lightning storm that sparks Victor's interest in electricity, Victor studying or performing experiments, the Creature's vivi-fication, the death of William, Justine's trial and execution, the confrontation between Victor and the Creature, the Creature being abused by villagers, the Creature and the De Laceys, Victor's assemblage and destruction of the female creature, the death of Clerval, the death of Elizabeth, and the Creature returning to Victor's deathbed. Illustrations depicting Victor's family and domestic life are few and far between. Even less common are illustrations that allude to the novel's epistolary structure or use of embedded narrative devices.[5] Rather, the novel as it is conveyed through successive sets of illustrations follows a conventional narrative trajectory of rising action, com-plication, conflict, falling action, and resolution. So, while the ostensible (or assumed) goal of illustration might be to illustrate the prose, we see already that decisions regarding illustration have a significant impact on readers' impression of the novel. That the same scenes are depicted over and over by different illustrators for different editions published by different presses fosters the impression that they *are Frankenstein*. Through repetition and reinforcement, these scenes become *Frankenstein's* lexicon.

In the discussion that follows I consider the process by which a visual lexicon develops – specifically, the process by which illustrators convey consensus regarding what a scene looks like. I also consider the role that illustrated abridged editions play in reinforcing *Frankenstein's* lexicon. While any of the above-mentioned scenes would demonstrate this process, I focus on the Creature's vivification, as it is perhaps the most iconic event in our cultural memory and serves as a poignant metaphor for the 'createdness' of the *Frankenstein* lexicon. Most illustrated editions of *Frankenstein* contain at least one image related to this event and many offer more than one. After addressing some ways in which illustrators build on each other's work, I consider differences among the sets of illustrations. As I see it, if commonalities establish what 'counts' as *Frankenstein*, variations in perspective and focus establish what the novel means. That is, the illustrations may prioritise similar scenes, but they offer distinct interpretations of those scenes and, by extension, of the novel.

Mary Shelley devotes three chapters to Victor's education and increasing interest in natural science and chemistry, yet her description of the Creature's creation is famously brief:

> It was on a dreary night of November that I beheld the accomplishment of my toils. With an anxiety that almost amounted to agony, I collected the instruments of life around me that I might infuse a spark of being into the lifeless thing that lay at my feet. It was already one in the morning; the rain pattered dismally against the panes, and my candle was nearly burnt out, when, by the glimmer of the half-extinguished light, I saw the dull yellow eye of the creature open; it breathed hard, and a convulsive motion agitated his limbs. (Shelley 53 [Ward, 1934])[6]

The ambiguity of the Creature's vivification is heightened by the scene's emphasis on impaired vision. Victor 'beholds' his creation, but does not see him clearly, due to the late hour and the 'half-extinguished light'. This impairment carries through the novel as Victor refuses to convey the particulars of his reanimation process. Stage and film adaptations, by contrast, typically amplify this moment, exploiting its spectacular potential. While the actual animation of the Creature occurs off stage in Peake's *Presumption*, changing coloured lights in the laboratory window suggest, Forry points out, 'a portent of the pyrotechnic emphasis in later adaptations' (16). Whale's famous scene unfolds dramatically and chaotically, accompanied by a frenzy of sparks and electricity. Branagh's creation scene may be even more spectacular, involving as it does an 'enormous sack containing … electric eels that get injected into the sarcophagus of amniotic fluid at the moment of recreation', to borrow Heidi Kaye's description (65). Following Shelley's lead, some illustrators opt to conceal the process by which Victor animates the Creature and focus more on Victor's preparatory studies and his end result, while others, following stage and film adaptations, choose to depict the process.[7] Two early *Frankenstein* illustrators – Theodore von Holst (1831) and Carl Lagerquist (1922) – take their cue from Shelley. Holst offers an image of Victor fleeing from the recently animated Creature and Lagerquist offers one image of Victor studying a skeleton in his laboratory in preparation for his experiment and another of the Creature appearing at Victor's bedside. Thus, like Shelley, both allow that creation has taken place, but neither offers details of that process. Other illustrators are more explicit and depict the process of animation. Some, motivated by Victor's interest in discovering 'the elixir of life' (32 [Ward, 1934]) and drawing from the early stage productions, attribute the Creature's vivification to alchemical processes. Others, perhaps influenced by Victor's fascination with 'the subject of electricity and galvanism' and Whale's adaptation, suggest an electrical means of animation (33).

Figure 14.1 Nino Carbe's version of the Creature's vivification.

Differences in how illustrators depict the Creature's creation are best demonstrated through a comparison of two editions published in the 1930s, in the wake of Whale's film: the 1932 Illustrated Editions edition illustrated by Nino Carbe and the 1934 Smith and Haas edition illustrated by Lynd Ward. It is from Carbe's and Ward's sets of illustrations that most elements of the illustrated editions' visual lexicon evolve.

Carbe is the first illustrator to suggest the particular means by which the Creature is brought to life. Carbe's full-page illustration depicts the Creature (wearing neck electrodes) reclined on a wooden chaise surrounded by rigging and electrical cables, some of which feed into the chemistry apparatus on the table in the foreground. In this way, Carbe's image recalls both the stage and film adaptations in its allusion to alchemical and electrical means of revivification (Figure 14.1). Like Holst's and Lagerquist's creatures, Carbe's has not been stitched together and he is not disproportionately larger than Victor. Although Carbe situates his representation within an existing visual tradition, his depiction is definitely his own. For example, all earlier depictions of the animation scene focus attention on Victor, rather than the Creature. Shelley conceals the Creature until the moment he opens his 'dull yellow eye', and early stage adaptations, including Peake's and Kerr's follow suit and keep the Creature off stage until he is brought to life (Shelley 53 [Ward,1934]). The Creature is present in Whale's animation scenes but concealed under a sheet, and the scene's action focuses on Henry's movements and anxieties. Carbe's image turns the focus from the creator to the creation and, in doing so, adopts a previously unconsidered perspective that brings a sense of quiet and calm to the scene. Carbe anchors his depiction firmly in the tradition of print in various ways, such as using the convention of the pictorial initial as a device of foreshadowing. Carbe develops Victor's interest in chemistry over two pictorial initials, each of which forms the first letter of the first word of a chapter, and features objects related to alchemy and science (e.g., candles, books, beakers) that appear later in the full-page image of the Creature's birth. Several illustrators, including Lynd Ward and Everett Henry, also adopt the technique of using small illustrations to allude to Victor's growing interest in science.

Ward opts to conceal the method of the Creature's reanimation in his illustrations for the 1934 Smith and Haas edition and, instead, focuses on the surrounding events. Like Lagerquist, Ward offers an image of Victor in his laboratory prior to the experiment and another of the Creature appearing at Victor's bedside. The Smith and Haas edition is much more heavily illustrated than those including Lagerquist's, Holst's or Carbe's illustrations and, as a result, Ward is able to contribute to *Frankenstein's* visual lexicon more broadly and initiate a grammar that is adopted by subsequent illustrators. For example, Ward is the first illustrator to depict the lightning storm that sparks Victor's interest in electricity and he is the first to depict Victor digging through graves for raw materials: images that will become staples of subsequent illustrated editions of *Frankenstein*. Additionally, although Ward is not the first illustrator to depict the Creature appearing at Victor's bedside, he is the first to depict the scene from Victor's point of view. Lagerquist's illustration for the 1922 Cornhill edition utilises a third-person, proscenium perspective and depicts Victor reclined partially in bed, his right hand held to his temple in a gesture of horror as he beholds the Creature, who has pulled aside the bed curtains. By contrast, Ward places the viewer within the bedchamber, so that we, like Victor, see the Creature from low-angle perspective. This perspective heightens the horror of the moment and is adopted by many later illustrators, likely for this reason.[8]

The influence of Carbe and Ward is evident in virtually all subsequent illustrators' depictions of the Creature's vivification and its surrounding moments. Equally evident is the method by which each illustrator reinterprets Carbe and Ward and expands the visual lexicon. Like Carbe, Berni Wrightson opts to depict the Creature in the laboratory in his illustrations for the 1983 Marvel Comics edition. However, if Carbe's image stands out for its unexpected sense of calm, Wrightson's is notable for its tremendous energy and sense of action. Wrightson includes both Victor and the Creature in his image, framing them almost in close-up to draw attention to their expressions. While later illustrations will reveal the Creature to be physically much larger than Victor, in this image they appear comparable in size, both physically and in terms of their compositional weight. Unlike Carbe's illustration, which omits Victor, or Holst's illustration, which depicts Victor fleeing the Creature, Wrightson offers the uncommon view of Victor *beholding* his creation and registering what has occurred. The Creature appears to be pulling himself into a vertical position on the table as Victor, horror-stricken, leans in toward him. In this moment, Victor and the Creature mirror each other. We see Carbe's influence also in Wrightson's inclusion of scientific apparatus in the image – flat-bottomed flasks, test tubes, tubing, rope and skulls provide visual weight, anchoring the lower half of the image. However, whereas Carbe (and Ward) use the apparatus as short-hand communication for Victor's progress on assembling and animating the Creature, Wrightson uses the apparatus to indicate shifts in Victor's psychological state. The apparatus in Wrightson's image of the Creature's awakening occupies only the lower half of the image, and each piece is distinguishable from its neighbour. As the novel progresses, we see that the apparatus is not limited to Victor's laboratory but enters the frame in every scene involving science or experimentation. As Victor deteriorates, the apparatus becomes increasingly oppressive, almost camouflaging the characters in the scene in which the Creature confronts Victor for destroying his mate.

Like Ward, Everett Henry conceals the process of animation in his illustrations for the 1934 Heritage Press Limited Editions edition, focusing, instead, on the preliminary event of the lightning storm that heightens young Victor's interest in electricity, and the Creature's visit to Victor's bedside. Whereas Ward signifies the storm in a vignette placed at the conclusion of Chapter II that depicts lightning hitting a tree, Henry offers a full-page illustration of the scene (Figure 14.2). In Henry's image,

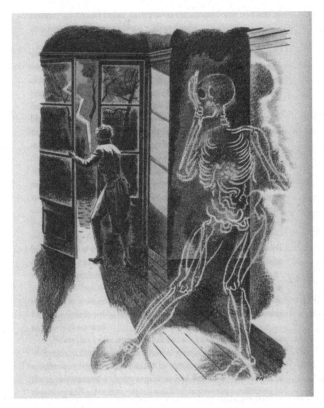

Figure 14.2 Everett Henry's enigmatic image of lightning striking the tree outside of Frankenstein's home.

Victor stands at the open door and watches the lightning sever a branch from a tree. Henry places the reader inside the room, looking over Victor's shoulder – a perspective that is adopted by several later illustrators, such as Wrightson and Pablo Marco Studios (1993). Victor stands in the image's background and, curiously, a skeleton, not mentioned in the chapter, stands at the foreground. Although the skeleton's presence is largely inexplicable, it may be intended to foreshadow Victor's interest in vivification, and to allude to his obsession with the occult, which is mentioned in the chapter. The skeleton might also be a stand-in for Destiny, which Victor mentions on the facing page: 'Destiny was too potent, and her immutable laws had decreed my utter and terrible destruction' (35).

Henry's depiction of the Creature visiting Victor's bedside is very different from Ward's, adopting as it does a third-person perspective and focusing solely on Victor. In this image, Victor sits up in bed, wide-eyed and startled by something, presumably the Creature, outside of the composition. Henry takes the theme of concealment further than any other *Frankenstein* illustrator by declining to depict the Creature. Instead, Henry only alludes to his presence through characters' facial expressions or with shadowy hands that loom in the periphery of the composition.

These few examples demonstrate that over time we see a consensus develop. Illustrators agree that the Creature's creation needs to be represented in some fashion and that certain elements should be present in this representation. We might imagine that illustrated editions of *Frankenstein* would lose vitality under the weight of repetition, but, as Linda Hutcheon has pointed out, part of audience pleasure of adaptation actually comes from repetition, but repetition with difference. Hutcheon writes that adaptation has 'the ability to repeat without copying, to embed difference in similarity' (174). Although illustrators opt to visualise the same moments and scenes, they differ (often significantly) on what these scenes *mean*. Each edition conveys its own visual agenda that impacts on our reading of the illustrations and the novel. For example, each illustrator's depiction of the processes of creation reveals much about the novel's attitude toward Victor and the Creature and the novel's tone in general. Kamilla Elliott comments on the process by which different adapters mould similar information to different ends. Using Branagh's film as an example, Elliott draws a parallel between adapters and literary critics: 'Like these [literary] critics, Branagh cuts and pastes episodes from the novel into a feminist binder, adding feminist scenes where literary critics have added feminist critical commentaries. Just as critical articles select and explicate passages to shape a new narrative, so too' an adapter 'selects, cuts, pastes, and juxtaposes pieces of the novel' into a particular 'critical narrative' (142). Illustrators cut and paste aspects of the novel into particular binders in much the same way, adding, amplifying, or altering information when necessary to meet the larger point. The number of illustrations devoted to visualising a particular scene or moment relative to the number of illustrations in the edition, the elements emphasised in those images, and the tone, all contribute to readers' understanding of the edition's larger agenda. In the next section I will look at some ways in which illustrators convey their particular arguments.

Carbe's *Frankenstein* is very much the Creature's story: he appears in nineteen of the approximately twenty-seven woodcuts included in the edition.[9] Carbe's portrayal is sympathetic and underscores the Creature's isolation: thirteen of the nineteen illustrations depict him alone. Carbe's illustrations also suggest that the Creature is largely misunderstood. Hitchcock writes that Carbe 'envisioned Frankenstein's monster as diabolical: fleshy in form and evil in expression, with a sinewy physique, sharpened nails, foreshortened forehead, upraised brow, humped nose, and vampire incisors, top and bottom, revealed by a slack lower jaw' (167). While Hitchcock's physical description is accurate, her overall assessment of the depiction seems to overlook its intentional incongruities. The Creature's appearance is coded as demonic, yet he is placed consistently in postures and environments that challenge this characterisation and play on readers' prejudices and misconceptions. For example, Carbe does not portray the Creature engaging in violent behaviour, but, rather, regularly portrays him communing with nature (Figure 14.3). While many illustrators depict the scene in which Felix De Lacey attacks the Creature, Carbe adapts instead the subsequent

Figure 14.3 Carbe's Creature in nature.

scene, in which he retreats to the woods, 'fatigued with excess of bodily exertion, and sank on the damp grass in the sick impotence of despair' (Shelley 140 [Carbe, 1932]).[10]

In Carbe's image, the Creature sits in the grass wearing an expression of hopelessness. His nakedness coupled with the stylised landscape that grows up around him suggests his vulnerability as well as the simplicity of his desires. The incongruity between the Creature's demonic appearance and the peacefulness of the natural environment in which Carbe places him draws attention to the novel's larger tension between the physical and behavioural. Upon meeting William, the Creature reflects that prejudice is learned. He admits that 'an idea seized me, that this little creature was unprejudiced, and had lived too short a time to have imbibed a horror of deformity' (148). Carbe's Creature may be 'deformed', but he is not inherently evil, and in characterising him in this way Carbe asks readers to reflect on their own preconceptions and, by extension, on the novel's dominant themes and conflicts.

Like Carbe, Wrightson offers a sympathetic portrayal of the Creature, but a portrayal that is much more in line with the avenging anti-hero common to action comics and graphic novels. Wrightson's Creature is often alone and on the periphery of human society. For example, although Wrightson offers several images of events that occur during the Creature's time at the De Lacey cottage, he does not depict the De Lacey family. Rather, he shows the Creature reading and observing the family through the aperture in his hovel, and gathering wood. Wrightson underscores the Creature's outsider status by depicting him, literally, always on the outside of community in which he longs to participate.

More interesting than Wrightson's depiction of the Creature, though, is his rendering of the novel's more peripheral outsider characters. He depicts Safie arriving at the cottage on horseback, but the title of the image – 'the trial … deprived them of their fortune, and condemned them to perpetual exile' – underscores her ejection from society, not her acceptance into the De Lacey family. Wrightson also offers an illustration of Ernest Frankenstein, the middle brother, who factors into several domestic scenes in Shelley's novel, but who is not the focus of any dramatic moments. No other illustrator, to my knowledge, offers a depiction of him. He is too young to be Victor's confidante and is, thus, less interesting than Clerval or Elizabeth. Likewise, he is not a target of the Creature's revenge and is, thus, less interesting than William, Justine, Clerval, or Elizabeth. Wrightson's illustration highlights this negligibility. The prose that his image illustrates comes from Elizabeth's letter to Victor, in which she relates that Ernest 'looks upon study as an odious fetter; his time is spent in the open air, climbing the hills or rowing on the lake' (Shelley 43 [Wrightson, 1983]). Wrightson's illustration offers an impressive expanse of natural landscape. Ernest stands in the composition's middle ground, his back to the reader, almost invisible on the horizon between field and mountain. His positioning coupled with his anonymity (i.e., we do not see his face) draws attention to his correlative value in the novel. At the same time, the mere act of representing Ernest recasts his role as important. Ernest's ease in manner and eagerness to commune with nature's mysteries (rather than dominate its secrets) characterise him as his brother's polar opposite and, perhaps, a more sympathetic brother to the Creature. Additionally, Ernest is the sole survivor of the Frankenstein family (or one of two, if we include the Creature), and the recipient of the legacy of grief that his brother's actions bestow. Wrightson shifts readers' attention momentarily from the narrative tensions developing between Victor and the Creature and focuses it on the peripheral characters impacted upon by this tension and its horrific effects.

Although Justine plays a more pivotal role than Ernest, she is also an outsider character. As Bouriana Zakharieva points out, 'The solitude of man, the lack of communality, the mechanisms of exclusion and scapegoating are at the bottom of the drama of not only the Creature, but other characters, too,' including Justine (423). Neither a fully fledged member of the Frankenstein family, nor a valued member of her own family, Justine's status is rather liminal and positions her well to become a pawn in the Creature's revenge. Wrightson highlights Justine's dual allegiances in two illustrations: one depicting her at her mother's grave and one that depicts her execution. Like Ernest, Justine is portrayed from behind in both images and her face is concealed, thus underscoring their similarities. Elizabeth writes to Victor that Justine's mother had 'died on the first approach of cold weather, at the beginning of this last winter' (47). Wrightson's image offers a high-angle vision of Justine in the snow-covered graveyard, head bowed before her mother's grave. Justine also has her back to the reader in Wrightson's depiction of her execution. This pose grants her some anonymity at the same time that her partial nudity underscores her sexual appeal/threat for both Victor and the Creature. Ernest's hikes and Justine's visit to the graveyard are not part of Victor's memory but are conveyed through Elizabeth's letter to Victor (which Victor recounts to Walton and Walton recounts to his sister, Margaret); this narrative remove is underscored by Wrightson's illustrations.

The vision of *Frankenstein* conveyed in Barry Moser's illustrations for the 1984 Pennyroyal Press edition is a little more abstract than that offered by the other illustrators, largely due to Moser's use of portrait and still-life. Unlike the modes employed by other illustrators, which strive to convey the illusion of action or a snapshot of action, Moser's technique emphasises stasis and pause – qualities that support the illustrations' larger cause and effect-related theme. This theme is first evident in the connection between the edition's frontispiece illustration, 'A Stream of Fire', which depicts the lighting storm Victor witnesses as a young boy, and one of its title page illustrations, 'The Blasted Stump', which depicts the tree that is decimated by that storm.[11] Thus paired and placed at the novel's opening, these images foreshadow the pattern of action and consequence that will determine the novel's plot. Importantly, 'The Blasted Stump' also faces the novel's epigraph from *Paradise Lost* – 'Did I request thee, Maker, from my clay / To mould me man? Did I solicit thee / From darkness to promote me?' This juxtaposition helps to focus readers' attention less on the glories and wonders of Victor's experiment than on the consequences.

The theme of cause and effect is alluded to also in Moser's depiction of the Creature's reanimation. Rather than illustrate the moment of creation, Moser, like Ward and others, illustrates a moment immediately before and immediately after. The first illustration, 'The Lifeless Thing', occupies half a page and provides a close-up of a right hand, presumably the Creature's, resting on a sheet. The title of the image alludes, of course, to Victor's explanation: 'I collected the instruments of life around me, that I might infuse a spark of being into the lifeless thing that lay at my feet' (51). Moser's decision to allow the hand to stand in synecdochically for the Creature underscores its symbolic potential as the instrument by which the Creature commits the murders of William, Justine, Clerval, and Elizabeth.[12] The page on which 'The Lifeless Thing' appears faces a full-page image titled 'Victor's Dream of His Mother', which depicts a body covered in a sheet – save for a portion of the left side of the face – in which worms crawl in the creases. The illustration's title alludes to Victor's confession that: 'I thought that I held the corpse of my dead mother in my arms; a shroud enveloped her form, and I saw the grave-worms crawling in the folds of the flannel' (52). Thus, Moser brackets the actual moment of birth with images of before and after.

Moser repeats this pairing of images with variation in his depiction of the assemblage and destruction of the female creature. Compositionally, Moser's 'The Female Daemon' resembles strongly 'The Lifeless Thing', in that it features a close-up of a feminine left hand on a sheet. The shift in titles and hands underscores the threat posed by the female. The title 'The Lifeless Thing' draws attention to Victor and the moment before he animates the corpse, when he still has the opportunity to change the course of events. The title 'The Female Daemon', by contrast, suggests that the female is already alive and has already a fixed identity. The change in hands seems to highlight Victor's change in perspective. The right hand of the male connotes the hope Victor has for his Creature, the first of 'many happy and excellent natures [who] would owe their being to me,' whereas the left hand assigns a literal sinisterness to the female who might propagate a 'race of devils' (47; 178). 'The Female Daemon, Ravaged', which depicts the female creature after Victor destroys her, recalls 'Victor's Dream of His Mother', explicitly; the sheets are folded and draped in exactly the same way and the figure's posture is the same. This similarity highlights the link between Victor's mother's life-giving potential, which he tries to emulate, and the female creature's life-giving potential, which he must destroy.

Although several of Moser's portraits and still lifes do not fit into neat cause-and-effect pairings, they are weighted with symbolic value. Moser has indicated that, in these portraits, 'you never see the whole figure because I wanted to leave that to the imagination of the reader' ('Barry'). For example, Moser's first illustration of Victor depicts him as an adult, wearing spectacles, a top hat, and scarf. This characterisation seems fairly unremarkable, yet the right half of Victor's face is in almost complete blackness. This lighting effect, coupled with his spectacles (part of Moser's characterisation), alludes to Victor's short-sightedness and divided self. Juxtaposed against prose in which Victor relates details of his youth, particularly his advanced studies and the death of his mother, the image seems to foreshadow future events. Moser depicts the Creature over a series of nine portraits, eight of which punctuate the section of the novel in which the Creature relates his history to Victor. Each portrait is roughly the same in size, yet each is lighted differently and, thus, offers a different view of the Creature's face (which, I should mention, is very clearly formed of decomposed flesh). Unlike Moser's other portraits which are titled by name (e.g., 'Victor Frankenstein', 'Henry Clerval'), most of these portraits are titled with phrases from the Creature's story that, when considered cumulatively, outline a causal trajectory. For example, the first portrait is titled 'All men hate the wretched', the third is titled, 'My organs were indeed harsh', the fourth, 'No father had watched my infant days', the fifth, 'Hateful day when I received life!' and the sixth, 'Cursed, cursed creator!' Thus, the series begins with the Creature making a statement that expresses mankind's general attitude toward him, which is followed by a reflection on why this may be (e.g., his constitution, faulty parenting) and then a curse on Victor specifically. Although Moser does not depict narrative moments or characters engaging in action in the same way as other illustrators, these portrait techniques prevent the representations from coming across as static.

Like illustrators before him, Moser alludes to Victor's growing interest in science and vivification via images of or alluding to chemistry apparatus and grave robbing. Moser's still life technique provides an uncommon view of these moments by divorcing the apparatus and the raw materials from their application. For example, the tools in Moser's 'M. Waldman's Instruments' appear harmless enough, initially (Figure 14.4). The image breaks a line of text that reads: 'He then took me into his laboratory,

Figure 14.4 Barry Moser's 'M. Waldman's Instruments'.

and explained to me the uses of his various machines; instructing me as to what I ought to procure, and promising me the use of his own, when I should have advanced far enough in the science not to derange their mechanism' (43). The presence of the image here deranges, in a sense, the mechanism of the prose. The sense of disturbance is compounded by the eye that looks out from one of Waldman's instruments, presumably a reflection of Waldman's, but the lack of contextualising information creates the impression of an independent consciousness.

Like Ward and Wrightson, Moser draws attention to Victor's collecting of raw material, but does so in a more grisly manner. Ward depicts Victor digging in graveyards and Wrightson depicts him examining cadavers, but both artists focus the attention of the illustration on Victor engaging in an activity and obscure the particulars of that activity – i.e., the materials. In 'Victor's Midnight Labors', by contrast, Moser omits Victor from the scene and emphasises, instead, the raw materials, including at least two severed heads and several arms and legs hanging from hooks. This image stands out not only for its graphic quality, but also for its similarity to a later illustration of Justine's execution and for its allusion to the composite nature of the Creature – a fact elided by most illustrators. Whereas the body parts in 'Victor's Midnight Labors' are particularised visually but generalised nominally, Justine is generalised visually and particularised nominally in 'Justine Moritz, Executed'. Her body appears in silhouette against a background of horizontal lines, an amorphous shape; only her right hand is illuminated. Moser's illustrations remind us that the difference between what is revealed and what is concealed in illustrated editions of *Frankenstein* shapes significantly the tone and focus of the edition. Both Moser and Ward may offer an illustration of grave digging, for example, but Moser's decision to depict the various decomposing body parts minus Victor, and Ward's decision to depict Victor minus the decomposing body parts, results in editions with very different messages.

In thinking about the relationship between revealing and concealing, I would like now to turn briefly to illustrated abridgements. While I am not able to address this genre as fully as I would like in this chapter, I will offer a few general observations as they relate to issues of adaptation, the visual lexicon, and literacy. I included five illustrated abridged editions in my sample group: The Step-Up Classic Chillers edition adapted by Larry Weinberg and illustrated by Ken Barr (1982), the Peter Bedrick Books edition abridged by Wendy Hobson and illustrated by Caroline Church (1989), the Great Illustrated Classics edition adapted by Malvina G. Vogel and illustrated by Pablo Marcos Studio (1993), the Oxford Bookworms Library edition retold by Patrick Nobes and including illustrations by Lynd Ward (2001), and the Dalmatian Press Junior Classics for Young Readers edition adapted and condensed by Bethany Snyder and illustrated by Miracle Studios (2011). With the exception of the Peter Bedrick edition, each of these editions offers a version of *Frankenstein* that has been adapted for a third grade reading level, i.e., a reader who is at least seven years old.[13] These editions differ from those addressed earlier in this chapter, primarily in that, whereas those already discussed offer visual adaptations of Shelley's prose, the abridged versions offer visual adaptations of adapted prose. Yet their contributions to *Frankenstein*'s lexicon are surprisingly similar.

Earlier I claimed that illustrations in illustrated editions prioritise certain moments and that, in doing so, they offer a very particular view of the novel. The abridged versions do a similar thing on the level of the prose as well – they highlight particular moments as essential to *Frankenstein*. Two online customer reviews of the Step-Up Classic Chillers edition highlight this issue. One reviewer explains that he bought the book for his eight-year-old daughter and it gives 'all the import[ant] parts without [losing] the true story' (Gary). Another comments that 'The story, of course, was "watered down" and just gave the basics' (T. Wood). Opening the edition reveals that the epistolary format and Walton-as-frame are not included in the story's 'basics', and neither is the Creature's narrative voice.[14] This edition employs Victor's first-person narrative voice throughout. Some of the abridged editions bullet the 'important parts' in the table of contents. For example, the Oxford Bookworms edition's table of contents includes: 'Victor Frankenstein's Story', 'The Monster's Story', 'Victor Frankenstein's Story', and 'Captain Walton's Note'. Similarly, both the Great Illustrated Classics edition and the Dalmatian edition impart the 'story's basics' through the table of contents, highlighting major plot points in chapter titles, such as 'Creating the Monster', 'The First Murder', 'The Monster Begins His Tale'. In this way, these abridged editions telegraph what 'counts' as *Frankenstein* through both prose and visual markers.

The versions of *Frankenstein* offered in abridged editions geared toward young readers are unlikely to offer graphic or visually disturbing information, not without attenuating it in some manner. The Oxford Bookworms edition includes Ward's illustrations from 1934, but only *some* of them. For example, the edition includes Ward's image of the Creature strangling William, but it does not include the image of the Creature at Victor's bedside. While William's death is clearly violent, Ward's image conceals William's body beneath the Creature's large hands. By contrast, Ward's bedside image does not depict a violent act, but the Creature's penis is clearly visible. In omitting this illustration but including that depicting William's death (as well as several others that allude to violence), the edition makes a clear distinction between acceptable and unacceptable content and, by extension, versions of the novel. The 'frank and (for the time-period) disturbing homoerotic content' that Grant F. Scott observes in Ward's coding of the Creature's body (208), becomes de-emphasised as the body is coded for young readers as physically but not sexually threatening.

The Oxford Bookworms edition is not the only abridged edition to attempt to offer an unambiguous visual depiction of the Creature. Many illustrators code the Creature as visibly monstrous, but do so in ways that are exaggerated enough to alleviate some of the threat and make him less scary. For example, Miracle Studios' Creature for the Dalmatian Press is visibly stitched together but otherwise fairly human looking and frequently depicted as smiling. Ken Barr's version of the Creature for the Step-Up Classic Chillers edition appears to be a cross between Boris Karloff in the 1931 film and the Incredible Hulk. Caroline Church's version in the Peter Bedrick edition resembles both a knobby troll and The Fantastic Four's The Thing. In both Barr's and Church's versions, the Creature is large and hulking, but lacking the agility that contributes to the threat posed by Ward's and Wrightson's creatures. That Barr's and Church's characterisations recall familiar 'monsters' or monster-types also renders them less menacing.

While it may appear that a divide exists between illustrated editions of Shelley's novel and illustrated abridged editions, we see the latter demonstrating an awareness of and reinforcing the *Frankenstein* lexicon in several ways, including shared symbolism. For example, although the context differs for each, Barr and Church both borrow from Carbe and use the background of the illustration to reflect psychological turmoil initiated by the action in the foreground. We see this, for example, in Carbe's illustration of Victor's Montavert ascent. Victor hopes that this trip will have restorative powers. He relates: 'The sight of the awful and majestic in nature had indeed always the effect of solemnising my mind and causing me to forget the passing cares of life' (96). Carbe portrays Victor hunched over on horseback, slowly making his way through the terrain. A vague impression of the Creature's face looms in the background, suggesting the unlikelihood that Victor should find rest and foreshadowing his encounter with the Creature. Barr and Church employ similar techniques. Barr's illustration of the scene in which Victor flees the monster and his laboratory and encounters Clerval on the street features an enlargement of the monster's head looming in the background. Church's use of this technique is closer to Carbe's stylistically, largely due to her attempt to replicate a woodcut aesthetic and her use of horizontal lines and high- and low-contrast. Church illustrates the scene in which Victor, recently released from prison for Clerval's murder, sails from Ireland with his father. Victor relates a nightmare he had on board, in which he imagines 'the fiend's grasp in [his] neck'. The sky in the background of Church's illustration of this moment bears the image of the Creature holding Victor's throat. Victor's father wakes him and the text notes, ironically, that 'the dashing waves were around, the cloudy sky above, the fiend was not here' (Shelley 102 [Church, 1989]).

The abridged editions also reinforce *Frankenstein*'s visual lexicon through in-jokes and intertextual references. For example, Miracle Studios includes an illustration of Victor digging in a graveyard, in which a wooden cart holding a body is partially visible, as is a tombstone bearing the name 'Wrightson'. This allusion has several possible connotations: the illustrator might be suggesting that he or she has conjured or 'unearthed' Wrightson in his or her own images or that Wrightson is 'dead and buried' and this edition lives as the new version of *Frankenstein*. Or the illustration might be suggesting that his or her *Frankenstein* is a hybrid of pre-existing *Frankenstein* texts, including Wrightson's. This last suggestion becomes more plausible when considered against the other illustrations' intertexts. Miracle Studios' depiction of the creation moment, for example, recalls Branagh's film in the decision to immerse the Creature in a large tub of fluid. In addition, the illustration depicting the female creature invokes

Whale's *Bride of Frankenstein* (1935) in terms of her hairstyle and the cloth that wraps her arms and torso. Whether or not young readers pick up on these references is not important. As Hutcheon has pointed out, audiences approach adaptation with different levels of 'knowing', and '[f]or unknowing audiences, adaptations have a way of upending sacrosanct elements like priority and originality' (122). For unknowing readers viewing Miracle Studios' illustrations, these intertexts are not intertexts, and they do not signal the illustrations' derivativeness or deference to an original. Rather, they are the original against which readers' subsequent experiences with the Frankenstein Complex will be assimilated.

The recent publication of *Gris Grimly's Frankenstein* (2013) indicates that popular interest in illustrated editions of the novel continues. That Grimly's edition features a foreword by Wrightson is a suitable reminder of the circuitous evolution of adaptation. Wrightson tells Grimly's readers, 'I illustrated the story more than thirty years ago. Just my own visual interpretation, one more in the long line of interpretations – on stage, on film and in print.' He relates that, since the publication of his edition, 'I've been told by many people that it was my pictures that drew them into the book … and that they wouldn't have been able to read it at all had it not been for my illustrations pulling them along. I realized that I had done something much more than just decorate a favorite story: I had created a gateway into the book for the reader' (x–xi). Wrightson claims that Grimly's edition offers the same service; that it will bring readers into the story. Illustration has been called many things (e.g., decoration, supplement, interference, addition), yet the metaphor of the gateway may illuminate why so many illustrated editions exist and continue to be produced: each edition provides its own way into the novel. In his introduction to Wrightson's edition, Stephen King admits to having 'laid aside' Shelley's novel in his youth, and speculates that he might not have done so if had he picked up an illustrated edition (9). Had young King read *Frankenstein* through Wrightson's comics lens the novel might have resonated. Moser's graphic portrait style might resonate with another reader and Carbe's aestheticism with another. In teasing out qualities of Shelley's prose, illustrated editions hone readers' attention at the same time that they broaden the range of possible significations, textual and contextual connections.

As Hitchcock has pointed out, 'Mary Shelley conjured up the character, and, as in a culturally driven game of telephone in which each new utterance contains new meaning, we make it into the story we need at the moment' (9). Although each utterance may contain new meaning, 'some thread of consistent meaning weaves through them all' (10). Yet, as the successive sets of illustrations demonstrate, even this thread of consistency is varied in texture. More important than the thread or the *Frankenstein* of a particular moment is the weave, the larger network or complex in which all of these versions exist simultaneously, each contributing to our larger understanding of *Frankenstein* and its cultural impact.

Notes

1 See, for example, Susan Tyler Hitchcock's overview of the impact of Whale's film and Bouriana Zakharieva's essay, which claims Whale's film 'has accounted for the clichéd popular perception of the Monster' (416).

2 Hitchcock provides a brief overview of some *Frankenstein* illustrators, such as Carbe, Ward, and Henry (see pages 164–169), and Grant F. Scott provides an in-depth consideration of Gothic and homoerotic themes in Ward's illustrations. Scott situates Ward's illustrations within a visual conversation that includes *Frankenstein*'s early stage productions, early illustrations by Holst and Lagerquist, and Ward's own *Wild Pilgrimage* (1932).

3 Throughout this chapter I use the term 'lexicon' to refer to the inventory of images and impressions associated with *Frankenstein* in the popular imagination as well as the inventory of scenes, characters, and moments that illustrators commonly depict.

4 Whale's film adapts not only Shelley's novel, of course, but also Peggy Webling's play (1927); see Forry (90–100) and Hitchcock (138–162).

5 While few illustrations allude to the novel's epistolary structure, several editions include illustrations of letters or of characters reading, and indicate shifts in narrative voice via typographical signifiers. For example, the Dalmatian Press edition includes Walton's letters and an illustration of Walton writing. It also includes letters to Victor from Elizabeth and Alphonse and indicates the shift in genre and voice via italics. The Oxford Bookworms edition and the Great Illustrated Classics edition omit the epistolary frame but indicate shifts from Victor's narrative to the Creature's by employing a different font. The Great Illustrated Classics edition also includes letters to Victor from Elizabeth and Alphonse, as well as illustrations showing the letters being delivered and Victor reading them. *Gris Grimly's Frankenstein* includes Walton's, Elizabeth's, and Alphonse's letters and renders each in distinctive handwriting.

6 Unless otherwise indicated, the pagination of this chapter's citations corresponds to that of the particular edition under examination.

7 As Thomas Leitch points out, 'every film adaptation follows the early theatrical adaptations … in transforming this episode into a pivotal scene,' *Film Adaptation and Its Discontents*, 208.

8 Berni Wrightson, Pablo Marcos Studios and Gris Grimly each depict this moment and, like Ward, align the reader's point of view with Victor's, perhaps to engender sympathy or to foster identification. Wrightson's image is very similar to Ward's, and both emphasise the Creature's muscularity and imposing stature. Pablo Marcos Studio's depiction of this scene for the Great Illustrated Classics edition downplays the threat presented by the Creature at the bedside by clothing him and softening his expression. Grimly depicts the bedside scene over five panels in *Gris Grimly's Frankenstein*, one of which offers a view of the Creature from within the bed chamber, very similar to Ward's illustration.

9 This number excludes the pictorial initials with which Carbe begins each chapter.

10 Ward, Henry, Barr, Church, Pablo Marcos Studios, Miracle Studios, and Grimly all depict the Creature's encounter with Felix, and, with the exception of Henry and Grimly, all depict the confrontation as explicitly violent.

11 Moser's edition follows the 1818 version of Shelley's text and is divided into three volumes, each with its own frontispiece.

12 Several illustrators emphasise hands. In addition to vignettes of disembodied hands, each

of Ward's figures has large, powerful hands. Scott links this characteristic to what he sees as Ward's homoerotic theme (Scott 212). Similarly, Grimly's figures have enlarged, bony hands which stand out due to the pink tint used as a highlight, which contrasts against his dominant palette of muted greens and yellows.

13 Dalmatian is geared for a 3.5 reading level, which it defines as 'Ages 7 and up'. Step-Up Classic Chillers is geared for a 3.4 reading level. The Oxford Bookworms edition is also Stage 3 or 1,000 headwords or content words. The Renaissance Readers' programme materials explain that these numbers refer to the 'textual difficulty of a book' but not necessarily the maturity level of the content. See 'Using'.

14 The Oxford Bookworms and Great Illustrated Classics editions also omit Walton as a framing device, though the Oxford Bookworms edition concludes with a note from Walton.

Bibliography

Albrecht-Crane, Christa and Dennis Cutchins. 'Introduction: New Beginnings for Adaptation Studies.' *Adaptation Studies: New Approaches*. Madison: Fairleigh Dickinson UP, 2010. 11–22.

'Barry Moser's *Frankenstein*.' The Bakken Museum. 2013. 25 January 2014.

Elliott, Kamilla. *Rethinking the Novel/Film Debate*. Cambridge: Cambridge UP, 2003.

Forry, Steven Earl. *Hideous Progenies: Dramatization of* Frankenstein *From Mary Shelley to the Present*. Philadelphia: U of Pennsylvania P, 1990.

Gary. 'great bok [*sic*] for beginners.' Rev. of *Frankenstein*. By Mary Shelley. Ill. Ken Barr. Adapted by Larry Weinberg. Step-Up Classic Chillers. New York: Random House, 1982. Amazon.com. 11 January 2014.

Grimly, Gris. *Gris Grimly's Frankenstein*. New York: Balzer + Bray, 2013.

Hitchcock, Susan Tyler. *Frankenstein: A Cultural History*. New York: W.W. Norton, 2007.

Hutcheon, Linda. *A Theory of Adaptation*. New York: Routledge, 2006.

Kaye, Heidi. 'Feminist Sympathies Versus Masculine Backlash: Kenneth Branagh's *Mary Shelley's Frankenstein*.' *Pulping Fictions: Consuming Culture Across the Literature/Media Divide*. Ed. Deborah Cartmell et al. London: Pluto, 1996. 57–71.

King, Stephen. 'Introduction to the Marvel Edition of Frankenstein.' *Frankenstein; or, the Modern Prometheus*. By Mary Wollstonecraft. Ill. Berni Wrightson. New York: Marvel, 1983.

Leitch, Thomas. *Film Adaptation and Its Discontents: From* Gone With the Wind *to* The Passion of the Christ. Baltimore: John Hopkins UP, 2007.

———. 'Twelve Fallacies in Contemporary Adaptation Theory.' *Criticism* 45.2 (Spring 2003): 149–171.

Oates, Joyce Carol. Afterword. 'Frankenstein's Fallen Angel.' *Frankenstein; or the Modern Prometheus*. Ill. Barry Moser. Pennyroyal Press. Berkeley: U of California P, 1983. 241–254.

Scott, Grant F. 'Victor's Secret: Queer Gothic in Lynd Ward's Illustrations to *Frankenstein* (1934).' *Word & Image: A Journal of Verbal/Visual Enquiry* 28.2 (2012): 206–232.

Shelley, Mary Wollstonecraft. *Frankenstein; or the Modern Prometheus*. Ill. Theodore von Holst. London: Henry Colburn and Richard Bentley, 1831.

———. *Frankenstein; or the Modern Prometheus*. Ill. Carl Lagerquist. Boston: Cornhill Publishing, 1922.

————. *Frankenstein; or the Modern Prometheus.* Ill. Nino Carbe. New York: Illustrated Editions, 1932.

————. *Frankenstein; or the Modern Prometheus.* Ill. Everett Henry. New York: Heritage Press, 1934.

————. *Frankenstein; or the Modern Prometheus.* Ill. Lynd Ward. New York: Harrison Smith and Robert Haas, 1934.

————. *Frankenstein; or the Modern Prometheus.* Ill. Ken Barr. Adapted by Larry Weinberg. Step-Up Classic Chillers. New York: Random House, 1982.

————. *Frankenstein; or the Modern Prometheus.* Ill. Berni Wrightson. New York: Marvel, 1983.

————. *Frankenstein; or the Modern Prometheus.* Ill. Barry Moser. Pennyroyal Press. Berkeley: U of California P, 1984.

————. *Frankenstein; or the Modern Prometheus.* Ill. Caroline Church. Abridged by Wendy Hobson. New York: Peter Bedrick Books, 1989.

————. *Frankenstein; or the Modern Prometheus.* Ill. Pablo Marcos Studio. Adapted by Malvina G. Vogel. Great Illustrated Classics. New York: Baronet Books, 1993.

————. *Frankenstein; or the Modern Prometheus.* Ill. Lynd Ward. Retold by Patrick Nobes. Oxford Bookworms Library. Oxford: Oxford UP, 2000.

————. *Frankenstein; or the Modern Prometheus.* Ill. Miracle Studios. Condensed and Adapted by Bethany Snyder. Franklin, TN: Dalmatian Press, 2011.

Stam, Robert. 'Beyond Fidelity: The Dialogics of Adaptation.' *Film Adaptation.* Ed. James Naremore. New Brunswick: Rutgers, 2000. 54–76.

St Clair, William. ''The Impact of Frankenstein.'' *Mary Shelley in Her Times.* Ed. Betty T. Bennett and Stuart Curran. Baltimore: Johns Hopkins UP, 2000. 38–63.

'Using Readability Levels to Guide Students to Books.' Renaissance Learning. 2006. http://doc.renlearn.com/KMNet/R001005421GD6336.pdf (accessed 25 January 2014).

Wood, T. 'A book that even second graders love to read! A Must Read!' Rev. of *Frankenstein.* By Mary Shelley. Ill. Ken Barr. Adapted by Larry Weinberg. Step-Up Classic Chillers. New York: Random House, 1982. Amazon.com. 4 December 2011.

Wrightson, Berni. 'Foreword by Berni Wrightson.' *Gris Grimly's Frankenstein.* New York: Balzer + Bray, 2013.

Zakharieva, Bouriana. 'Frankenstein of the Nineties: The Composite Body.' *Frankenstein.* By Mary Shelley. Ed. Johanna M. Smith. Boston: Bedford/St. Martin's, 2000. 416–431.

15

'The X-Men meet Frankenstein! "Nuff said!"':
adapting Mary Shelley's monster in superhero
comic books

Joe Darowski

'"THE" X-MEN MEET FRANKENSTEIN?" Perish the thought!' (Douglas 309). Thus begins a letter found in 'Mutant Mail-Box', the official letter column of *The X-Men* comic book in the 1960s. The letter writer, Scott Douglas, is responding to a story featured in *X-Men* #40 (1968), titled 'The Mark of the Monster'. In that issue, the X-Men encounter the notorious Frankenstein Creature. Douglas's reaction to the tale is mixed. While initially sceptical about an encounter between the X-Men and the Creature, he felt that 'it was a successful meeting after all', but also confesses, 'I'm still not sure whether I personally like the story or not' (309). Douglas further asks that Marvel keep classic monsters out of its comic books, a request that the editor penning the response assures him isn't even needed: 'don't worry about any more monsters popping up in our mags for a while! We just decided to toss in Franky one time for kicks!' (309).

The appearance of Frankenstein[1] in an X-Men comic book may seem a novelty (and the story itself is peculiar), but Frankenstein's Creature had already appeared in several other comics and continues to appear in various comic-book publications to this day. These appearances range from direct adaptations of Mary Shelley's novel to the appropriation of characters from the original story into any number of comic-book genres, from horror to comedy to superhero.

Like those in other media, comic-book adaptations of *Frankenstein* represent varying degrees of fidelity to their source texts. Many adaptations seem to appropriate the larger popular-culture conceptions of the Creature rather than the actual content of the novel. In the case of *The X-Men* #40–42, issue #40 features a visually iconic Frankenstein's Creature in a superhero adventure with little connection to Shelley's novel, while issues #41 and 42 create a two-part storyline that has many thematic associations with the novel but makes no overt references to either Frankenstein or his Creature. *X-Men* #40 is influenced more by the iconography of the 1931 James Whale film adaptation, as well as other comics' stories that appropriate aspects of the novel, while *X-Men* #41 and 42 (February–March 1968) are actually more engaged with the ideas and themes of Shelley's novel, although they carry no explicit references to that text. In addition to Shelley's novel and cultural conceptions of Frankenstein's

Creature, perhaps one of the largest influences on the adaptations of the Creature that appear in *X-Men* #40–42 is the existence of the Comics Code Authority. Its strict guidelines for comic-book content heavily influenced the plot, tone, and presentation of these *Frankenstein*-inspired superhero tales.

In order to properly contextualise the use of Frankenstein's Creature in an *X-Men* comic book, some familiarity with other adaptations and the history of the comic-book industry is necessary. This is particularly true because more traditional versions of Shelley's Creature had appeared in comic-book form previously, but were not allowed to be published in the 1960s when these X-Men tales were produced.

The comic-book industry's history is generally divided into three periods: a Golden Age, from the late-1930s to the mid-1950s; a Silver Age, from the mid-1950s to the mid-1980s; and the 1980s into the 2010s, although there is little consensus about how to categorise this most recent era. One of the earliest versions of *Frankenstein* to appear in comic books was created during the 1940s by Dick Briefer. Briefer's interpretation of *Frankenstein* was a curious instance of trial-and-error experimentation, quite fitting for a comic book from the Golden Age, when the industry was still establishing conventions and expectations.

Briefer's version of *Frankenstein*, first published in an anthology comic book, *Prize Comics*, and later in a solo series titled *Frankenstein*, changed significantly during its run (Wright 59). Initially the Creature was portrayed as a horror character, one that would 'tear bystanders apart' (Bark). Briefer's *Frankenstein*, with a first appearance in *Prize Comics* #7 (December 1940), is one of the earliest known horror comic books published in the United States (Eaton). This represented a precursor to a genre that would become immensely popular with comic-book fans in subsequent decades, and ultimately alter the course of popular-culture history when, in the 1950s, the US government began investigating whether horror and crime comic books influenced juvenile delinquency (Howe 30).

Briefer's Creature roamed contemporary New York City in the 1940s and battled several of *Prize Comics*' costumed crime fighters. During World War II, the Creature 'was brainwashed into hating Nazis' and became a pseudo-hero (Bark). But the changes to the character did not end there. After being a figure of Gothic horror and then a Nazi-hunter, the character experienced perhaps its most unexpected transformation, becoming a 'cutesy kid's character' as the *Frankenstein* comic book became a slapstick comedy (Bark). In the final incarnation by Briefer, in the early 1950s, the comic returned to a more serious horror series for just over two years. In returning to the horror genre in the early 1950s Briefer was following an industry trend away from superhero and comedic comic books.

The comic-book industry was defined by superheroes in the early Golden Age. Empowered do-gooders resonated with audiences during the Great Depression and later during World War II, but following the war, crime and horror comic books eclipsed superheroes in popularity. Many publishers naturally pursued what was selling, abandoning the superhero genre for tales of terror and crime. As Lance Eaton puts it, 'An entire generation of readers had grown up with superheroes and light-hearted fare, but the brutalities of war meant that the more gentle comic books of the late 1930s and 1940s would not engage an audience' (19). However, while the content of comic books was maturing, if you will, the reputation of the industry for producing content that appealed to children remained. The disconnect between content intended for more mature audiences and a perceived market of children and adolescents made some powerful people uneasy. Dr Fredric Wertham published *Seduction of the Innocent: The Influence of Comic Books on Today's Youths*, linking the reading of comic books with juvenile delinquency, and in 1953 the United States Senate Subcommittee on Juvenile Delinquency held hearings to determine whether comic books were corrupting the youth of America. In 1954, to appease their critics, the comic-book publishers agreed to a self-censoring board, the Comics Code Authority (CCA), that essentially regulated horror and crime genres out of existence during the Silver Age (Howe 31). The influence of the CCA waned in the 1970s and 1980s before disappearing entirely in 2011, but its impact on the late Golden Age and the early Silver Age, particularly for horror comic books, cannot be overstated. Horror comics would not reappear from Marvel comics until 1971.

Both before and during the reign of the CCA many other comic-book publishers also created versions of *Frankenstein*, or adapted the familiar Gothic characters to inhabit new worlds. DC Comics, for instance, has a Frankenstein's Creature that appears multiple times in its wide-ranging superhero continuity. Initially appearing a single time in a Batman story from 1948's *Detective Comics* #135 before disappearing for several decades, DC's character became a superhero in the 2000s with appearances in *Seven Soldiers of Victory* and *Frankenstein: Agent of Shade*. As DC Comics' online database describes the character, 'Eventually he became a government agent, smiting down supernatural threats with his flaming sword and flintlock pistol' ('Frankenstein', DC Wikia). Although the *Agent of Shade* series lasted for only sixteen issues, the character occasionally appears in other titles from the publisher.

There have also been comic-book adaptations that much more closely reflect their literary and cinematic source material in terms of plot and characters, although as adaptations they are still independent products from the 1818 novel or the many film adaptations, filtered as they are through the eyes of new creators. In 1945, for example, the comic-book series *Classic Comics*, later known as *Classics Illustrated*, published a direct adaptation of Mary Shelley's novel. *Classics Illustrated* was a part of a movement in the comic-book industry to publish more uplifting and educational content. In addition to publishing comic-book adaptations of literary classics, the series would include author biographies and some additional educational information (Goulart 206). In 2008 Penguin Classics began to publish graphic novel-length adaptations of classic literature, using the series name *Classics Illustrated Deluxe*, and *Frankenstein* was the third volume in that series. Following the 1971 loosening of the CCA's restrictions on publishing horror-themed content, Marvel Comics had success with various horror titles, including *The Tomb of Dracula* and *Werewolf by Night*, so it also introduced *The Monster of Frankenstein* in 1973. The first four issues of the series were an adaptation of Shelley's novel, although subsequent issues brought the Creature into Marvel's established continuity, and it started appearing in Marvel's superhero comic books. This 1970s series ignored the company's own continuity, however, as it was not the first time Frankenstein's Creature had appeared in Marvel's superhero comic books. As mentioned earlier, an entirely different interpretation of the Creature had appeared in a 1968 issue of *The X-Men*. Much like the film industry, comic-book publishers produced myriad interpretations of the iconic Creature and his creator, but the version presented by Roy Thomas and Don Heck in early 1968 stands out, partly due to several identifiable influences on their interpretation of the Creature, but also because of the limitations placed on Marvel Comics by the CCA.

The X-Men meet Frankenstein

Marvel Comics followed industry trends, and when superhero comics waned in popularity, they stopped publishing them, which 'was okay with [Stan] Lee, as long as *something* was popular' (Howe 27). Marvel would turn to Westerns, sci-fi, and 'movie-matinee-style monster' comics (Howe 35). But in the early 1960s, Stan Lee and his artistic collaborators, including, most notably, Jack Kirby and Steve Ditko, began to publish superhero adventures again, and revolutionised the genre. In quick succession the Fantastic Four, Incredible Hulk, Thor, and Iron Man were all introduced in an ever-expanding narrative world that became known as the Marvel Universe. At this time, Marvel introduced two new superhero teams to comic-book readers. One – the Avengers – combined several of its most popular heroes into one team, but the other consisted of wholly original characters.

In 1963, Jack Kirby and Stan Lee's *The X-Men* #1 was published by Marvel Comics. The series departed from most previous superhero tales in that the origins of the various characters were not centred on alien births, personal tragedies, mythological roots or scientific accidents. The X-Men series featured 'mutants', people who were simply born with different abilities than everyone else around them. These abilities or superpowers generally manifested as the characters reached puberty. Throughout the 1960s the series featured a team that primarily consisted of Cyclops, Beast, Angel, Iceman, and Marvel Girl, who were all mentored by Professor Xavier, also known as 'Professor X'.

Lee and Kirby were prolific creators in the early 1960s, however, and had many other projects on their plates. *The X-Men* wasn't selling particularly well, so after less than two years it passed on to other creators. Thus *The X-Men* #40, featuring a story called 'The Mark of the Monster', was written by Roy Thomas and drawn by Don Heck.

As with many issues of *The X-Men* from the 1960s, the story opens with the team training and trading barbs with one another. Soon, Professor Xavier summons his students, the X-Men, to his office, and reveals that he believes Frankenstein's monster has recently been discovered. Iceman protests that the monster is just a myth, but Professor X chides him for not reading the novel, then suggests that this is exactly what a 'complacent mankind' has always thought, implying that people have been lax in not keeping their guard up concerning Frankenstein's monster (Thomas, 'The Mark'). On the one hand, the idea that a fantastic creature is real makes more sense in a narrative universe populated by Spider-Man and the Incredible Hulk, but on the other hand, this assertion is absurd. Why should his students, or mankind in general, have assumed Shelley's novel was non-fiction? No answer to this question is provided in the comic.

The cause of Professor Xavier's concern is a body encased in ice that scientists in the Arctic have discovered and are bringing back to the fictional New York Museum. Xavier explains that he has always had a theory that Frankenstein's monster is real, and the X-Men guess that the Creature must have been an early mutant, an explanation that would tie in with the themes that pervade this particular comic-book series. The X-Men characters are not revered and idolised in the way most other heroes are; they are hated and feared because they are different from normal humans. Whereas Iron Man is a normal man in a suit of armour, and Captain America represents the peak fitness humanity can achieve (albeit aided by World War II-era performance enhancers), the X-Men are perceived as freaks and mutants. While prejudice is not as much of a defining theme in the series during the Silver Age as it would become later, by 1968 the X-Men had already experienced expressions of fear from 'normal' humans in their adventures. Thus, assuming that a creature that was chased by mobs with burning torches and pitchforks was an early mutant could have been a unique twist on Frankenstein's Creature for this superhero adventure.

However, Xavier instead theorises that the Creature was really an android that had been *built* by one of the earliest mutants, a mutant who would have had a 'super advanced brain' (Thomas, 'The Mark'). The origins of Professor Xavier's theories are never explained to the reader, but the reason for an android rather than a traditional cadaver-collected Creature likely lies with the CCA. Throughout the 1960s the CCA's restrictions were still quite strong and explicitly forbade the inclusion of 'Scenes dealing with, or instruments associated with, walking dead, torture, vampires and vampirism, ghouls, cannibalism and werewolfism' (Nyberg 167). It is likely that the CCA would have considered the traditional version of Frankenstein's Creature too closely associated with 'the walking dead' and thus the issue would not have received the necessary Seal of Approval to be sold on news-stands. A few years later, use of a more traditional Frankenstein's Creature would clearly have been allowed. In 1971 the CCA released updated guidelines that included the following concession:

> Vampires, ghouls, and werewolves shall be permitted to be used when handled in the classic tradition such as Frankenstein, Dracula, and other high caliber literary works written by Edgar Allan Poe, Saki (H.H. Munro), Conan Doyle and other respected authors whose works are read in schools throughout the world. (Nyberg 172)

It seems highly probable that the idea of the android origins of the Creature was meant to ensure an easy approval from the CCA.

The X-Men and Professor X, perhaps familiar with the tropes of the science-fiction genre when it comes to creatures encased in ice – Frankenstein's Creature had been thawed from the ice just a few years earlier in Hammer's *The Evil of Frankenstein*, for instance – realise that if the monster is freed from the ice it may revive. Fearing the rampage that they suspect would result from this, the X-Men go to the museum to stop a scientist from thawing the Creature. They are, of course, too late, and a battle with the Creature ensues, followed by a chase to a shipping barge, and the eventual destruction of the Creature, which does turn out to have been an android. However, it was not created by a mutant from an earlier era; rather, it had been built by aliens to explore the Earth. The aliens wanted to see how their creation was received by the natives of the planet before they initiated contact. As Marvel Girl exclaims, it 'was the first interstellar ambassador!' (Thomas, 'The Mark'). Professor X surmises, 'Evidently it went berserk, Jean – thru some malfunction – and became a menace to Earthmen! The aliens pursued it to our polar regions where [...] it was helpless' (Thomas, 'The Mark'). This theory is presented as fact to readers, although how this conclusion was reached is uncertain. Interestingly, although Mary Shelley and her novel are frequently mentioned in the issue, the X-men continually refer to the Creature as an urban legend, rather than as a work of fiction.

Clearly, this is anything but a direct adaptation of Shelley's novel, although Mary Shelley is explicitly referenced in the story, beginning with the mention of a home-work assignment that Iceman had not completed. Unlike many other superhero teams, the X-Men, at this point in Marvel continuity, are adolescents enrolled in Professor Xavier's School for Gifted Youngsters. 'I see you haven't read the *novel*, Bobby – which I *assigned* last spring! In it, Victor Frankenstein *pursued* his grotesque creation into the *Arctic regions*! And *there* – near the top of the world – he *died*!' (Thomas, 'The Mark'). At the end of the story Professor X muses that they'll never know how Mary Shelley learned about the Creature, nor is there any indication as to why she wrote a novel which conspicuously does not feature aliens from a tropical planet, nor an android. When asked if he reread the novel in preparation for the story, Roy Thomas, who taught high school English before becoming a comic-book writer, explained, 'I first read the novel *Frankenstein* in high school. Never taught it or studied it in school. For research I might have looked at the novel to get a fact or two straight, but that would have been about it' (Thomas, 'Re: Inquiry'). It seems certain that he at least reviewed the novel, because its final lines, 'He was soon borne away by the waves and lost in darkness and distance!' are accurately quoted and attributed in the comic book (Thomas, 'The Mark').

While the use of the Creature, explicit references to Mary Shelley, and exact quotations from the novel make it clear that *Frankenstein* served as some manner of source material for the storyline in 'The Mark of the Monster', there are also other influences at play. The popular Universal film adaptation supplied some of the visual look of the Creature; Don Heck's art includes the famous neck bolts and flattened head that Boris Karloff made iconic in his portrayal of the Creature. Similarly, a scene in the comic book when the scientist waves his hands in the air declaring 'He lives! The monster lives!' (Thomas, 'The Mark') bears more in common with the Universal film than with Shelley's novel. Thomas also cites an EC Comics story from *The Vault of Horror* #22 (December 1951–January 1952) as a direct inspiration for the idea to have polar explorers discover Frankenstein's Creature ('Re: Inquiry'). The *Vault of Horror* (*VoH*) story seems to be one of many stories loosely inspired by the novel, the cover even proclaiming, 'In this issue, the old witch reveals the startling rediscovery of the authentic Frankenstein Monster!' (Feldstein). The Frankenstein story in *VoH* #22, titled 'The Monster in the Ice!', was written by Al Feldstein and drawn by Graham Ingels. In this comic book two American explorers in the Arctic are warned by an Eskimo not to go where there is a body trapped in the ice. They, of course, ignore this warning and go and dig the body out, remarking that this body in the ice reminds them of Mary Shelley's *Frankenstein*. The Creature revives when it is thawed out and they realise that they must trap it again, so they dig a hole through the ice to water and lure the Creature there. Unfortunately, the Creature drags them both down into the water with it, where they perish. In classic EC Comics style, the story ends a year later as the US Air Force has decided to build a base at the same site, and some airmen spot bodies trapped in the ice and begin to dig them out. This story was published in late 1951, the same year that the film *The Thing from Another World* (1951) was released, providing another potential source of influence. Although Thomas makes no mention of *The Thing*, the classic sci-fi film has many similarities with the EC Comic story described above. In the film, the US Air Force discovers a crash-landed alien craft near the North Pole and brings a body, frozen in ice, back to base. The ice thaws, the creature escapes, and mayhem ensues. Whether this was a direct influence on Thomas's story or not (although the Thing's Frankensteinian look in the film suggests it), it is further evidence that this was recurring trope in sci-fi stories from the 1950s and 1960s.

Thomas also cites another, earlier comic as influencing his tale, a Batman story from 1948 called 'The True Story of Frankenstein' (Thomas, 'Re: Inquiry'). Published in *Detective Comics* #135, this comic was written by Edmond Hamilton with art by *Batman* co-creator Bob Kane. The story is, again, a strange one. Batman and Robin travel back in time and have an adventure with a 'Baron Frankenstein'. Mary Shelley observes the action, then writes a novel that fictionalises some aspects of the story, but removes the time travellers, because the 'true' story she witnessed would never be believed. In this instance the time travel of Batman and Robin sets off a sequence of events that ends with a giant man in a trance-like state rampaging through a village. The only element that seems to be shared between the *X-Men* issue and this Batman adventure is the idea that a fantastic occurrence inspired Mary Shelley to write her novel. This concept would later be used in *Frankenstein Unbound*, a 1973 novel by Brian Aldiss, in which a modern-day man travels back in time and meets both Mary Shelley and Frankenstein's Creature. Thomas also mentioned that he always thought of *X-Men* #40 as 'The X-Men Meet Frankenstein' because *Abbott and Costello Meet Frankenstein* (1948) was one of his favourite pairings ('Re: Inquiry'). The pairing of the classic monster with an established franchise into a sort of mishmash of stories in a new genre is shared between this movie and the comic book.

Despite several identifiable sources of influence, there are also unique aspects to the Creature that appears in Thomas and Heck's story. In alignment with the superhero genre, this Creature displays several unique powers. For example, it can shoot lasers out of its eyes, perhaps a homage to the opening credits of James Whale's film, which features a still image of rays shooting from a monster's eye. The X-Men's foe also has magnetic feet. Little explanation is provided for the unique abilities the Creature possesses, but possibly these were incorporated to provide visually interesting options for the artist. In this era, it was not uncommon for a supervillain to be introduced, display a visually arresting set of powers, be defeated by the heroes, and rarely or never be seen again.

It should be noted that this particular interpretation of Frankenstein, aside from deviating significantly from the source material, is not an effective story. Despite the reputation comic books have as disposable, adolescent entertainment with little literary merit, the Silver Age of comics produced many fantastic issues that hold up well in terms of entertainment value and narrative complexity. This, however, is not one of them. Thomas himself admitted that he wished 'the Frankenstein story had turned out better' ('Re: Inquiry'). Subjectively, I found the pacing dull and the story contrived. Objectively, there are problematic aspects, from minor details to the larger narrative, that detract from the issue's quality. In the end, 'The Mark of the Monster' is not really an adaptation of *Frankenstein* at all, but a generic and uneven superhero adventure that borrows the name of a character from the classic novel without addressing the themes, concepts, or issues that made the novel so enduring.

The next two issues of the series, however, share more thematic affinities with Mary Shelley's novel than does the previous example, although Thomas has no recollection of 'consciously' trying to explore Shelley's themes in the storyline (Thomas, 'Re: Inquiry'). In discussing this two-part story, I will borrow the term 'affinities' from Dennis Perry's work on Alfred Hitchcock and Edgar Allen Poe, wherein he notes that influence studies are a particularly thorny issue even when authorial intent has been stated, but in some works 'similarities clearly exist, though we can't possibly know how they got there' (1).

X-Men #41, titled 'Now Strikes ... the Sub-Human', also written by Roy Thomas and drawn by Don Heck, opens with a new villain, Grotesk: The Sub-Human attacking a subway train that Iceman and Beast are riding. This monster appears without any explanation and, after a quick battle with Iceman and Beast, disappears into a series of ancient underground tunnels. His origin is then revealed to readers. He came from an ancient civilisation that lived beneath the Earth's surface, one of about a dozen such underground civilisations that are, or were, thriving just beneath Manhattan in the Marvel universe. The civilisation decided to go to the surface to conquer humans and enslave them, but just as they were about to do this, some unspecified disaster destroyed most of the underground cities. Grotesk, who was known as Prince Gor-Tok at the time, tried to rally the survivors of his people, but a mysterious illness brought on by radiation following the disaster killed them all, including his wife, and Gor-Tok was left alone. Grotesk now believes the disaster and subsequent radiation sickness were brought on by humans from the outer world. In a Cold War-era comic book, the idea of radiation wiping out a civilisation bent on conquering another part of the world would resonate with readers who lived in fear of nuclear war, should the temperature of the Cold War turn hot.

Readers are also introduced to a scientist named Dr Hunt, who has invented a machine called the Nuclear Oscillotron, which can 'create Earth tremors' (Thomas, 'Now Strikes'). In order to prove himself to other disbelieving scientists, Dr Hunt activates his machine, which causes tremors that Grotesk can feel in the underground tunnels he calls home. In a paranoid leap of 'logic', Grotesk decides that the tremors he is feeling must be an attack from the surface world, and vows to kill whoever is causing them. Having seen Hunt successfully demonstrate his machine, the other scientists are appalled, and warn Dr Hunt that his unnatural machine could destroy the world. While Shelley's novel included debates and warnings about certain kinds of science, the threat largely remains at an individual level, unless Victor had finished his creation of the female creature. But in a world that has seen single bombs kill thousands, the scale of the threat to the world by Dr Hunt's actions is elevated to an extinction-level threat to humanity.

Angered by Hunt's use of the machine, Grotesk seeks out the source of the tremors he has been feeling. Although it is never explained how, Grotesk goes directly to the university where the machine is housed, in an attempt to take the machine to his underground lair, but it has been moved by Dr Hunt. Grotesk returns to his lair, where Cyclops and Beast, having found his base in the underground tunnels, confront him. Grotesk handles Beast and Cyclops easily, but suddenly receives a mental image of Dr Hunt operating the machine where it is now located. Grotesk goes to the site and finds Professor Xavier, who has disguised himself as Dr Hunt and used his mental powers to summon him. In what is perhaps a flaw in Professor X's plan, Grotesk is now in the room with the very machine he had been seeking but was unable to find, and he quickly throws Xavier aside and activates the machine, turning it up to full power in the hope that it will destroy the Earth. The X-Men arrive and a classic superhero-style fight ensues. In an effort to speed the machine's planetary destruction, Grotesk increases its power to dangerous levels and the machine explodes, killing both Professor X and Grotesk.

This two-part story, surprisingly, shares far more affinities with Shelley's work than 'The Mark of the Beast'. There is a scientist playing god, who unleashes a new life form that hunts him down and destroys him. Actually, there are two instances of scientists meddling with natural forces that inspire Grotesk to attack mankind. The first is obviously Dr Hunt, using his machine that creates earthquakes (the benefit of such a machine is questionable in any instance), and with his dying breath Xavier reveals that it was underground atomic tests which released the radiation that wiped out Grotesk's people. This revelation addresses contemporary concerns of the era. The concern about the threat of the fictional earthquake machine functions as an all-too-real allusion to controversial underground nuclear testing.

An additional affinity with *Frankenstein* is Grotesk's anger at his condition as the only member of his species. His wife has been killed, and, like Frankenstein's Creature who seeks a female companion for much of the novel, Grotesk is lonely. The 'monsters' in both works are not motivated by a lust for power or notoriety as the scientists are, but by a desire for companionship/affection. The death of Professor X represents another plot point shared with the novel. This is the first death of a hero in the X-Men comic books, and it comes at the hands of a monster raised from the Earth due to man's scientific arrogance. When Denny O'Neil became the writer of the series Professor Xavier's death was undone in *X-Men* #65 (February 1970), the first return from the grave for the X-Men, although that became a recurring trope of the franchise in future decades (O'Neil). Death as punishment for mankind's hubris permeates Shelley's novel to the point of oppressiveness, making the 'The Death of Professor X' perhaps further evidence of the comic's borrowing from Shelley's death-littered novel.[2]

When writing about the idea of influence studies, Dennis Perry noted that the subject is inherently 'thorny', and perhaps a recognition of 'affinities' could be more fruitful than a search for influence (1). In the end, the two-part 'Death of Professor X' storyline seems to share more affinities with Shelley's *Frankenstein* than the issue that lifted a character directly from the novel. In this sense, *The X-Men* #41–42 is arguably more of an adaptation of Shelley's novel than 'The Mark of the Monster'. 'The Mark of the Monster' borrows from other Frankenstein stories, from the Universal film to an EC Comics horror story, but little from the original source. In these stories, it is the shared themes that more directly link the X-Men to *Frankenstein* than the actual use of characters from the novel. 'The Mark of the Monster' may have borrowed a character name from Shelley's novel, but 'The Death of Professor X' is closer to an adaptation of *Frankenstein*.

Notes

1 As seen in the letter already cited, many of the references to 'Frankenstein' in comic books fall prey to the classic error of popular culture and conflate the Creature from Mary Shelley's novel with Victor Frankenstein, the Creature's creator. When speaking of 'Frankenstein' appearances in comic books, it is the Creature who appears, rather than Victor Frankenstein, unless otherwise noted.

2 Roy Thomas was not through with adapting books into comic books following these stories. He would go on to adapt Robert Howard's Conan the Barbarian stories into a very popular and respected series for Marvel Comics. He would also frequently include literary allusions in his subsequent work, such as including Percy Shelley's poem 'Ozymandias' in the

conclusion of the first story featuring the robotic villain Ultron (Thomas, 'Behold ... The Vision!').

Bibliography

Bark, Jasper. 'Dick Briefer's Frankenstein.' *This Is Horror*. This is Horror, n.d.

Douglas, Scott. Untitled letter to editor in 'Mutant Mail-Box.' *The X-Men Omnibus* Vol. *2*. 309. NY: Marvel Comics, 2011.

Eaton, Lance. 'The Horror Narrative and the Graphic Novel.' *Critical Insights: The Graphic Novel*. Ed. Gary Hoppenstand. Ipswich, MA: Salem Press, 2014.

Evil of Frankenstein, The. Dir. Freddie Francis. Perf. Peter Cushing, Sandor Eles, Peter Woodthorpe, Katy Wild, Duncan Lamont, and Kiwi Kingston. Hammer Film Productions, 1964.

Feldstein, Al (w) and Ingels, Graham (a). 'The Monster in the Ice!' *The Vault of Horror* #22 (December 1951). NY: EC Comics.

'Frankenstein.' *DC Wikia*, n.d. http://dc.wikia.com/wiki/Frankenstein.

Frankenstein. Dir. James Whale. Perf. Boris Karloff, Colin Clive, Mae Clarke, and John Boles. Universal Pictures, 1931.

Goulart, Ron. *Great American Comic Books*. Lincolnwood, IL: Publications International, 2001.

Howe, Sean. *Marvel Comics: The Untold Story*. New York: HarperCollins, 2012.

'Mutant Mail-Box.' *The X-Men Omnibus Vol. 2*. 309. New York: Marvel Comics, 2011.

Nyberg, Amy. *Seal of Approval: A History of the Comics Code Authority*. Jackson, UP of Mississippi, 1998.

O'Neil, Dennis (w) and Neal Adams (a). 'Before I'd Be Slave...' *X-Men* #65 (February 1970), NY: Marvel Comics.

Perry, Dennis. *Hitchcock and Poe: The Legacy of Delight and Terror*. Lanham, Maryland: Scarecrow Press, 2003.

Thing From Another World, The. Dir. Christian Nyby. Perf. Mararet Sheridan, Kenneth Tobey, Douglas Spencer, Robert O. Cornthwaite, and James Arness. RKO Pictures, 1951.

Thomas, Roy. 'Re: Inquiry Regarding X-Men/Frankenstein.' Message to Joseph Darowski. 19 February 2014.

Thomas, Roy (w), John Buscema (p), and Marie Severin (p). 'Behold ... The Vision!' *Avengers* #57 (October 1968), NY: Marvel Comics.

Thomas, Roy (w) and Don Heck (a). 'The Mark of the Monster!' *X-Men* #40 (January 1968), NY: Marvel Comics.

———. 'Now Strikes ... the Sub-Human!' *X-Men* #41 (February 1968), NY: Marvel Comics.

———. 'If I Should Die ...!' *X-Men* #42 (March 1968), NY: Marvel Comics.

Wright, Nicky. *The Classic Era of American Comics*. London: Psion Books, 2008.

16

Expressionism, deformity, and abject texture in *bande dessinée* appropriations of *Frankenstein*

Véronique Bragard and Catherine Thewissen

Introduction

IN MARY SHELLEY'S NOVEL the central and most enigmatic moment in the life of Victor Frankenstein's Creature is unquestionably its birth. When Victor Frankenstein faces his living Creature for the first time, he is excited by his success, but this short moment of fascination soon turns into a fearful experience of sour repulsion and disgust. The Creature's assemblage emerges as a daunting mixture of life and death, self and other. The mystery driving this scene has led to a great number of interpretations and reimaginings. Novelists, filmmakers, comic-book writers and artists in endless other media have been haunted by the Creature-turned-monster. Its composite quality can in many ways be read as an exceptional example of the abject, which, as Julia Kristeva puts it, 'disturbs identity, system, order'. She argues that the abject 'does not respect borders, positions, rules', and remains 'the in-between, the ambiguous, the composite' (4). Is it the Creature's deformed body that repulses or scares Victor, for instance, or its nearly human shape? The monster's body is uncanny in its tallness, its texture, and its status as a recomposed corpse – not quite human, but too close for comfort, the same and yet other. Disability-studies approaches to *Frankenstein* have emphasised this composite aspect: 'What is found to be truly horrifying about Frankenstein's Creature is its composite quality, which is too evocative of the fragmented body' (Davis 2414).

Ever since the first comic-book adaptations of *Frankenstein* in the 1940s, the strange composite nature of Victor Frankenstein's Creature has been the central point of numerous visual rewritings which work to unveil the sensory aspect of the abject which Shelley's text explores. Victor Frankenstein's Creature was first adapted as a comic book in the 1940s, the 'Golden Age of Comics' and superheroes (Wright 54; Rogel 18). Shelley's progeny became a simplified comic-book character alongside Batman, the Flash, the Green Lantern and Captain America (Wright 43). In these comics 'Frankenstein' became, not the creator of a monster, but the rejected Creature itself, made up of the refuse of humanity, and, more often than not, these early comic-book creatures chose good over evil and even fought the forces of evil. More recently, the Creature has been revived in comics that highlight some of the more complex issues raised in Shelley's original. For instance, Gary Reed and Frazer Irving's black-and-white adaptation, *Mary Shelley's* Frankenstein*: The Graphic Novel* (2005), explores the aspect of shared culpability for the Creature's actions; *The Cobbler's Monster: A Tale of Gepetto's Frankenstein* (2006), by Jeff Amano, and *Frankenstein: The Prodigal Son* (2008), by Dean Koontz, expose Frankenstein's inability to cope with loss and his resultant wish to rec-reate life, echoing recent associations between Frankenstein and genetic engineering.[1] Still other adaptations of the novel open the way for new and unexpected associations. Gris Grimly's *Frankenstein: The Modern Prometheus*, for instance, makes use of punk Gothic elements, skeletal shapes and Holocaust-related imagery to reinforce issues of injustice and exclusion. Very different from all of these are *Frankenstein* adaptations in the world of Francophone *bande dessinée*[2] (BD). Under scrutiny in this chapter are Marion Mousse's Gothic expressionistic recreations in *Frankenstein de Mary Shelley* (2008), Denis Deprez's intimate textural approach in *FrAnKeNsTein* (2003), and Alex Baladi's black-and-white deformed lines in the feminist *Frankenstein, Encore et Toujours* (2001).

The above list of graphic adaptations of Shelley's novel, while not exhaustive, is representative of a peaking phenomenon: graphic adaptation of canonical literary texts. Contemporary culture, as Christa Albrecht-Crane and Dennis Cutchins argue, 'loves to adapt' (12). Library and bookshop shelves are increasingly filled with graphic adaptations of classics of world literature. Yet, in spite of this long history, adaptations have typically been looked down on, often considered as 'lesser' or 'poorer' versions of the original. Like Frankenstein's Creature, 'adaptation is creativity's stepchild, always vying for validation, never catching up to its originating source' (Bryant 47). When adaptation studies first emerged in the 1950s, it was haunted by fidelity criticism that took the source text as an absolute and indisputable model, while adaptations were merely inferior copies. That second-class status applies especially to comics. In 1998 critic Jacques Samson denounced the fact that a graphic adaptation

> a beau être porteuse d'une sensation de plénitude il n'en reste pas moins qu'elle ne pourra jamais être absolument unique, c'est-à-dire dépasser cet état de fait qui la rend seconde par rapport à un texte remier qui en est la source profonde, la matrice.... L'on attend de cet autre texte, qu'il demeure en tout point, en toute mesure, conforme, fidèle à celui qui l'a inauguré et qui a fondé son désir et son mouvement d'écriture. (235)[3]

Adaptations were constantly pitted against this 'matrix', this source text, and discussed not in terms of their creative value, but in terms of their faithfulness or narrative similarity to the source text: the adaptation was tagged as 'successful' if it remained faithful, or as 'unsuccessful' if it had veered away from the original narrative (Samson 15–16).

However, adaptation studies has recently opened up this binary base in favour of a real, dynamic interrelationship between the source text, the adaptation and other possible productive influences. Adapting a text into another medium, for instance a novel into graphic works of art, as in the case of *Frankenstein*, has led to questioning the uniqueness of each work/medium. Adaptations illustrate the fact that genres and media are not cordoned off from each other but, rather, interact in potentially productive ways. This is what Thierry Groensteen calls 'la transécriture' (transwriting) or 'la transmédiatisation' (transmedia) (275). For Groensteen, translating a text from one medium into another is no longer about faithfulness to the original, but about a whole series of transformations:

> L'adaptation est, au sens strict, la reincarnation d'une oeuvre OE1 [l'oeuvre originale] dans un média différent de celui qui servait originellement de support. Cette 'transmédiatisation' … ne peut toutefois s'effectuer sans que les autres déterminés de OE 1 en soient plus ou moins altérés. D'abord parce que changer de media équivaut, par définition, à changer de signifiants, donc de texte. C'est à ce niveau particulier que la notion de « transécriture » prend toute sa valeur. (275)[4]

In other words, Groensteen suggests that one needs to take into account the specificity, the conventions, the characteristics and modal constituents of each medium. Adapters choose in the precursor text 'the various meanings and sensations they find most compelling' and adapt those chosen sensations to their new creative text (Albrecht-Crane and Cutchins 16). In this sense adaptations/appropriations are best considered as 'responses to other texts that form a necessary step in the process of understanding' (17); they may be understood as interpretations, 'readings', or 'paths' that adaptors chose to develop.

Transposing a text into another medium also necessarily involves changing the discourse of the source text. Groensteen explains that a specific form of discourse is attached to each medium. 'Each media', he writes, 'involves a different organisation of discourse, whereby the content cannot go untouched' (275). This change in discourse also derives from the audience's expectations of a particular medium. Readers of *Frankenstein*, the novel, and *Frankenstein*, the graphic novel, will have different expectations in terms of discourse organisation. Also, as Groensteen further argues, adaptations can be strongly influenced by other adaptations of the same work. He writes, 'L'adaptation d'un roman pourra ainsi emprunter des éléments à la correspondence ou la biographie de son auteur. Elle pourra aussi tenir compte d'adaptations ou d'illustrations que ce texte a déjà suscitées antérieurement' (277).[5] He suggests that we must study the meanings and sensations which artists have chosen to reconfigure, as well as the intertextual forces at play.

Central to the works under consideration, and certainly one of the sensations the artists in question have chosen to adapt, is the concept of the abject. Abjection was defined by Julia Kristeva in her ground-breaking *Powers of Horror*, which addresses the role of abjection. The abject is defined by Kristeva as follows:

> There looms, within abjection, one of those violent dark revolts of being, directed against a threat that seems to emanate from an exorbitant outside or inside, ejected beyond the scope of the possible, the tolerable, the thinkable. It lies there quite close, but it cannot be assimilated. It beseeches, worries and fascinates desire, which, nevertheless, does not let itself be seduced. (2)

Abjection, as Kristeva argues, is a vital and determinative process in the function of the subject. On a psychological level, the experience of the abject is 'a threat' (2) to the individual. The abject, by definition, threatens the boundaries of the self, and is, by its essence, unassimilable and therefore inherently disruptive. It cannot, however, be objectified. This is one of the unrelenting features of the abject as identified by Kristeva: it is not a subject, nor is it an object, but it displays features of both. As Rina Arya explains in her book *Abjection and Representation*, 'it exists between these two states, where it cannot be discretely separated from the subject and where it lurks object-like but without becoming an object' (4). The abject hovers at the boundary of 'the possible, the tolerable, the thinkable', (Kristeva 1) but is itself unassimilable, which means that we have to contemplate its otherness in its proximity to us, although we cannot completely understand it. It is, in fact, the other that comes from within that we have to reject and expel in order to protect our boundaries. The inability to separate entirely the abject from the self, or to objectify the abject, contributes to the complex relationship we have with it. It 'beseeches, worries and fascinates desire', Kristeva tells us (1), and we are both repelled by the abject because of fear and yet attracted to it through our desire.

Perhaps the single object most closely associated with the abject is the corpse, and the tension between desire for and rejection of the abject corpse/body is precisely what is at the heart of Shelley's *Frankenstein*. First drawn to his Creature for its beauty in Shelley's novel, Victor is almost immediately overwhelmed by abjection and ultimately rejects his own creation because it 'beseeches, worries and fascinates desire, which, nevertheless, does not let itself be seduced. Apprehensive, desire turns aside, sickened it rejects' (Kristeva 1). The Creature Frankenstein creates pushes the boundaries between life and death, fragmentation and unity, self and other.

Piecing together cultural myths and images: Mousse's Gothic expressionism

One way of representing or conveying the abject has been the depiction of fear in those experiencing it. Fear is the very natural consequence of the abject moment of existential disruption. As Arya notes in her study of *Abjection and Representation*, 'We turn away from something that causes disgust because we do not want to be in contact with it; we fear it and it is perceived to be dangerous because of its powers to contaminate or pollute by contact or ingestion' (38–39). Abjection, 'unlike disgust, involves fear because of the threat to the sense of self' (38). Marion Mousse's Frankenstein *de Mary Shelley*, an illustrated story in three volumes, enacts the threat to the reader's self-integrity. Diegetic emphasis is laid on fear via doubles, surprise, suspense, madness, and the breakdown of the body, and these elements are conveyed through the use of dark Gothic expressionism and black-and-white angular shadows.

Mousse's Frankenstein *de Mary Shelley* opens with the image of boats trapped in the frozen water of the Arctic Circle. Walton and his crew, hoping to achieve their

dream of discovering a secret path to the North Pole, wait patiently for a thaw. The
sailors, instead, rescue the desperate Victor Frankenstein, compared by Walton to
Coleridge's Ancient Mariner whose fate it was to roam the earth as punishment for
shooting the albatross. In Mousse's highly intertextual adaptation, Walton repeatedly
recurs as a character at transition points in the narrative, reminding the reader that
the story is ultimately Walton's. While the three volumes of Frankenstein *de Mary
Shelley*[6] are, plot-wise, close to Shelley's text, Mousse's text also includes numerous
popular, iconic, cultural, and historical references. In an interview, the French artist
explains that although his adaptation references the historical contexts of the novel,
he 'was more interested in the way a new era looked at religion and the place of man
in nature: in other words, … was more interested in Victor's torment than in his
creature'[7] (Mousse, 'Rencontre', our translation). In many ways, Mousse played the
role of Victor Frankenstein or Mary Shelley as he pieced together his various readings
into a single text.

Mousse emphasises the historical context of *Frankenstein* through the use of cir-
cumlocutions, or anticipatory 'mini-episodes' that are not found in Shelley's text.
These give substance and context to the politics and belief system of the nineteenth
century. In one episode, as the reader gets to know the young Victor, Frankenstein's
mother discusses the secrets of creation with the local priest, thereby emphasising
the religious system in place in the nineteenth century. This episode, which is not in
Shelley's novel, makes Victor's challenging act of creation all the more transgressive.
Another mini-episode features a young Victor Frankenstein and his friend, here called
Henry Chevalier (Clerval in Shelley's text), playing at being knights fighting each other
(Vol. 1, 19). Henry crushes a snail, an act that disgusts Victor and foreshadows the
paradoxes of his creation, which involves recreating life but also toying with it. In this
anticipatory scene, Victor emerges as the benevolent one who is shocked and angry
at his friend's behaviour against nature, and yet he is later the one who will subvert
nature's rules.

Mousse's style is close to German expressionistic woodcuts, which themselves
engage with the Gothic. His illustrations stress angular lines and a dark atmosphere
that reveal the obscure side of Victor's experiment and the tormented minds of both
Victor and his Creature. As the author comments in an interview,

> pour moi 'Frankenstein' c'est Victor, le créateur, ses affres, ses affects, tous très sombres
> et désespérés. Je voulais une ambiance sombre donc, mais plus encore lourde et étouf-
> fante pour exprimer le côté inéluctable et oppressant de la folie dans laquelle le héros ne
> peut plus éviter une fois 'l'expérience réussie'. Le noir cache tout. Il est le mystère fait
> forme, on peut tout y mettre, le lecteur tout imaginer.[8] (Phibes)

Visually speaking, Mousse draws the characters with sharp lines that delineate their
faces. In some cases he creates characters who change and develop from the innocent,
happy-go-lucky people they were to the tormented, dramatic, alienated figures they
become. Their faces, and especially their eyes, at first reflect a sense of innocence

and kindness that radically contrasts with the dark colour that surrounds them. This darkness emphasises the obscure and tormented side of both Victor and his Creature. Mousse confides that he was drawn to Shelley's tale because there was no real adaptation that was faithful to the original in the sense that it told the story of the creator facing a changing world (Phibes). Mousse also makes use of the expressive possibilities of angular lines, sharp-pointed forms, and contrasting patches of black and white to convey fear and anxiety as well as mental and ethical agitation.

Mousse's version reveals itself to be a complex intermedial cultural text that reshapes and adapts various media, reinforcing a déjà-vu experience for readers, and echoing the doubles central to the diegesis. Mousse enmeshes in the text the ways in which popular culture has appropriated the figure of the Creature, which has had a long life of its own. Whale's influence clearly operates at the visual level in Mousse's work, but also on the diegetical level. Volume II, for instance, reframes the controversial film scene wherein the Creature throws the young Maria into the lake, a scene which is absent from Shelley's text and which was censored when the Whale film was released in 1931. Mousse inserts this scene just after an episode in which the Creature witnesses Felix and Agatha bathing and playing in the river. This creates a certain echo between the two scenes and reveals a desire on the part of the Creature to experience a similar bonding. As figures 16.1 and 16.2 illustrate, the Maria scene blends the two versions of the Creature: on the one hand we see Whale's naive monster with his innocent eyes, and on the other hand, the vengeful, tormented, greenish Creature from later in the novel which echoes the popular comic-book image of Marvel's Hulk (Figures 16.1 and 16.2).

Mousse's work also enters into dialogue with other cultural intertexts like canonical forms of painting, appropriating famous Romantic artists to establish graphic and diegetic intertextual connections. In Volume III, page 14, the reader will easily recognise Caspar Friedrich's 'Wanderer above the Sea of Fog' (1818), a painting that conveys both the pride of Romantic imagination and the feeling of insignificance of the individual (Figure 16.3). Victor is depicted looking at the valley in the fog. Yet the following eight vignettes present him in several positions that convey his deep torment. Victor cries in at least one of them, and two depict a landscape without him. The final image in this series depicts Victor from a bird's-eye point of view, apparently sobbing. Although Mousse's work does not engage with the abject experience per se, it points to the potential of BD to mediate intervisuality and create a sense of fear in the face of latent abjection.

Stitching the abject in deformed lines: Baladi's *Frankenstein Encore et Toujours*

The next two sections scrutinise the ways in which two other graphic novels, beyond exploring the signification possibilities of the Frankenstein myth, use the capabilities of the visual and of comics sequences, and more specifically texture and lines, to further

Figures 16.1 and 16.2 The two sides of Frankenstein's Creation, Mousse, Vol. II, 31.

Figure 16.3 Victor in a fog both physically and psychically, Mousse, Vol. III, 14.

complicate the singular system of graphic signification. In many ways and in many adaptations the Creature's deeds become abject and disgusting, particularly when he transgresses moral codes and starts killing. Deprez's and Baladi's works radically break away from this fear-oriented representation of the abject. They experiment with texture, deformity, liquidity, and graphic silence to unveil *Frankenstein*'s core abject affect, which is firmly rooted in the corporeal. These two graphic creations belong to the new wave of French-speaking BD published by Francophone independent collectives (Dozo and Preyat 13). Of note is the fact that Denis Deprez belongs to the Fréon group created in the 1990s (Baetens 98), a group that represents a typical avantgarde stance within the field of the graphic novel, combining technical and formal experiments, a hands-on and do-it-yourself approach to editing, and a clear political and artistic commitment. These collectives made the conscious decision to dissociate themselves from mainstream publishers, whose concern is more with economic viability than with artistic freedom and who therefore tend toward the reproduction of stereotypically comic materials and young male fantasies (Dozo and Preyat 13).

In Baladi's *Frankenstein, Encore et Toujours*, which is set in contemporary Ingolstadt, the monster becomes a catalyst for the traumatic memories of two young girls, isolated and lost in a dark and empty city where they discover an old copy of Shelley's novel and ultimately identify with her Creature. The tone of the monochrome graphic novel is introspective and deals predominantly with the psychological state of these two young girls, lost in an empty, urban landscape. Far from scientific experiments or the question of the ethical responsibility of the creator, here the Frankenstein narrative is reduced to the solitary figure of the Creature struggling for social integration. As the title *Frankenstein, Encore et Toujours* (*Frankenstein Again and Again*[9]) reveals, Baladi underscores the persistence and cultural recycling of themes introduced by Mary Shelley in *Frankenstein*. Baladi's text also stresses the contemporary appeal of the tale, since the main character so closely identifies with the Creature.

The text opens up on the image of a pile of trash left on the side of the road, and the next page illustrates the new, recycled lives of these objects. The next panels introduce the two protagonists, young women, aimlessly walking the city's bare streets one afternoon. Eva and her friend, who is portentously unnamed, chance upon a cardboard box at the foot of an apartment building, the detritus of a move. The box contains a dog-eared copy of *Frankenstein* with handwritten notes throughout the margins. As Eva peruses its pages, her room-mate becomes frozen in puzzled shock, merely from having recognised the book's title. This first step into the graphic novel highlights the meta-narrative nature of Baladi's adaptation: a canonical text of English literature can, just like the other objects in the trash, have another life and be adapted to new contexts. The book the two girls discover is itself a palimpsest and a montage of memories, notes, photographs, and bits and pieces.

The two protagonists grab the book and start discussing its meaning. Eva's friend reveals her interpretations of the injustices at the heart of the novel, including the story of Safie, the young Arab woman. Baladi's version allows the young woman to tell her own version of the story, unveiling the text's metafictional adaptation approach. Within this *mise-en-abîme*, Baladi's characters slowly come to identify with the Creature, who seems to visually resemble both the stitched-together social environments in which they live as well as their own exaggerated and deformed bodies. Eva, for instance, has a bigger nose than most of the other characters, as well as a lanky, awkward frame (Figure 16.4). She says she has no friends, and is unemployed and chronically depressed. This stitch motif is also found in the objects that surround the two women, a physical characteristic that highlights the social and psychological instability of the protagonists.

Eva's nameless room-mate appears to be 'normal', and the reader may commend her at first for befriending poor, unappealing/unattractive Eva. But, as the novel unfolds, the reader learns that she is even more damaged than Eva. The figure of the Creature, with its deformed face and stitches, appears in Eva's hallucinations and

Figure 16.4 Eva becomes visually identified with Frankenstein's monster from Alex Baladi's *Frankenstein, Encore et Toujours*.

provokes introspection and, ultimately, darkly existential self-discovery. Part of this discovery involves an inner journey that occurs mostly in dreamtime, but the characters also experience a waking nightmare that finds reality decaying at every turn. The protagonists may be doomed to lives of wretched loneliness, their stories broken into pieces, their identities fragmented.

For both these girls, the Creature acts as a catalyst for the expression and confession of their self-disgust, solitude or trauma. As Eva's unnamed room-mate tries to decipher the marginal notes in the book, she comes to believe that they reveal a horrifying truth about why her ex-boyfriend, an artist and undocumented immigrant, has disappeared. Eva, on the other hand, speaks with the Creature, confessing her lack of emotions and her fear of nothingness, visually evoked in a dark panel. It is the Creature, in fact, who confronts both girls with their own internal turmoil and helps them to act on it. The Creature is here portrayed as a benevolent being that helps them to approach their own personal alienation; the real monster in this text is the (sub)urban milieu that isolates and alienates. Baladi reveals a city that is as bare as the lives of the two lonely women who live in it. Eva wants to blame the city for the disconnection that she, the Creature, and her room-mate feel. Again, black-and-white expressionism pinpoints a deep anxiety and a world where every person is dehumanised. Eva wonders why she stays in the city and decides to leave, but the last panel portrays her paralysed in place, looking at the city's river. She recognises that her room-mate will not leave either.

Eva's friend fears an even more traumatic downfall, a repetition of the collapse she experienced some years earlier. We discover that she had a nervous breakdown that led to her self-mutilation and alienation. The young girl keeps hallucinating, imagining that her boyfriend, Michel, has been kidnaped by a Dr Frankenstein figure who has, perhaps, dismembered him, though the real Michel also appears in the text. He seems to be with friends, ignoring her and considering her mad. The Creature works as a catalyst that brings this repressed trauma to the fore. Eventually readers are confronted with an image of the nameless room-mate that reveals her deep, emotional wounds, as well as her constant fear of her own abject self (Figure 16.5). The inside of her body, its texture and liquids, are brought outside, leaking or liquefying into pus or sweat. The girl ultimately becomes a monster for the others in the narrative, and probably for herself as well.

Despite the fact that the storylines of the two women diverge early and are radically different, neither gets a happy ending. This is a tale of patchwork people, the stitches of their emotional scars the only things left holding them together. While one of the girls is led to explore her powerlessness to influence the direction of her life, the other delves into her deeply buried traumatic past and her abandonment four years earlier by her boyfriend. Baladi's text offers no answers to the problems these young women are forced to face, but he foregrounds the dangers of social and self-abjection. Indeed, this graphic novel exposes the idea that there may be no cure for loneliness. Mary Shelley's *Frankenstein* is rewritten by Baladi as a critique of modern ostracism, a function of the disconnection between people in an increasingly schizophrenic age. Far from a

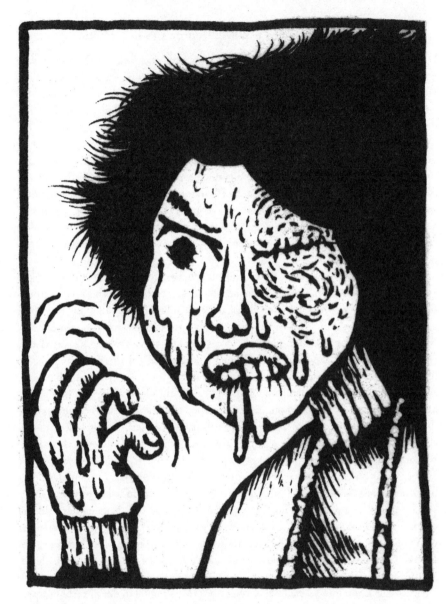

Figure 16.5 The shocking reveal of the nameless room-mate's physical and emotional wounds from Alex Baladi's *Frankenstein, Encore et Toujours*.

philosophical tale of scientific experiment and irresponsibility, Baladi's adaptation uses the Creature figure as a metaphor for this tormenting solitude that is made visible in the corporeal deformed lines of the black-and-white expressionist panels that convey both emptiness and deep anxiety.

Flesh and coloured texture: Deprez's *FrAnKeNsTein*

Deprez's *FrAnKeNsTein*, unlike Baladi's work, returns the focus of the text to the Creature and his creator. The artistic cover of *FrAnKeNsTein* presents a ghostly, skeletal, Karloff-like face that epitomises two important aspects of his work, namely the fact that it brings together styles and experiments in drawing and that these drawings delve deeply into the terrifying, abject aspects of Shelley's text. Even the title of the piece visually conveys in its shape and mixture of letters the monstrous, composite, destructured nature of the Creature/adaptation. Far from the image of the mad scientist in his high-tech laboratory, Deprez's graphic representation opens with Walton's story but quickly moves to Frankenstein's laboratory on a stormy night. The gradual zoom-in and the steady intensity of the red colour of the panels draw the reader into Victor Frankenstein's lab, which is nothing but a timber-framed house. The reddish colour used throughout the creation scene already hints at a kind of danger zone, an uneasy place of madness.

Central to Deprez's work is the resemblance between the eyes of Victor and the eyes of the Creature, which suggests inalienable ties. The first two rectangular panels of the creation scene show a Victor full of pride, standing up, deciding the fate of his as yet inanimate creation. These images indicate Victor's power over his Creature. His words, 'Un puissant flux va inonder tes chairs froides et ténébreuses. Tu vas vivre!' (A powerful current is going to flood your cold and dark flesh. You are going to live!) illustrate Deprez's elliptic rewriting of Shelley's text (11). The reddish colour, reminiscent of fire stolen from the gods, and used throughout the creation scene, hints at the madness and uneasiness of the scene, and culminates when the eyes of the Creature and the creator meet. The fourth panel is larger, and includes the two characters, Victor Frankenstein and the Creature, both with yellow eyes. This visual similarity exposes the two protagonists' uncanny doubleness, and seems to counter Slavoj Žižek's observations that Shelley's monster's 'Nontransparent', 'depthless' eyes block our access to the 'soul', to the infinite abyss of the 'person', thus turning it into a soulless monster: not simply a non-subjective machine but, rather, an uncanny subject that has not yet submitted to the process of 'subjectivization' which confers upon it the depth of 'personality' (240). The eyes drawn by Deprez, on the other hand, suggest not the Creature's uncanniness, but its similarity to Victor. The next panels depict Victor waking up after a long, nervous sleep. The focus is on his own fearful eyes again. He leaves his laboratory exclaiming 'those eyes' (16), alluding to this disturbing aspect of the Creature.

Deprez's *FrAnKeNsTein* delves into the intimate maze of a creature and its creator, both in pain. This pain is rendered graphically through the use of layers of colour and distorted figures. Doubleness, repetition, visual silence, images of death, and ghostly figures are used to convey the instability of the experience of both the Creature and its creator. But the abject is also suggested by the form, colour, and textures of the paintings. As Jan Baetens writes, 'Le glissement de l'action à la couleur: le sens des images

dépend moins de ce qui est représenté que de la tonalité chromatique: la métamor-
phose des couleurs dominantes, débarrassées de leurs valeurs réalistes ou symboliques
conventionnelles, suscitent un rythme formel'[10] (Baetens *Othello*). Deprez's characters
speak with a poetic and elliptic language but his Creature also communicates mostly via
the expressionistic metamorphosis of its colour texture that expresses the Creature's
in-betweenness.

The real force of Deprez's work is in his deeply intertextual/intervisual experimentation. Many of his vignettes remind the reader of the raw imagery of Francis Bacon
or Edvard Munch, Ernst Kirchner's abstract expressionism, Mark Rothko's multiform
paintings, and John Constable and Claude Monet's colourful knife-painting. Deprez's
art enters a world that is not only personal, inward looking, and deeply intimate, but
that exposes the abject, the sense of strangeness/déjà-vu at the heart of *Frankenstein*,
not only at the diegetic level but in its visual materiality which generates disgust and
instability in the reader. More specifically, he makes use of colour texture and layers
to carry layers of existential angst. These fuzzy colour blendings ultimately expose
the instability of borders of body-abjection. The very cover of the piece and vignettes
depicting Victor are cases in point. The face of the Creature is presented as a half-dead,
half-present, half-skeleton, half-flesh Karloff-like ghost emerging from an abyss of
darkness and emptiness (Figures 16.6 and 16.7). The movement of the painting knife
suggests an act of body sculpting and shaping while evoking deletion and erasure.
Deprez's Creature remains wraithlike and incomplete, qualities that accentuate its
abject nature. The novel's cover conveys layers of life and death, pleasure and pain,
superimposed to convey the protean effect engendered by the experience of abjection.
One must here emphasise how the corpse, as described by Kristeva, 'is the utmost of
abjection. It is death infecting life. It is something rejected from which one does not
part, from which one does not protect oneself as from an object' (*Powers* 4). Linked
with the violation of moral codes such as purity, the body of the Creature remains here
visually in between living flesh and corpse.

While the creation scene analysed above is still rather figurative in essence, the
Creature's personal story is rendered using a more abstract style of drawing. Action-
based panels are replaced by understated, silent, emotion-focused representations of
the Creature/creator. The viewer's introspective, intimate graphic journey into the
Creature's experience starts with a graphic representation of the Creature reminiscent
of Rothko's signature style, the multiform, in which blurred blocks of various colours,
devoid of landscape or of human life, seem to possess their own life force. Deprez's
multiform in *FrAnKeNsTein*, in contrast to Rothko, makes use of a human shape in the
background: Deprez fuses together Rothko's design for the multiform and merges it
with Frankenstein's Creature, so as to create this lasting image of the Creature with
a red hue, red being, in Rothko's world, a colour symbolising energy and ecstasy.
Drama is found in the contrast of colours and thickness radiating against one another.
The creation act central to Shelley's text is here in a constant *mise-en-abîme* because of
the way the thickness of the colours is constantly moulded to convey the disruption of

Figures 16.6 and 16.7 Denis Deprez's impressionistic Frankenstein monster à la Boris Karloff from *FrAnKeNsTein*, Éditions Casterman, 2003. © Casterman. Reproduced by kind permission of the authors and Éditions Casterman.

boundaries between body and emptiness, between creator and creature. Deprez also establishes a tension between the expressionistic images analysed above and several impressionistic illustrations that are often used to portray Frankenstein's brother William and a happy Romantic age that is over. The intervisuality of Deprez's work is dense, as most vignettes refer to other paintings, other artistic styles, and other filmic productions, including Victor Erice's *The Spirit of the Beehive* (1973), a Spanish film in which a young girl is obsessed with the figure of Frankenstein's Creature. The clay house from that film is found in several of Deprez's panels. Read closely, Deprez's *FrAnKeNsTein* is itself a most composite and disjointed piece.

Deprez's piece moves away from moral codes of responsibility found in Mousse's or Baladi's adaptations. For Deprez both Creature and creator suffer and reflect each other's anger in an intimate relationship close to a Jekyll and Hyde doubleness. The Creature is presented as a more full-fleshed man with a crooked grin who identifies with Satan (48–49) or the beast of the Apocalypse. The panels depicting the Creature become thick with paint, showing the layers of fingerprints they are made of. This technique gives flesh and presence to the Creature that becomes alive and malignant, yet never quite complete. Deprez improvises visually, alluding to a Creature that is escaping his creator, the drawing taking on a life and orientation of its own. When the Creature is rejected from the De Lacey cottage after a discussion with the blind man, he is portrayed as being chased by huge dogs in a reddish darkness (39–40). As he screams in defence, he is turned into a beast himself with the jaw of the dogs that had hunted him. It is the image, its shapes, and colours that further build the diegesis. In a departure from Shelley's novel, Deprez's text ends with Walton continuing his trip North ('Dear Margaret, We're still heading North'), turning a blind eye to Victor Frankenstein's cautionary tale.

The visually abject plays a significant role in Deprez's illustrations. Deprez visually dissects the corpses retrieved from the cemetery, opened up by Victor as he creates the Creature's mate, and this evisceration creates an instance of attractive aversion. The inside parts of the body are made visible, as in the depiction of the skin of the abdomen being stitched together (42–43). Other scenes reinforce this abjectness. Red paint resembling blood, for instance, is visually spilled over the vignette in the episode in which the Creature strangles Elisabeth. The abject experience is not only depicted in its consequences and circumstances, it is also conveyed by the form of the medium and is designed to affect the audience by moving beyond representational limits. Deprez manages to convey the very abjection of the body experience thanks to his constant avoidance of colour limits, its transgression of body margins that cause repulsion and disruption (Figure 16.8).

Deprez's and Baladi's works go further in experimenting with the visual, rephrasing the textual, and confirming a creative work where 'the image resists its traditionally inferior position' (Baetens 'Of Graphic Novels' 115). Several panels focus on body parts to convey body trauma and disorientation, often via texture, blood, tears, bodily wastes, fluidity, and gender ambiguity. The images are not so much of the dejected,

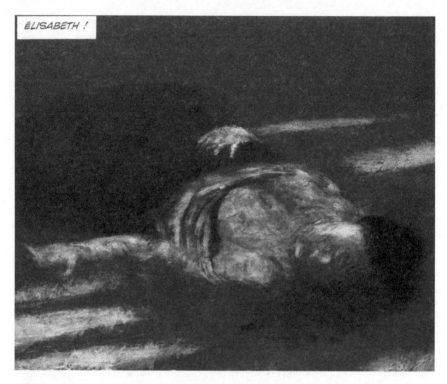

Figure 16.8 Deprez suggests the abjectness of the bloody body of the murdered Elisabeth from *FrAnKeNsTein*, Éditions Casterman, 2003. © Casterman. Reproduced by kind permission of the authors and Éditions Casterman.

pieced-together stranger, but of a wounded, disfigured, lonely woman or man, whose external scars mirror internal torments. Both texts can be examined in the light of Lennard J. Davis's essay, 'Visualizing the Disabled Body: The Classical Nude and the Fragmented Torso', which emphasises that the Creature's 'body is a zone of repulsion' (2414) wherein 'the disruption of the skin's surface immediately translates into a threat of touching, of being touched' (2415) and engendering repulsion, fear, and attraction. The Creature's body in Baladi's work is disabled and abject for both the narrator, who cannot stand her own body, and the reader, who is confronted, via the compelling visual, with this sense of the abject conveyed by disproportion, scars, deformity, and, often, incompleteness. Baladi's protagonist's repulsion and self-loathing is bodily present in her mutilated eye, which she hides behind a lock of her hair until it is revealed at the end. The mirror image she receives is one of a gruesome skeletal Creature made of bones, stitches, and scars; a victim, rather than an evil presence. And Baladi's Creature, in turn, becomes a traumatised yet tender victim with whom the protagonist identifies.

Deprez's depiction of the abject is quite different. Deprez challenges the repression of materiality on the part of Victor himself, who fears his own senses and falls ill and ghostly once he is threatened. Baladi's work takes the point of view of the Creature who, in Shelley's original, wakes up to his senses and materiality, but here denies and mutilates this corporeal function. Baladi's approach conveys abjection in black and white, using deformed lines and profound emptiness, while Deprez's panels convey an equal sense of abjection with colour, texture, and layers of paint. The monochromatic nature of Baladi's artwork stresses the depth and reality of marginalisation. This technique resembles the work of Marjane Satrapi in which, according to Chute, 'The visual emptiness of the simple, ungraded blackness in the frames shows not the scarcity of memory, but rather its thickness, its depth; the "vacancy" represents the practice of memory, for the author and possibly for the reader' (144). In the case of both Baladi and Deprez the visual breaks away from text to communicate a sense of abjection with images, an alteration which reflects the work's weaving together of the process of memory and disjuncture.

Composite comics approaches: framing the unframable abject

Mary Shelley's Creature is made of parts of corpses, a composite image which is reproduced at the formal level since Shelley's *Frankenstein* is made out of numerous literary, philosophical, artistic, and political references. In many ways, both the Creature and the text in which it is represented exemplify the very act of adapting, of creating new texts/bodies with older/other parts. The texts analysed above make use of this dialectic and expand on the composite nature of literature and the potential of intermediality to embrace transtemporality. The déjà-vu experience made possible via the numerous intertextual references enhances the uncanny experience of the reader. In many ways, the composite nature of comics, made out of panels, pages, vignettes, and intertexts most perceptibly echoes the paradigm of the composite.

However, the abject never disappears. Both Baladi's and Deprez's unsettling aesthetic and material approaches use the visual and the materiality of lines and painting to convey the abject, the sense of instability. Both authors understand this and arguably intensify the sophistication of texture to impact on the body of the audience. The use of layers of colour or the deformity of the black-and-white shapes gives a corporeal materiality to the abject which is in itself primarily physical and hardly possible in words. If Mary Shelley's text was apt to convey things with words, the graphic novel suggests in very few sequences the very central abjection linked with the scary experience of the famous Creature–creator encounter. In many ways, it reasserts the power of the visual that is central to graphic novels.

Although the abject remains outside of the boundaries of the aesthetic and/or cultural per se, the experimentation of Baladi and Deprez challenges this unrepresentability. Despite the potential dangers of such an engagement with the audience's affect, the work of these artists manages to convey the abject, which, despite its actual unrepresentablility, can only be experienced with the senses and corporeality. Yet, as Hal Foster asked, 'Can the abject be represented at all? If it is opposed *to* culture, can it be exposed *in* culture? If it is unconscious, can it [be] made conscious and remain abject?' (114). Foster situates the interest in trauma and the abject, popular in the 1990s, as a reaction against consumerism and as an attempt to reclaim the body from the age of the digital, but his observations may also apply to Mary Shelley's novel. The texts analysed here emphasise the corporeal and the abject nature of birth/separation, an experience which links these texts to the Frankenstein Network.

   Frankenstein is not only a story of the social ostracism of a Creature who is repulsive, as it has often been interpreted. In the eyes of twenty-first-century readers, *Frankenstein* and its adaptations can be stories of 'meeting your meat', as Paul Outka puts it, of the encounter with organicity (40). The creative works analysed above expose the psychological, cultural, and corporeal experience of abjection. The graphic renderings in these novels highlight the experience of abjection and materially echo Outka's analysis of the organic sublime in *Frankenstein*, the unsettling awareness of one's materiality, which in Shelley's novel 'supplants the romantic sublime' (20) and which is increasingly present in our posthuman society. As Outka further points out, 'the organic sublime, as exemplified in the creature, resolves that instability by collapsing the human and the natural into each other, in both the literal and metaphorical sense, of a larger material field' (21). More than in Shelley's text, this collapse is central to Deprez's work, taking place, as it does, not in the sublime landscapes of the Alps but mostly on the beaches of a Leon Spilliaert painting. It is this materiality of a post-human and post-natural world that Baladi and Deprez are ultimately pointing to. Their works address the instability of borders not only in the relationship between creator and Creature, but more largely between human, animal, and post-human.

Notes

1 See Jed Mercurio's *Frankenstein* (2007), in which a female doctor, Victoria, works on an advanced stem cell research project.
2 In the French-speaking context, the term 'bande dessinée' (BD) is used as an umbrella term. The term 'comics', mostly associated with the anglophone world, is often used with superheroes. 'Graphic novel' is used to distinguish more serious works aimed at adults. In this chapter we use BD and graphic novel interchangeably to refer to a corpus that belongs to both traditions.
3 A graphic adaptation 'may well bring with it a sense of plenitude, the fact remains that it can never be unique; that is to say move beyond its status as second compared to the first text that is its original source, its matrix. The second text is naturally expected to be faithful in every way to the one that preceded it and which founded the desire to read and to be written in the first place'. (Our translation)
4 Adaptations are, strictly speaking, the reincarnation of the original work into a different media. This 'transmediatisation' cannot be done without alterations to the precursor text. Because changing media implies changing the signifier and, by extension, the text, it is at this particular level that the notion of 'transwriting' takes all its value. (Our translation)
5 The adaptation of a novel can borrow elements from the author's correspondence or

biography. It can also be influenced by previous adaptations or other illustrations of the text. (Our translation)

6 Mousse's title is a clear echo of Kenneth Branagh's *Mary Shelley's* Frankenstein (1994). In that film the title reconnects the film with Shelley's novel, but the film involves a complete rewriting of the narrative.

7 'Mais c'est davantage le regard d'une époque nouvelle sur la religion et la place de l'homme vis à vis de la nature qui m'intéressait: davantage les affres de Victor que de sa créature, en somme.'

8 For me Frankenstein is Victor, the creator, his torment, his emotions, all very dark and desperate. I wanted a sombre atmosphere then, but even heavier and more stifling to express the inevitable and oppressive side of the madness he cannot escape from once 'the experiment has succeeded'. Blackness hides everything. It is mystery made visible in which one can see everything, in which the reader can imagine anything. (Phibes, our translation)

9 The title for the English language version of this graphic novel is *Frankenstein Now and Forever*.

10 The shift from action to colour: the meaning of the images depends less on what is represented than the chromatic tonality: the metamorphosis of dominant colours, stripped of their realist meanings or conventional symbolic meaning, convey a formal rhythm.

Bibliography

Albrecht-Crane, Christa, and Dennis Ray Cutchins, eds. *Adaptation Studies: New Approaches*. Madison, NJ: Fairleigh Dickinson UP, 2010.

Amano, Jeff, Craig Rousseau, Wayne Faucher, Giulia Brusco, Kristyn Ferretti. *The Cobler's Monster: A Tale of Gepetto's Frankenstein*. Berkeley: Image Comics, 2006.

Arya, Rina. *Abjection and Representation: An Exploration of Abjection in the Visual Arts, Film and Literature*. New York: Springer, 2014.

Baetens, Jan. 'Denis Deprez, *Othello*,' Ed. Casterman, coll. *Un Monde*. www.vlrom.be/pdf/044baetens.pdf.

————. *Formes et politique de la bande dessinée*. Leuven: Peeters Publishers, 1998. 132.

————. 'Graphic Novels: Literature without Text?' *English Language Notes*, 46.2 (2008): 77–88.

————. 'Littérature et bande dessinée. Enjeux et limites.' *Cahiers de Narratologie*16.[online] 25 May 2009. http://narratologie.revues.org/974 (accessed 22 July 2014).

————. 'Of Graphic Novels and Minor Cultures: The Fréon Collective.' Yale French Studies 114, *Writing and the Image Today* (2008): 95–115.

————. 'Olivier Deprez et les frontières de la bande dessinée.' *Relief* (2014), 2.3, 381–397.

Baladi, Alex. *Frankenstein, Encore et Toujours*. Atrabile, 2001.

Baldick, Chris G. *In Frankenstein's Shadow: Myth, Monstrosity, and Nineteenth-Century Writing*. Oxford UP, 1990.

Bryant, Clive, ed. *Frankenstein, The Graphic Novel*. Towcester: Classical Comics, 2008.

Chute, Hillary. *Graphic Women: Life Narrative and Contemporary Comics*. New York: Columbia University Press, 2010.

Davis, Lennard J. 'Visualizing the Disabled Body: The Classical Nude and the Fragmented Torso.' *Enforcing Normalcy: Disability, Deafness, and the Body* 1st Edition (US, 1995) reproduced in *The Norton Anthology of Theory and Criticism*. Ed. Vincent B. Leitch. New York, 2001, 2393–2421.

Deprez, Denis. *FrAnKeNsTein*. Tournai, Belgium: Casterman, 2003.

———. Interview. *Khimaira World*. 1 July 2003.www.khimairaworld.com/frankenstein-par-denis-deprez/.

Dozo, Björn-Olav and Fabrice Preyat. La bande dessinée francophone belge au present, la bande dessinée contemporaine. Dossier dirigé par Björn-Olav Dozo and Fabrice Preyat, le cri, textyles no 36–37, *revue des lettres belges de langue française*. 36–37 (June 2010): 2–42.

Duncan, Randy. 'Image Functions: Shape and Color as Hermeneutic Images in Asterios Polyp.' Ed. Matthew J. Smith and Randy Duncan. *Critical Approaches to Comics: Theories and Methods*. New York: Routledge, 2012. 43–55.

Eisner, Will. *Comics and Sequential Art*. Tamarac, FL: Poorhouse Press, 1985.

Foster, Hal. 'Obscene, Abject, Traumatic.' *October* 78 (1996): 106–124.

Gaudreault, André and Philippe Marion. 'Transécriture et Médiatique Narrative: L'enjeu de l'intermédialité.' *La Transécriture: Pour une Théorie de l'adaptation. Littérature, cinéma, bande Dessinée, théâtre, clip*. Ed. André Gaudreault and Thierry Groensteen, Québec: Editions Nota bene, 1998. 31–52.

Groensteen, Thierry. 'Tentative de recapitulation reisonnee', *La Transécriture: Pour une Théorie de l'adaptation. Littérature, cinéma, bande Dessinée, théâtre, clip*. André Gaudreault and Thierry Groensteen, eds. Québec: Editions Nota bene, 1998.

James, Louis. *Frankenstein's Monster in Two Traditions, Frankenstein, Creation and Monstrosity*. Ed. Stephen Bann, London: Reaktion Books, 1994. 77–95.

Kristeva, Julia. *Powers of Horror: an Essay on Abjection*, New York: Columbia University Press. 1982.

Lorfèvre, Alain. '"Othello" Revu aux Couleurs de Denis Deprez.' La Libre, July 2004.

McKinney, Mark, ed. *History and Politics in French-Language Comics and Graphic Novels*. UP of Mississippi, 2011.

Mousse, Marion. Frankenstein *de Mary Shelley*. Paris: Delcourt, 2008.

———. Interview. *Scenario* April 2008. www.sceneario.com/interview/FRANKEN STEIN+par+Marion+MOUSSE_FRANK.html.

———. 'Rencontre avec Marion Mousse – Auteur de *Frankenstein*.'www.bdencre.com/2008/02/1067_rencontre-avec-marion-mousse-auteur-de-frankenstein/.

Outka, Paul. 'Posthuman/Postnatural: Ecocriticism and the Sublime in Mary Shelley's Frankenstein' *Environmental Criticism for the Twenty-First Century*. Ed. Stephanie LeMenager, Teresa Shewry, and Ken Hiltner. London: Routledge, 2011. 31–48.

Phibes. 'Frankenstein par Marion Mousse: Interview réalisée par Phibes.' April 2008. http://www.sceneario.com/interview/frankenstein-par-marion-mousse_FRANK.html (accessed January 2018).

Reed, Gary and Frazer Irving. *Mary Shelley's Frankenstein: The Graphic Novel*. Puffin Graphics. New York: Byron Preiss Visual Publications. 2005.

Rogel, Thierry. 'Sociétés et pensées.' *Sociologie des Super-Héros*. Paris: Hermann publishing, 2013.

Rushing, Janice and Thomas Frentz. 'The Frankenstein Myth in Contemporary Cinema.' *Critical Studies in Mass Communication* 6.1 (1989): 61–80.

Samson, Jacques. 'L'autre texte,' *La Transécriture: Pour une Théorie de l'adaptation. Littérature, cinéma, bande Dessinée, théâtre, clip*. Ed. André Gaudreault and Thierry Groensteen. Québec: Editions Nota bene, 1998. 233–248.

Scarry, Elaine. *The Body in Pain: The Making and Unmaking of the World*. New York: Oxford UP, 1985.

Wright, Bradford W. *Comic Book Nation: The Transformation of Youth Culture in America*, Baltimore: John Hopkins UP, 2001.

Žižek, Slavoj. *Tarrying with the Negative: Kant, Hegel, and the Critique of Ideology*. Durham, NC: Duke UP, 1993.

Part V

New media adaptations of *Frankenstein*

Assembling the body/text: *Frankenstein* in new media

Tully Barnett and Ben Kooyman

Introduction

A s the other chapters in this collection attest, the chilling tale which Mary Shelley concocted on a dark night in Switzerland in 1816 has maintained a narrative urgency through the intervening centuries, its afterlife sustained through adaptation and transformation via the dominant and/or cutting-edge technologies of each era. This long history of adaptation has continued into new media platforms, creating opportunities to consider how the themes of the novel interact with notions of hybrid textuality, new media identities, and the boundaries of the human offered by an engagement with digital frameworks for storytelling. This is in addition to the great extent to which the themes pursued in the text resonate with contemporary concerns around biotechnology, genetic modification, and the threat of a posthuman future. Shelley Jackson's CD-ROM-based multimedia work *Patchwork Girl, by Mary / Shelley and Herself* (1995), composed and published in the early days of hypertext enthusiasm, is an early new media work that grapples with Shelley's novel and its themes, while Dave Morris's highly esteemed iPad 'app' adaptation of *Frankenstein* (2012) is an example of a maturing digital media format treatment.

New media adaptations like these provide unique opportunities for generating thematic resonances between Shelley's original printed work and newer technologies of reading. Both of these texts exhibit a marked preoccupation with the material conditions of Shelley's original composition and explicitly incorporate them, whether thematically through Jackson's equation of hypertext navigation with writing and quilting, or visually through Morris's visual evocation of print literature. Moreover, Shelley's novel, the Creature at its centre, and the new media technologies that adapt it are all inherently hybrid beings, assemblages of disparate component parts linked together. In looking for material to tell old stories in new forms, Jackson and Morris see in Shelley's *Frankenstein* a narrative that is itself hybrid and speaks both thematically and materially (that is, in its format) to present concerns. Their transformations of Shelley's work thus intertwine their mediums of adaptation – reading formats that are assemblages, which destabilise the boundaries between humanity, technology, and textuality – with the story's themes and content, forging opportunities for commentary on new media itself. In addition, these texts blur traditional boundaries between the author and reader-user, often positioning the reader-user in the role of author or in disparate subject positions both empowering and disempowering, enabling not only new modes of reading but also, potentially, new reader interpretations of Shelley's canonical work. These works also offer commentary on the body and its integrity, gender, and scientific advancement. Jackson and Morris find within the formats and navigation of their works ways to dramatise these themes and situate their performed reading of the source material within a contemporary context of scientific advancement and concerns that speak to, but also depart from, those of Shelley and her contemporaries in the early nineteenth century.

Adaptation in the new media age

Stable notions of authorship, textual coherence, and the writer–reader relationship are frequently undone by adaptation, where sources of authorship multiply, texts are unbound and rebound, and writer–reader functions blur. Adaptation studies has risen to address these complexities since 2000, transcending its previous narrow focus on the fidelity or infidelity of adaptations to engage in the pragmatics and politics of the adaptation process, as advocated by various scholars in the field (Hutcheon; Kooyman; Leitch; McFarlane; Sanders). The emergence of hypertext, new media, and technologised forms of writing and reading open this discourse to even more complex considerations of authorship, intertextuality, and textuality itself. For example, hypertext – the medium to which Shelley Jackson's *Patchwork Girl* belongs – offers a completely different form of textuality to print literature and film (the two dominant media when it comes to adaptation studies), one which thoroughly disrupts perceptions of authorship, linear narrative, and textual stability applicable to those media. In 1997 George P. Landow, one of the pre-eminent hypertext scholars of the period, commented that 'hypertext blurs the boundaries between reader and writer' (4) and argued that as 'a fundamentally intertextual system, [it] has the capacity to emphasise intertextuality in a way that page-bound text in books cannot' (35). Meanwhile, app-based storytelling – the medium to which Dave Morris's app belongs – has been characterised as 'a loose conglomeration of phenomena such as the Internet, digital television, interactive multimedia, virtual reality, mobile communication, and video games' (Huhramo and Parikka 1).

These new formats alter the traditional reading experience and enable new textual possibilities which further blur the boundaries between media as well as between authors and readers. For example, the New Book Press has created a series of e-books based on Shakespeare's *Macbeth*, *A Midsummer Night's Dream* and *Romeo and Juliet* that combine play-text and performance, with one side of the screen featuring Shakespeare's script and the other featuring a recorded performance of that script by actors shot in close-ups that resemble Victorian portraiture (Brown). Such a text collapses the boundaries between media by combining play-script, video, stage performance, and electronic textuality, while it also challenges traditional understandings of authorship. The authors for one of these works could include Shakespeare, the e-book designers, the performers, and even the reader, who authors their reading experience by alternating between modes of textual transmission. Consequently, scholarship of adaptation hinging on the straightforward translation of one text into another, from one medium into another, from one author to another, proves insufficient. As noted by Michael Ryan Moore, in a discussion of how adaptation theory needs to be reconceptualised in the light of more interactive media practises, 'traditional theories of adaptation rely on the preservation of plot, characters, and themes, [but] new media protocols stress our own role in constructing media use, and therefore, in constructing a landscape for novel adaptation' (191).

In her book on adaptation, Linda Hutcheon likens the repeated adaptation and circulation of certain canonical texts to genetic evolution: 'like genes, they adapt to those new environments by virtue of mutation – in their "offspring" or their adaptations. And the fittest do more than survive; they flourish' (32). *Frankenstein*, it goes without saying, is one of these 'fittest' and has enjoyed one of the most varied and resilient cultural afterlives through multiple adaptations. Jackson's *Patchwork Girl* and Morris's *Frankenstein* contribute to the continued circulation and preservation of *Frankenstein* in contemporary culture, as well as mirror their surrounding media and cultural tides. Moreover, they exemplify the critical interests of, and provide ideal objects of analysis for, contemporary adaptation scholars. For example, Phyllis Frus and Christy Williams, among others, advocate looking at radical adaptations of texts such as these as 'transformations' rather than simply adaptations, and use the scientific analogy of 'metamorphosis' to rationalise this: 'When a caterpillar has reached maturity, it transforms into a butterfly – an entirely new form that is based on the earlier form. In literary transformations, the new texts may be based on an older one, but the reader or viewer may not recognise the connection' (3). *Patchwork Girl* is an exemplary instance of transformation, given its multi-faceted status as not simply an offshoot of Shelley's *Frankenstein* but also a rewrite, prequel, sequel, free variation, and biography. *Patchwork Girl* also supports Julie Sanders' contention that while adaptation appears outwardly to be 'an inherently conservative genre', it 'can also be oppositional, even subversive' (9). Sanders notes the 'ability of adaptation to respond or write back to an informing original from a new or revised political and cultural position' and the 'capacity of appropriations to highlight troubling gaps, absences, and silences within the canonical texts to which they refer ... giving voice to those characters or subject-positions they perceive to have been oppressed or repressed' (98). As will be discussed shortly, Jackson's hypertext engages in a gender-centric dialogue with the *Frankenstein* mythos, reinforcing Shelley as author, highlighting the aborted female Creature as character, and utilising hypertextual reading practices coded as traditionally feminine (e.g. sewing, patchworking) which are also incorporated thematically.

This hybridising of form and content also hints at the other boon that *Frankenstein*, as an archetypal text of transgressive science and commentary on scientific advancement, offers both adapters and scholars of adaptation: an opportunity to comment on the changing conditions of textuality by illuminating correspondences between technologies of reading, technologised reading, and the form and themes of Shelley's novel. The novel *Frankenstein* is, as Fred Botting has observed, an assemblage of parts: 'Fragmented, disunified, assembled from bits and pieces, the novel is like the monster itself' (*Gothic* 102). Botting's view of the original novel's material and thematic use of assemblage may also help to explain why the text continues to resurface in popular culture in multiple and dynamic ways. This correspondence between the novel's fragmented form and its own antagonist assembled from multiple parts is reflected in the themes and form of *Patchwork Girl* as well as hypertext itself. Story and medium thus complement one another and offer opportunities for commentary and critical engagement not achievable in print. And while Morris's *Frankenstein* app is superficially a less radical work than *Patchwork Girl*, it is nonetheless representative of the potential of apps to merge classical and contemporary textual forms and practices in dynamic ways.

Shelley Jackson's *Patchwork Girl* (1995)

Hypertext fiction, now more frequently called electronic literature, developed in the 1980s alongside advances in personal computer usage and software packages. The program HyperCard, appearing for the Macintosh system in the 1980s, was a programming tool that allowed users to develop hypermedia systems in the pre-World Wide Web era. HyperCard allowed users to manipulate information and incorporate graphics and other elements using clickable hyperlinks to move around a database of text. The program allowed computer users to create an interface for others to access information in a range of ways and to build interactive programs without programming knowledge or ability. Independently, a range of users saw the potential for literary and creative production in this programming tool and began generating what they called hypertext literature. Michael Joyce released *afternoon, a story* in 1987 and Stuart Moulthrop released *Victory Garden* in 1991, to name just two signature works of this medium.

Hypertextual literature uses embedded links within sections of the text, known as lexias, to create multi-linear pathways through the text. The more links within a lexia, the more potential pathways through a text, resulting in multiple different versions of a work so that, potentially, no two readings are the same and no two reading experiences are identical. At the time, theorists argued that hypertext provided a radical new experimental form of literature (Landow; Snyder; Douglas); however, these theorists also saw in this experimental fiction connections with a tradition of literature that coexisted with and predated print. For example, they identified correspondences between hypertext and the codex as a non-linear, intratextual and targeted form of reading where readers access specific parts of the text independently of its chronological assembly. Moreover, many famous works of print literature contain inherently hypertextual components, such as Laurence Sterne's *Tristram Shandy* (1759–67) and

James Joyce's *Ulysses* (1922) and *Finnegan's Wake* (1939). However, even though these works contain elements of hypertextuality, most notably non-linearity and digressive tangents, they are nonetheless typically associated with and presented in a format that dictates chronological reading – a printed work where the reader starts at one end and finishes at the other – and readers typically read these works in the specific order dictated by the authors and publishers, thus following a single authoritative vision of the text's structure. The key difference that hypertext as a medium provides is a genuinely non-centralised ordering of the material free of the author's overriding framing, so that any one pathway through the story is as legitimate as any other. As noted by George P. Landow, 'all hypertext systems permit the individual reader to choose his or her own centre of investigation and experience. What this principle means in practice is that the reader is not locked into any kind of particular organisational hierarchy' (38). This results, Landow suggests, in a 'potentially democratic' medium of storytelling, where 'no one discipline or ideology dominates or founds the others' (89). Hence hypertextual reading not only places command of the reading experience in the reader-user's hands, it significantly multiplies the possibilities of authorship, given that each reader will navigate through and arrange the core ingredients of the text differently. However, it is worth noting that more recently critics have pointed out that hypertext fiction, as with all other structural experiments, still provides one linear way through the text, no matter how random the choosing of that order might be. See, for example, Liestol, cited in Aarseth (43).

Regardless of this debate, hypertextual reading clearly engenders fundamentally different reading practices than those used for printed literature. Indeed, according to N. Katherine Hayles, hypertextual reading 'initiate[s] and demand[s] cyborg reading practices':

> Because electronic hypertexts are written and read in distributed cognitive environments, the reader necessarily is constructed as a cyborg spliced into an integrated circuit with one or more intelligent machines. To be positioned as a cyborg is inevitably in some sense to become a cyborg, so electronic hypertexts, regardless of their content, tend toward cyborg subjectivity. Although this subject position may also be evoked through the content of print texts, electronic hypertexts necessarily enact it through the specificity of the medium. ('Flickering Connectivities' par. 13)

Landow's and Hayles' views here represent a trajectory of thought from the early days of hypertext – Landow was involved in the critique of hypertext from its earliest days – to a more nuanced, perhaps even second-generation view of electronic literature in the work of Hayles. Hayles' use of the figure of the cyborg here emerges from a strong debate in gender studies as can be found, for example, in Donna Haraway's 1985 essay 'The Cyborg Manifesto' (*Simians*). While drawing on the tradition of science fiction in which Frankenstein's Creature is often considered the first cyborg, Haraway uses the figure of the cyborg to construct a metaphor for agency in a particular technological and economic environment (180–181).

With its emphasis on the assemblage of independent textual parts into a disjointed but unique whole, hypertextual reading mirrors the work of Victor Frankenstein in assembling individual body parts into a disjointed but unique material body, namely that of his creation. This correspondence between Frankensteinian scientific enterprise and hypertextual literary enterprise provides the thematic subtext for Shelley Jackson's *Patchwork Girl*, in which, as noted by Hayles, the title character is 'an assemblage rather than a unified self' ('Flickering Connectivities' par. 24) and the text itself is 'also seamed and ruptured, comprised of disparate parts with extensive links between them' ('Flickering Connectivities' par. 23).

Jackson's 1995 work of hypertext literature is a multimedia artwork stored and disseminated on CD-ROM. It elaborates on its precursor text, Mary Shelley's *Frankenstein*, by positing a fictional framework in which it was Mary Shelley herself who created the female Creature that Victor Frankenstein abandons. The story casts Shelley and her creation as lovers, and chronicles their relationship as well as the Creature's subsequent travels and retreat to Death Valley at age 175 to decompose. However, a large portion of the reading experience for the reader-user entails the assemblage of those aforementioned textual parts, coded here as body parts, to create the titular Patchwork Girl. This process collapses the already tenuous distinctions between author and reader, creator and creation in the hypertext domain, as well as collapsing the boundaries between author, reader, user, Victor Frankenstein, and Mary Shelley herself. This unsettling of boundaries is signalled from the outset via the authorial credit to 'Mary/Shelley and herself', which blurs distinctions between Mary Shelley, Shelley Jackson, and the female Creature.

Shortly after the release of *Patchwork Girl*, Robert Coover described it as a 'pioneer narrative hypertext', and the work has been analysed and discussed by many academics over the two decades since its publication (e.g. Hayles; Hackman; Clayton; Latimer; Sundén). Part of the work's fundamental appeal is how, as mentioned above, it thematically equates the practices of hypertextual reading and writing with the Frankensteinian science of Shelley's text. In Jackson's work, the body parts of the titular Patchwork Girl must be sewn together by the reader to progress the narrative in the same way that the lexias, the basic units or sections of a hypertext, are sewn together to create a story. In tasking the reader-user to carry out this sewing work, Jackson relinquishes her own traditional authority and control as author and assigns the responsibility to the reader-user to create meaning, as well as metaphorically casting the reader-user in the roles of both author Mary Shelley and Frankensteinian scientist. This sewing work is carried out by clicking and navigating through the text, and each reader will follow a slightly different pathway, thereby creating a slightly different story and slightly different understanding of the work. Because of this, there can be no authoritative version of *Patchwork Girl*, supporting Landow's assertion that the hypertext medium is uniquely democratic, redistributing the traditional balance of power within the text from writer to reader-user.

Upon entering Jackson's CD-ROM-based work, the reader-user is confronted with a black-and-white sketch of the protagonist, where dotted lines indicate the scars of being sewn together from disparate parts. This image reappears, in different ways, throughout the text: a hand or a torso will be displayed, or a head attached to a leg. In this way Jackson uses the format of hypertext to provide visual clues to guide the reader, as well as textual clues. Despite the comparatively textual nature of *Patchwork Girl* in comparison to other hypertexts that contain a higher proportion of images, the immediate graphics of the text indicate that it is a new and different format from the more familiar printed book. The narrative structure has five elements, or sections: 'a graveyard', 'a journal', 'a quilt', 'a story', and '& broken accents'. Our focus here will be on the first three of these.

While there is no doubt that *Patchwork Girl* is hypertextual in its most literal sense, and that reader-users can forge strikingly different pathways through it, there is also a degree of linearity underpinning Jackson's work. The first lexia in the section titled 'a graveyard', itself called 'graveyard', is very clearly an introductory statement and an invitation – even challenge – to the reader-user. Jackson's protagonist states, 'I am buried here. You can resurrect me, but only piecemeal. If you want to see the whole, you will have to sew me together yourself.' This immediately establishes and intertwines the functions of reader, writer, user, and creator. Following this prelude the reader-user will arrive at 'headstone', which outlines the protagonist's many body parts. Clicking on the name of each part opens a short lexia that recounts the story of the person from whom the body part derived. We learn, for example, that the Creature's right leg comes from Jennifer, a socialite of the nineteenth century for whom 'it was only bound in laces and tight bodices that she dared go down to breakfast; unbound, she might tear all to shreds' ('right leg'). Continuing the notes, we learn that the creature's trunk comes from a dancer named 'Angela, a woman of low birth but high sights … [who] saw rightly that the language of the body also has its accents, low and high' ('trunk'). While there are some male body parts (Walter's incisors, Roderick's liver) and some animal parts (Bossy the cow's guts mixed with human Mistress Anne's guts), the majority of the body parts come from female cadavers, and through the assemblage of these parts and prior histories, a patchwork identity, fragmented and multi-faceted, is forged for the Patchwork Girl. The piecemeal assemblage of the female Creature is symbolically aligned with the piecemeal reading practices engendered by hypertext. Elsewhere the narrator states that 'Assembling these patched words in an electronic space, I feel half-blind, as if the entire text is within reach, but because of some myopic condition I am only familiar with in dreams, I can only see that part most immediately before me, and have no sense of how that part relates to all the rest' ('this writing'). This evokes and contrasts with the traditional geography and navigation of printed literature – where the reader is free to flip forwards and backwards by the turning of the page, but is also steered more overtly in their reading experience by the author's established narrative trajectory – and accentuates the challenges and dynamism inherent in hypertextual reading.

Jackson's decision to focus on Frankenstein's abandoned female creature, and her use of predominantly female body parts with women's stories attached to them to construct her Patchwork Girl, is significant. As mentioned earlier, the adaptation process provides a platform for authors to talk back to and address canonical works of literature (Sanders 98). Linda Hutcheon notes that 'there are manifestly many different possible intentions behind the act of adaptation: the urge to consume and erase the memory of the adapted text or to call it into question is as likely as the desire to pay tribute' (7). Jackson's text both pays tribute to and calls into question the gender politics of Shelley's novel, and provides the reader-user with what Hutcheon would characterise as 'an extended intellectual engagement with the adapted work' (8). While much has been made in *Frankenstein* criticism of the links between Mary Shelley's biography – specifically her experiences with childbirth and of growing up without a mother, who herself had died in childbirth – and her novel's motifs of creation, monstrosity, and man usurping woman's role as vessel for childbirth, less has been said about the actual role of women in *Frankenstein*'s world. Botting identifies correspondences between the role of women and that of the Creature in that both 'are identified firmly as others' (*Making Monstrous* 11). He elaborates, 'the monster speaks out against prevailing social practices, [while] women's voices are limited and constrained' (111). He also notes that 'the women in *Frankenstein* rarely speak out in voices of discontent and certainly do not clamour for better treatment or equal status. They remain securely within their families performing their domestic duties as wives, mothers, sisters and daughters' (100). In *Patchwork Girl*, Jackson creates a space not only for the female Creature that was aborted by her creator in Shelley's original text, but also for Mary Shelley herself to engage with her aborted creation and, possibly, with her own complicated biography. Moreover, in giving voice to the multiple body parts from whom the Patchwork Girl is assembled, Jackson introduces a multiplicity of other women's voices and histories straddling social classes and other identity markers into the female-authored but male-dominated fictional world of *Frankenstein*. These are the women denied voices throughout both Shelley's work and the social reality and broader literature of Shelley's time. The voices and text attached to these body parts also emphasise the textuality of the body. Jackson equates bodies with writing text and characterises language as assemblages which are 'composed from a limited number of similar elements, a kind of alphabet, and we have guidelines as to which arrangements are acceptable, are valid words, legible structures, and which are typographical or grammatical errors: "monsters"' ('bodies too'). The fact that these body parts carry text, and that their assemblage helps to assemble both the Patchwork Girl's body and the narrative of *Patchwork Girl*, further reinforces the mirroring of bodies, identity, text, and hypertext throughout.

Another key section of *Patchwork Girl* is 'a journal', which adopts the narrative voice of Mary Shelley herself and, consequently, is central to the text's gender commentary. The section titled 'a story', meanwhile, adopts the voice of the Patchwork Girl and chronicles her life post-Shelley. The journal at the centre of this section chronicles Shelley's reunion with her female Creature and forging of a relationship which is initially that of parent–child but is ultimately sexual. Jackson depicts this relationship between creator and creation as non-combative – and indeed warm and positive – in sharp contrast to that between Shelley's Victor Frankenstein and his creation. When Shelley writes of the reunion between creator and creation in her novel, she depicts Frankenstein's repulsion:

> I trembled with rage and horror, resolving to wait his approach and then close with him in mortal combat. He approached; his countenance bespoke bitter anguish, combined with disdain and malignity while its unearthly ugliness rendered it almost too horrible for human eyes. But I scarcely observed this; rage and hatred had at first deprived me of utterance and I recovered only to overwhelm him with words expressive of furious detestation and contempt. (Shelley 122–123)

In contrast, Jackson weaves an ethical dimension into Shelley's emotional response to her female Creature, writing 'I felt variegated emotions churning in my breast: tenderness, repugnance, fear, and profound responsibility, both anxious and prideful' ('a journal'). This exemplifies Hutcheon's point about rewriting canonical texts in order to revise them and introduce alternative and/or contemporary viewpoints. By writing that Shelley feels 'profound responsibility' for her creation, Jackson is directly addressing the point on which Victor Frankenstein is most frequently condemned, namely his evasion of responsibility for his creation. Jackson thus reinserts into the Frankenstein mythos the parental – and, obviously, maternal – impulse that Frankenstein lacked, which resulted in his creation's ostracism and subsequent retribution. In *Patchwork Girl*, that violent rejection is transformed first into familial and then sexual love for the creation, and ultimately a blurring of boundaries between creation and creator. Shelley reminisces, 'I wish that I had cut off a part of me, something Percy would not miss, but something dear to me, and given it to be a part of her. I would live on in her, and she would know me as I know myself' ('female trouble'). The fictional Shelley does eventually do this: she and her companion exchange flaps of skin with each other, collapsing the borders between creation and creator in a symbolic bio-textual ritual akin to an exchange of blood. *Patchwork Girl* also asserts that the reader-user, previously engaged in the act of assembling her from pieces of others' bodies, will themselves ultimately be collapsed with their creation, stating, 'You will all be part of me. You already are: your bodies are already claimed by future generations, auctioned off piecemeal to the authors of further monsters' ('universal'). The reader-user is thus identified both as assembler and as future meat for assemblage, indicating that their authorial command of this multimedia work is ultimately transitory, and symbolically reasserting Jackson's ultimate overriding authorship.

In the 'a journal' section, Shelley reminisces on the creation of her Creature: 'I had made her, writing deep into the night by candlelight, until the tiny black letters blurred into stitches and I began to feel that I was sewing a great quilt, as the old women in town do night after night' ('written'). This is perhaps the most explicit evocation within the text of the correspondences between Frankensteinian science, hypertextual reading and writing and the art and craft of sewing or quilting – an activity that is 'characteristically feminine' according to Hayles ('Flickering Connectivities', par. 33). This emphasis on sewing, Landow suggests, also 'permits us to see … the degree to which the qualities of collage – particularly those of appropriation, assemblage, concatenation, and the blurring of limits, edges and borders – characterise a good deal of the way we conceive gender and identity' (204). The section titled 'a quilt' reinforces this by being, essentially, a quilt of quotations relevant to *Patchwork Girl*. For example, in the lexia titled 'labor', Jackson weaves her text with Shelley's,

> With an anxiety that almost amounted to agony, I collected the instruments of life around me, that I might infuse a spark of being into the lifeless thing that lay at my feet, *a personage known as 'a proper woman'*. It was already one in the morning; the rain pattered dismally against the panes, the Glass Cat was lying before the mirror and the Patchwork Girl lay limp and lifeless upon the bench. ('labor')

Jackson adopts different fonts and textual forms to signify that different passages of text derive from different sources, as seen in this quotation. Clicking on any piece of text from the lexia provides the list of sources for these quotes: the plain text comes from Shelley's *Frankenstein*, the italics from Hélène Cixous, and the bold text from L. Frank Baum's *The Patchwork Girl of Oz* (1913), from which Jackson also derived her work's title. Shelley and Baum are frequent sources of quotations throughout this section, along with other authors as well as theorists of hypertext and gender. This intertextuality reinforces Landow's contention that hypertext as a literary tool lends itself to intertextuality (35). Moreover, it mirrors the fact that the Patchwork Girl herself is an assemblage of different body parts, texts, and identities, as was the original source material. Levine and Knoepflmacher note of Shelley's novel's evolution,

> Working from a parlour game ghost story contest, out of a mind cluttered with an extraordinary profusion of serious reading, with a political philosophy she derived from her father and from her dead mother's writings, the science she learned from [Percy Bysshe] Shelley, the moral ideas she adopted from all three, Mary Wollstonecraft Godwin Shelley fashioned [her story]. (Qtd in Botting, *Making Monstrous* 73)

Other notable texts which are part of the fabric of Shelley's novel include the Bible, Greek mythology, Dante's *Divine Comedy* (1472), Milton's *Paradise Lost* (1667), and Coleridge's *Rime of the Ancient Mariner* (1798). The real Mary Shelley thus practised the art of quilting various sources into a textual whole, much as Jackson does in the section 'a quilt', and the reader-user does so to navigate *Patchwork Girl*. These acts of assemblage create further resonances between past and present, and between Shelley, Jackson, Frankenstein, and the reader-user.

Linda Hutcheon argues that 'an adaptation is not vampiric: it does not draw the lifeblood from its source and leave it dying or dead, nor is it paler than the adapted work. It may, on the contrary, keep that prior work alive, giving it an afterlife it would never have had otherwise' (176). Jackson's *Patchwork Girl* – an offshoot, sequel, rewrite, free variation, and 'transformation' of Shelley's work in the sense advocated by Frus and Williams – continues this tradition. It also uses its medium of adaptation, hypertext, to generate numerous intertextual and extratextual resonances: between Frankenstein's creation of his Creature, Shelley's writing of the novel and her female creature, and our assemblage of both the titular Creature and the hypertextual narrative; between sewing and writing and reading via hypertext; and between bodies, textuality, identity, and hypertextual reading practices. While the age of hypertext enthusiasm from which it originated has subsided, the work remains relevant in other ways. For example, Paul Hackman advocates for *Patchwork Girl*'s topicality as 'an increasingly relevant meditation on the relationship between print and digital media, rather than as a paradigmatic work of a literary movement' (85–86), and he asserts the value of reading its relationship to print as dialectical rather than oppositional (105). In other words, Hackman suggests, Jackson's work is not the harbinger of textual revolution that hypertext was commonly predicted to be, but an enabler of dialogue about the possibilities and limits of the precursor medium.

Like many of the digital artworks created since the invention of the personal computer, however, whether for floppy disk, CD-ROM or the internet, ongoing accessibility is a concern for *Patchwork Girl*. While *Patchwork Girl* is protected to some extent – more than many other digital works of the 1980s and 1990s – by its publication by Eastgate Systems, a company developed to publish what it calls 'serious hypertext', it is still victim to the same evolution of digital tools that prompts the obsolescence of earlier technologies. This situation is even worse for browser-based artworks such as Melinda Rackham's *carrier* (Barnett, 'Monstrous Agents') and is something now being addressed in a range of initiatives, such as Melanie Swalwell's *Play It Again* website (Stuckey, Swalwell, and Ndalianis) and Oliver Grau's *ADA: Archive of Digital Art*, amongst others. Thus, while Jackson's text contributes to the dissemination of Shelley's mythology in contemporary popular culture and its media specificity is central to its content, this media specificity also represents a potential impediment to its continuing circulation and shelf life. This prospective threat awaits many texts of this technological era that are intensely media specific, including Dave Morris's *Frankenstein* app.

Dave Morris's *Frankenstein* (2012)

Concurrent with the rise of smartphones and tablets has been the proliferation of apps, or mobile applications. In addition to the numerous functional and recreational apps that stormed the App Store in the days since the iPad was released, literary apps have emerged and are increasingly common. The medium provides authors and designers with new opportunities – some consistent with hypertext, others digressing from this precursor – to release literary texts from the shackles of their original bindings. Siobhan O'Flynn observes:

app designers begin to break away from the convention of the book as a material object of bound pages and utilise the affordances of the iPad as a screen that can display multiple content zones simultaneously. These rich media components can make what exist in the material book as footnotes, for example, dynamic elements that can deepen the experience of a work through audio, visual, and video stimuli and source material. (204)

Yet, at the same time that developers and designers seize the opportunities afforded by the app medium, the conventions of the book are frequently integrated into their design; as O'Flynn suggests, the best examples 'play with the material form of the book, integrating elements of film animation and touch-screen gaming with the conventions of the material book' (200). Indeed, the iOS Human Interface Guidelines posit materiality and resemblance to physical form as a desirable attribute of i-design, instructing developers to 'When appropriate, add a realistic, physical dimension to your app. Sometimes, the more true to life your application looks and behaves, the easier it is for people to understand how it works and the more they enjoy using it' (qtd in Galey et al. 25). Apparently, while we can take the text out of the book, we cannot quite take the book out of the text. The symbols for the iBooks app and eBook Downloader apps, for example, signify traditional textuality (an open manuscript and a bookshelf, respectively), and as Galey et al. note, 'Apple's marketing of the iBooks e-reading app … emphasises the interface's continuity with book forms' (26). Meanwhile, the iPhone Kindle app icon is a silhouette of a person reading a book beneath a tree, and while the reading device held by the silhouetted figure could be electronic or print, the pastoral scene evokes images of more traditional reading environments.

A number of scholarly research projects have also emerged which study the intertwining of traditional book forms and new technologies of reading. One of these undertakings is the ArchBook project, an ongoing, online, open essay collection chronicling the emergence of specific design features throughout the history of books, spearheaded 'with an eye to the continuities and discontinuities the feature might have with digital reading environments' and a 'specific goal of informing digital design' (Galey et al. 21). Another project is Implementing New Knowledge Environments (INKE), through which representatives of both electronic and print culture collaborate on prototypes for digital reading environments (Galey and Ruecker). This attachment to the material form of the book even as technological progress surpasses its possibilities is evident more generally in modern e-book culture (Barnett, 'Platforms for Social Reading'). Dave Morris's app adaptation of *Frankenstein* exemplifies this, representing both a transformation of Mary Shelley's literary text and continuity with the work's prior material forms.

Morris's app follows the plot of Shelley's novel, but tweaks the story's trajectory to fit a very systematic structure: the story is divided across six parts, each containing three chapters. Part One establishes the character of Victor Frankenstein and chronicles the creation of his Creature, while Part Two chronicles the Creature's survival in the wilderness, his courting of and eventual rejection by a peasant family, and his intellectual development. Part Three charts Victor's return to Geneva and the murder of his brother; Part Four depicts his reunion with the Creature and creation of a mate at its bidding; Part Five presents Victor's short-lived marriage to Elizabeth; and Part Six charts his pursuit of the Creature to their mutual end. The reader-user advances through the story using a 'choose your own adventure'-style mechanism, making decisions which inform the sequence and, in some instances, the outcomes of story incidents.

While the plot generally follows Shelley's original and Morris borrows some of her prose, there are a number of significant narrative digressions. For example, where the female creature is aborted by Victor before being invested with life in Shelley's novel, in Morris's app the sentient female Creature commits suicide after comprehending her monstrosity at the end of Part Four. In Part Six, meanwhile, Walton and the crew of his ship all die, whereas in Shelley's novel they are the surviving witnesses to the final confrontation between Frankenstein and his progeny. Both these incidents have popular-culture precedents. In Kenneth Branagh's *Mary Shelley's Frankenstein* (1994), for instance, Helena Bonham Carter's reanimated Bride commits suicide after comprehending her monstrosity. Kenneth Branagh is actually cited in the credits of Morris's app, so it is likely Morris was familiar with the 1994 film. Meanwhile, most film adaptations jettison Walton and his expedition entirely, so killing them off is no radical digression. These departures from Shelley's narrative point to an agenda of continuity and contrast, familiarity and dissonance, one which most directly benefits users acquainted with Shelley's source, whose knowledge allows them entry into a conversation between the texts, the source materials and biographical information.

Of course, such digressions are routine in adaptations of Shelley's novel, and Morris's app acknowledges its status as the latest in a long line of adaptations of *Frankenstein* by gesturing towards other versions of the story. For example, where the process of the Creature's assemblage and creation is obscured in Shelley's novel, Morris takes a cue from the countless film adaptations of the novel in making the apparatus and process of creation a little clearer, as well as deploying the line 'It is alive' (Part One), a clear homage to the cry of 'It's alive!' immortalised by James Whale's *Frankenstein* (1931). This intertwining of different versions of *Frankenstein* attests to Frus and Williams' observation that 'Many transformations [of stories] work from multiple texts, not just a single one' (5) – as previously evidenced by *Patchwork Girl*. In the words of Julie Sanders, 'adaptations perform in dialogue with other adaptations as well as their informing source' (24). Sanders argues that where adaptations are concerned, 'The spectator or reader must be able to participate in the play of similarity and difference perceived between the original, source, or inspiration to appreciate fully the reshaping or rewriting undertaken by the adaptive text' (45). In short, knowing an original helps readers get the most out of an adaptation. Frus and Williams, however, suggest that 'While knowing about the older text enriches our reading of a transformation, our interpretation does not depend on it' (4). That is to say, pre-existing knowledge of a text is not a guarantor of a rich reading experience, nor is lack of familiarity necessarily a handicap. Ultimately, whether this holds true or not will depend on the adaptation itself: where arguably it is essential to possess a working knowledge of *Frankenstein* to derive the most from *Patchwork Girl*, it is less essential in the case of Morris's more linear and streamlined app adaptation. Even so, familiarity with the original source lends digressions like those discussed above a certain frisson and charge of the new. Moreover, by openly embracing the intertextual and narrative possibilities in adapting a story as oft-told and familiar as *Frankenstein*, Morris rightly posits Shelley's story as a shared myth or textual network that is open to play.

This theme of continuity and transformation in the app's content is mirrored in its form and design, which embrace both traditional textuality and the possibilities afforded by the new medium. The app delights in the juxtaposition and intertwining of old and new textual forms. For example, traditional textuality is emphasised in its layout and design: words and text are presented in old-fashioned typeface on an old-fashioned parchment background, and the work is peppered with images that signify traditional textuality, such as drawings from antiquated anatomy books, extracts from maps, and illustrations of places and voyages. The very first image on opening the app is also a book, explicitly tying the story of *Frankenstein* to its textual precursor. On touching the image, the colour of the book fluctuates lightly, suggesting the book is a living, breathing, embodied object (its blood-red colour further signifies this) or, conversely, that the app itself serves to animate and bring the traditionally static text to life.

This fetishising of traditional literary forms is also incorporated into the story content: in Part Two, the reader-user is tasked with developing the Creature's consciousness, and literary works and the diary of Victor Frankenstein are central tools in the formation of this consciousness. This is consistent with Shelley's novel, where, as Botting notes, the Creature's identity is constructed 'on the basis of his literary identifications' (16). The Creature finds a trunk containing three books: *Paradise Lost*, *Plutarch's Lives*, and *Jefferson's Travels*. The reader-user is asked which one they want the Creature to read first, and we reader-users selected *Paradise Lost*. Following a description of this work, we were then asked if the Creature is like Adam or Satan; we chose Adam. Such reader-user choices guide both the education and characterisation of the Creature and the reader-user's own interpretation of the text. For example, a subsequent reader-user question/choice posed to us was 'Did you [the Creature/reader-user] anger your father so that he cast you out?' which invites the reader-user to further develop their own interpretation of the story as well as guiding the subsequent characterisation of the Creature. This question/choice also means the reader-user's interpretation and the Creature's intellectual development are explicitly framed through reference to Milton's work, meaning that allusions to traditional printed objects are framing the reading and interpretation of contemporary electronic ones.

However, while traditional textuality is evoked in design and content, the choose-your-own-adventure-style storytelling mechanics, whilst also having precedents in traditional textuality, are distinctly twenty-first century, and similarly impact on the reader-user's experience and interpretation of the text. As indicated above, after each passage of text – with passages varying in length – the reader-user is presented with a question/storytelling choice and some options to choose from which will impact on how a scene or character arc progresses. These questions include queries directed at Victor or the Creature (about their actions, opinions, or more philosophical matters), dialogue options for a character to steer a conversation in two possible directions, and in some cases a combination of the two. For instance, in Part Five, which centres on Victor's doomed marriage to Elizabeth, reader-user choices include arming Victor against the Creature or simply submitting to fate; enjoying the wedding night or being resigned to whatever the Creature has in store; going upstairs with Elizabeth or loitering downstairs; and, after Elizabeth has been slain, going out to hunt the Creature or staying with the murdered bride. Elizabeth's demise itself, however, cannot be circumvented; like *Patchwork Girl*, the path, though flexible and digressive, is nonetheless ultimately predetermined.

In guiding the storytelling, the reader-user occupies a shifting position, alternating between confidante, conspirator, guide, and helpless observer. At some points the reader-user will actively guide the narrative, while at other times they inhabit a more fly-on-the-wall role, merely asking questions that generate certain actions and outcomes. In some instances the reader-user serves as Victor's or the Creature's conscience, but in others they are powerless to affect the narrative outcome. For example, at times certain actions are fixed in stone, and the reader is presented with only one storytelling option. In Part Three, Victor receives a letter regarding his brother William, and the sole action option is 'Read it at once'. On reading about his brother's death and being implored to return to Geneva, the sole action option is 'Of course we must' (Part Three). Other instances where no alternative choices are offered include the Creature's burning of the De Lacey household (Part Two), and early in the story when Victor tries to articulate his scientific ambitions to his friend Henri and muses 'I want so much for Henri to understand', but the sole response offered is a defeated 'He will never understand' (Part One). The notion of 'agency mechanics' has been applied to video games to describe the alternation between player autonomy and fixed narrative incidents and how this generates experiences which 'oscillate between empowerment and disempowerment' (Habel and Kooyman 1). Similar agency mechanics are at work in Morris's app, which alternates between empowering the reader-user with certain choices and disempowering them by removing storytelling agency at key points. While fixed narrative events like the burning of the De Lacey home could still have been arrived at through posing narrative choices with two or more options, robbing the reader-user of alternative options lends these moments a decisive fatalistic charge, fitting for a novel about humanity's hubris.

This alternation between empowered agent and disempowered observer, and the ambiguous subject position of the reader-user, is further reflected in how the reader-user is addressed throughout. Much of the text is written in first person and focuses on Victor. In these sections Victor speaks to the reader-user and, as indicated above, the reader-user inhabits the role of confidante, co-conspirator, analyst, or helpless observer depending on the scene in question. Sometimes the reader-user will be ignored, sometimes Victor will directly address them ('Will you walk with me?'), and sometimes they will be positioned as part of the action ('We can cut through these back streets') (Part One). However, where most of the app focuses on Victor's perspective and closely follows the chronology of Shelley's novel, in Part Two the focus shifts to the Creature, dramatising in present tense the incidents which the Creature recounts in past tense to Victor when they meet in Geneva in Shelley's novel. This contrast and the dissonance it generates – both between the app sections themselves and with Shelley's source text – is made more jarring by the fact that the delivery switches from first person to second person in this section. From the outset of Part Two the reader-user is, as mentioned earlier, tasked with steering the development of the Creature, and is asked 'Do you concentrate on what you can see? Or on your hearing? Or on developing your coordination?' This use of second-person positions the reader-user, previously an adviser to and observer of Victor Frankenstein, in the role of his creation.

Linda Hutcheon contends that 'telling the same story from a different point of view ... can create a manifestly different interpretation' (8). *Patchwork Girl* attests to this, using the minor character of the aborted female creature as a means of exploring themes either absent from or marginalised in Shelley's original. This is also evident, to a lesser degree, in Morris's app. While Shelley's novel has three threads of first-person narration – Walton's, then Victor's, and then the Creature's – the Creature's narration of his story in that work is located within the broader frame of Victor's narration (i.e. Victor narrates to Walton what the Creature narrated to him), and is thus subordinated to and coloured by Victor's narration. By partitioning the Creature's interactions with the De Laceys and intellectual development into its own separate section, and presenting it in present as opposed to past tense, Morris's app invests this material with greater significance and immediacy than previous iterations. Furthermore, the equation of the reader-user with the Creature through the use of second-person direct address generates greater empathy for the creature's plight. Whilst reading Victor's diary and discovering Victor's contempt for his creation, the reader-user is told 'The minutest description of your odious and loathsome creation is given, in language which vividly paints your maker's horrors and renders yours indelible. You feel sick but cannot tear your eyes away' (Part Two). Elsewhere, Morris writes 'You scurry back thirsty to your lair, pulling the twigs and leaves behind you as if that might shut out the scrutiny of some immense, unseen, celestial eye that is somehow judging you. And if such an eye exists, what does it make of you?' Of the reader-user options presented, we selected 'That you are hideously ugly?' which generated the response 'You are. More than ugly: monstrous' (Part Two). This constant assertion of the Creature's malignant status and corresponding equation of the Creature with the reader-user heightens sympathy for – or masochistic identification with – the Creature, allowing reader-users who typically regard the Creature as villainous to re-evaluate and forge new connections with the story. This reinforces Frus and Williams' notion that 'telling a story from a different perspective [can be used] as a way to engage themes and issues left out of the previous version' (4), a point previously evidenced by *Patchwork Girl*.

As mentioned earlier, scene and character choices made by the reader-user throughout help them to develop and determine their own interpretations of the text. Morris's app tasks the reader-user with authorial and interpretive decisions at several key points. For example, during the Creature's education, when it learns that humans possess both good and evil capacities, the app asks 'You must have seen enough of mankind by now to judge which side is dominant?' and then provides the options of 'Good' or 'Evil'. When we selected 'Evil', the response generated was 'You surmise that the true nature of man is malicious, and it is only through the laws and the invented punishments of Heaven that it has been possible to tame him' (Part Two). Later, when the Creature asks Frankenstein for a companion, once again two options are presented: 'Pretend to agree for the time being' or 'It has a genuine right to ask you for a mate' (Part Four). Such questions, in addition to generating alternative plotting or character outcomes, task the reader-user with choosing between alternative interpretations of the story and grappling with larger moral and thematic questions raised by the text: is humankind evil or simply flawed, does the Creature truly deserve a mate or not, and so on. Hence the reader-user is not passively digesting or even simply guiding the story of *Frankenstein*: they are working through their own interpretation of the story as they progress through it. No doubt many readers' choices at key junctures will differ from those we have chronicled above, and while these different choices may all lead to the same narrative outcomes, their interpretations of the text and thematic outcomes will differ, based upon their interpretive trajectories.

Alan Galey and Stan Ruecker, in making their argument for designers to be credited as authors in the digital age, contend that authoring in the traditional sense is now 'only one activity among many, including *designing, manufacturing, modifying, reading*' (408, emphasis in original). The inclusion of the reader in this statement, and the incorporation of reader-user functions into storytelling apps like Morris's *Frankenstein*, is symptomatic of the shift towards interactivity in the digital-reading era enabled by smartphones, tablets, and other devices which encourage reader interaction and electronic communities of readers (Barnett, 'Social Reading'). By asking the reader-user key questions which determine characterisation and scene directions, the app furnishes the reader-user with various opportunities to impose their own authorship upon *Frankenstein*, most frequently by positioning the reader-user as a moral (or immoral) compass for the characters. Even so, as with *Patchwork Girl*, the reader-user never truly attains the status of reader-user-*author*, as they are limited by fixed plot points and certain storytelling mechanisms. Moreover, unlike *Patchwork Girl*'s hypertext, where the reader-user can digress in radical directions, when navigating Morris's app the reader-user remains bound to the linear chronology of Shelley's text. However, this flirtation with authorship followed by the retraction of authorial privilege at decisive narrative points – the aforementioned oscillation between empowerment and disempowerment – is central to the experiential appeal of the app. So too is the constant shifting of subject positions from confidante to co-conspirator to helpless observer. As mentioned earlier, Hayles argues that hypertext and other types of technologised reading engender 'cyborg reading practices' (i.e. more machine-like reading). Donna Haraway, in her famous manifesto for cyborgs, characterises her work as 'an argument for pleasure in the confusion of boundaries' (150); that is to say, an argument for destabilising traditional writer-reader hierarchies enabled through newer, more technologically savvy ways of reading. Cyborg reading practices invite the human reader to be 'spliced into an integrated circuit with one or more intelligent machines' (Hayles, 'Print is Flat' 85). This confusion of boundaries for the cyborg reader-user of Morris's app is multi-faceted and potentially pleasurable: there is confusion between the roles of confidante, co-conspirator, and helpless observer; between empowerment and disempowerment; between being inside and outside the narrative action; and between the functions of reader, user, and author in navigating the text. Pleasurable, too, is the confusion of textual forms inherent in the adaptation of a traditionally printed literary work into an electronic form, particularly one that appropriates traditional textuality in its design whilst enabling interactive reading experiences difficult or unwieldy to approximate in print publication.

These confusions are consistent with Morris's agenda of continuity and transformation alluded to earlier, and this intertwining and creation of assemblages between old and new is actually a central thematic preoccupation of the app. While we tend to think of *Frankenstein* as a period novel due in part to the multitude of contemporary adaptations which adopt its period setting, as well as to equate it with the Gothic literary tradition (a body of work which frequently looked back to bygone horrors), Shelley's novel was in fact a thoroughly modern composition reflecting Romantic sensibilities. Fred Botting writes:

> there are no Gothic castles and evil aristocrats, nor any hint of the supernatural. Artificial creation is produced by scientific endeavour and technique, along with Romantic imagining. With its allusions to readings of the French Revolution … its references to alchemy and science, its location in modern Geneva, the novel dispenses with older Gothic trappings. (*Limits of Horror* 117–118)

In short, Shelley's finger was firmly on the pulse of her times, a pulse which continues to beat, given the timelessness of many of the novel's themes and its continued deployment in interrogations of modern scientific advances and anxieties. As Botting, among others, has noted, 'the continued circulation of historical figures of terror and horror [like Frankenstein and his monster] gives form to contemporary fears about technological, scientific and biological innovations' (*Limits of Horror* 43). Morris's app preserves the source novel's period setting, yet from its outset asserts Victor's progressive and forward-looking scientific thinking in a way that mirrors today's technological and digital reading climate. Early in Part One he enthuses to the reader-user, 'Now consider the events that are sweeping across the world. A spirit of confidence, optimism, bold enquiry. Men dare now. In my own endeavours, I seek discoveries as revelatory as those of Copernicus and Columbus. It is a new world.' While ostensibly talking about the scientific accomplishments of the eighteenth century, Victor could also be talking about the staggering technological landscape of the twenty-first century, to which Morris's app belongs. And while Victor criticises art and architecture as accomplishments that 'do not advance understanding' (Part One), suggesting that he would find little value in an artistic creation like Morris's adaptation of Shelley's literary work, the fact remains that Morris's app embodies – at least in the realm of storytelling – the spirit and potential of a new world, specifically new media and its potential for adapting and forging new possibilities from older works. Ironically, like *Patchwork Girl*, Morris's app's cutting-edge media specificity puts it at risk of obsolescence as that media rapidly evolves. However, preservation concern for apps has grown in the last few years. The Smithsonian has begun collecting and storing apps made for tablets and mobile phones as part of its collection, creating a challenge for collections managers who have to now consider not only how to appropriately store and catalogue such works but also how to ensure reader-users can access and use them in a manner approximating the way they were intended to be used (Thompson).

Conclusion

Jackson's *Patchwork Girl* and Morris's *Frankenstein* testify that Shelley's novel – as a ubiquitous canonical work, as a commentary on scientific advancement and its impact on humanity, and as itself an inherently hybridised construction – provides fertile ground for new types of adaptation as well as commentary on those very mediums of adaptation through the intertwining of medium, message, and navigation. In its conflation of Frankensteinian science, hypertextual reading, and the crafts of sewing and quilting, and in its collapsing of boundaries between the reader-user and 'Mary/ Shelley and herself', Jackson's work provides a multi-faceted meditation on gender, the body, identity, intertextuality, and hypertext itself. And in its merging of old and new textual forms, its posing of questions to advance its narrative, and its alternation between empowering and disempowering the reader-user, Morris's work guides readers in developing and determining their interpretations of Shelley's *Frankenstein* and attests to the potential of mobile applications for forging new reading opportunities. While their intense media specificity potentially endangers their continued availability and access, much as *Frankenstein* saw Prometheus unbound, Jackson and Morris unbind *Frankenstein*, textually speaking, from the page, showing the potential for the text both to be reinvigorated by adaptation and to invigorate the mediums to which it is adapted.

Bibliography

Aarseth, Espen J. *Cybertext: Perspectives on Ergodic Literature*. Baltimore, MD: Johns Hopkins UP, 1997.

Barnett, Tully. 'Monstrous Agents: Cyberfeminist Media and Activism.' *Ada: A Journal of Gender, New Media and Technology* 5 (2014a). July 2014. http://adanewmedia.org/2014/07/issue5-barnett (accessed 17 November 2015).

———. 'Social Reading: The Kindle's Social Highlighting Function and Emerging Reading Practices.' *Australian Humanities Review* 56 (2014): 141–162.

———. 'Platforms for Social Reading: E Material Book's Return.' *Scholarly and Research Communication* 6.4 (2015).

Botting, Fred. *Making Monstrous: Frankenstein, Criticism, Theory*. Manchester, UK: Manchester UP, 1991.

———. *Gothic*. London: Routledge, 1996.

———. *Limits of Horror: Technology, Bodies, Gothic*. Manchester, UK: Manchester UP, 2008.

Brown, Neil Porter. 'All the World's a Page.' Harvard Magazine July–August 2014.

Clayton, Jay. 'Frankenstein's Futurity: Clones, Replicants, and Robots.' *The Cambridge Companion to Mary Shelley*. Ed. Esther H. Schor. Cambridge: Cambridge UP. 84–99.

Coover, Robert. 'Literary Hypertext: The Passing of the Golden Age (Keynote Address, Digital Arts and Culture, Atlanta, Georgia).' *Nick Montfort.com*. 1999. http://nickm.com/vox/golden_age.html.

Douglas, J. Yellowlees. *The End of Books – or Books without End?: Reading Interactive Narratives*. Ann Arbor: U of Michigan P, 2000.

Eastgate *Eastgate: Serious Hypertext*. Eastgate Systems, Watertown MA, 2010.www.eastgate.com/.

Frus, Phyllis and Christy Williams. 'Introduction: Making the Case for Transformation' Ed. Phyllis Frus and Christy Williams. *Beyond Adaptation: Essays on Radical Transformations of Original Works*. Jefferson, NC: McFarland, 2010. 1–18.

Galey, Alan, and Stan Ruecker. 'How a prototype argues.' *Literary and Linguistic Computing* 25.4 (2010): 405–424.

Galey, Alan, Jon Bath, Rebecca Niles, and Richard Cunningham. 'Imagining the Architectures of the Book: Textual Scholarship and the Digital Book Arts.' *Textual Cultures* 7.2 (2012): 20–42.

Grau, Oliver. Archive of Digital Art. https://www.digitalartarchive.at/nc/home.html.

Habel, Chad and Ben Kooyman. 'Agency Mechanics: Gameplay Design in Survival Horror Video Games.' *Digital Creativity* 25.1 (2013): 1–14.

Hackman, Paul. '"I Am a Double Agent:": Shelley Jackson's Patchwork Girl and the Persistence of Print in the Age of Hypertext.' *Contemporary Literature* 52.1 (2011): 84–107.

Haraway, Donna. *Simians, Cyborgs, and Women: The Reinvention of Nature*. New York: Routledge, 1991.

Hayles, N. Katherine. 'Flickering Connectivities in Shelley Jackson's *Patchwork Girl*: The Importance of Media-Specific Analysis.' *Postmodern Culture* 10.2 (2000).

———. 'Print Is Flat, Code Is Deep: The Importance of Media-specific Analysis.' *Poetics Today* 25.1 (2004): 67–90.

Huhramo, Erkki and Jussi Parikka. 'Introduction: An Archaeology of Media Archaeology.' Eds

Erkki Huhtamo and Jussi Parikka. *Media Archaeology: Approaches, Applications, and Implications*. Berkeley, CA: U of California P, 2011. 1–21.

Hutcheon, Linda. *A Theory of Adaptation*. New York: Routledge, 2006.

Jackson, Shelley. *Patchwork Girl Mary, Shelley and Herself/Shelley Jackson*. Computer software. Eastgate Systems, Watertown MA. 1995.

Kooyman, Ben. 'The Pedagogical Value of Mary Shelley's Frankenstein in Teaching Adaptation Studies.' Ed. *Fear and Learning: Essays on the Pedagogy of Horror*. Aalya Ahmad and Sean Moreland.. Jefferson, NC: McFarland, 2013. 245–263.

Landow, George P. *Hypertext 2.0: Being a Revised, Amplified Edition of Hypertext: The Convergence of Contemporary Critical Theory and Technology*. Baltimore: Johns Hopkins UP, 1997.

Latimer, Heather. 'Reproductive Technologies, Fetal Icons, and Genetic Freaks: Shelley Jackson's *Patchwork Girl* and the Limits and Possibilities of Donna Haraway's Cyborg.' *MFS Modern Fiction Studies* 57.2 (2011): 318–335.

Leitch, T. 'Adaptation Studies at a Crossroads.' *Adaptation* 1.1 (2008): 63–77.

McFarlane, Brian, 'Reading Film and Literature.' Eds Deborah Cartmell and Imelda Whelehan. *The Cambridge Companion to Literature on Screen*. Cambridge, UK: Cambridge UP, 2007. 15–28.

Moore, M.R. 'Adaptation and New Media.' *Adaptation* 3.2 (2010): 179–192.

Morris, Dave. *Frankenstein*. App, Inkle Studios, Profile Books, London. 2012. Software app.

O'Flynn, Siobhan. 'Epilogue.' Linda Hutcheon, *A Theory of Adaptation*. 2nd Edition. New York: Routledge, 2012. 179–206.

Sanders, Julie. *Adaptation and Appropriation*. London: Routledge, 2006.

Shelley, Mary. *Frankenstein; or, The Modern Prometheus*. London: Penguin, 1994 [1818].

Snyder, Ilana. *Hypertext: The Electronic Labyrinth*. Carlton South, Vic.: Melbourne UP, 1996.

Stuckey, Helen, Melanie Swalwell, and Angela Ndalianis. 'The Popular Memory Archive: Collecting and Exhibiting Player Culture from the 1980s.' Ed. Arthur Tatnall, Tilly Blyth, and Roger Johnson. *Making the History of Computing Relevan*. Berlin: Springer, 2013. 215–225.

Sundén, Jenny. 'What if Frankenstein('s Monster) was a Girl? Reproduction and Subjectivity in the Digital Age.' Ed. Anneke Smelik and Nina Lykke. *Bits of Life: Feminism at the Intersections of Media, Bioscience, and Technology*, Seattle: U of Washington P. 2008: 147–162.

Thompson, Clive. 'How Does a Museum Acquire an iPad App for its Collections?' *Smithsonian Magazine*. September 2013.

Adaptations of 'liveness' in theatrical representations of Mary Shelley's *Frankenstein*

Kelly Jones

Two productions of stage adaptations of Mary Shelley's *Frankenstein* emerged in the UK in the spring of 2011, both of which made explicit reference to their liveness in performance. The National Theatre in London production was based upon Nick Dear's stage adaptation of the novel and was directed by celebrated filmmaker, Danny Boyle. It featured acclaimed popular television and film actors Benedict Cumberbatch and Jonny Lee Miller. As part of its theatrical run, the production was commissioned, on a couple of occasions, to be transmitted live into various cinemas across the country as part of the National Theatre Live (NT Live) initiative. The other production was televised on BBC3, a channel associated with popular, experimental, and, at times, rather subversive entertainment directed at its target audience of '16–34 year olds' (BBC Trust 1). This was an open-air performance, transmitted live at Kirkstall Abbey in Yorkshire, entitled *Frankenstein's Wedding: Live in Leeds* (written by Chloe Moss and directed by Colin Teague and Trevor Hampton). It was intended as an interactive performance experience in which audience members at the event were asked to dress as wedding guests and the characters recorded their reactions to the events in the narrative via a social-networking site, Twitter, throughout the performance. Both productions shared some important similarities, including their insistent endeavours to distance themselves from early film representations of the novel and to highlight the plight of Frankenstein's creation. Both promised a sense of fidelity to Shelley's novel by portraying an articulate Creature. More significantly here, however, both productions were also emphatic in their engineering a sense of the 'live' theatrical event that could reach a wider audience, making the adaptations accessible for spectators beyond those who shared the performance venue with the actors.

However, while the National Theatre production was slick, rehearsed, had undergone a vigorous series of previews, and could be controlled by its theatrical environment, *Frankenstein's Wedding* was sprawling and chaotic, a hybrid of various texts such as popular songs, web-cam links, pre-filmed exposition sequences, and dramatic exchanges between the characters. The need for improvisation and direct audience address, the interactivity of the project, and the unreliable performance conditions of an open-air, collaborative performance, meant that there was an ever-present sense of chaos about to erupt. In this sense, the BBC3 production shared much in common with its patched-together antagonist.

This chapter will compare these two theatrical reimaginings of Shelley's tale both with each other and in terms of their relationship with Shelley's novel. Moreover, it will offer a fresh perspective on how each production adapted and constructed the sense of 'liveness' of the theatrical event in transmission, thereby, rather aptly, playing with the ontological concerns with the controlled constructions of liveness which lie at the heart of the Frankenstein Complex itself.[1] Finally, this chapter will open up the question: how can an engagement with the Gothic offer an appropriate lens through which to foster a significant and vigorous understanding of the contemporary constructions of liveness?

Liveness, performance, and adaptation

In his book, *Liveness and Recording in the Media*, Andrew Crisell seeks to account for the value that is placed on the quality of liveness in television and radio broadcasting. He explains that 'the crucial element of liveness is temporal: co-presence in *time*' (original emphasis), and that '[c]o-presence in space without temporal co-presence is almost meaningless because if two people are not temporally co-present they cannot be spatially co-present' (14). He continues:

> it follows that the most interesting objects of live coverage are those that manifest the process of temporal existence, for instance by moving or making noises. They should, in other words, be living. This explains why the words *alive* ('possessing life') and *live* ('conveying presence') can sometimes be hard to distinguish. (14, original emphasis)

For Crisell, then, the special quality of liveness relies upon its cognisance of human presence: 'for nearly all of us, the most interesting living things are other humans, but even if what we see on the television are merely inanimate objects or animals, they will be made intelligible or interesting to us only by a human presence.' (14–15) Perhaps, then, we can understand that a primary characteristic of liveness is its ability to provide a temporal co-presence with something that possesses life.[2] Crisell describes the characteristics of liveness in the broadcasting media here, and his comment about the lack of a necessity for co-presence in the space seems at odds with the theatrical experience of liveness in which there is, importantly, a physical co-presence between performers and audience. Without this, Matthew Reason asks: does theatre become something other than theatre (95)? In his 2006 book, *Documentation, Disappearance and the Representation of Live Performance*, Reason explains that recordings of live performance have generally served the purpose simply of documenting an otherwise ephemeral event, but he points out that recordings of performance, whilst useful as a tool of performance analysis, fail in themselves to provide satisfactory entertainment (73–91). This is true, in part, because theatre is, in the words of Herbert Blau, 'always at vanishing point' (Blau 28). In a statement that persuasively colonises the kind of liveness that is particular to theatrical performance Reason argues that viewing live performance and the performance as recorded 'reminds us that the live is a particular medium of its own – it is its own kind of technology', and that 'Screen representations of theatre and dance performance ... make an implicit statement about not so much the loss or absence of liveness, but about the otherness of liveness. They assert that the live is a medium, a technology and a verb in its own right' (110).

However, the contemporary emergence of 'cinema livecasts' has opened up questions about the ways in which it is possible for audiences to experience the liveness of performance. In his book, *Live to Your Local Cinema: The Remarkable Rise of Livecasting*, Martin Barker addresses the advent of cinematic 'livecasts', and is one of the incipient number of scholars to have explored the important aesthetic, cultural, and phenomenological consequences of these new 'live' events.[3] Appropriately, like Victor Frankenstein's Creature, 'livecasting' lacks a single specific name and a precise generic identity, which, as Barker illustrates, serves to underline its alterity and the 'still-unsettled questions about these events' cultural status' (10). Known variously as 'event cinema', 'alternative content cinema' and 'simulcasts', amongst other labels, these are names given in diverse attempts to describe the live broadcasting of theatrical, or in some cases, music or sporting events (Barker 2). In a further contextualisation of the space of the reception of the 'livecast', if not a clearer definition of its nomenclature, Bernadette Cochrane and Frances Bonner allude to its 'distinct component' that 'involves presentation in cinemas' (121–122). Janice Wardle, meanwhile, opts to use the nostalgic term 'outside broadcasts' to describe the live broadcasting of theatrical events and thereby appropriates the employment of the term as used in the 1920s with the advent of BBC radio and, later, television, and 'the initiative to extend the audience for cultural events, made possible by new broadcasting technologies' which 'challenged and expanded listeners' understanding of the appropriate place(s) to engage with high culture such as opera and music' (135). Whilst this use of yet another name extends the consideration regarding the label to be attached to these broadcasts, Wardle's focus on the space of the reception and the co-presence of the cinematic audience is helpful in defining the primary characteristics of these events. She writes, 'at the heart of the decision to broadcast to cinemas, as opposed to transmitting via television or to produce a DVD ... is refocusing on the sense of place for these performances, with a celebratory insistence on the significance of public theatrical space', and adds, 'television may provide the stylistic model for the 'liveness' but cinema provides the public space' (136–137, 139).

The initiative to broadcast live events to theatres started in December 2006 with the New York Metropolitan Opera's production of Mozart's *The Magic Flute*, 'beamed to 100 digitally equipped cinemas in the USA, the UK, Canada, Norway – and, with a delay, Japan' (Barker 2). The UK's National Theatre, inspired by the success of the project, made its own foray into the enterprise of 'livecasting' in 2009 with its broadcasting of *Phèdre*, starring Helen Mirren, in which the staged performance was filmed and transmitted live to cinema audiences. This has been followed by twenty other productions to date, including *London Assurance* (2010), *One Man, Two Guvnors* (2011), and *King Lear* (2014). Despite their regularity, David Sabel, Head of Digital at the National Theatre, explains that these broadcasts are not meant to supplant the theatre experience: 'We've always seen NT Live as a complement to the live experience, not a replacement.' (Youngs n.p.)

How, then, is an experience of liveness in one medium (in a theatre) different to that of another (in a cinema)? 'Livecasting' opens up important questions in the field of adaptation studies, not just in adapting the apparatus of one medium to facilitate the mediation of another, but in the adaptation of the experience of liveness itself and, as Barker asserts, its 'mode of delivery' (91). He argues that the unprecedented rise of the livecast with its 'not-quite-liveness' (10) has encouraged a revision of the ways in which we understand and experience liveness. To this end, Barker presents a comprehensive survey regarding critical debates in the fields of theatre and performance studies, television studies, film studies, music studies, sports psychology, comedy studies, and virtual performance, as he demonstrates that the concept of 'liveness' has attracted considerable critical attention within the scholarly disciplines attached to these various media. 'Liveness matters', he writes, '[b]ut *how* it matters varies mightily ... according to which area of public and academic thinking you turn to' (41, original emphasis). Barker complains that assumptions about the audience's experience of – and relationship to – liveness remain largely theoretical in the arguments of critics, and that scholars fail to engage in actual audience research. However, Barker's central bugbear is that debates concerning liveness have hitherto focused upon what is special about particular media, and this has led to a lack of cross-fertilisation and, more worryingly in the context of theatre and performance studies, a pessimism regarding the threat of other mediations of liveness to the perceived sacrosanctity of the immediacy of the liveness in theatrical performance. This is most fervently articulated by Peggy Phelan, for whom 'theatre becomes itself through disappearance' (146). She argues that the theatre's ontological definition, 'its life' (146), and thereby, perhaps, its Benjaminian auratic quality, lies in its ephemerality; that its power to engage and transform its participants resists capture, documentation, and representation. For Phillip Auslander, who contentiously challenges Phelan's essentialism, 'liveness' must be seen as a historical concept, constructed through a culture conscious of the 'recorded' and the 'non-live':

> Prior to the advent of those technologies (e.g., sound recording and motion pictures), there was no such thing as 'live' performance, for that category has meaning only in relation to an opposing possibility. The ancient Greek theatre, for example, was not live because there was no possibility of recording it. (Auslander 56)

He speaks, having appropriated Baudrillard's 'characterization of the mass media as the cultural dominant of contemporary, western(ised) societies' (5), of the idea of the live increasingly being impeded by the domination of other mediation, specifically, the televisual. Barker, again, however, critiques the gloom of Auslander's argument, avowing that mediatisation can enhance, rather than hinder, the experience of live-ness. He also challenges the idea of the sanctity of live theatrical performance. Barker asserts the usefulness of Christopher Balme's distinctions of intermediality and the need to embrace the interdependence of media, but argues that this realises these media as separate forms and experiences.

Barker contends that livecasts force us to consider 'new ways of "doing liveness"' (71). This petition to consider new ways of thinking about the live seems appropriate to a consideration of adaptations of a story that warns of the dangers of constructing a new sense of life, liveness, and the lack of responsibility of a parental figure in engendering this new way of 'doing liveness'.

BBC3's *Frankenstein's Wedding ... Live in Leeds*

To intentionally coincide with the cosmic event of the moon's closest proximity with the Earth since 1992, as well as, perhaps, with the year's Royal Wedding, BBC3 commissioned a performance event, 'combining drama and music inspired by Mary Shelley's gothic masterpiece' to focus upon the nuptials of Victor Frankenstein ('Victor') and Elizabeth Lavenza, and to be transmitted live on national television on 19 March 2011.[4] The collaborative project between BBC3, BBC North, and BBC Cymru Wales was inspired by the successes of previous live-beamed broadcasts tel-evised by BBC3, *Manchester Passion* (April 2006) and *Liverpool Nativity* (December 2007). Whilst these broadcasts were not cinematic livecasts, it is significant that the first initiatives appear to have emerged earlier in the same year as the New York Metropolitan Opera's inaugural foray into event cinema.

Set in present time, the production relocated Shelley's story from early nineteenth-century Europe to 'credit-crunch Britain', in which Victor's father, Alphonse, a surly, self-made businessman complains of 'pissing money up the wall' in a bid to impress with a society wedding, held at the family home. Located in Kirkstall Abbey in the northern English city of Leeds, the performance site was adorned as a hybrid between a wedding venue and a rock festival. The action was sprawled across various loci around the Abbey: with a 'main stage' set up to house the wedding reception area, and from which contemporary popular performers, dressed as the wedding entertainment, would perform live music to the 12,000-strong audience who had gathered for the event. Haunted by the background roar of the live 'theatrical' audience, 'backstage', television cameras were seemingly permitted access to all areas: Victor's laboratory, Elizabeth's dressing room, the chapel in the grounds (where the wedding would take place in front of selected guests), the graveyard where young William Frankenstein was buried, as well as various other clandestine corners where the action could unfold.

BBC3, the channel that commissioned the performance, championed its com-mitment to using 'the full range of digital platforms to deliver its content and to build an interactive relationship with its audience' (BBC Trust 1).[5] The channel stressed the live interactivity of the event, which, for the audience present, included dressing up in wedding outfits, and participation in a Flash-mob-style wedding dance, a choreographed sequence taught in workshops prior to the performance by Leeds-based company Phoenix Dance Theatre. For the television audience, the invitation for live interaction was presented in the opportunity to follow live online tweets from one of the show's characters, Justine, Elizabeth's best friend and maid of '[dis]honour', played by Jemima Rooper. The adaptation brazenly sought to exploit the celebrity appeal of its actors such as Lacey Turner, who played Elizabeth, an actress who had recently left the popular soap opera *East Enders*, and David Harewood, who played the Creature, who had appeared in popular television series, *Doctor Who* and *New Tricks*. There were plenty of special 'turns' from popular musicians and personalities, such as Reggie Yates, a popular television actor, presenter, and radio disc-jockey who here played Giles, both wedding planner and compère to the music acts, and who provided the show's choric presence, welcoming the viewers in the early stages of the perfor-mance, interacting with the characters, and directing the viewer through the narrative sequences. The attempt to court popular appeal was further enhanced through the use of contemporary music, used either to underscore the dramatic action, in the grand tradition of melodrama, or as part of the action itself, as in musical theatre. Songs such as the Kaiser Chiefs' 'I Predict a Riot', and Billy Idol's 'White Wedding', sung vari-ously by the wedding band and Justine and Giles, exploited the dramatic tensions in the lead-up to the ceremony, while Athlete's 'Wires' was sung by Victor as he wrenched his second creation from its life-support mechanisms.

Andrew Gower played a youthful, exuberant Victor, at pains to state that he stands 'utterly opposed to any forms of human violation' and that his experiments are intended to 'serve humanity' rather than to provide its curse. As the production begins we learn that Victor has already given life to the Creature, and is now putting the fin-ishing touches on his mate. David Harewood, interviewed prior to the performance, revealed that the production was taking a more 'modern approach' to the rationale behind Victor Frankenstein's project, and that the Creature was 'not sewn together using body parts', but instead 'was genetically created in a lab'. Harewood, in the same interview, spoke of the production's innovation in its fleshing-out of the Creature as a sentient and cognisant being:

> Hollywood has envisaged the Creature with a bolt through his neck and fairly dumb, inar-ticulate, whereas Shelley writes a Creature that is articulate, speaks fluent French, reads *Paradise Lost*, can comprehend the world around him, can understand the world around him, and that … has … led me to play this character as if he's basically a two-year-old, a very strong, very intelligent two-year -old. (Harewood 2011)

To counter Victor Frankenstein's purported medical philanthropy, and the Creature's eloquence, the production appeared to offer a clear-cut ethical standpoint against the artificial creation of human life by depicting Henry Clerval, confidant here to both Victor and Elizabeth, as a man in holy orders, responsible for con-ducting the marriage ceremony and a vessel to provide a moral touchstone and an explicit confrontation between scientific advancement and traditional Christian values. Surprisingly, and out of compass with the protagonist we meet in Shelley's novel, Victor, even with the consciousness of the Creature's murderous instincts, seemed, in creating a female mate, to feel no horror in the proliferation of his efforts in making artificial life, confident that the 'flaw' in the creature – the 'cognisant brain' – will not affect 'future specimen', and as the audience watched him document his latest experiment, he told the camera, 'through trial and error, I'm getting closer to my goal'. What this goal was never quite became clear, and, having initially refused the Creature his request for a partner, he appeared to have revoked this decision. The narrative itself was disorientating and contradictory at times, perhaps the effect of transferring the novel to another medium. Unable to condense the entirety of the novel to an hour and a half of stage-time, this adaptation instead delivered its spectacular horrors in quick succession.

This is not to suggest that such an adaptation becomes inherently inferior in quality to its source material. Linda Hutcheon warns that an adaptation should be seen as 'a derivation that is not derivative – a work that is second without being secondary' (Hutcheon 9). In this vein, Albrecht-Crane and Cutchins argue that, by definition, there are necessary differences between the source text and the adapted text in a new medium, and that 'Adaptation studies ought to focus on the space of disjunction between texts and media to ask what that space, that necessary difference, enables' and that 'the crucial move here is the suggestion that, in their intersection, novels and films (and many other forms of adaptations across media) inhabit a sort of cross-fertilization that is both artistically productive and affirmative of difference' (20). If the finer details of the narrative were left neglected or ambiguous in this production, the performance medium enabled its actors to deploy the melodramatic potential of representing the emotional consequences of Victor's transgressions. Furthermore, the focus upon the rapid unravelling of emotional chaos, which the live nature of this performance opened up, allowed for the audience to be plunged into the disorientating experience of Victor's nightmare as it unfolded in real time.

This sense of disorientation seeped into the format of the performance with its 'patched-together' merging of live action and pre-filmed sequences. There was live footage of the wedding and its chaotic preparations: the arrival of guests, the bride's pre-wedding anxieties, the revelation of Elizabeth's pregnancy to both Henry and, later, Victor, and the disruptive appearance of the Creature who comes to claim his own bride. This live action was interspersed with presentations of Victor's video-diaries which recorded and revealed his experiments, pre-filmed footage of William's murder, the Creature's prior encounter with his maker, in which he implores Victor to create a companion for him, and pre-filmed footage of the Creature, some sequences supposedly taking place in the present, some in the past, as he interacted with the homeless and the dispossessed on the streets of central Leeds. These particular sequences mapped the cityscape, but with shaky camera angles, uncanny close-ups, and optical illusions. The camera lens unhinges its focus in one scene as it shows, from the Creature's perspective, the city from above, by daylight, from atop a spiral tower. The viewer is plunged into a sense of Gothic disorientation, claustrophobia, and disturbance in the way the camera makes sense of the space. This pre-filmed footage also served to incorporate the broadest possible focus on the extreme ends of the social spectrum. The television viewer, voyeur of each end of this spectrum, was positioned in a space between these two extremes of social 'Otherness'. The television viewer was distanced from the menace of society's vagrants as they watched the pre-filmed sequences that took place outside the Abbey through the lens of social realism, a perspective that was reinforced through the added sense of gritty, non-theatrical, 'fly-on-the-wall', 'slice-of-life' documentary. Back in the Abbey, however, the television audience was also detached from the live 'theatrical' audience at this society wedding in their ostentatious parade of costumes that resembled *Rocky Horror* meets *Masque of the Red Death* in a spirit of excess that, as Fred Botting (1996) reminds us, lies at the heart of the Gothic experience.

The project's relationship to the Gothic, in fact, is key to an understanding of both the spirit of the production and its differences from the National Theatre enterprise. Contemporary Gothic theatre has received relatively scant scholarly attention. Emma McEvoy, one of the very few scholars in the field, explains the significance of literary adaptations in the genre[6] when she suggests, 'It is worth pointing out that many examples of the Gothic (as might be expected because of the phenomena of transmission and framing) on the modern stage are adaptations – from novels, short stories or films' (McEvoy 215).

McEvoy further explains that 'Much Gothic theatre thrives on its incorporation of other media and a sense of generic trespass' (215). This assertion is supported by what Fred Botting argues is the Gothic's preoccupation with borders, limits, and transgression, made manifest in novels like Shelley's, in their 'concerns about the limits, effects and power of representation in the formation of identities, realities and institutions', and that 'Gothic devices are all signs of the superficiality, deception and duplicity of narratives and verbal or visual images' (14–15). McEvoy notes that the success of many contemporary 'Gothic' theatrical experiences, such as Stephen Mallatratt's *The Woman in Black*, an adaptation of Susan Hill's novel, is largely attributable to the playing with 'frames', the audience's ways of seeing and making sense of the narrative, and how the audience are immersed in the deceptiveness of theatricality itself which distorts and destabilises how an audience can make sense of what it is experiencing. For this reason, she explains, 'Site-specific performance and instillation have proved to be fruitful modes for the Gothic' because of their ability to exploit 'the manipulation of real-time experience within a Gothicised space' (McEvoy 215). If we expand upon this, then the immersive and experiential nature of site-specific performance, manipulating the phenomenology of time and space, can elicit, amongst its spectators, a sensual, primal, and thrilling biological response to the production, as Kathleen Irwin explains:

where physical traces of a building's past operate metaphorically to render absent present [*sic*] and function to introduce the spectator into other worlds and dimensions of our world that are *other*. The material traces evoke worlds that are intangible and unlocatable: worlds of memory, pleasure, sensation, imagination, affect and insight. (37)

As Irwin's quotation serves to illustrate, there is a Gothic rhetoric that the discipline of site-specific performance studies itself employs in exploring the relationship between place and performance. Mike Pearson uses the term 'the host and the ghost' to describe the relationship between the site and the performance that it accommodates:

Site-specific performances rely upon the complex superimposition of a number of narratives and architectures, historical and contemporary. These fall into two groups: those that pre-exist the work – of the host – and those which are of the work – of the ghost. (95–96)

Cliff McLucas elsewhere elaborates: 'The host site is haunted for a time by a ghost that the theatre-makers create. Like all ghosts it is transparent and the host can be seen through the ghost' (128). With the implicit reference to the 'host' as visual receptacle and relic, portal to an ephemeral, spiritual, non-bodily entity, there is a pseudo-Catholic lexis at work here, which again, as Robert Mighall tells us, resonates with the Gothic in the genre's obsession with the medieval past:

The celebration of what is modern or progressive in history (according to a Protestant, liberal, or enlightened view of progress), easily shades into an identification and condemnation of what is 'historical' or anachronistic in the present day. Such troubling reminders of the 'dark ages' as the worship of relics, belief in miracles, the persistence of the Inquisition or the power of the Pope, occur in both historical and topographical accounts, contemporary with the emergence of Gothic fiction. Such accounts help to reinforce Protestant identity, but also evoke the frisson of confrontation that structures the narrative and dramatic effects of Gothic fiction. (6)

Though ambiguous as to whether *Frankenstein's Wedding* constitutes a site-specific performance, links with a medieval Catholic past are displayed through the host setting of *Frankenstein's Wedding* in the grounds of Kirkstall Abbey (which, with a poignant irony, was reportedly the inspiration for Thomas Love Peacock's satire *Nightmare Abbey* published in 1818, the same year as Shelley's novel, and which takes aim, amongst its various targets of derision, at Percy Bysshe Shelley, husband to Mary). Moreover, in exploiting the associations between place and a 'return of the repressed' medieval Catholic past, *Frankenstein's Wedding* builds upon the remit of *Manchester Passion* (2006) and *Liverpool Nativity* (2007), productions which sought to geographically map a dramatic retelling of biblical stories onto the cityscape and to foster both a communal celebration of the city and an interactive experience for the audience. These productions emulated the staging of the medieval mystery-cycle plays produced by the city guilds in the fourteenth to sixteenth centuries to celebrate the Catholic festival of Corpus Christi (Richardson and Johnston 14). *Frankenstein's Wedding* engenders a format[7] similar to the medieval mystery-cycle plays, which were performed at various stations, spread across the city, on wagons, rather like *tableaux vivants*, and which played out dramas from the Fall of Man to the Last Judgement. Crowds of spectators could watch the drama in any chronological order they chose.

With its similarly dispersed loci of dramatic action, and its loose sense of sequential order as the narrative travels backwards and forwards between present time and past time, recorded sequences and live action, there was a sense of messiness to the experiential nature of this production and one reviewer, who was in the live audience, complained that it was not always clear what was being experienced:

> The most thought-provoking parts of Colin Teague's production are those that have been filmed in advance. Sequences showing Frankenstein's creation performing acts of charity among the homeless are evidently an attempt to humanise the monster. But outside the abbey, it is hardly any easier to form a judgment of David Harewood's performance than it would be watching the current National theatre production from a vantage point on Waterloo Bridge. [...] As a technical feat, BBC3's enterprise is undeniably impressive. But as an audience member, you feel strangely isolated and incidental to the main event. It may be one of those occasions when you just had to be there – at home, watching it on TV, that is. (Hickling, n.p.)

The television viewers, although they had privileged perspectival access, were also privy to the mishaps of an unruly live performance, such as microphones cutting out and camera shots obscured by props. Harewood's Creature, conscious of a misplaced chair upstaging his murder of Elizabeth, was impelled to desolate the unfortunate article out the path of the television audience's visibility before delivering the death blow. This sense of jeopardy, the sense of the performance-gone-wrong, offers perhaps a refreshing antidote to the tight control exercised over the contemporary, highly spectacular commercial theatre of the mega-musical, produced by the likes of Cameron Mackintosh. Dan Rebellato terms this style of polished production 'McTheatre' as he likens the spectacle to the 'standardisation, organised through franchising and automation' similar to the fast-food enterprise that provides the prefix to this type of theatre (101) and points out that:

> a founding principle of McDonald's was that every Big Mac, wherever you were in the world, would taste the same. Cameron Mackintosh similarly – and commendably – insisted that his shows should not become any less professional or polished the further in time or space they were from the first press night. However, as the production process becomes more and more automated, what begins as a guarantee of quality ends as a guarantee of predictability. (102)

Frankenstein's Wedding, by comparison, seemed very conscious of its unpredictable 'liveness', its possibility of failure, its singularity as a unique performance event for both the theatrical audience and the television audience. It was, in short, very much aware of its patched-togetherness and its potential exposure of human error.

The National Theatre's *Frankenstein*

By comparison, the National Theatre's production of Dear's play appeared to be controlled, clinical, precise, and polished. Evasive in its claims of adaptation, Dear appears on the published play-text as its author, although the play is 'based on the novel by Mary Shelley'. The production premiered on 22 February 2011 on the stage of the Olivier Theatre, following a series of previews, and thereafter followed a couple of nationwide livecasts in March 2011 as part of the NT Live initiative. The filmed performances of Dear's play were later re-released to coincide with the celebrations of the fiftieth anniversary of the National Theatre in 2012. Since then there have been further annual screenings to coincide with Hallowe'en festivities.

The chief ploy of the production was its dependence upon the casting of the two leads, Victor Frankenstein and the Creature. Cumberbatch and Lee Miller alternated roles throughout the production run. To this end, perhaps it is necessary to see the productions as different adaptations of the play, depending upon the casting of the primary roles. However, the actors' rotating of the two lead roles was ostensibly used to underscore the idea of the Gothic double, and the uncanny similarities between the monster and its maker and to play with the master/servant, parent/child dichotomy at work in Shelley's story. Nevertheless, Lee Miller seemed to excel in the role of the Creature with his 'animalistic, plaintive, primitive' performances (Libby Purves 172), and Cumberbatch, as many critics agreed, was the most advantageously cast as the aloof, 'semi-autistic genius with a chip of ice at his heart' (McGinn 175). This was, perhaps, a felicitous casting choice to this extent, that Cumberbatch's Victor seemed to have been 'ghosted', to employ Marvin Carlson's phrase, 'so that audience reception of each new performance is conditioned by inevitable memories of this actor playing similar roles in the past' (58). That is, the actor was haunted by his performance as the remote, precise, emotionally challenged detective, Holmes, in BBC1's *Sherlock*, the nemesis of the Gothic nightmares of contemporary London, employing his powers of deduction with a clinical detachment, and dispassionate logic.[8]

Set in the early nineteenth century, in keeping with the setting of Shelley's novel, the production focused, even more so than *Frankenstein's Wedding*, on the story and perspective of the Creature as based upon the narrative that Shelley presents in the second volume of her work. In an interview mediated by 'National Theatre Discover', Dear emphatically states that his play sought to distance itself from the James Whale film productions, which he complains, 'deny the Creature a voice'. He states, 'we do start with the moment of creation but not told from the perspective of the scientist which is how it is usually told, but from the perspective of the experiment, rather than the experimenter' (Dear 'Nick Dear').

Following his 'birth' on stage, in which he erupts from a makeshift womb, the Creature wanders into an unreceptive and newly industrialised city, where he is greeted by the hellfire sermons delivered from the lips of austere preachers, the hissed threats of the wretched and dispossessed who cross his path, and the calamitous steam-engines, spewing electrifying sparks. Shunned by all who greet him, the Creature takes refuge in nature, screeching with joy at the touch and taste of rain, the feel of grass, and the glow of the sun. Thereafter follows the Creature's encounter with De Lacey, his subsequent rejection by Felix and Agatha (who are here man and wife rather than siblings, with the Safie plot omitted altogether), his murder of William, and his encounter with Victor. Following this meeting, the play revises its focus to its other protagonist with Victor's flight to the Hebrides to create (and then to destroy) the Creature's bride, and his subsequent wedding to Elizabeth. In a ghoulish scene set in the bridal suite, a scene imagined but not depicted in the novel, the audience watch a perverted substitution of a wedding night, as the Creature usurps and appropriates the role and status of his master, raping and murdering Elizabeth, triumphantly exulting in his rite of passage to his maker, 'Now I am a man' (72). The play concludes with a pursuit across the frozen arctic wastes, the Creature driving on the creator, oscillating between taunting his broken spirit and goading him to continue the chase.

The geographical scale of the play, in contrast to *Frankenstein's Wedding*, honoured the global sweep of the novel, with the action unfolding across European locations from Lake Geneva to the Scottish Hebrides to the northern abyss. Representative time, too, is played out in more epic dimensions – the events taking place over three years. Unlike *Frankenstein's Wedding*, with its claustrophobic confinement of the action to real time, with recorded filmed flashbacks, Dear's adaptation, although set in the past, embraces the future, always advancing, so says the Creature, echoing his master's earlier warning: 'We can only go forward, we cannot go back' (*Frankenstein* 76). Relentlessly onward-facing, the production ran for two hours *sans* interval, necessarily, as with *Frankenstein's Wedding*, streamlining the narrative of the novel.

This condensing of the novel drew complaints from several reviewers who, in generally favourable appraisals, bemoaned the play's rapid exposition and its downplaying of some of Shelley's themes, because of its choice to foreground the Creature's perspective. Susanna Clapp, for instance, objects that 'Dear's script is monster-oriented to the point of drowning out the notion of experimental excitement' (173). Henry Hitchings was even more incensed, complaining that 'things we should be shown we are told instead' (Hitchings 170). This condensing of the narrative, however, did not necessarily equate to a faster pace to the action, and, amongst the praise lavished upon the aesthetics and individual performances in the production, many critics also decried the lack of velocity in Dear's adaptation. Particular blame was directed at the opening of the show, a ten-minute sequence in which the audience, with the patience demanded of a new parent, watch the Creature's 'birth' and subsequent efforts to learn to stand, walk, and laugh.

Audience behaviour during the livecasts was necessarily heavily regulated in a tightly scripted and immaculately plotted production which left no room for improvisation and interaction between performers and audience. Despite the invitation for the theatre audience members to ring, en route to their seats, the bell that hung, tantalisingly, over the auditorium aisle, even this was an exercise in controlled participation.[9] Once the performance began, the aisle was commandeered by the performers, who colonised the ringing of the bell. The space too, was rigorously controlled, as set designer Mark Tildesley's multiplex of special effects, the chandelier of light bulbs which shivered above the stage, the spluttering locomotive, the elemental effects of rain and snow, smacked of the visual effects usually associated with the mega-musical. These automated ocular splendours relied upon mechanical precision and impeded any licence of improvisation from the actors. This situation led Susannah Clapp to teasingly remark, 'Tildesley's exuberant engineering is not above swagger and showmanship: that chandelier, and the bell hanging over the stalls … are so prominent that if we weren't at the National the words "Andrew Lloyd Webber" might be murmured' (173–174). Presented on the Olivier stage, the theatrical space itself was explicit in its finitude, with its celebrated fan-shaped layout which exposes everything to the spectator, and its famous revolve; this was a production which, in the crudest of terms, showed its backside to its audiences. There were no covert nooks or crannies, no labyrinthine excesses, and to this extent, the production seemed to resist the Gothicised sprawl that characterised the BBC3 venture.

The need for this regulation was perhaps ameliorated by the intention to film the live event, with a finely tuned, considered camera arrangement that would capture the visual sweep of the production for cinema audiences. Martin Barker notes these 'bravura moments' (15), 'created by editing, dissolves, and camera movements' (19). These included the introduction of the steam train, as well as other anamorphic patterned sequences that were best viewed from above and privileged the bird's-eye perspective, denying access for the theatrical audience.[10] Barker writes,

> Sometimes these high-angle shots themselves provide a special kind of aesthetic experience. Highly choreographed movements whose interrelations may hardly be visible to those attending the event can become visible through well-chosen high shots, emphasising cinema audiences' privileged access. (14)

This privileging happened again during the Creature's first experience of rain, and later when the eagle-eye shot captured the devastating moment of the Creature's rape of Elizabeth. But if the cinema audience were permitted special access for certain shots, at other times they were treated, conversely, to moments of disorientation and confusion. When these moments did occur, however, they were again carefully orchestrated. Filtered effects and out-of-focus shots were used to manipulate the audience's perspective so as to conceal what they were looking at, or to foreground the camera's focus on a certain performer.

Barker asserts the need for tightly plotted control over the space of the performance, since the cinematic audience's experience of the production must not obstruct the experience of the theatrical audience (and vice versa):

> Cameras must not obtrude for the present audience. No doubt this required some experimentation as to what worked and also what was accessible to the house audience.

However, livecasts are important enough that for the performance at which they are filmed, seats are removed to make space for cameras, and (with the National Theatre) a track for one mobile camera is installed. (13)

If the exposure of the theatrical or 'house audience' to the apparatus of filming was minimised, the consciousness of the cinema audience to the presence of the theatrical audience was also carefully controlled. Unlike the BBC3 venture, which promoted its interactivity between performers and theatrical audience, interaction between stage and house audience in this production was limited, with the audience expected to sit in silence throughout the production. Consequently, the camera's consciousness of the audience was restricted to the opening shots of the audience taking their seats, their applause at the conclusion of the play, the camera's sweep of the stage, taking in the first few rows of the auditorium at the opening of certain scenes, and the capture of the audience laughter in the more light-hearted exchanges between De Lacey and the Creature. Nevertheless, this reminder of the presence of the theatrical audience, albeit controlled, assisted in the simulation of a theatrical experience in a cinema, the manufacturing of a sense of liveness as these shots were 'important for the "guarantee" they provide of the event's simultaneity' and the 'proof of liveness' (Barker 13). This controlled attempt to immerse the audience in a sense of the 'live' was a poignant enterprise, given the nature of the subject material.

Controlling 'the live'

Here, then, are two live broadcasts of theatrical performances of adaptations of Shelley's *Frankenstein*, both mediating and attempting to construct a phenomenology of liveness for an audience which is not physically co-present. There are distinct differences between the two productions, and the clinical precision of the National Theatre production sharply contrasts with the sense that events are unfolding as they are happening in *Frankenstein's Wedding*. The latter repeatedly drew attention to its framing – its construction – of liveness, ever conscious of its intermediality, and, in certain scenes, even brazenly exploiting the presence of a camera. As Alphonse Frankenstein, for instance, welcomed the crew of *Look North*, a local BBC news station, they caught his transition from antagonistic father-of-the-groom to smarmy host as he realised the cameras were rolling. The project embraced the idea of the narrative unfolding live, 'brought to you as it happens', like a breaking news story. The action was *presented* as live to conceal the act of dramatic representation, with its live 'here-and-now-ness' ingrained in how the audience were to experience and understand the narrative. Whilst scenes had been rehearsed, because of the large-scale and unique nature of the event, there was a sense of messiness in the production of the work that echoed the chaos of its narrative. In *Frankenstein's Wedding*, the separate components – the live, interactive elements, the mimetic dramatic episodes which demanded the reverential silence conventionally expected of theatrical audiences, and the pre-recorded film sequences – seemed patched together and the production was all too conscious of its stitches.

Martin Barker contends that livecasts foster considerations of 'new ways of "doing liveness"' (71). Paradoxically, if we consider here the medieval 'Gothic' legacy that *Frankenstein's Wedding* uses in its formatting, this can assist us in understanding the differences between these two productions and the ways in which they 'do' liveness. In *Author's Pen and Actor's Voice*, Robert Weimann describes the bifold perception of the experience of liveness of the theatrical event for early modern performers. These performers had to negotiate between their commitment to the dramatic mimesis, 'the imaginary, represented world-in-the-play' (55), and their allusions to the actual world in which the play is a fiction. These allusions to the actual world expose the materiality and constructedness of the theatrical event – its 'now-ness' – as actors interact with the audience and consciously expose the actor behind the character and the act of performance, what Weimann calls the more explicitly presentational, 'play-ing-in-the-world' (55). These two modes of playing, as Weimann explains, descend from the legacy of medieval performance practices with their conjoining of popular, unscripted performance and dramatic text, nowhere more forcefully illustrated than in the medieval Catholic mystery-cycle plays with their division of the *locus*, the area on the wagon where the fictional drama would play out, and the *platea*, the space in front of the wagon, where the performers could embrace a freedom to interact with the audience and where the boundaries of the world and the play became much more permeable. While the self-conscious theatricality that Weimann speaks of here is not exercised to this extent (the actors in *Frankenstein's Wedding* never attempt to draw attention to the fictionality of their characters), Weimann's idea of the dichotomy between 'playing in the world', inviting the audience to be conscious of the idea of playing, and the representational 'world in the play' in which the play invites the audience to suspend their disbelief, offers perhaps a useful way of understanding what is happening in *Frankenstein's Wedding*. His descriptions of the mystery-cycle plays help to define the slippage between the real world and the world of the fiction experienced in *Frankenstein's Wedding* as the seams between the two dramatically burst.

The National Theatre's *Frankenstein* was much more tightly stitched together. Although a live broadcast, the performers never strayed out of the 'world of the play', and the action was contained in a mimesis that neither audience could penetrate. In other words, there was liveness, but this was live *representation*: it denied the presen-tational aspect that the BBC3 venture embraced. At no point were the audiences to believe that the events were actually happening, and the need to suspend their disbelief simply underlined the consciousness that this was a fictional world in a play.

Nevertheless, despite the stark differences between the productions, both adapta-tions have been preserved for posterity, their liveness captured on camera to be revived for future screenings.[11] Both production teams fostered a control over the liveness of the productions, at least for the livecast audiences, through their positioning of the cameras, used to pre-edit the action that was planned and 'staged'. The pre-set camera/editing suite controlled and directed the 'live' viewing experience (indeed the language of editing itself with its reference to 'cuts', 'headshots', 'splicing' is not dissimilar to the language of surgery, although, ironically, this language itself is rendered ephemeral by the new use of digital editing). A live recording and a recording of a live theatrical event, because of this pre-conditioned editing, each boast an inevitable ability to outlast the ephemerality of the event itself and to outlive its 'flesh and blood' creators. However, there is restricted access to the afterlife of each production, rather like the limited access to the theatrical event. The filmed recording of each production is confined to the institutional vaults: neither is available to own on DVD.[12] In the case of the NT Live's *Frankenstein*, a digital download is accessible only in the National Theatre Archive in London. *Frankenstein's Wedding*, while it remained 'live' on BBC iPlayer for a limited period of time after the initial transmission, has since been deactivated, so that access to the production remains largely confined to the academic facilities of Box of Broadcasts and similar institutional repositories. Scattered fragments are available on YouTube and the digital TV recorders of television audiences who had the foresight to capture the programme and keep hold of it. But neither recorded work is free to move within the wider public sphere. This quality of control over the now dead 'liveness' of these recordings, how it is contained and revived – how it behaves – poignantly evokes the aspirations of Shelley's Victor Frankenstein.

We might ask, however, do these productions lose their value if they are not completely live? Although revived at the whim of its creators, as the NT Live production was to celebrate the fiftieth anniversary celebrations of the National Theatre, is there something special about the liveness in its simultaneity? Andrew Crisell suggests as much in his assertion that the desire for the live is for the reassurance that we are not alone, an assertion that neither the audience nor the actor is dead:

> And perhaps it is not too fanciful to suggest that in the world of new media – a largely solitary and interactive one in which we perform things at times to suit ourselves – the growth of chat rooms, blogs and tweets, with the aim of prompting instant responses and spontaneous conversations, is the hankering for a liveness that is otherwise becoming hard to find. In our separate worlds, we want to know what others are doing at this moment, and that is often not very different from a craving for human contact. (16–17)

To this end, if we can postulate the television or cinematic audience member as the post-digital human – as the Creature seeking a connection with other live beings – even if it is via the digital apparatus that both enforces this need and enables them to feel the value of liveness, perhaps there is much to be said as to why these experiments in live theatrical broadcasting chose to use the adaptation of the story that they did.[13]

Notes

1   Here I capitalise on the useful definition that Dennis Perry and Dennis Cutchins offer in the Introduction to this book as they define the 'Frankenstein Complex' as 'the personal idea of Frankenstein that each of us carries within' (6).

2 An exception here might be live music with is potential for 'captured and recorded live-ness' (Barker 57).

3 Two recent symposia demonstrate the emerging scholarly interest in these events: 'Live Theatre Broadcast Symposium' at the Department of the Theatre, Film and Television at the University of York, UK (June 2015) and 'From Theatre to Screen and Back Again!' at De Montfort University, Leicester, UK (February 2014).

4 www.bbc.co.uk/bbcthree/programmes/genres/drama/schedules/2011/03/20.

5 In March 2014, with the BBC under pressure to make planned budget cuts, the decision was taken to broadcast the channel exclusively online, discontinuing its presence within television schedules from February 2016 (www.bbc.co.uk/news/entertainment-arts-35578867).

6 See also Babbage for a discussion of the Gothic drama and adaptation.

7 See Twycross for a detailed explanation of the medieval mystery-cycle pageant arrangement.

8 Remarkably, Lee Miller too was cast as Holmes in an American television series, *Elementary*, which premiered on CBS in September 2012.

9 The idea of 'controlled participation' is inspired by Millie Taylor's analysis of audience engagement in the British pantomime performance where 'the breaking of the physical barriers between performer and audience also allows the audience to feel that it is more fully a participant and not separated from the world of the performers', but, she warns, 'the opportunities for breaking down the barriers, whether physical or cultural, between audience and performer, could lead to anarchy and are therefore carefully controlled' (123).

10 Boyle's choreography might seem to have anticipated his staging of the smoke chimneys of the Industrial Revolution in the Opening Ceremony of the Olympic Games in London 2012.

11 At the time of writing, NT Live had just announced the 'Encore' screening of *Frankenstein* across nationwide cinemas in the autumn of 2014 (http://ntlive.nationaltheatre.org.uk/productions/16546-frankenstein).

12 In response to the 'huge amount of interest in making the broadcast available on DVD', David Sabel, in the NT Live Tumblr blog, posted an official statement to confirm that 'this is not the wish of the artists involved' and that 'if you are a fan of anyone involved in the creation of Frankenstein or the National Theatre, [*sic*] we would ask that you respect their wishes and decision, and hope that you will continue to support National Theatre Live in your local cinema'.

13 The author would like to express her thanks to the National Theatre Archive, London and to Dr Andrew Westerside.

Bibliography

Albrecht-Crane, Christa and Dennis Cutchins, eds. *Adaptation Studies: New Approaches*. Madison, NJ: Fairleigh Dickinson UP, 2010.

Auslander, P. *Liveness: Performance in a Mediatized Culture*. London: Routledge, 2008.

Babbage, Frances. 'Heavy Bodies, Fragile Texts: Stage Adaptation and the Problem of Presence'. *Adaptation in Contemporary Culture: Textual Infidelities*. Ed. Rachel Carroll, London: Continuum, 2009, 11–22.

Balme, Christopher. 'Surrogate Stages: Theatre, Performance and the Challenge of New Media.' *Performance Research* 13.2 (2008): 80–91

Barker, Martin. *Live To Your Local Cinema: The Remarkable Rise of Livecasting.* Basingstoke, Hampshire: Palgrave, 2013.

BBC News. 'BBC Three Moves Online after Final Night as TV Channel'. BBC News: Entertainment and Arts. 16 February 2016. www.bbc.co.uk/news/entertainment-arts- 35578867.

BBC Trust. *BBC Three Service Licence.* BBC Trust, September 2013. http://downloads.bbc. co.uk/bbctrust/assets/files/pdf/regulatory_framework/service_licences/tv/2013/bbc_three_sep13.pdf.

Blau, Herbert. *Take Up the Bodies: Theatre at the Vanishing Point.* Urbana, IL: University of Illinois Press, 1982.

Botting, Fred. *Gothic.* London: Routledge, 1996.

Carlson, Marvin. *The Haunted Stage: The Theatre as Memory Machine*, Ann Arbor: U of Michigan P, 2003.

Clapp, Susannah. 'Review of *Frankenstein.*' *Observer* 27 February 2011. *Theatre Record*, 12–25 February 2011, 173–174.

Cochrane, Bernadette and Frances Bonner. 'Screening from the Met, the NT, or the House: what changes with the live relay'. *Adaptation* 7.2 (2014): 121–133.

Crisell, Andrew. *Liveness and Recording in the Media.* Basingstoke, Hampshire: Palgrave, 2012.

Dear, Nick. *Frankenstein.* London: Faber and Faber, 2011.

Dear, Nick. 'Nick Dear on Frankenstein'. National Theatre Live. 24 June 2014.http://ntlive. nationaltheatre.org.uk/productions/16546-frankenstein.

Frankenstein's Wedding. BBC Three, 19 March 2011.

Frankenstein. By Nick Dear, based on the novel by Mary Shelley. Dir. Danny Boyle, Olivier, National Theatre, London, 17 and 24 March 2011.

Harewood, David. Interview. 'Meet the Cast of Frankenstein's Wedding!' YouTube. 17 March 2011. https://www.youtube.com/watch?v=PMq3wzp6yAw.

Hickling, Henry. 'Frankenstein's Wedding – Review'. *Guardian.* 20 March 2011. www.theguardian.com/stage/2011/mar/20/frankensteins-wedding-review.

Hitchings, Henry. 'Review of *Frankenstein.*' *Evening Standard* 24 February 2011. *Theatre Record*, 12–25 February 2011, 170.

Hutcheon, Linda. *A Theory of Adaptation.* 2nd Edition. London: Routledge, 2013.

Irwin, Kathleen. 'The Ambit of Performativity: How Site Makes Meaning in Site-Specific Performance.' University of Art and Design, Helsinki, 2007. PhD Thesis.

McEvoy, Emma. 'Contemporary Gothic Theatre'. *The Routledge Companion to Gothic.* Eds Catherine Spooner and Emma McEvoy. London: Routledge, 2007.

McGinn, Caroline. 'Review of *Frankenstein.*' *Time Out London* 3 March 2011. *Theatre Record*, 12–25 February 2011, 175.

McLucas, Clifford, 'Ten feet and three-quarters of an inch of theatre'. *Site-Specific Art.* Ed. Nick Kaye, London, Routledge, 2000, 125–37.

Mallatratt, Stephen. *The Woman in Black: A Ghost Play.* London: Samuel French, 1989.

Mighall, Robert. *A Geography of Victorian Gothic Fiction: Mapping History's Nightmares*, Oxford: Oxford UP, 1999.

Pearson, Mike. 'Special Worlds and Secret Maps: A Poetics of Performance'. *Staging Wales: Welsh Theatre 1979–1997.* Ed. Anna-Marie Taylor. Cardiff: U of Wales P.,1997. 85–99.

Phelan, Peggy. *Unmarked: The Politics of Performance*. London: Routledge, 1993.

Purves, Libby. 'Review of *Frankenstein*.' *The Times* 25 February 2011. *Theatre Record*, 12–25 February 2011, 172.

Reason, Matthew. *Documentation, Disappearance and the Representation of Live Performance*. Basingstoke and New York: Palgrave, 2006.

Rebellato, Dan. 'Playwriting and Globalization: Towards a Site-Unspecific Theatre.' *Contemporary Theatre Review*, 16.1 (2006): 97–113.

Richardson, Christine and Jackie Johnston. *Medieval Drama*. Basingstoke and London: Macmillan, 1991.

Sabel, David. 'Official Statement re: Frankenstein DVD/Bootleg Recordings.' National Theatre Live. 26 June. http://ntlive.tumblr.com/post/27833520736/official-statement-re- frankenstein-dvd-bootleg.

Taylor, Millie, *British Pantomime Performance*. Bristol: Intellect, 2007.

Twycross, Meg. 'The Theatricality of Medieval English Plays.' *The Cambridge Companion to Medieval English Theatre*. Ed. Richard Beadle, Cambridge: Cambridge University Press, 1994. 37–84.

Wardle, Janice. '"Outside Broadcast": Looking Backwards and Forwards, Live Theatre in the Cinema – NT Live and RSC Live.' *Adaptation*, 7.2 (2014): 134–153.

Weimann, Robert. *Author's Pen and Actor's Voice*: *Playing and Writing in Shakespeare's Theatre*. Eds Helen Higbee and William West. Cambridge: Cambridge UP, 2000.

Youngs, Ian. 'Sir Alan Ayckbourn voices fears over theatre screenings'. BBC News. 11 June 2014. www.bbc.co.uk/news/entertainment-arts-27761568.

Frankenstein's pulse: an afterword

Richard J. Hand

THIS COMPREHENSIVE COLLECTION OF chapters demonstrates the thrilling range and diversity of Frankenstein Studies. Mary Shelley dreamed up the story in the Regency era, within a group of writers who together form one of the key crucibles in the history of Romanticism. Infused with classical and literary allusion, her story may be a metaphor for the French or Industrial Revolutions; it may be an exploration of contemporaneous science or the gendered psyche; it may be a deeply personal psychoanalytical narrative. It is all – and yet none – of these things. What is for certain is that when Shelley brought her monster to life, she also started a key cultural heartbeat, the pulse of which continued to beat long after publication. And it is beating still: *Frankenstein* continues to loom over us, sometimes it frightens us, sometimes it amuses us, sometimes it may even – through its sheer sense of marvel – genuinely enrapture us.

In the two centuries since it was written, Shelley's myth of the scientist and the definitive man-made monster has prevailed: in their symbiotic relationship, they have continued to need, despise and adore each other in their tale of creation, destruction, and pursuit. Just as the old seafarer in Samuel Taylor Coleridge's *Rime of the Ancient Mariner* (1798) is cursed to tell his sorry tale again and again – and burden the listener in the process – so popular culture has endlessly retold the story of *Frankenstein*. Like all great myths and legends, *Frankenstein* thrives through its adaptability. *Frankenstein* has straddled the modern genres of horror and science fiction more successfully than any other single tale, but it has also spanned contexts much wider than that. From Halloween costumes to digital games; from cartoons and caricature to amateur content on YouTube, *Frankenstein* is never far away, an essential myth in the modern consciousness.

Frankenstein is extraordinarily diverse in its range and manifestations. Bobby 'Boris' Pickett and the Crypt Kickers' novelty song 'Monster Mash' (1962) has been the making of millions of Halloween parties, with its playful Gothic narrative of Frankensteinian experimentation recounted through the lead singer's impeccable Karloff impersonation. As well as one-hit wonders, the 1931 Universal film creates the same monster that the six-year-old Ana (Ana Torrent) beholds in absolute terror and fascination in

The Spirit of the Beehive (Victor Erice, 1973). The children's culture franchises *Scooby Doo* (1970 onwards) and *Goosebumps* (1992 onwards) have made innumerable allusions to – and appropriations of – *Frankenstein*. At the other end of the spectrum of popular culture, *Frankenstein* dwells at the heart of the sexual liberation in *The Rocky Horror Show* (Richard O'Brien, 1972) and even stalks the arena of outright pornographic spoofs such as *Fuckenstein* (Joanna Angel, 2012), a female-directed black-and-white adult parody which, with its 'silver screen' aesthetic, attempts to be as allusive to Universal Pictures as it is uncompromisingly explicit. In this regard, adaptations of *Frankenstein* can be as excessive and transgressive as a director can possibly imagine or get away with, exploiting its taboo ingredients of grave robbing, dissection and body parts, unethical science, and bloody revenge. After all, beneath the immediate tale of the scientist and his creation, it is a story about bodies and flesh, about heightened emotions and passions, about shameful secrecy and paradigm-changing genius.

At the same time, reworkings of *Frankenstein* can be as downright silly as one might possibly wish: countless sketch shows have 'hit the ground running' with instantly recognisable scenarios of mad scientists and their creations or direct parodies through the appropriation of the iconography of Karloff and the Universal Pictures style. The successful and elaborate parody *Young Frankenstein* (Mel Brooks, 1974) has been mentioned several times in this collection, and so another comic example will serve us well. In Rod Serling's post-*Twilight Zone* television series *Night Gallery* (1969–73), Frankenstein's Creature offers a moment of light relief. Each broadcast of *Night Gallery* features a portmanteau of plays, interspersing its tales of horror with comic interludes. One such comedy is 'Junior' in a broadcast in October 1971 in which a sleeping couple are awoken by the plaintive cries of a young child wanting a drink of water. 'It's your baby!' says the wife, ejecting her husband from the bed. As the father approaches the crib we see the 'baby': a Karloffian monster, gigantic in its crib, despite its childlike wail. It is a simple if not facile sketch, less than two minutes in duration, but it functions successfully in its deployment of cliché and recognisable iconography. In its sparse dialogue, we accept that the monster is indeed Frankenstein's 'baby' and the title of 'Junior' captures the synonymity of Frankenstein as Doctor and Frankenstein as Monster. Squeezed between intense tales of alienation and arachnophobia ('A Fear of Spiders') and the militaristic brutalisation of troublesome children ('The Academy'), this sketch about the baby-monster is grotesque, yet strangely comforting. Significantly, the other ironically humorous short piece in the broadcast is 'Marmalade Wine', a tale of a deranged surgeon (in other words, another type of Frankenstein) who experiments on his unsuspecting house guest.

However, television's use of *Frankenstein* need not just be parodic. In the twenty-first century scientific advances and speculation surrounding transplantation, genetic manipulation, bio-technology, and robotics has led to ethical debates and enthusiasm in equal measure. As in the best of science fiction, these scientific ideas are extrapolated into powerful speculative fiction. One striking example is 'Be Right Back' (Channel 4, 2013), an episode of Charlie Brooker's television series *Black Mirror*, in which a

Figure A.1 Martha (Hayley Atwell) begins to come unglued as her dead husband (Domhnall Gleeson) returns as a man-made simulacrum ('Be Right Back,' *Black Mirror*, written by Charlie Brooker, directed by Owen Harris Channel 4, 2013).

bereaved woman purchases a bio-synthetic model of her husband which downloads all the extant digital material of her late husband (from video, social media, and elsewhere) and becomes a seemingly faultless imitation of the dead man (Figure A.1). The experiment is inevitably doomed to fail: despite his seeming perfection (and, in some respects, 'improvement' on the original), the resurrected figure– like Frankenstein's Creature – is not human and never will be.

Once she has recovered from her grieving, the widow comes to regard her reconstructed partner in horror. In the haunting finale, the living simulacrum is placed in the attic to be looked at on rare occasions alongside dusty photographs and other souvenirs. 'Be Right Back' is an effective reimagining of *Frankenstein* for the twenty-first century which raises equivalent ethical issues, inasmuch as ubiquitous digital presence does not equate to the vital essence of humanity any more than Dr Frankenstein's assemblage of reanimated body parts does.

Frankenstein continues to infuse popular culture. The 69th Edinburgh Festival Fringe – the world's largest arts festival – offered, for instance, plenty of *Frankenstein* culture. In a range of venues, a number of theatre companies aimed for Fringe success with original approaches to the *Frankenstein* myth. Golden Fire Theatre Company's *Making Monsters* offered a satirical take on the writing of *Frankenstein*, with an intense Mary scribbling her ideas amidst the infantile partying of Byron, Percy Shelley, and Claire Clairmont. The Canny Creatures Theatre Company's new adaptation of *Frankenstein* began, arrestingly, with the monster, already created, breaking for freedom. The Provisional Players' *Frankenstein: A New Play* started its narrative even later in Shelley's plot as we witness the expedition to the North Pole which stumbles across the distraught Frankenstein, clinging to the ice. Striking a contemporary note, Shade Theatre's *ADAM – The Modern Frankenstein* made the protagonist a computer programmer who strives to create artificial life in an attempt to rebuild his reputation after causing the stock market to crash. Away from theatre, in the arena of stand-up comedy, Richard Todd's Fringe act was promoted entirely in Frankensteinian terms, his routine presented ironically as a tragedy of ambition that needs to be appeased now that it has risen in life. Similarly, a performer called 'Tape' worked with the Gravel Road Show to offer a hybrid of clowning, devising, and performance art in 'the creation of a pop-cultural Frankenstein'. Meanwhile, festival-goers frequented Edinburgh's *Frankenstein* public house, an astonishing Gothic structure and environment which featured a life-sized animatronic monster which descends from the rafters and jolts into life on an hourly basis. The *Frankenstein* pub was a Fringe venue itself, presenting *Dr Frankenstein's Spooky Disco*, a daytime cabaret show suitable for children aged two-years old and up; while at nighttime the venue hosted a strictly adults only *Rocky Horror Night* with playful activities and cabaret hosted by, of course, Dr Frank N. Furter.

As well as being detected in every creative context imaginable, *Frankenstein* continues to loom over other realms. Just as Mary Shelley's novel emerged in a time of major crisis, the abiding relevance of her tale is clear in this contemporary era of angst. In the USA, 2016 was an election year and the surprise success of Donald Trump in securing the Republican Party nomination led more than one commentator to turn to *Frankenstein* for allusion. Robert Kagan opined in the *Washington Post* that 'Trump is the GOP's Frankenstein monster. Now he's strong enough to destroy the party' (*Washington Post*, 25 February 2016). Other critics went further in coining the name 'Trumpenstein'. This predictably included numerous left-leaning satirists, but even Steve Deace – in the usually Republican-sympathising *Conservative Review* – agreed with them when he described Trumpenstein as a 'monster created by a feckless GOP' (*Conservative Review*, 23 July 2016). Of course, it is worth noting that other satirists have attempted to locate the monster elsewhere, with Democrat candidate Hillary Clinton cast as *The Bride of Clintonstein* (*A Double Take Presidential Primary Rib*, July 2016).

Outside of the USA, a major news story with political impact has been the UK's referendum about whether to remain in the European Union. It was a heated campaign which resulted – in June 2016 – in the decision to leave the EU. Generally, pundits assumed that the anti-EU campaign ('Brexit') would lose and the arguments and rhetoric they deployed (principally in regard to immigrants and refugees) were seized upon by critics with articles in British newspapers such as Dan Hodges' 'Not even the immigration Frankenstein can save the Brexit mob now … but that won't stop them setting him loose' (*Daily Mail*, 24 May 2016). At the same time, the Brexit campaign decided to draw on the same allusion, creating the somewhat awkwardly named 'FrankenEUstein' to represent what they perceived as the 'monster' that united Europe has become in a political experiment gone wrong (*Social Democracy for the 21st Century*, 24 June 2016). World commentary on the UK referendum included Canada's oldest newspaper, *Chronicle Herald*, presenting a caricature titled 'Brexit Frankenstein' in which a headless Frankenstein monster wears a Brexit T-shirt as it attempts to read a book called 'Getting Ahead' (*Chronicle Herald*, July 2016). This satirical cartoon reflects the perception that, despite the passion that infused the Brexiteers and their supporters, their arguments lacked intellectual credibility and a coherent plan of action, should their campaign win.

Political campaigns come to an end in either success or failure, just as arts festivals, plays, and films come to an end. *Frankenstein* will continue to frighten us, titillate us, amuse us. It can be a mythos and iconography that can safely entertain our children but also haunt our consciousness about where and who we are, what we have done, and what the future may hold. The 'yellow eye' that opens and stares at its creator in Mary Shelley's magnificent novel continues to stare at us and shows no sign of blinking. And if we turn away in disdain or close our eyes in fright, we can still hear that unnatural pulse beating, inexorably.

Bibliography

Black Mirror: 'Be Right Back'. Channel 4, 1 February 2013.

Chronicle Herald. 'Brexit Frankenstein.' *Chronicle Herald*, July 2016. http://tinyurl.com/zua2ynn (accessed 20 August 2016).

Conservative Review. 'Enter Trumpenstein: The Monster Created by a Feckless GOP.' *Conservative Review*, 24 July 2016. http://tinyurl.com/zwalhjm (accessed 20 August 2016).

Daily Mail. 'Not Even the Immigration Frankenstein Can Save the Brexit Mob now … but that Won't Stop Them Setting Him Loose.' *Daily Mail*, 30 May 2016. http://tinyurl.com/hbu8gls (accessed 20 August 2016).

Double Take Presidential Primary Rib, A. 'The Bride of Clintonstein.' *A Double Take Presidential Primary Rib*, July 2016. http://tinyurl.com/j8g6uws (accessed 20 August 2016)

Night Gallery. NBC, 6 October 1971.

Social Democracy for the 21st Century. 'FrankenEUstein.' *Social Democracy for the 21st Century*, 24 June 2016. http://tinyurl.com/hfpl2ha (accessed 20 August 2016).

Washington Post. 'Trump Is the GOP's Frankenstein Monster.' *The Washington Post*, 25 February 2016. http://tinyurl.com/zcbuq73 (accessed 20 August 2016).

Index

Note: 'n.' after a page reference indicates the number of an endnote on that page.